THE
DEAD SEA
SCROLLS

THE DEAD SEA SCROLLS

Understanding Their Spiritual Message

STEVEN A. FISDEL

JASON ARONSON INC.
Northvale, New Jersey
Jerusalem

First Jason Aronson Inc. softcover edition—1998

This book was set in 11 pt. Berkeley by Alpha Graphics of Pittsfield, New Hampshire.

Copyright © 1997 by Steven A. Fisdel

10 9 8 7 6 5 4 3 2 1

Library of Congress Cataloging-in-Publication Data

Fisdel, Steven A.
  The dead sea scrolls : understanding their spiritual message / by Steven A. Fisdel.
    p. cm.
  ISBN 1-56821-973-3 (hardcover)
  ISBN 0-7657-6023-1 (softcover)
  1. Dead sea scrolls—Theology. 2. Qumran community. 3. Judaism—
History—Post-exilic period, 586 B.C.-210 A.D. I. Title.
  BM487.F54 1997
  296.1'55—dc21
                                                                    98-49938

Manufactured in the United States of America. Jason Aronson Inc. offers books and cassettes. For information and catalog write to Jason Aronson Inc., 230 Livingston Street, Northvale, New Jersey 07647.

CONTENTS

1

A BRIEF
HISTORICAL OVERVIEW

The most important and valuable aspects of the Dead Sea literature are the spiritual perspectives presented. Across a span of over
two millennia, it is the message of the scrolls that still speaks directly
to our hearts and our minds. It is on these spiritual views, articulated
in the Qumran literature, that we will focus our attention during the
course of this work.

Before going into the question of the nature of the scrolls and
their specific contents, it is best to deal with a bit of history first. It is
important to be able to put the literature of the Dead Sea Scrolls into
a firm historical framework. With a clear historical perspective, it is
far easier to understand the material and its messages, allowing us to
work with it fully and effectively.

In this chapter, I would like to provide the reader with a concise, historical backdrop for viewing the scrolls in their proper context. This should make our later, technical examinations of the Dead
Sea literature far more comprehensible.

The best place to start is always at the beginning. So let's begin
by perusing the biblical period, the time of the emergence of the Jewish people onto the stage of world history.

1

A Historical Overview of the
Two Jewish Commonwealths

The First Jewish Commonwealth was established in Israel during early biblical times. The Jews took possession of the Land of Israel under Joshua sometime around 1400 B.C.E. They remained in possession of the country until the Babylonians destroyed the Kingdom of Judah in 586 B.C.E. According to the biblical record, during the first four centuries (as the people of Israel settled the Land), the Israelites lived as a confederation of tribes united by religion and by common historical experience.

The Kingdom of Israel was founded under David and Solomon around 1000 B.C.E. Under King David, a professional standing army was created, replacing the tribal conscriptions that were the rule during the preceding period of the Judges. David captured Jerusalem and established it as the capital of the entire country. Toward the end of his reign, David relocated the Sanctuary, along with the Ark of the Covenant, from Shilo (where the Tabernacle was established in the days of Joshua) to Jerusalem, the new capital. These actions effectively ended the tribal confederation, which was the political, economic, and religious structure of the Israelites since the days of their arrival in the Land.

Elected as kings by all of the twelve tribes, the monarchy was firmly established in Israel under Saul and David. David and Solomon, his heir, ruled an empire, Israel having conquered or subdued most of the neighboring countries. Four centuries of warfare came to an end, by the end of David's reign. During the reigns of David and Solomon, their rule extended from the borders of Egypt to those of Syria. Under David, the empire was established. During Solomon's reign, peace prevailed. Prosperity followed. As a result of the country's economic strength and political stability, King Solomon was able to build the First Temple in Jerusalem and thereby to centralize religious worship.

After Solomon's death, the country split into two Jewish kingdoms, with Israel comprising the ten northern tribes and Judah comprising the two southern tribes. Tribal rivalries and cultural tension had existed for a long time between the northern and southern tribes. Loss of strong leadership, political insensitivity to the needs of the north by Solomon's heir Rechavam, and interference by the Egyptians (whose expansionist aims may well have been threatened by a strong, centralized Jewish state) allowed the simmering tensions to explode.

Two Jewish states emerged as the northern tribes opted for independence from the south and from Jerusalem.

In the subsequent era of their mutual existence, the two kingdoms co-existed, sometimes peacefully and sometimes not, for approximately three hundred years. At the beginning of the seventh century B.C.E., the Kingdom of Israel in the north was destroyed by the Assyrians as they expanded westward, building an empire of their own. The fate of the ten northern tribes is not fully known. They disappeared from the stage of history.

A century later, the Kingdom of Judah was to disappear. At that time Nebuchadnezzar, the King of Babylonia, broke the power of Assyria. Nebuchadnezzar marched his armies through the Near East in the process of establishing an empire for Babylon. In this process, the Babylonians conquered Judah and destroyed the First Temple. Jerusalem was captured and destroyed in 586 B.C.E. Large elements of the population, particularly the upper classes, were removed from the country and brought to live in Babylonia, in exile.

For seventy years the Jews were in exile in Babylonia. At the beginning of the fifth century B.C.E., Babylonia was conquered, in turn, by the Persians. The first Persian emperor, Cyrus, allowed the Jews who wished to, to return to Jerusalem and to reestablish the province of Judea on behalf of the Persian empire. Under the guidance of Ezra the Scribe and the Jewish governor Nehemiah, Jewish life in Judea was rebuilt. During this time, permission was given to the Jews to rebuild the Temple, as well.

The reality of the Second Temple era, which encompassed the period of the Persian empire and the Greco-Roman period, was very different from that of biblical times. Under the domination of foreign empires, there were no kings in Israel. There was no nobility. Judea was a province. It was no longer an independent country. Leadership devolved onto the priesthood. As a result of the centrality of Jerusalem, the capital, and the reestablishment of the Temple, with its centralized worship, the priesthood became the central power in the reconstituted Jewish community. Priests served as both the religious leaders of the community and the intermediaries between the government and the Jewish population. During the period of the Second Temple, the internal structure of the Jewish Commonwealth was, in a very real sense, a theocracy.

There was also another important difference. For centuries, the prophets of Israel conveyed God's message to the people. One of the most frequent refrains in biblical prophecy was the message that the people's propensity to serve other gods alongside God and to emulate the practices of the idolaters was polluting the Land and violating the Covenant. They prophesied consistently that the utter destruction of the State would be the result of not repenting of their ways and not returning to the service of God. They could not, in the long run, violate the terms of the Covenant without disastrous results ensuing.

First, the Kingdom of Israel was destroyed and the ten northern tribes disappeared. Later, when the Judean State in the south was annihilated, the population was dragged into exile. During the pain of the Exile, the Jews came to take the prophetic message to heart. Thus, when the Jews returned to Jerusalem to reestablish the Temple and their presence in their homeland, idolatry had vanished from Israel.

For almost two centuries, life developed and matured in Judea under the protection of the Persian Empire. During that time, the life of the community revolved around the Temple, the sacrifices, and the priesthood. The study of the Law of Moses proliferated and became a way of life. The life of the people was secure and predictable. A deepening religious lifestyle and spiritual reality took root in Judea.

Toward the end of the fourth century B.C.E., a monumental and totally unanticipated shift took place. Events took place that were forever to redefine the face of civilization in general. These changes and developments were also to impact strongly on the evolution of Judaism. The Greek armies of Alexander the Great suddenly and irrevocably swept through the Near East. Hellenism had arrived.

The ensuing struggle, which developed between the culture of the Greeks and the religion of Israel, was to prove to be mammoth both in its proportions and in its impact. In Judea, the faith of Israel eventually carried the day. However, it did so only after a long and bitter life and death conflict that set Jewish life and thought moving irreversibly in new directions.

The Greeks under Alexander captured the entirety of the Near East and created an empire that extended from Greece and Macedonia in the West to Egypt in the south and to India in the East. After Alexander the Great died, his empire split into three smaller empires—the Macedonian, the Syrian, and the Egyptian. The Seleucid dynasty of Syria and the Ptolemaic dynasty of Egypt, which were Alexander's successors in the Near East, were to battle each other for over a century and a half, contesting for power.

At the beginning of the second century B.C.E., Antiochus III decisively defeated the Egyptians and proceeded to establish definitive control over the majority of the Near East. The question of sovereignty over Lebanon, Judea, Samaria, the Transjordan, and the Negev—in short, the entire land bridge between Asia and Africa—was settled. It was now the domain of the Syrian Greek empire of the Seleucids.

At this juncture the members of the Hellenistic party in Jerusalem (who wished to see Jerusalem and Judea assimilated into the dynamic, cultural, and economic federation of Greek civilization) saw their chance to triumph over their traditionalist co-religionists. They looked to further their ends by seeking out the favor of the Seleucid court. If they could be confirmed in power in Jerusalem by the Greek government, Jerusalem could be hellenized.

With the ascension of Antiochus IV to the Seleucid throne in 174 B.C.E., the tension between the hellenizers and the traditionalists escalated into crisis. Antiochus, for his own reasons, was very interested in the hellenization of Judea. His father, Antiochus III, had fought a major war in the East, attempting to seize Greece. He lost the conflict to the Greek city states and their very powerful ally, Rome. The Romans, once they gained a military foothold, solidified their political hold over Greece. Now, a new and very serious threat was posed to the Seleucid empire—the possibility of Roman conquest.

As a result, Antiochus IV was intent on solidifying political power within the empire itself. Part of that program required the hellenization of the land bridge between Asia and Africa—that is, the cultural, economic, and political absorption of Lebanon, Samaria, Judea, and the Trans-Jordan. The desire of the hellenizers in Jerusalem to meld Judea into the Greek economic and political mainstream clearly dovetailed with the designs of the Seleucid emperor. However, the attempts by the Hellenistic party in Judea to seize power produced an explosive situation. The actions of the Hellenistic party led first to a forced acculturation of Jerusalem and Judea by the hellenizers, assisted by foreign troops from Syria. When internal resistance proved to be substantial, the situation ultimately deteriorated into a full and ruthless suppression of Judaism by Antiochus. The resulting events triggered a quarter of a century of armed resistance aimed at overthrowing Greek overlordship.

The ensuing conflict was initiated and subsequently led by the Maccabees, the sons of Mattathias the priest. Their struggle began as an attempt to secure religious freedom. As the struggle deepened and spread, the objectives of the conflict broadened. Ultimately, the Maccabean conflict led to victory. It resulted in the establishment of a free and independent Israel under the leadership of their descendants, the Hasmoneans.

The Hasmonean kings ruled Israel for about a century. Not since the days of the last kings of Judah had the Jews been an independent people. During that time, the original Jewish province of Judea (now a fully sovereign state) was vastly enlarged to encompass other areas of the Land, uniting Jewish groups all over Israel. Areas such as Samaria, the Galilee, Idumea, et cetera, were either absorbed by conquest or influenced through diplomacy. The Hasmonean kings worked hard to solidify the country politically, economically, and religiously. The Hasmoneans united in their persons both the High Priesthood and the crown of secular authority. They operated on equal political footing with the kings of Syria and of Egypt.

The precious reality of freedom was not to last. The political independence of the Jews was lost eventually, when the Roman general Pompey was invited to the country to settle a dynastic dispute between two brothers. Pompey's solution to a difficult set of circumstances was to reduce Judea to the status of being a satellite client state of Rome's.

With independence snatched away from them and with the introduction of the Roman yoke, the situation of the people in Judea deteriorated from difficult to desperate. Over the course of time, conditions in Israel under the Romans shifted in stages from strained relations to intolerable suppression. The change was gradual but both inexorable and dramatic.

During the Roman Civil War, the Jews in Judea and Egypt supported Julius Caesar in his struggle against Pompey. The Jews went so far as to rescue Caesar and his army physically, when Ptolemy double-crossed him and held him hostage in Alexandria. Caesar was very grateful for the timely support. He expressed his gratitude to the Jews by confirming the High Priest, Hyrcanus, as ethnarch of the Jews. Caesar, in determining the status of the Jews, officially left the legal system of the Jews in place, giving Jewish Law and religious practice a rather unique status within the newly emerging Empire.

When Hyrcanus died, the governor, Antipater, engineered his son Herod to the throne in Judea. Herod (later to be referred to as The

Great) was well-received by the Romans—though not by the Jews. Herod was an Idumean and only half Jewish. He was not a Hasmonean and had no blood ties either to the monarchy or the priesthood. Herod was, however, very acculturated. He had deep ties to the Roman aristocracy and to the Greco-Roman lifestyle. He was a close friend of the Emperor Augustus and was familiar with many leading Romans.

The Jews, in large part, felt that a foreigner should not sit on the throne in Israel. Few could forget that Herod had secured the throne by destroying any remaining traces of the Hasmonean lineage and by adeptly playing the Greco-Roman power game politically. It was very clear that Herod owed his very position to Rome. He went to great lengths during his long reign to promote his own independence, to enhance his political power base, and to ingratiate himself to the highest levels of the Roman imperial government. For this, he was both feared and hated.

Although Herod's rule was that of an iron and bloodstained fist, he did maintain a remarkable degree of freedom from Rome. His policies and force of personality successfully managed to protect the Jews from the rapaciousness and greed so characteristic of direct Roman rule. As long as Herod was alive, Judea maintained a semi-independent state, ruled by a strong individual who was viewed as a friend of Rome.

Over time, however, the political and social status of the Jews in Israel deteriorated under the Romans. Under Simon the Hasmonean, in the days when Israel was still independent, the state of Judea was a "socius," an ally of Rome. When Pompey terminated her independence, Judea was reduced to the status of a conquered state. Under Caesar, her position was elevated to that of a client state of the Romans.

With the death of Herod, the Emperor Augustus (who was a close personal friend) largely honored Herod's last wishes and divided up his domain among his children and heirs. Eventually, however, the disturbances in Judea and the inability of Archelaus (one of Herod's heirs) to control the situation led Augustus to depose him and to make Judea into a Roman province to be ruled directly by Roman procurators, who were responsible to Rome for maintaining both imperial control and enforcing law and order.

As a result of the degenerating situation and of the increasing restiveness of a people longing to return to the freedom they once so cherished, the Roman rule over Israel grew continually harsher. The Romans neither understood nor necessarily sympathized with Jewish belief or religious practice. The desire of the Jews to become free and independent was viewed as seditious and as a threat to the political stability of the Empire.

Roman economic exploitation of the country under the procurators was oppressive in the extreme and what political favoritism might be shown once in a while never benefited the majority of Jews. The Roman occupation of Judea was callous, self-serving, and ruthless.

In the first century of the Christian Era, events began to accelerate. During this entire period, strong messianic hopes began to emerge and make themselves felt in Israel. The nation's expectations of imminent salvation began to soar. Both anticipatory preparation and agitation for the Coming of the Messiah were the order of the day.

Over the century, despair had given way to desperation. As the Jews were economically squeezed dry, politically crushed underfoot, and culturally burdened under heavy and sustained assault, the yearning for freedom and independence flared from a fire into a conflagration. With the example of the Maccabees before them, the people waited for a redeemer. Many sought the Messiah.

The *Piska De Rav Kahanah*, a collection of rabbinic discourses dating from late antiquity and reflecting older oral traditions, expresses rather poignantly the reality of Roman rule in Israel. The Third Discourse focuses on Deuteronomy 25:17–19. Here, God commands Israel not to forget what the Amalekites did to them in the desert and makes it clear that at the appointed time, God will blot the enemy out permanently, their crimes being so heinous.

As is common in rabbinic literature, references to Amalek are often interpreted to mean Rome. The discourse stresses that Israel is to remember what the Amalekites did. Three of the sins indicated in this discourse are the introduction of depravity into Israel, the castration of the Jews (that is, the emasculation of the people and the State), and the willful destruction of the Temple and of Jerusalem.

The message being conveyed here is that Rome subjugated Israel, a free and proud people, devastated it culturally and politically, reduced the nation to abject servitude, and attempted to destroy its religious heritage and thereby discredit God. By and large, a careful reading of this period in the works of the historian Josephus gives one a very similar picture.

Josephus makes it clear that many Jews of his generation felt that they were very close to the End of Days. The End meant that God's judgement was imminent and that judgment would bring the coming of the Messiah. In fact, the entire period from Pompey's conquest of Judea in the mid-first century B.C.E. to the Bar Kochba Revolt in 132 C.E. was an escalating crescendo of increasing agitation, one of constant expectation of the coming of the Messiah and the final deliverance of Israel.

In the year 66 of the Christian Era, the dam finally broke with the onslaught of the First Revolt against Rome. The Jews rebelled openly and sought to make a clean break with the Empire. The objective was to reestablish full Jewish independence. The reaction of Rome, in response, was swift and brutal.

Though it may seem that the action taken by the Jews was merely suicidal, one should keep several things in mind. First of all, the Empire was still young and somewhat vulnerable. Augustus effectively became the first emperor in Rome in 12 B.C.E., when he assumed the position of Pontifex Maximus after the death of Lepidus. When the Judean Revolt erupted in 66 C.E., the empire was only eight decades old. In Rome, the Emperor Nero was forced from the throne and near-anarchy was to grip the government for some time.

Although Rome had a long history of conquest, the Empire established by Augustus was not even a century old as yet and had never been forced to contend with a full-blown secessionist insurrection. Were the Jews successful, the pattern would be set for other subject nations to follow suit. This could easily entail the loss of Egypt, which was one of the breadbaskets of the Empire, or the loss of Syria, the buffer against the East. Moreover, the region Judea inhabited and influenced was the vital land bridge between Asia and Africa. Launching a secessionist revolt in Judea meant initiating a life and death fight not only for the Jews, but also for the Empire.

During the First War against Rome, which lasted from 66 to 73 C.E., a desperate and protracted struggle emerged. Eventually, the Romans recaptured the entire country, but it was through a long and bitter contest. In the process of subduing the country, the Temple was completely destroyed and the entire city of Jerusalem leveled. The Roman generals responsible for the destruction of the country and the capital were heralded as great heroes. Both Vespasian and his son Titus were to be elected successively as emperors.

In the six decades that separated the First Revolt from the Second, the country rebuilt itself and the population gradually recovered. However, changes had taken place. Jerusalem was in ruins and the

Temple was gone entirely. The political and economic status of the area deteriorated even further, for now Judea was a conquered country and legally the full possession of Rome.

Despite the defeat, the determination to be free did not die or even diminish necessarily. Rather, opposition to Rome stiffened. Under the reign of Trajan, the Jews fermented an uprising in North Africa, widely supported by the Egyptian and Libyan peasantry, which tapped the anger and deep frustration of the disenfranchised. The ensuing upheaval strained the resources of the Roman army and left entire regions of North Africa devastated and desolate in its wake.

In 132 C.E., the Jews in Judea made another attempt to break the yoke of Rome. It was a very well-organized and strategically planned revolt that broke out under the leadership of a Messiah figure. Simon bar Kosivah, known popularly as "Bar Kochba" (the Son of the Star), assumed the title of *Nasi* of Israel and led Israel in yet another attempt to become a free people.

The Second Revolt against Rome proved to be even more devastating than the First. During this intense and very bloody conflict, the Roman army was faced with such enormous resistance that the country had to be reduced on a city-by-city basis. During the course of the war, civilian losses were staggering and the emperor Hadrian had to take the unheard-of step of coming to the region to personally lead the Roman troops. Moreover, a very large part of the entire Roman army had to be diverted from all over the Empire to put down the uprising in Judea.

By the time the war was over, some of the finest of the Roman legions at the disposal of the Empire were either decimated or completely wiped out. The war proved very costly for both sides. The Roman army suffered staggering physical losses and the financial cost of war nearly bankrupt the Roman government. A clear indication of how devastating the war had been is revealed in Hadrian's final communication. In his victory communique to Rome, Hadrian conspicuously omitted the standard, traditional statement used by victorious consuls from the earliest days of the Republic: that he and the army were well.

In the aftermath of the war, Hadrian's wrath was unbounded. He set out on a deliberate course to destroy Jewish life in Judea and to depopulate the country of Jews. He proscribed the practice of Judaism entirely in Judea and the surrounding territories. Practice of

Judaism was outlawed and made a capital offense. Intense persecution of the Jews followed. Hadrian renamed the region "Palestine." He rebuilt Jerusalem as a Roman city. He named the new city "Aelia Capitolina" and forbade Jews entry into the city. On the site of the Temple, Hadrian built a temple to Jupiter. His program was thorough and complete.

The devastation of the war, the intense persecution of the Jews that followed under Hadrian's rule, the deliberate policy of depopulating the country of Jews, and the rapid economic collapse of the country all effectively coalesced to destroy Judea. Thus ended the Second Jewish Commonwealth.

The Importance of the Scrolls of Qumran

The scrolls found by the shores of Dead Sea belong to the period of the Second Jewish Commonwealth. As will be discussed in the next chapter, it is my view that the scrolls were diverse in origin and reflect a broad spectrum of Jewish belief, representative of the times.

The period of the Second Commonwealth encompasses an era of great theological development in Israel. The literature of Qumran reflects a world of deepening commitment, of spiritual searching, and of theological innovation. It illustrates poignantly the religious and intellectual climate prevalent in Israel, as Judaism interacted with Greco-Roman civilization. It is within this climate of evolving religious thought that both rabbinic Judaism developed and Christianity was born.

Under the threat of potential cultural and religious extinction brought by the onslaught of Greco-Roman civilization, the people of Israel sought to redefine their ancestral heritage. They endeavored not only to preserve Judaism but also to strengthen their faith and develop Judaism's principles more deeply. The Jews sought to incorporate these principles and beliefs more effectively into the practice of their daily lives.

The insight we are provided with, when examining these scrolls, is far-reaching. This is true, in large part, because the literature is so diversified. The Qumran material can be classified into several different types of literature that are related to each other, yet are very distinct in character from one another.

Among the most important and historically significant scrolls are those that are Sectarian in nature. Scrolls like the Damascus Covenant, the Community Rule, the War Scroll, et cetera, appear to be products of a specific religious grouping within Israel at this critical point in time. As will be discussed subsequently, there were a number of different Jewish groups flourishing during the Second Commonwealth.

These Sectarian documents shed great light on a specific theological and social group within Israel. This is of great importance in and of itself. Prior to the discovery of the Dead Sea Scrolls, we had little information regarding the beliefs, practices, and way of life of any of the non-Pharisaic groupings in Israel during the Greco-Roman period. The Pharisaic view of Judaism, from which rabbinic Judaism evolved, was only one of several influential streams of thought during this theologically rich period in Jewish history. The emergence of this material provides us with a much broader context for understanding Jewish life and thought in this critical period of time.

These scrolls also tell us quite a bit about the difference in belief and practice between the Sectarians and other groups in contemporaneous Israel. This is particularly true when their doctrines are compared with the theological beliefs and religious practices of other groups operating in Second Temple Israel, with which we are familiar from other ancient Jewish sources.

However, not all of the scrolls are necessarily Sectarian in nature. Among the Qumran literature, several other types of documents are present in large numbers. There are fragments and scrolls comprising sections of biblical books. There is an entire genre of apocalyptic literature focusing on the End of Time and the advent of Messianic salvation. There are copies of non-canonical and apocryphal books constituting wisdom literature and historical material. There are scrolls that focus on legal material and ritual observance, and there is even material that is esoteric in nature.

The scrolls, therefore, shed great light on this most important period in the history of humanity and the history of religion and faith. Written over centuries during a pivotal point in the development of Judaism, the scrolls offer us a glimpse into the hearts and minds of the people and provide vastly important information regarding the trends in Jewish thought and belief, which led directly to the creation of Christian belief and which helped form the rabbinic Judaism that has characterized Jewish life in much of the world for almost two thousand years.

The Sadducees, the Pharisees, the Essenes, and Others

Before delving into the origins of the Dead Sea Sect, it is important to outline briefly the various religious groupings that dominated the religious and political scene in Israel during the Second Commonwealth.

It is my opinion that it is not really accurate to refer to the Judaism of the Second Commonwealth. The truth of the matter is that it is far more appropriate to speak of the Judaisms of the period—that is, in the plural. It seems very clear that there were a number of diverse approaches that characterized the outlooks, beliefs, and practices of this era.

The development of Jewish belief and practice at this time was multifaceted and not strictly linear. There were definitely uniform assumptions that underpinned all of the various approaches to Judaism that were being experimented with in Israel. However, when it came to theological belief and the practical implication of Mosaic law in day-to-day life, there was wide variance in expression.

The first century Jewish historian Josephus tells us that from the Hasmonean period on, there were several religious divisions within Judean society. He classifies them as the Sadducees, the Pharisees, the Essenes, and the Zealots.

In his book, *Pharisees, Scribes and Sadducees*, Anthony Saldarini makes a very important observation and assessment. He points out that Josephus applies the term *hairesis* to these groups. This Greek term can mean "adhering to a way of life advocated by a specific school of thought or philosophy."

Unlike the characterization of these groups as sects, it is more accurate to realize that what Josephus was trying to express to his Greco-Roman audience was that within Israel there were diverse groupings, representing several different approaches to Jewish belief and practice.

It seems very likely that there may well have been a number of different groups and approaches operative within each one of these general tendencies. It is not necessarily true that Josephus was talking about either established institutions or necessarily fixed groups when he spoke of the different philosophies within the Jewish world. Rather, the labels he uses—Sadducee, Pharisee, Essene, and Zealot— describe several different ways of life, not four different sects.

That there were variations within each of these groupings seems obvious when one considers some of the other groups mentioned in the literature of the time. Groups such as the Nazirites, the Evionim, the Haverim, the God-fearers, the Baptisers, et cetera, are mentioned in early rabbinic literature. In the Gospels, a distinction is made between the Pharisees and the Scribes. Indeed, the early followers of Jesus must have constituted yet another group.

It is very difficult to determine, based on the available information that we have, whether the authors of the Sectarian literature discovered at Qumran were actually Essenes or whether they were a distinct group related to the Essene movement. What is clear is that they were far closer in belief, orientation, and practice to the Essenes than to any of the other groupings with which we are familiar from contemporaneous writings.

So, let's take a moment to define and to describe each of the three general approaches to Judaism from the Greco-Roman period, as we currently understand them. We must bear in mind that these are very likely broad definitions of approach. Each approach may well have encompassed a wide variety of different groups within the social, political, and spiritual world of the Second Jewish Commonwealth.

The two groups, or schools of thought, within Judaism mentioned most prominently in *Josephus*, in the *Mishnah*, and in the Gospels are the Sadducees and the Pharisees. These two groups seemed to be the ones tied most directly to Jerusalem.

The Sadducees are most often indicated as being close to the seat of power. Evidence in *Josephus* seems to indicate that the Sadducees drew heavily from the ranks of the priesthood and from the upper classes, although by no means exclusively. The term "Sadducee" derives from the name "Zadok." In all likelihood, this is a reference to Zadok who was a disciple of Antigonus of Soho.

In the *Mishnah*, the collection of Israel's oral and legal traditions compiled in the beginning of the third century C.E., there is a description of the evolution of Jewish law from the time of Moses to the time of the *Mishnah*'s completion. It mentions Antigonus of Soho as being one of the leading authorities during the Greek era. A contemporaneous work, *Avot de Rabbi Natan*, informs us that Antigonus had two disciples, Zadok and Boethius, who interpreted his teachings to mean that there was no future life after death and no resurrection.

Josephus tells us that the Sadducees denied the concept of the survival of the soul and did not believe in associating anything connected to evil with God. God transcended evil altogether. His realm was beyond good and evil. Therefore, God was not sitting in judgment over human souls in the next world. Rather, the Sadducees dismissed the idea of a future process of reward and punishment entirely. However, the Sadducees did argue that man had complete freedom of will and the freedom to choose between good and evil. It would appear that they were harkening back to the concept implicit in the Hebrew Scripture: that man is rewarded or punished for his behavior through the course of events in his life on earth. If man obeys God, he prospers; if not, he suffers.

Josephus points out clearly that the Sadducees believed in a strict and rather literal interpretation of the Law of Moses. They opposed the tendency to interpret the laws too extensively. They denied the validity of the oral legal tradition entirely. It would seem that the Sadducees took the approach that if something was not stated in the Bible directly and clearly, then it was not an issue.

This approach differed substantially from that of both the Pharisees and the Essenes. From the time of Ezra and Nehemiah at the beginning of the Second Temple period, when the Jews returned from the Babylonian Exile, the Jewish people faced a growing concern. Many biblical laws were no longer clear, in terms of what they meant or how exactly they were supposed to be observed. It became necessary, on one hand, to interpret the laws Moses handed down at Sinai and make them applicable to a changing society.

On the other hand, new situations began to develop that biblical law did not specifically address, and answers to these concerns had to be extrapolated. The Pharisees led in the direction of interpreting and extending the biblical laws to contemporary life. They did so by arguing for the existence of an Oral Law in Israel.

The concept was that even in the days of Moses, there were traditions and practices set down and established that were not written down, per se. Rather, they were transmitted orally and passed down from generation to generation. These traditions were discussed and elaborated over time. Since they were passed down over the generations, they were to be considered as authoritative.

The Torah, the Five Books of Moses encompassing the Law from Sinai, was referred to as the Written Law. The traditions and interpretations of the laws of the Torah were distinguished by being called the Oral Law.

The Pharisees, we are told, held theological positions that were at odds with the Sadducees. They believed strongly in Providence. That is, they believed in God's continual interaction with humanity and

His direct involvement in Creation. They held that man had free will and an individual could yield either to good or to evil. The choice was his. In response to man's actions, God rewarded a person for the good he accomplished and also punished him for his mistakes and his sins.

This was a very important Pharisaic doctrine. The Pharisees took the doctrine to the point of asserting the survival of the soul beyond the grave. Moreover, they affirmed that Divine Judgment is passed on each soul when it crosses to the Next World. Every soul is imperishable. Yet it must take full responsibility for its life and actions in the temporal, physical world. The souls of the righteous merit a high place in the World to Come. Eventually, in the End of Days, the souls of the righteous will merit passing back into physical bodies, but the souls of the wicked suffer eternal punishment.

In terms of numbers and distribution, Josephus tells us that the Sadducees generally had the support of the upper classes and that the Pharisees had more influence among the broad population. One of the most important reasons for this, he points out, is that the Pharisees were considered to be the most accurate interpreters of the Law. This may reflect where the term "Pharisee" actually stems from. The Hebrew term for "Pharisees" is *Perushim*. The word comes from the verb *pairaish*, one of its meanings being "to explain or expound." The Pharisees were the expounders of the Law—those teachers and sages who interpreted the Law for the people.

In turning to the Essenes, a different picture emerges. Outside of the Qumran material, most of what we know of the Essenes from ancient literature comes from the Jewish historian, Josephus, and the great contemporaneous Jewish philosopher, Philo of Alexandria. Both sources stress that the Essenes strived for piety and that the intensity of their pursuit distinguished them, because it led to several striking behavioral characteristics.

The Essenes tended to live in organized communities and developed a regimented lifestyle. They devoted themselves exclusively to agriculture. Their communities had specific regulations that governed their lives and their relationships to each other. Deference was shown at all times to superiors and silence was highly cherished. The Essenes were well-known as healers and for their ability to forecast the future accurately.

The Essenes practiced community of property, community of worship and prayer, and community of discussion and decision-making. They were known for their ardent study of ancient literature and their expertise in expounding the hidden meaning of Scripture. They held the Law of Moses to be sacred and were very strict in their observance of the laws.

In terms of their beliefs, as outlined in the ancient sources, we are told that the Essenes were very rigorous in their devotion to the Law of Moses and that they sought to extend the priestly way of life to the entire community. The religious life of the communities was, in fact, dominated by priests and was patterned in close accordance with the levitical purity laws in the Bible.

The Essenes strongly adhered to the belief in a life after death, in which the righteous were rewarded and the wicked were doomed. The presence of God in the world was emphasized, and destiny played a strong part in the affairs of man.

As we will see subsequently, it is very clear that those responsible for authoring the Sectarian literature discovered on the shores of the Dead Sea certainly were far closer to the Essenic school of thought and its approach to Jewish faith and observance than to either that of the Sadducees or the Pharisees. As we delve deeper into the beliefs and practices of the Sectarian literature, it will become clearer where the lines of demarcation are between the various groups, as well as where there are similar underlying assumptions.

Before journeying into the realm of the Sectarian literature, it is important to gain clear insight and a sharp focus on one of the most essential and fundamental beliefs in Judaism and one that without question underpinned all of Jewish thinking during this period—the primacy of the Law of Moses.

2

THE PRIMACY OF THE LAW

At the very core of Judaism is the Covenant. From the very inception of the Hebrew faith, beginning with Abraham himself, the foundation of the relationship between man and God was the Covenant. What constitutes mankind's relationship to God in Jewish experience is the Covenant.

What do we mean by a covenant? Quite simply, a covenant is a contractual agreement between two parties. Two independent parties come together and define their relationship through an agreement on mutually binding conditions. They formally undertake to fulfill the obligations agreed upon under the terms of the contract. There are mutual benefits that are derived from fulfilling the terms of the contract and penalties imposed for violation of its terms, as well.

In biblical experience, the reality of Covenant was developed over time. In the beginning, after the Flood, God made a covenant with Noah, who represents the progenitor of a reconstituted humanity. God affirms the principle that direct judgment of human conduct by God, as a norm, would not be workable at mankind's current level of development. The standard by which God judges is such that few people would be able to meet the criteria and survive. At the time of the Flood, God had judged humanity and it fell so seriously short of the mark that only one man and his family were fit to escape the judgement and the cataclysm that sealed it.

With regard to this point, God makes an agreement with Noah, who represents mankind as a whole. God will not intervene directly in the judgement of mankind, in order to allow humanity to develop. From this point on, it is man's responsibility to correct his own mistakes. Whatever damage man does, it is his responsibility to rectify. God is giving the earth and its bounty to humanity, with the proviso that it is to be respected.

God is giving mankind freedom of will and dominance in the world, with the understanding that man will have to regulate his own behavior. God undertakes not to routinely intervene in the administration of justice. Breaches within the norms of proper human conduct will be subject to the jurisdiction of human justice, rather than to Divine Judgement.

The Covenant with Noah, found in Genesis 8:20–9:17, is significant for several reasons. First, it is the original covenant, the prototype. It is directed toward all of humanity and is intended to be eternal. It is a statement of God's commitment to mankind and it establishes a clear precedent—namely, that from God's point of view, when God undertakes a course of action toward mankind, humanity has certain obligations to fulfill in return. Moreover, the obligations are carried out through a set course of action.

"Never again will I doom the world because of man, since the devisings of man's mind are evil from his youth. Nor will I ever again destroy every living being, as I have done. So long as the earth endures, seed time and harvest, cold and heat, summer and winter, day and night, shall never cease" (Genesis 8:20–22).

First, God states what His decision and commitment are to humanity. He is forgoing Divine Judgement as a norm for dealing with human iniquity and, instead, is establishing natural laws to govern the world.

God then states what is to be expected from mankind in exchange. "Be fertile and increase, filling the earth. . . . everything with which the earth is astir . . . they are given into your hand. You must not, however, eat flesh with its life-blood in it. For your life-blood, too, will I require a reckoning. Of every beast will I require it. Of man, as well, will I require a reckoning for human life, of every man for that of his fellow man" (Genesis 9:1–5).

God gives mankind dominion over the earth and all of its life forms. God expects that man will respect their integrity, even when he needs to utilize them for his own needs. Moreover, God is going to hold all creatures accountable for their natures. In man's case, this has several implications, the first being justice. Every man is responsible for his fellow.

The importance of this reality cannot be overemphasized. The biblical view, evident throughout the Hebrew Scriptures, is that the very basis of mankind's relationship to God is steeped in morality, in honoring the integrity of each person, because every human being is made in the image of God. Mankind is expected to honor its fundamental relationship to the Creator through the exercise of moral behavior and the continual pursuit of justice.

In this earliest of covenants, God sets out several laws binding on all of humanity. Humanity is to be fruitful, to take charge of the earth, to respect other life forms, to acknowledge God, to refrain from murder, and to administer justice. In rabbinic tradition, these laws are referred to as the Covenant of Noah. The Talmud delineates this Covenant as consisting of seven laws: the commandment to promote justice, and the prohibition of idolatry, of sexual misconduct, of blasphemy, of murder, of cruelty to animals, and of theft.

What is important to understand is that the central feature in a divine covenant is the reality that God is responding to human needs. The covenant is being made primarily for the benefit of mankind. God, on his part, is undertaking to fulfill several self-imposed conditions. God undertakes to obligate Himself to fulfill certain principles and expects, in return from humanity, observance of the laws that He is setting out.

Two extremely important factors must be kept in mind and understood fully. First, the core of these commandments and ordinances are the moral laws. Second, they have an eternal validity. In all of the biblical covenants, the core element is the moral law. This is true of the seven Laws of Noah. This is true of the Sinai Covenant. The Ten Commandments stand as the core of the Covenant made at Mount Sinai. Six of the Ten Commandments are moral laws.

Moreover, all of the biblical covenants were made between man and God, not between individuals. The Covenant with Noah was made with all of mankind. The Covenant with Abraham, Isaac, and Jacob was with them and their descendants. The Covenant of Sinai was made with the entire people of Israel. They were all initiated by God and made with God. The implications here are very clear.

First, the divine covenants are inclusive. Noah's Covenant takes in all of humanity. The Sinai Covenant encompasses all of Israel and embraces all who are willing to voluntarily take on its obligations. Potentially, that could include most or all of humanity. Second, regarding the duration of the covenants, there is no time limitation. Noah is contracting the arrangement with God on behalf of all the future generations of humanity. God covenants with the entire people of Israel on Mount Sinai. The Covenant is binding on all future generations of the people of Israel, not merely the generation that was present. In the covenants articulated to the patriarchs and the Covenant at Sinai, God's promise is spelled out in terms of future generations and for all times. From the beginning it was clear that divine covenants are based on moral law and are eternal.

The Covenant with Noah was the first. Another covenant arrangement emerges later between Abraham and God. This particular agreement is reiterated to his grandson Jacob. In this Covenant, a new element emerges. In the Covenant initiated with the patriarchs, God is seeking to make Himself known in a world that has completely lost touch with Him. Amidst a world that is totally dominated by idolatry, God makes a Covenant with Abraham, Isaac, and Jacob.

The terms of this agreement are simple and rather straightforward. God is asking Abraham and his descendants to accept God alone as God and to act as His representatives to the other nations of the earth. Abraham and his descendants are to act in accordance with God's law. By doing so, they will be blessed and their children will multiply and be blessed. They shall prosper and, through their example and through contact with them, all the nations of the earth will be blessed.

In chapter 12 of Genesis, Abraham is told that he is being taken from his native land and brought to the land that God will give to his descendants as a perpetual heritage. He is told, in chapter 15, that his descendants will be oppressed in a strange land for four hundred years and then will be settled in the Land. God identifies Himself as *El Shaddai* in chapter 17. God tells Abraham that the Covenant will be established if he continues to walk in God's ways and is blameless. The sign of the Covenant being made is to be the circumcision of the male foreskin. The agreement is to be eternal.

When Jacob encounters God's presence in Beth El, the same Covenant is reiterated and expanded. Jacob accepts God as the only

God. As a result, Jacob is told that his children will inherit the Land. Jacob asks that God protect him and provide for him as he departs outside of the Land. He requests that at the appropriate time, he be brought back to the Land.

Jacob also voluntarily adds two conditions to the agreement, on his own initiative. First, he stipulates that he will tithe one tenth of what he earns back to God in thanksgiving. Second, he affirms that the stone, which he has anointed with oil, will serve as the foundation for a sanctuary to God, to be built upon his return.

As we will see, the Covenant made between God and Jacob played an important role in the future Messianic expectations that are reflected in the Dead Sea literature. What is important to note here is the extension of the covenant arrangement. Noah's Covenant was very simple and binding immediately upon all of mankind. The Covenant with Abraham and Jacob reflects on the future of mankind.

God is laying the groundwork to set up a specific group of people to promote recognition of God in the human world. God's objective is to elaborate in more concrete, demonstrable terms what He expects ultimately of all humanity. This brings us to "The Covenant," the covenant made at Mount Sinai.

Chosenness and the Covenant at Sinai

Before going into the Sinai Covenant, it would be wise to clear up a longstanding misconception regarding the role of the Jews in the world. This misconception revolves around the concept of "chosenness."

In biblical literature, the Jews are described by God as an *Am Segulah*, who are to function as a nation of priests and a holy people. Unfortunately, this term has often been translated as "The Chosen People." However, in Hebrew, if one wished to say "chosen" in the sense of "choicest, prime, or best," the term would rather read *Am Nivhar*. The phrase *Am Segulah* is more accurately translated "The Designated People."

"Designated" is not the same as "choicest." Rather, it signifies being given a specific role to play in a larger context. The people of Israel, the people of the Covenant, are to be a separate nation whose function it is to be a role model. They are to be a nation of priests who illustrate the relationship between mankind and the Creator, as He envisions it. The objective of the Covenant is to establish the people as a working model. This model is to affirm and articulate God's expectations of humanity. It is designed to point the direction back toward reestablishing the Kingdom of God on earth, the relationship God had originally with Adam and Eve.

The Covenant made at Mount Sinai is the extension of the Covenant initiated with Abraham and refined with Jacob. The Hebrews, the children of Israel, are extracted from Egypt by God for several different reasons. In the first place, God acknowledges their suffering and asserts that the term of their enslavement is over. It was in Egypt, over a period of centuries, that the offspring of Jacob's sons developed into tribes and became a people, cemented together by common experience and by a common fate.

Second, the experience of servitude was to condition the people emotionally for all time. After four centuries of slavery, the imprint would be deep and permanent. Subsequent generations would cherish being a free people after having spent centuries in abject slavery. The people would cherish freedom, justice, equality, and choice. This was part of the standard that the Law of Sinai was intended to establish in human consciousness.

God was taking the Children of Israel out of Egypt to be free. This was essential to the Covenant. Only a free people can voluntarily undertake to make a commitment. God brings the Israelites to Sinai as a free people, so that they are fully in a position to accept willingly the contractual obligations that would be incumbent upon them and their descendants as a result of accepting the Covenant.

God was intent on making his Presence in the world known and understood. He wanted to set up a specific group of people to be identified with Him, in order to illustrate certain principles connected with the true relationship between man and God. In order to do so, nothing could be more to the point than the dramatic events that took place as a result of God's direct manifestation in human history.

God took the Israelites out of Egypt with a show of force that is unparalleled in its extent and drama to this very day. God revealed His full Presence to the people at Mount Sinai, making the Covenant with them directly. He spoke to Moses face-to-face, one on one. He guided them through the desert for forty years. During those many years, the Israelites had to rely directly on God for their very sustenance and survival. God's hand could be discerned in all of the miracles that happened along the way, in the continual guidance of the people by God through the agency of Moses, and by the defeat of their enemies.

God took the Israelites out of Egypt to give them the Law—the Law of Moses being the expanded terms of the Covenant agreement. Under the Sinai Covenant, God is to be their God. The Children of Israel, in turn, are to act as His Designated People, serving as a light and a model to the nations. The message and the paradigm are to be reflected in their conduct. They are to be holy because the job they are performing is of the utmost importance to God.

In exchange for God's protection and blessing, the Israelites are to serve God by observing the Law of Moses, as given and accepted at Mount Sinai. The Covenant consists of 613 commandments. The commandments are the terms of the Covenant. One fulfills the Covenant by observing the commandments and the ordinances that God set down for the people in the Torah, in the Law.

The Law is the constitution of the people of Israel and it is their mandate from God. Observance of the Law is the very basis of the relationship between Israel and God. Israel's obligation to God is met by adherence to the Law of Moses and by consistency in upholding it.

The Torah, the Law of Moses, encompasses all areas of human life. The Torah includes civil law, criminal law, family law, ritual law, priestly law. What is most significant about Mosaic Law is, not only does it effectively encompass all human experience—more importantly, it is all based on moral imperative.

Roman Law and Jewish Law

In order to better understand the Covenant and its core nature, it would be useful to compare it to Roman law. In Roman law, from which most Western law is derived, the underlying principle is that property is nine-tenths of the law. What is actually meant by that is simply that the vast majority of secular law involves protecting people's property rights, delineating ownership, and determining the relationship between the claims of the individual and that of the state.

The Roman legal system's basic concern is with the protection of property. Material well-being is held up as the highest good a society can bestow on its people. Ensuring material security is the primary motivation in the Roman system of law and order. Every aspect of human life is defined as rights and privileges. The organization of human life and the preservation of order are structured, in the Roman system, through human legislation. Human will crafts the law into a comprehensive system of social order and property protection.

By contrast, biblical law is founded on an entirely different basis that is reflected often in the Hebrew scriptures. "Justice, justice shall you pursue," states God, in Deuteronomy 16:20. The biblical emphasis is on justice and on righteousness. "Justice" and "righteousness" are the same term in Hebrew. The word *tzedek* embraces both concepts.

Acting righteously is the fulfillment of one's obligation to God. We honor God by treating our fellow human beings honestly and uprightly. The Covenant is to serve as a guide to moral behavior. This message is both paramount and consistent throughout biblical literature. The emphasis of biblical law is morality. Justice and righteousness are the heart of the Covenant.

Unlike Roman law, biblical law was not legislated. It was revealed to the people of Israel by God in an unparalleled event at the foot of Mount Sinai. By accepting the Law, the Torah, Israel becomes both a nation and a designated people. Both their relationship to God and their function with reference to the other nations of the world are established simultaneously. The Law is Israel's constitution and its mandate at the same time.

The Triumph of the Covenant

During the Greco-Roman period (from the conquest of the Near East by Alexander the Great until the destruction of the Jewish State under the Roman Emperor Hadrian, from the third century before the Christian Era until the middle of the second century of the Christian Era), the relationship of the Jewish world to the Law and its observance went through a long process of evolution.

For two centuries prior to the coming of the Greeks, the Jews lived under the Persian Empire and were allowed to reconstruct both the Judean State and the Temple in Jerusalem. The reconstructed Jewish community in Judea was governed by the priesthood in Jerusalem and by the Law. The Torah became the primary focus of the people's lives.

From the very beginning of the resettlement, Ezra the Scribe set up a system of teaching the laws of the Torah to the people, which routinely included interpreting the provisions of the Law. It was the widespread belief that the destruction of the State and the Temple by the Babylonians, three quarters of a century before, was the result of God's wrath at Israel for abandoning observance of the Law—a mistake not to be repeated at any cost.

Observance of the Law, therefore, became the core of Jewish life as the State and the Temple were being reestablished. Moreover, the leadership of the Province of Judea fell to the priesthood. They served as the intermediaries between the people and the government, since political control remained firmly in the hands of the Persian satraps and governors. Since a substantial part of the Law is ritual, heavily involving the priesthood, this tended to reenforce the centrality of the Law in the new state of Judea.

With the passage of time, the Law became ingrained as a way of life fundamental to the existence of the people of Israel. With the coming of the Greek armies came Greek values and the Greek way of life. Hellenism, the culture and way of life of the Greeks, spread rapidly throughout the Mediterranean and beyond, during the third and second centuries B.C.E. This confrontation between Hellenism and Judaism produced one of the most severe crises ever faced by the Jews.

Particularly within Jewish communities living in Israel, tensions soon ran very high and were ultimately to reach an explosion that was to have very far-reaching consequences. Since Hellenism and Judaism represented two extremely different value systems and worldviews, a choice had to be made in terms of allegiance toward one direction or the other.

The cultural facets of Greek life appealed broadly to many people. The new emphasis on art and music, theater and architecture, thought and philosophy, athletics and competition were to have an irresistible pull. Jews living outside of Israel not only embraced much of Greek life but also sought to harmonize Jewish belief, thought, and practice with Hellenistic culture into a workable synthesis.

The Greeks created a universal civilization in the Western world, by uniting inhabitants of diverse cultures into a homogeneous body through the spread of Hellenism. The seat of Hellenistic civilization was the polis, the Greek city-state. Each city within the Greek world shared the same political structure, the same cultural norms, and the same institutions. Moreover, Greek cities were all united to each other through strong commercial ties.

Hellenism was a culture and a total way of life. Its function was to create a universal civilization through strong political and economic urban ties, reinforced by cultural norms and standards that were consistently recognized as the basis of civilized society and that, as such, permeated all levels of the social order and all aspects of life.

Within Judea, a chasm developed in response to this new reality. On one side were those Jews who were mesmerized by this new way of life. They were drawn strongly by the desire to become part of this new universal culture. Many of these Jews were also aware of the tremendous economic advantage that would exist if Jerusalem were to become a Greek polis and become absorbed into the international fraternity that was developing.

This meant that the Jews would have to embrace Greek culture completely. Many were willing to do so. Many were not. The single biggest obstacle, as far as observant Jews were concerned, was the reintroduction of idolatry into Israel. The core of Greek culture was the religion of the Greeks. Greek mythology not only dominated art, music, and architecture, but religious practice, civil administration, and business as well.

It was the reversion of their fathers to idolatry that constituted the most serious breach of the Covenant with God and, in the opinion of the Prophets, led to the destruction of the biblical State and the First Temple. The specter of idolatry reemerging in Israel meant rebellion against the Covenant, an abandonment of God, and the certain destruction of people and State, to many Jews.

The fear that embracing Hellenism would mean the end of Judaism and would threaten the very existence of the Jewish people was based on a very real threat. Hellenism did not offer cultural assimilation to the Jews or accommodation of their beliefs and their way of life. Rather, Judaism was threatened with cultural and religious extinction. Such fear was quite justified. It was often substantiated by the behavior of those Jews who sought to assimilate with the dominant Greek culture. Hellenizers, as they were called, often abandoned observance of the Law, and spurned, ridiculed, and oppressed those who sought to remain loyal to the traditional way of life. They frequently called in Greek assistance when attempting to impose their will on the general population or to suppress opposition by force.

Two opposing ways of life were vying for control in Israel. One path sought to extract itself from its people's past and nullify the

Covenant, in order to merge with the surrounding civilization. Adherents of the other path strove to remain a distinct people with a distinct history and a sacred mission. The traditional Jews saw as their very purpose the fulfillment of the Covenant made with God at Mount Sinai.

The centrality of the Covenant, the primacy of the Law, was the issue that was to tear the Jewish community in Israel apart for almost two centuries. Was Israel to remain a covenant community or was it to redefine itself as a constituent people in the world of Greek universality?

In terms of political clout and economic leverage, the hellenizers among the Jews held the upper hand for quite some time. The conflict began to come to head and assume crisis proportions at the beginning of the second century B.C.E. At that time, the Hellenistic party began making increasingly bold moves to take over the priesthood and wrest complete political control in Jerusalem.

Their actions led successively to the exile of the High Priest Onias III, to a corruption of the priesthood, to the attempt to make Jerusalem a Greek polis, and, finally, to the military and political intervention of the Seleucid king, Antiochus IV of Syria.

The removal of Onias III, who was highly revered and a very strong advocate of the traditions of Judaism, paved the way for the rededication of Jerusalem as a Greek polis. Antiochus, who wished to solidify his hold over the Greek empire he had recently inherited, was anxious to foster such a move.

When resistance broke out, Antiochus moved in an army to occupy the country. By force of arms, the Greek army attempted to promote compliance with the process of hellenization and to prohibit the practices of Judaism altogether. The hellenizers became the official, ruling party in Jerusalem. They were strong allies of Antiochus, helping to enforce the proscription of Judaism and the hellenization of Jerusalem. In reaction to this violation of the Covenant, Mattathias (a priest from the town of Modin) and his five sons (known as the Hasmoneans) led a revolt against the Seleucid Greek government.

In the course of a quarter century, not only did the Hasmoneans succeed in defeating the Greeks, they established a fully independent Jewish state. As a result of the long struggle and the rather complete victory, the primacy of the Law as the basis of Jewish life was no longer a contested issue. The Hasmoneans had begun as defenders of the faith and as upholders of the Covenant. They ultimately proved victorious militarily and politically. The Hasmonean dynasty effectively maintained and ruled a strong, independent Israel for almost a century. During that time, the Hellenists disappeared from the scene. The Covenant prevailed.

3

THE NATURE OF THE QUMRAN MATERIAL AND THE ORIGINS OF THE SECT

Among the many documents found in the Dead Sea literature, an entire genre can be identified that forms an organic whole and possesses a uniqueness quite its own. This genre of the literature reflects the specific views, social organization, and approach to observing the Covenant that is characteristic of a distinct group within Jewish society during the Greco-Roman period. Traditionally, this group has been identified with the Essenes, mentioned by the historian Josephus as one of the four major philosophical and theological groupings within Jewish society in the Land of Israel at that time.

Scholarly opinion on the subject, however, is not unanimous. Some are of the opinion that the group portrayed in this literature is an offshoot of the Essenes. Other scholars have postulated that this group was actually another division within Jewish society, which, prior to the discovery of the scrolls, was previously unknown to us. If that is the case, this group could be termed the Dead Sea Sect, as opposed to being seen as Essenes.

Whichever way one chooses to look at it, this group of people constituted a specific segment of Jewish society during the Greco-Roman period. It had its own unique organization. It possessed its own doctrines and had its own way of interpreting and observing the commandments of the Covenant. As such, this group needs to be seen its own light and spoken of in its own context. For that reason, I shall refer to this group simply as the Sectarians.

The Origin of the Sect

In the Damascus Covenant, the Sect seems to refer to itself as "the Sons of Zadok" (in the Zadokite document from the Cairo *Genizah* and in Qumran Manuscript Db, fragment 6, column 1, for example). The Sons of Zadok are said to have left the Land of Judah and are regarded as constituting the Elect of Israel. The scrolls refer to "the remnants of Israel," frequently in the same connection. This alludes to a belief by the members of the Sect that they were the True Remnant of Israel—that is, they saw themselves as the saving remnant that would return to the Law and be saved, as was prophesied by Isaiah.

The concept of a saving remnant implies either that most of the people have been corrupted and/or destroyed or that a core influential group within the community had been. It implies, as well, that the majority had abandoned the true observance of the Law. They had been led astray. Therefore, only a small group of penitents, returning to the true path, would be capable of saving themselves and, ultimately, the people, by leading them back to the proper relationship with God and with His Law.

The term "Sons of Zadok," which appears in the Damascus Covenant, parallels the term *Zadokim*, used in early rabbinic literature. The *Zadokim* are the Sadducees. The group referred to in *Josephus* and in the Gospels as the "Sadducees" is termed the *Zadokim* in rabbinic literature.

The name of Zadok is familiar to us from the Hebrew Bible; Zadok was the High Priest under King David. It was David who brought the Tabernacle and the Ark of the Covenant from Shilo to the new capital, Jerusalem. It was King David who established the worship ceremonies in Jerusalem. Although his son Solomon actually built the Temple in Jerusalem, it was David who drew up the plans in all their details. Hence, it was under the auspices of the High Priest, Zadok, that the Temple services were inaugurated and established.

This would suggest that the term "Sons of Zadok" is a reference to a priestly group. The name harkens back to the High Priest Zadok. It also suggests that there probably was some direct connection between the Sect, which called itself "Sons of Zadok," and the *Zadokim*, the Sadduccees of contemporaneous literature. In examining the scroll literature, it is not difficult to surmise that the Sect members were originally a Sadducee breakaway group.

The scrolls make it very clear that the founding members of the Sect were, indeed, priests. The Damascus Covenant states that a group of priests left Jerusalem and went to settle in Damascus. They were joined by Levites and other Jews who shared their feelings and beliefs when the Sectarian community was established. The Damascus Covenant, the Community rule, and the War Scroll all make it very clear that the role of the priesthood is central to both the organization and the theology of the group.

This fact is very surprising and highly significant. Since the days of Zadok, the priesthood was tied intimately to the Jerusalem Temple. The sacrifices, prayers, and rituals performed on behalf of the entire people were dependent on and synonymous with the priesthood. Outside the Temple, the priests had no function nor authority.

For a group of priests to move away from Jerusalem was tantamount to making a complete break with the Temple and severing connection with all established religious authority. They were effectively leaving the traditional framework of Temple ritual. This was both a very dramatic move and a drastic measure. What would have impelled a whole group of priests to walk away from their traditional responsibilities, give up their status in society, and seek to redefine their purpose in a foreign land?

Prior to the discovery of the Dead Sea Scrolls in 1947, a medieval copy of the Damascus Covenant Scroll appeared during the excavation of a very old Karaite synagogue in Cairo, in the early 1920s. Rabbi Solomon Schechter, who headed the project, referred to the document as the Zadokite Fragments. The answer to these questions may be found in the prologue to the Damascus Covenant. Some of the recently released scrolls confirm two very salient facts evident in the Zadokite Fragments that were found in the Cairo *Genizah*. When taken literally, these facts are of great importance regarding the origin of the Sect.

Until the emergence of the Cave 4 scrolls, the prologue to this unearthed copy of the Damascus Covenant (labeled as Zadokite Fragments and recovered in the Cairo *Genizah*) was thought to be a medieval interpolation added to the ancient text. However, scrolls of the Damascus Covenant from Cave 4 of Qumran, it turns out, provide the same prologue—indicating that this information is not the invention of some pious scribe from the Middle Ages. Rather, it is ancient information accurately preserved.

This ancient information sheds great light on the emergence and nature of the Sect. It needs to be examined carefully. First, the statement is made in the prologue that the period of God's Anger ended 390 years after the Destruction of Jerusalem by Nebuchanezzar of Babylon, at which time God caused a root to sprout in Israel.

The period of God's Anger refers, then, to the period beginning with the Destruction of Jerusalem and extending through a period of several centuries into the Greek era. That being the case, the root that God caused to sprout is, in all likelihood, the remnant that leaves the Land of Judah and settles in Damascus—that is, the core group of priests who established the Sect.

Second, it is stated that these people wandered in the wilderness as blind people for twenty years, until which time God saw their devotion and sent the Teacher of Righteousness.

Three hundred and ninety years after the Destruction of Jerusalem in 586 B.C.E. would bring us to 196 B.C.E. as the time of the Sect's emergence. Moving forward another twenty years, 176 B.C.E. is stipulated as the arrival point of the Teacher of Righteousness. These are highly significant dates.

The period around 196 B.C.E. was the point when the Seleucid monarchy solidified its permanent control over Judea and the rest of Coele-Syria in the aftermath of Antiochus III's victory over the Egyptians at Panion in 199 B.C.E. Since the division of Alexander's empire after his death, Judea, Samaria, the Galilee, and Trans-Jordan (the land bridge between Asia and Africa) were the scene of a constant struggle for control between the Seleucid Greeks in Syria and the Ptolemaic dynasty in Egypt. In 196 B.C.E., the contest was over. The Syrians took permanent, unchallenged control after the Egyptian defeat.

The destruction and dislocation the war caused in Judea must have been serious, since Antiochus makes it a point to send money and supplies to Judea to rebuild Jerusalem and several other cities devastated by the war, in appreciation for the support he received from the Jews during the conflict. As refugees departing a war zone racked by considerable destruction, it would be logical for the Sect's founders, the priests and their followers, to seek safe haven by moving to the land of the victors.

Since the Sect was being formed by priests, Levites, and Israel-ites disenchanted by the developments in Jerusalem and seeking to distance themselves from the Temple and from the Jerusalem priest-hood, movement to security beyond the borders of Judea was the logical course of action. Hence, the emergence of the Sect in Dam-ascus was the result of a combination of factors. It was the result of war and dislocation, and it was born out of a desire to find safe haven beyond the political, economic, and social reach of the Jerusalem hierarchy.

The Identity of the Teacher of Righteousness

To understand the motivation for this break with Jerusalem, it is very important to focus on the identity of the Teacher of Righteousness, who appears and establishes the community's doctrines. The Dam-ascus scroll points out that the group wandered around in Syria, in the desert, for twenty years until the arrival of the Teacher of Righ-teousness.

Though it may also imply that a physical component was in-volved, the comment in the scrolls about wandering in the desert for twenty years before the arrival of the Teacher of Righteousness appears as a reference to a lack of spiritual direction. It is clear that the Teacher of Righteousness established the doctrines and way of life of the Com-munity, which were to remain in place until the Day of Judgement and God's revision of the Covenant terms.

It is entirely possible that the Sect's founders had a general motivation for separating from Jerusalem, but no clear cut program—that they were swept up by the course of events. It would seem that their raison d'etre was supplied with the appearance of the Teacher of Righteousness. The question then becomes: Who was the Teacher? Here the scroll's dating of events gives us a strong clue.

If indeed the Teacher of Righteousness appeared in 176 B.C.E., we have a probable answer. At this point in time, two opposing fac-tions were locked in an intense power struggle in Jerusalem. One fac-tion, led by the Tobias family, aimed at the hellenization of Jerusalem and, hence, of Judea. Their aim was to adopt Greek culture, belief, and practice. Their objective thereby was to assimilate Judea into the burgeoning international order. The other faction centered around

Onias III, the High Priest. This group sought to preserve traditional Jewish beliefs and practice and to maintain Judea's theocracy. They resisted hellenization adamantly, seeing it as the antithesis, and possible nemesis, of Judaism.

Fearing the outbreak of a civil war and in the face of Syrian support for the Hellenistic party, Onias left for Syria to plead his case and affirm his loyalty to King Seleucus. He sought to be confirmed as the sole legitimate High Priest. That year, 176 B.C.E., King Seleucus was murdered, and by the end of the year, Antiochus IV ascended the throne. Onias was in Syria for quite some time during the commotion and the subsequent changeover.

Antiochus IV, who favored the hellenization of Judea for his own political reasons, was not well-disposed toward Onias at all. Onias made little headway with the new king. Later, upon learning of a plot against his life, Onias fled to permanent asylum in Egypt. Subsequent to Onias' escape, the Tobias family succeed in establishing his brother, Jason, as High Priest. This was a radical break with tradition. The High Priestly office was always one filled by inheritance, being passed down directly from father to son. Although Jason was of the High Priestly family, he gained the office by political appointment obtained through bribery, not by priestly succession.

Within a short time, the Tobias family managed to engineer yet another coup. One of their kin, Menelaus, purchased the right to be High Priest from Antiochus and eventually secured the post with the assistance of armed force from Syria. Here, another major breach with tradition occurred. Not only was Menelaus an appointed High Priest, a post secured through payoff and the use of armed force, but he could not even claim to be of High Priestly lineage.

The Hellenistic party had engineered the forcible removal of Onias III from the High Priesthood, first replacing him with Jason and later with Menelaus. This was a radical disruption of tradition and law. Since the days of Zadok, the High Priesthood was occupied by members of the High Priestly family and the position was passed down from father to son. Neither of these conditions were met by Menelaus. Moreover, the determination of who would be High Priest was now being made by force of arms and by a foreign power. The priesthood and the purity of the Temple and the services had been compromised.

It is not hard to understand why Jews could come to regard the High Priesthood as illegitimate and corrupted at this point. It is highly probable that the Sectarians of the Damascus Covenant felt that they were the only true remnants of legitimate priesthood, being untainted by the corruption that ensued. Considering that the group refers to itself as the Sons of Zadok, it is also possible that the core group of founding members were not just priests, but also members of the High Priestly family.

It seems reasonable to believe that during his stay in Syria, Onias III connected with the Sect. The hellenization of Judea, and the subsequent corruption of the priesthood it was producing, may well have been the reasons leading the founders of the Sect to take the drastic step of breaking away from Jerusalem altogether. The removal of Onias from the High Priesthood would have only strengthened their convictions that society, the priesthood, and the Temple were being corrupted.

Moreover, the Sectarian community, now twenty years old, still lacked a focus and a purpose. Support for Onias III would have been extremely strong among the Sectarian community. It is obvious that his opinions and his authority as the legitimate High Priest of Israel would be respected greatly. Anything he said or taught would be taken to heart. Not only because of who he was, but also because the community thirsted for direction and doctrine.

The effect of his deposition and the realization that the Temple and the High Priesthood had been violated by the actions of the hellenizers and the government in Syria may well have had a profound impact on Onias III. The experience of losing everything, in all likelihood, forced him to rethink his position, his beliefs, and his view of the future.

As a result of his experience, it would appear that Onias redefined his own role, the role of the community, and the vision of Israel's future, in new and daring terms. His teachings, insight, and vision would have an enormous impact on the doctrines and way of life of the Sectarians. The guidelines and beliefs Onias set down were to lay the course and determine the direction of the Community for centuries to come. It would provide them with a clear and cogent purpose.

The stature of Onias III should not be underestimated. Onias represented the last truly legitimate High Priest, whose person could be regarded as sacred and whose words would be honored. This would be particularly true in view of what certainly would have appeared to the Sectarians as the complete corruption of the priesthood and the discrediting of the Temple.

In the Second Book of Maccabees, Onias III is portrayed as a High Priest of enormous standing and stature. Onias' reign is characterized

as one of unbroken peace and total fulfillment of the Law. He is said
to be a man of great piety and possessed of a hatred of wickedness
(chapter 3). He is seen standing shoulder-to-shoulder with the prophet
Jeremiah in Judah's vision (chapter 15).

The equation of Onias III with the Teacher of Righteousness also
explains another interesting correlation. If one reads the accounts of
the beliefs and ways of life in the writings of Philo of Alexandria and
Josephus regarding both the Essenes and the Therapeutae, one is
struck immediately by the close similarities between them. It would
seem that there is some relationship between the two groups.

When Onias III fled to Egypt, he was extended permanent asylum. He settled in Heliopolis, which had traditional connections to
both the Patriarch Jacob and Moses. There, Onias built a Temple to
the God of Israel and served as High Priest, until he was murdered,
being stabbed to death at the horns of the central altar.

It is the opinion of most scholars that the Qumran community
was either Essene or an offshoot of the Essene movement. If Onias
was the Teacher of Righteousness who established the doctrine and
organization of the Sect, then there is a direct, physical, and doctrinal
link between the Essenes and the Therapeutae of Egypt. That is, they
both would have been founded by the same leader, at around the same
time, as part of one long series of events.

This would mean that there was a logical reason for Onias' actions. Rather than being an enigmatic personality who inexplicably
built his own Temple and went into business for himself, Onias III
sought to preserve the purity of the Temple and the High Priesthood
during dark times. He established a way of life that was designed to
remain pure and uncorrupted until the coming of the End of Days
and the Restoration of the Temple Service under Divine directive.

The Book of 2 Maccabees records that Onias made public the
fact that Menelaus stole holy golden vessels from the Temple, in order
to make good on belated bribe payments to Antiochus. In other words,
Menelaus had promised a large bribe to the Syrian king, in order to
secure his appointment as High Priest. Unable to fully pay the bribe,
Menelaus resorted to stealing holy vessels from the Temple and using
them to pay the bribe. This fact, according to 2 Maccabees, was publicly disclosed by Onias III. As a result of the disclosure, Menelaus'
position was threatened seriously and he responded by having Onias
killed outside the confines of a foreign temple, in which he had
sanctuary.

That there is probably a strong grain of truth to this story is very clear. However, this is not the entire story surrounding Onias' death. Onias' disclosure may, indeed, have provoked a major crisis, becoming a catalyst for the decision to eliminate Onias permanently. However, considering the fact that Menelaus was a usurper, Onias' continued existence would always be a potential threat to Menelaus' position. This incident may only have been the straw that broke the camel's back.

It appears also that certain details of the account are garbled. In particular, it is highly unlikely that any pious Jew, let alone a High Priest, would seek sanctuary in a pagan temple. That would amount to tacit acknowledgment of the power of the deity to whom the sanctuary was dedicated. It is far more likely that Onias was murdered in the Temple he erected in Heliopolis.

The continued existence of a legitimate High Priest, particularly one held in high public regard, would be a standing threat to usurpers such as Menelaus. Sooner or later, he would want Onias done away with. The temple in question, the one where Onias had sanctuary, was his Temple in Heliopolis. That is, it was his own sanctuary and it was on foreign soil. So, the reference to an alien temple, in this context, does not necessarily mean Onias took refuge in a pagan temple. Rather, it means he was out of reach for some time, being cloistered in his own compound in enemy territory.

There are several references in the scroll literature to the murder of the Teacher of Righteousness by the Wicked Priest. If the equation is made of Onias III with the Teacher of Righteousness, this would mean that references in the Habakkuk scroll, for example, which squarely place the responsibility for the murder of the Teacher of Righteousness on the shoulders of the Wicked Priest, refer to the High Priest Menelaus.

The Essenes, the Sectarians, and the Maccabean Wars

The struggle between Hellenism and Judaism in Israel during the second century B.C.E., which culminated in the Maccabean Revolt and the ensuing War of Independence, gave birth to new definitions of Jewish expression of which the Essenes, Sadducees, and Pharisees were all representative approaches.

At a symposium on recent developments in Dead Sea Scroll research during the 1992 Annual AAR/BSL Convention, Professor

Wacholder of Hebrew Union College indicated that the unpublished scroll fragments soon to be released contained evidence that illustrated that the Qumran Sect was already extant during the time of the Maccabean Wars. This being the case, such evidence would lend support to dating the founding of the Sect to this period of time, to the War of Independence.

In Fascicle Three of *A Preliminary Edition of the Unpublished Dead Sea Scrolls* (Wacholder and Abegg, 1995) appears Scroll 4Q477. This fragment, according to Professor Wacholder, could be titled "A List of Those Chastised by the *Yahad* (The Community)." This remnant is a list of names compiled by the leaders of the Sect, outlining important people in Israel whom the Sect condemns, viewing them as enemies. Among those mentioned in the scroll is the name of Johanan ben Mattityahu—that is, Jonathan, son of Mattithias. This would be the eldest of the Maccabee brothers.

Since the war with the Greeks was to continue for years after Jonathan's death and in view of the fact that Jonathan was murdered in 143 B.C.E., the Sect could not have been founded any later than that date. The list, obviously, had to have been compiled while Jonathan was still alive. He was being viewed as an active enemy.

If this is true, that the Sect was already in existence at the height of the Maccabean Wars, it would tend to confirm the premise held by the late Solomon Zeitlin. In his work *The Rise and Fall of the Judean State* Dr. Zeitlin argued that the Essenes were, in fact, the same group mentioned in the First Book of Maccabees, referred to as the *hasidim*. This group was of great importance in its assistance to Judah Maccabee. The *hasidim* are described as having formed the backbone of Judah's army throughout the struggle with Antiochus IV.

This connection has several important implications. The *hasidim*, or Essenes, either emerged at the time of the revolt against the Greeks or some time prior to it. Their primary motive for supporting the struggle was the attainment of freedom of religion. The *hasidim*/Essenes stood at the core of Judah's army during the outset of the struggle. This would mean that the *hasidim* were already a specific, identifiable group within Israel by this time and were motivated by strong doctrinal beliefs that they were prepared to fight for.

If one views the doctrines of Pharisees, Sadduccees, Essenes, and Zealots as philosophies—that is, schools of thought or categories for differentiating the many religious groups within Judea—then the Sectarian Community of the Dead Sea Scrolls would classify as an

Essene group. The emergence of the Sectarian Community, then, is tied to the struggle with Hellenism, and the group may well have been connected intimately with the Maccabean Revolt.

This contention is supported by evidence from the Second Book of Maccabees, if, indeed, Onias III was the Teacher of Righteousness and the doctrinal founder of the Sectarian Community. Right before his last great victory, his defeat of the Greek general Nicanor and the final rescue of Jerusalem, Judah has a vision. In this vision, Onias III appears along with the Prophet Jeremiah. Onias tells Judah that Jeremiah prays fervently for the welfare of the people and for Jerusalem. Onias hands Judah a golden sword, a gift from God. With this sword, God is empowering the Jews to defeat the enemy (2 Maccabees 15:12–16).

Judah's entire career is validated with this final, great victory. It is sanctioned by God, who sends a golden sword to Judah, empowering him to proceed and to triumph. The messengers of God with whom Judah is dealing are the prophet Jeremiah and the High Priest Onias III. The appearance of Jeremiah and Onias to Judah strengthen the resolve of the army to move from a defensive position to an aggressive one. The vision is the source of motivation for Judah's victory. The army resonates with these personalities. Their resolve is strengthened and their courage and determination are ignited. If the hasidim were Essenes and the Sectarian community was an Essene group, then it is clear why Judah's vision of Onias III would be a source of great inspiration, strength, and encouragement to Judah's forces.

When Antiochus V ascended the throne and wished to make peace, he did two things of note. Antiochus V granted complete religious freedom to the Jews, thereby reversing his father's policy. He also had the High Priest Menelaus executed and replaced by his brother Alcimus. If the Essenes and the hasidim were one and the same, it would explain their abrupt withdrawal from the struggle after Antiochus V granted the Judeans religious freedom.

The Essenes believed that the priesthood and the Temple both had been compromised. The High Priesthood was delegitimized since the Teacher of Righteousness, the last true High Priest, had been killed and the Temple Service discredited. Alcimus did not qualify legitimately for the position of High Priest, his status being no different from that of his brother, Menelaus.

The Essenes would have no interest, necessarily, in continuing to fight. The focus of the struggle now began to center on winning political independence. They would have little enthusiasm for this objective and even less for supporting the administration of the Temple under Alcimus as High Priest. Once religious freedom was guaranteed, their objectives had been met already. They were free to go their own way.

Based on internal evidence from the scrolls themselves, both published and unpublished, a number of historical questions can be answered plausibly, if one assumes the accuracy of the scrolls' testimony. The evidence leads to several conclusions: first, that the Sect left Judea after its conquest by the Seleucid dynasty; second, that the Sect was founded based on the determination by a group of priests and Levites that they could no longer be associated with the Jerusalem Temple; third, that the Teacher of Righteousness was in all likelihood the High Priest, Onias III, and that Onias established the doctrines that governed both the Sectarian Community and the Therapeutae (his doctrine may well have been the foundation for the entire Essene movement); and finally, that the Essenes emerged as a distinct group within Israel during the Maccabean Wars.

What the Qumran Caves Represent

Ever since the discovery of the scrolls, it has always been assumed that the Qumran caves represent the remains of a library. The conception was put forth and maintained that Qumran was a community settlement, probably of Essenes. It was thought that the community was monastic and permanently housed at the Qumran settlement. It was logical, therefore, to assume that the nearby caves housing the scrolls were the Sect's library. Both of these premises are open to question.

According to the archeological record, the complex at Qumran was destroyed by the Romans during the 66–73 c.e. War. On their march toward Jerusalem, the Romans went quite some distance out of their way to obliterate the complex. This poses an interesting question. If the settlement at Qumran was merely a desert community of monks who separated themselves from society, what would have prompted a deliberate military attack and the subsequent destruction of the complex? The Romans did not target innocent civilian populations.

If the *hasidim* were indeed the Essenes, it would explain the assault. The Essenes were not pacificists. Just as they had fought with Judah Maccabee against the Greeks a century and a half earlier, they may well have joined in the insurrection against Rome. Yet this fact does not warrant the assumption that there was a permanent residence of any sort at the Qumran site or that this was a monastic settlement.

One of the most puzzling aspects of the ruins at Qumran is that nowhere within the compound is there any archeological trace of living quarters. If Qumran was indeed the central base of the Essene community, a monastic center, this omission is very difficult to explain. There is another possibility that is more plausible.

During the Hasmonean period, fortifications were established in the vicinity of the Dead Sea to protect the southern boundaries of Judea against hostile assault from neighboring peoples. It is quite conceivable that Qumran was originally established for such a purpose and that over time it retained that function to one degree or another. That is, that the Qumran complex was part of a chain of fortifications established in Hasmonean times, which continued to protect the southern flank of Judea militarily through the first century.

During the onslaught of the War with Rome, the Zealots made it a point to seize highly strategic fortifications and locales. The forts and outposts along the Dead Sea would certainly qualify. In fact, it was the seizure of the fortress at Masada which triggered the War.

The garrisoning of troops at an outpost location required only billeting in tents. That would have been standard military procedure. Tents would not necessarily leave any archeological trace. Viewing Qumran from this vantage point, the complex was a military outpost, part of a larger chain of fortifications being connected with the major military base at Masada. During the War with Rome, Masada was the central base of the Zealots.

The vast majority of scrolls are predominantly religious literature. This makes no sense, if Qumran was a Zealot base. If one takes the position that it was a community of Essenes who lived in Qumran and were drawn into the conflict, this may explain the Roman assault and the religious nature of the literature. But then, the question of lack of permanent shelter begs the question.

There are other problems as well. When surveying various scrolls' positions and locations when they were found, there does not appear to be any logical order to the accumulation of books that were found in any of the caves individually. Moreover, the materials discovered obviously include a lot of books that were in general circulation among the Jewish community at large. Only a percentage of the scrolls are actually Sectarian in content.

It is also noteworthy that many of the scrolls were found in jars, packed with straw, and possibly sealed at one time. Moreover, the scrolls were scattered in a number of caves, randomly. Given the fact that there is no logical order or system apparent in the storage of the scrolls, and that they were packaged, it is far more likely that the scrolls were intended for storage rather than for continual usage.

An analogy suggests itself. Let us say that a fire breaks out in the wilds and grows out of control. The local fire-fighting forces are unable to contain it. The fire then moves toward a populated area. So officials begin to evacuate the residents. Residents will have only a short time to grab whatever valuables they wish to save and abandon the area. The fire, upon reaching the area, burns down all of the homes before it is finally contained, some days later. The displaced residents are going to seek a safe place to temporarily store their salvaged belongings until they can resettle.

With Judea being destroyed, the Temple gone, and Jerusalem in flames, it is quite likely that different groups came to the caves around Qumran to store sacred texts they had salvaged, anticipating that they could reclaim them when the war was over. In remote caves, buried in the desert near Zealot strongholds, they had some hope that these cherished books would be saved from the general destruction, later to be retrieved.

What we have here in the caves of Qumran, in my opinion, is an ancient repository, not a library. Archeologically, we have reclaimed storehouses of literary documents that were so highly valued they were singled out for rescue during the greatest catastrophe to befall the Jewish people.

That being the case, the scrolls of Qumran are a rare window into the past, presenting us with a cross-section of Jewish literature, which embraces much of Jewish society during the period of the late Second Temple. This is a period that was vitally important to the subsequent development of Judaism and the emergence of Christianity. For the very discovery of this priceless literature, we should be eternally grateful. We should be ever diligent in our pursuit of the meaning and messages it holds for us and for future generations.

The Importance of the Dead Sea Scrolls

It is my contention that most or all of the Dead Sea Scrolls are first-century copies and transcriptions of works that date back centuries, in the case of the non-Sectarian literature, and to the period of the Maccabees and the subsequent Hasmonean dynasty, in the case of the literature of the Sect.

If indeed the *hasidim* of 1 and 2 Maccabees are the Essenes, then the Essene community mentioned in the works of Pliny, Philo, and Josephus are the product of two centuries of evolution. Josephus mentions the Essenes of his own day as being actively involved in the War against Rome. The *hasidim* of the Maccabean period, the main support group of Judah Maccabee, certainly were active, aggressive fighters. Therefore, it should be no surprise that even such documents as the War Scroll could have been authored by the early Essenes.

The war against Rome was a life-and-death struggle. It was waged by the Jewish people in order to preserve its religious beliefs and traditions and to save its national existence from being obliterated by the regime of a ruthless and brutal foreign overlord. The aims and objectives, as well as the driving forces, underlying this desperate war of survival have very close parallels to the Maccabean Revolt.

It is, therefore, very probable that the literature of the Maccabean period was of intense interest to Jews during this period of religious transformation and social upheaval. It is also very likely that the beliefs, objectives, patterns, and strategies of the Hasmonean period were regarded as successful models to emulate during the war.

During the Enlightenment in Europe, classical literature was revived and intently studied, Greco-Roman art, architecture, philosophy, and science were studied intensively and openly emulated. Why? Because the spirit and the reality of contemporary seventeenth- and eighteenth-century European society had a close connection, on many levels, to the classical world and its worldview. There are numerous examples of such cyclical movement in history.

Why ignore the obvious possibility that Jewish society in Israel, during the period from the Roman conquest to the suppression of the Bar Kochba Revolt, looked back to the Maccabean period and its literature as the source on which to model its aspirations, direction, and goals? They were kindred realities. What is more, the Hasmoneans had succeeded in liberating Israel and saving Judaism. There is no better model than a successful one.

The two wars against Rome constituted an intense and pro-tracted struggle—one that involved the active participation of the entire nation in a life-and-death struggle, both in 66 C.E. and in 135 C.E. If the literature found at Qumran was held in such high esteem, with people reproducing the documents and risking their lives to save them from destruction, then it had become, at this point in time, the literature of the Jewish people as a whole. The Qumran literature reflected the hopes, the dreams, and the aspirations, both social and spiritual, of all Israel—not just the beliefs of a small, secluded, and self-defined group.

If we come to understand this fact and accept it, then the Dead Sea Scrolls offer us a much broader understanding of the political realities and spiritual concerns of the Jews and Judaism in the last two centuries of the Second Commonwealth. The scrolls will come to provide us with much greater information and detail about the spiritual concerns and religious debates that were current among the Jewish people at a very formative period of time in the development of Judaism and, subsequently, in the emergence of Christianity.

Hopefully, by dialoguing with this material and reintegrating it fully into the core religious literature of Judaism and Christianity, we will be able to expand our knowledge and appreciation of the past, on one hand, and, on the other, to use this sacred and valuable litera-ture as a theological and spiritual springboard into the future.

4

THE SECTARIAN LITERATURE: DEFINING THE PURPOSE, THE PERSPECTIVE, AND THE SELF-IMAGE OF THE COMMUNITY

In order to illustrate that the Community described in the Sectarian literature from Qumran was Essene, in the broad sense of the term, we need to examine carefully the understanding the Community had of itself. We need to validate that the Sectarian Community shared the same, general, overall religious viewpoint and the behavioral orientation attributed to the Essenes in the writings of Josephus, Philo, and Pliny.

It is important to reiterate that among any of the broad categorizations within Jewish belief during the Greco-Roman period, there were, obviously, diverse variant groups within each general category. For example, along with the Pharisees (according to the Gospels), there were the Scribes, whose views were similar to the Pharisees but who were a distinguishable group nonetheless. It is entirely possible that this group represented the early Rabbis.

Among the early Rabbis themselves, there were different schools of thought within the movement, such as the School of Hillel and the School of Shammai mentioned in the Mishnah. The School of Hillel and the School of Shammai differed halakhically on a number of different issues, with each School deriving its own interpretation of some of the laws and commandments. Both went their own direction in setting their own perimeters, in terms of rules for observance. Yet both Schools of thought were steeped in the Oral Law. Both were bound by it. Both Schools contributed to the development the *halakhah*. Both were Pharisaic in orientation.

Based on the scattered references in the *Mishnah*, it is very likely that such groups as the *Haverim*—who placed great emphasis on tithing and on strict observance of the laws of cleanliness and ritual purity—adhered to the Pharisaic view of religious life as well.

The group that Josephus calls the "Fourth Philosophy," the Zealots (whom Josephus blames for fermenting the revolt against Rome), was allied to the Pharisees in terms of its religious beliefs and orientation. Yet the Zealots represent a distinct theological grouping, in and of themselves. Presumably, this category, too, encompassed a number of different groups sharing a similar theological outlook. From Josephus' historical account, we know that during the first century, there were a number of Zealot groups who were often at such odds with each other that it bred violent confrontation.

The Sectarians of the Dead Sea literature were a group that seems to be Essenic. Solomon Zeitlin makes a very good case for identifying the Essenes with the group mentioned in the ancient sources as the *hasidim*. He points out that the *hasidim*, the pietists who supported Judah Maccabee during his fight against the Greeks, are called in the Book of the Maccabees the *Asidaioi*, which would be the Greek rendition of the word *hasidim*.

The term *hasid*, in Hebrew, means "pious" or "Pious One." Philo, in explaining the origin of the name "Essene," states that it derives from the Greek word *Osiotes*, meaning "holiness" or "piety." Josephus uses the same term, "Essene," to describe various individuals or groups that appear in his history. A third century Hebrew translation of Josephus, called the *Josephon*, consistently translates the epithet "Essene" as *hasid*. Whether the *hasidim* were a branch of Essenes or whether the two were interchangeable terms is not certain. However, it will become clear as we examine the sectarian scrolls that the Dead Sea Scroll Sectarians were a branch of the Essene movement.

Among the most extensive and most important of the scrolls that constitute the Sectarian literature of Qumran are the Damascus Covenant, the Community Rule, the War Scroll, and a letter referred to as the MMT. These documents speak to us of the community organization of the group, their philosophy, and their approach to the Law.

How the Community Viewed Itself

In the Damascus Covenant, an interesting commentary is made on a verse from the prophetic book of Ezekiel. Chapter 44, verse 15 states, "The priests, Levites, and the Sons of Zadok, who have kept charge of My Sanctuary, when the Children of Israel went astray, they shall offer Me fat and blood."

Since the Damascus Covenant refers to the Covenanters, the Sectarians, as the Sons of Zadok, it is not surprising that the document comments on this particular verse. The scroll equates the priests mentioned in Ezekiel with those whose hearts were converted among Israel and who left for the land of Damascus. The Levites are identified as those who subsequently joined the original group. The Sons of Zadok are said to be those who will stand triumphant at the End of Days.

We are told here that the Sectarians refer to themselves as the Sons of Zadok. The reference here is most likely to Zadok, the High Priest who served under King David. The implication is that among the original group that left Judea and emigrated to Damascus were priests who felt that they were descendants or followers of Zadok. This means that they saw themselves as remaining true to the highest traditions of the priesthood and that they remained uncorrupted and untainted. They were faithful when the rest of Israel was led astray. Hence, they and those who joined their ranks are the Elect of Israel. They will remain standing tall and their actions will be justified during the final redemption of Israel.

The scroll continues to say that these first men of righteousness were given a specific Interpretation of the Law of Moses. They were instructed in it thoroughly. Those who enter the Covenant are to adhere strictly to this interpretation of the Law until the completion of the Age of Wrath and the coming of the End of Days. By so adhering to the Interpretation, all of their sins will be forgiven. After the completion of the current Age, however, it will no longer be possible to join the House of Judah.

The members of the Covenant felt that they were the true House of Judah. As such, they were thereby bound to follow strictly the Interpretation of the Law of Moses, revealed and taught to them by the Teacher of Righteousness. Such adherence was necessary in order to obtain forgiveness from God for their sins and, presumably, to atone for the sins of Israel as a whole. This was their role, as the Sectarians saw it.

They, however, were not an exclusivist community. Anyone was able to join, if they did so before the Final Judgement of Mankind and provided they lived in accordance with the Interpretation that was set down. The Interpretation of the Law established by the Teacher of Righteousness was the constitution of the Community.

More is said about the origin and purpose of the Covenant Sectarians in another commentary on a biblical verse treated in the scroll. The Damascus Covenant quotes Isaiah 54:16: "The well which the Princes dug, which the nobles of the people delved with the stave."

The image in this verse is that of a well being dug and then probed with a stave. The diggers are said to be those who left Judea for Damascus. They are called princes because their reputations were impeccable. Their renown and integrity were unchallenged. The well that was dug and probed was the Torah, the Law of Moses. It was delved into by the Teacher of Righteousness, who established the true Interpretation that is to guide the community until the End of Days. The nobles of the people are all of those who live their lives abiding by the Interpretation until the Teacher of Righteousness returns at the final End-Time.

The Covenanters looked to the Interpretation of the Law, taught to the founders of the movement by the Teacher of Righteousness, as the whole basis and foundation for their way of life. It was to be a temporary way of life that would bring them through the dark days leading to the End of Time, the Final Judgement. Their adherence to the Law, via the Teacher of Righteousness' Interpretation, would atone for their sins and be the vehicle that led to the redemption of Israel.

What principles did the Interpretation spell out? What, exactly, was expected of the Covenant Community?

The Concerns of the Community

Two of the most central concerns of the community were to adhere to the Covenant—the Law of Moses, the Torah—and to keep away from the major snares of evil, ever present in the current Age of Darkness.

At the beginning of the Damascus Covenant, an interpretation is made of Hosea 4:16. "Like a stubborn heifer was Israel stubborn." We are told that this refers to the rise of "the Man of Derision," who flooded Israel with lies, attacked the righteous, justified the wicked, and removed the boundaries set down by the forefathers.

This great deceiver led many to violate the Law, the Covenant, which is portrayed as an eternal height and the way of righteousness. The implication is that the deliberate violation of Mosaic Law was justified by this "man of derision." The violation of the Covenant, which this leader of the people propounded, served to lead many astray and, consequently, provoked God's wrath. Our document clearly states that violation of the Covenant has triggered the Curse, the avenging sword of Covenant.

The curse being referred to is the Curse invoked by Moses in his final oration at the end of the Torah.

> See, I set before you this day, life and prosperity, death and adversity. For I command you this day to love the Lord your God, to walk in His ways, and to keep His commandments, His laws and His norms, that you may thrive and increase, and that the Lord, your God may bless you in the land you are about to enter and occupy. BUT, if your heart turns away and you give no heed, and you are lured into the worship of other gods, I declare to you this day that you shall certainly perish. You shall not long endure on the land which you are crossing the Jordan to enter and to occupy.
>
> I call Heaven and Earth to witness regarding you this day. I have put before you life and death, blessing and curse. Choose life, if you and your descendants would live, by loving the Lord, your God, heeding His commandments, and holding fast to Him. For thereby you shall have life and shall long endure upon the land that the Lord, your God, swore to Abraham, Isaac, and Jacob, to give to them. (Deuteronomy 30:15–20)

The view in the Damascus Covenant is quite clear. The forces of Darkness, represented by the Deceiver, through their teachings and their behavior ridicule the Law and lead the people to transgress the commandments. This, in turn, has triggered the operation of the Curse, which as part of the divine mechanism of reward and punishment, is built into the Law. Transgression of the Law has led to the dark times of suffering and persecution, injustice and violence.

One of the most important—indeed, most imperative—decisions a Jew was to make was to turn away from the realm of Evil and to avoid any further transgression of the Covenant. The Damascus Covenant makes several observations to support this truth.

First, God is said to have patience for those who turn away from transgression and He pardons them. Yet those who willfully depart from the Law and do not repent are consigned to the Angel of Death. God has always known there would be wicked and evil people and that many would be led astray. So God has always sent individuals anointed with the Holy Spirit, filled with divine inspiration, to proclaim the truth—that is, that the way to redemption is through repentance and a return to the Law, to the precepts God imparted at Mount Sinai, to the road God has asked the people to follow.

The Torah, the Law of Moses, states clearly that the people—both as individuals and as a nation—have a choice. They can choose to obey the injunctions God has laid down for those who have undertaken the obligation of the Covenant or they can choose to reject them. There are consequences related to either decision.

What the Covenant scroll tells us is that God is aware of the propensity of the people to be led away from their commitments. Therefore, God periodically sends inspired individuals to remind us of our obligations and then allows us the latitude to repent and return.

Those who do return to God and resume observance of the Law are the remnant of the faithful. They will be saved from the destructive consequences of rebellion. Those who stubbornly refuse to listen and willfully resist will be given enough rope with which to hang themselves. God will allow them to stray, and eventually, they will have to face the full consequences of their decision. The reader is told to choose that which God loves and reject that which He hates. We are instructed not to follow our own guilty inclinations or act on the lust in our eyes.

We are told that the Heavenly Watchers, those who (according to the account in Genesis) came down from Heaven and married the daughters of men, were acting out of lust and walked in the stubbornness of their own hearts. This led them to violate the commandments God had set down for them. As a result of this willful rebellion, His anger was kindled against them, and although they were physically as mighty as mountains and as tall and strong as cedars, they were utterly destroyed. They pursued their own will, corrupted humanity, and violated the commandments of God purposefully. God, in turn, destroyed them root and branch—so thoroughly, in fact, that no trace of them remains. It is as if they never existed.

We are reminded that when the Israelites were in the desert, after leaving Mount Sinai, they were brought to the borders of the land of Canaan and commanded to march into the country and possess it.

After hearing the fearful and distorted account presented by the spies Moses had sent in to scout the land, the people refused to move into Canaan. This was a willful refusal to fulfill the command of God, "Go up and possess the Land" (Deuteronomy 9:23). The people chose their own will over God's. God therefore destroyed that entire generation by consigning them to wander in the desert for forty years.

In contrast, the Damascus Covenant points out that Noah did not choose his own will, unlike his entire generation. He walked with God instead. Consequently, he was not only saved but became the progenitor of a renewed humanity. Abraham, Isaac, and Jacob were party to a Covenant with God. They followed God's commandments, and were counted as friends of God.

The Sectarians, the Damascus Community, believed—as did many other groups in the Jewish world—that observance of the Law was of paramount importance. It was the proper relationship between Israel and God, as well as the gateway to national survival and redemption. Their message was that to abandon observance of the commandments was willful rebellion against God. Violation of the Law led to the invocation of the Curse, which unleashed widespread suffering and destruction.

Their position was that only through repentance and return to the observance of the Law was there salvation. They believed that the Teacher of Righteousness revealed the mysteries of the Law to the founders of the Covenant Community in Damascus. Through adherence to the Interpretation set down by the Teacher of Righteousness, the holy remnant of Israel would be able to get through the current age of Darkness and facilitate the rebuilding of Israel. Ultimately, they would see the coming, final destruction of evil and the institution of peace, at the time of the Divine Judgment.

The question then arises, what exactly was the nature of this Age of the Dominion of Evil? What were the righteous supposed to work so hard to separate themselves from?

Dealing with Evil in the Age of Wickedness

The members of the New Covenant, made in Damascus, were instructed to separate themselves entirely from three major snares presented by the Sons of the Pit, the forces of Darkness. The first was the snare of wealth.

The primary evil connected with wealth was the manner in which riches were often obtained. The scroll specifically attacks any practice that results in enriching oneself through deception or violence. It also condemns deriving any benefit whatsoever from ill-gotten gain.

One such method of deriving ill-gotten wealth was the use of the vow. Deriving wealth from the result of a vow or an anathema meant, on a practical level, gaining financially by depriving someone else of the access to, and use of, something of value.

In Jewish practice, a vow was undertaken voluntarily either to establish the sanctity of something or to obligate oneself to demonstrate higher levels of personal religious commitment. By using specific verbal formulas, one consecrated something to God or imposed on oneself a restriction against doing something that otherwise would be permitted.

For example, by the use of a vow formula, one might undertake the obligation to refrain from eating meat for a period of one year. This would be done in order to show one's sincerity in asking forgiveness for a certain transgression for which one was repenting. One might also vow regarding an object. If one declared, for instance, that one's gold ring is under vow, then it is of the same status as a gift to the Temple. One has donated it to God as consecrated property. Hence, one no longer owns it. The ring is now a donation to God. This may be as a sign of thanksgiving for something that has happened, or, perhaps, as an act of charity.

The legal effect of the vow was that the object was effectively removed from the individual's possession and consecrated to God, either permanently or for a specified period of time. Therefore, the vowed object was consecrated property and not usable by any lay person. In the case of a self-imposed restriction—such as abstaining from eating meat for year—legally, it had to be upheld for the full term of the vow. Biblical law states very clearly that when one gives one's word, one is bound to fulfill it. Moreover, no person mentioned in the vow could benefit from the resulting action.

For example, using a ritual formula one could say, "Korban is my wheat field to me and my family for one year." In essence, what is being said is that for one year the wheat field is consecrated to God, that any benefit derived from it must go to the Temple, and that neither the vower nor any member of his family could use it or gain any benefit from it whatsoever during the entire one-year term.

The institution of the vow was open to the possibility of serious abuse. One could declare a valuable business asset under vow and thereby prevent a competitor, a family member, an employee, or even a business partner from having access to it or use of it. It was out-of-bounds because it was sacred. For that matter, no one could even derive any indirect benefit from it. The partner or competitor would be completely frozen out, rightly or wrongly.

One could also impose on oneself a course of inaction, through the use of a vow, which could have serious repercussions on other people. Both the *Mishnah* and the New Testament speak of the moral breach involved if one declares one's property under vow and proscribed to one's parents. Jesus views this action as a deliberate attempt to avoid having to sustain one's parents and regards it as a violation of the fifth commandment, to honor your father and mother (Mark 7:10–15).

Similarly, the *Mishnah* (*Nedarim* 9:1) specifically opens up the possibility of annulling this type of vow on the basis that it was undertaken in ignorance and, therefore, is not valid by its nature. The reasoning here is that it is a direct commandment from God to honor one's father and mother. To violate a direct commandment willfully is an extremely grave sin. The assumption is that no one would consciously do this if they fully understood the implications of what they were proposing. Here we have an example of a person misusing the vow to deprive others of material benefit for his own reasons and personal gain.

The Damascus Covenant maintains that robbing the poor and victimizing the widow or the orphan, making profit off of the Temple treasury, or accumulating wealth by vow and anathema are all unclean acts.

This is an interesting and important assertion. Much emphasis in biblical law is placed on separating oneself from, avoiding contact with, and the consumption of that which is unclean. Most of the cleanliness laws involve avoidance of contamination, such as contact with corpses, prohibitions against eating certain types of animals, and states of ritual uncleanliness. These refer to states of impurity that would render one temporarily unfit to come into the Temple or touch anything associated with it.

The Damascus scroll goes one step further and classifies the act of accumulating ill-gotten wealth, and the insidious practices often connected with such pursuits, as being equally defiling and equally repugnant to God. The concepts of cleanliness and purity are being extended and merged with the moral commandments of the Bible.

Being in a state of uncleanliness, in biblical law, meant that until the condition was corrected or remitted, one was temporarily unable to draw near to God's service. Biblical law is very explicit about the procedures that need to be taken to purify a person and render him or her pure and whole. Uncleanliness is a contaminated state, and while in it, one is cut off from the community. However, it is temporary and rectifiable.

Biblical law is emphatic about the gravity of the sins of oppression. One is not to take advantage of the poor, the orphan, or the widow. One is to treat the stranger as a full member of the community. One is to be honest in business and in weights and measures. One is to leave the corner of the field unharvested for the sustenance of the poor. One is neither to persecute one's neighbor, nor stand by idly when something happens to him. The list of such commandments is very long.

The Damascus Covenant, by determining that the violation of these basic social and moral laws render one unclean—in the same sense that one becomes ritually unclean from contact with certain types of severe contaminants—is very important in its implication.

What is implied in the scroll, quite simply, is that these social and religious laws are to be viewed as being designed to prevent people from falling into a moral state that will preclude them from the community of Israel and from the service of God. The sense here is that violation of the moral laws in the Bible renders one spiritually unclean in the same way that contact with concrete contaminants renders one physically unclean. Just as physical contact with impure things contaminates an individual physically, moral transgression is seen as spiritually defiling.

It is important to realize that spiritual uncleanliness can be removed. If we understand the scroll correctly, spiritual defilement is erased and corrected by repentance and by a return to the observance of the precepts of the Law. Spiritual contamination is cleansed by holding fast to the Law and its Interpretation, through the difficult days that mark the culmination of the Age of Darkness.

The second major snare the scroll defines is that of fornication. In the technical language of the scrolls, the term Z'nut, "fornication," refers to forbidden sexual relationships. Proper sexual conduct within the context of marriage is a most important issue in the sectarian scrolls. The concern here is with practices that the Sectarians feel are misinterpretations of the intent of the Law that, inadvertently, can lead to incest. Here again, we are dealing with how the Law is to be accurately interpreted and applied to daily life.

Two practices are attacked as incest in the Damascus Covenant. The first is the practice of an uncle marrying his niece. In biblical law, quite a few different types of relationships are clearly spelled out as forbidden and incestuous. The law clearly states that a man cannot marry his aunt because she is close kin. However, nothing specifically states that a woman is forbidden to her uncle in marriage.

The approach taken by the Sadducees, the Pharisees, and later by the Rabbis was that if something is not specifically forbidden in the Torah, it is permissible. The difference between the Sadducees and the Pharisees was that the Sadducees went no further. The Pharisees, on the other hand, felt that if there were oral traditions connected with a law or commandment and its observance or if there were practices relating to it that could be deduced from Scripture, those practices were binding as well.

Both the Pharisees and Sadducees viewed the silence on the question of an uncle–niece marriage as permitting the possibility. Apparently, the custom was widespread at the time. The Sectarians objected vehemently.

Their position was very clear. They argued that even though the commandments are conventionally phrased in the masculine form, they are directed to all of Israel. In this case, a man cannot marry his aunt on the grounds that she is close kin. It would stand to reason, then, that the same premise should be binding on women as well. The corollary of this commandment would be that a woman cannot marry her uncle because he is close kin.

> There are also those that defile the Temple, in that they do not distinguish properly the [laws of the] Torah, having sexual relations with she who is witnessing a menstrual flow or [in the case of] a man who marries the daughter of his brother or the daughter of his sister. Moses said, "You shall not marry your mother's sister, for she is your mother's kin." The laws of incest are written for males, but they also apply to women. Therefore, if you uncover the nakedness of your brother's daughter, it is also the nakedness of your brother, her father, for she is kin. (Lohse transcription, CD 5:6–11)

The Damascus Covenant also delineates another form of sexual sin, this being a man who takes more than one wife. That is, the Damascus Covenant condemns polygamy as a sexual transgression. Fornication is described here as taking a second wife while the first is still alive. Polygamy is seen as a violation of Divine Law. Emphasis is placed on two being the natural number for union. The scroll points out that the animals were brought to the Ark at God's command in pairs.

The implication is that these animals were to preserve the animal kingdom and that proper procreation was the result of monogamous pairing, as ordained by God. The scroll then extends the concept to mankind itself, by referring to the statement in Genesis 2, that male and female He made them, and by quoting Deuteronomy 17:17, "A man shall not multiply wives unto himself."

A third specific illustration of fornication appears in the MMT letter.

> Regarding the fornication that is done among the people, for they are a holy people, as it is written, "Israel is holy" and regarding his dress, it is written that it is not to be *sh'atnez* [a mixture of wool and flax], and that the seed of his field and vineyard are not to be of mixed variety, for they are holy and the sons of Aaron are the Holy of Holies. As you well know, that some of the priests and the people are intermingling and mixing and defiling the holy seed, even their seed with fornication. . . . (Eisenman and Wise transcription, 4Q 394–398, part 2:83–89)

In this document, it is fornication as sexual transgression, in a different sense, that is being portrayed. At first glance, it would be tempting to assume that the issue being addressed is one of intermarriage. However, upon closer scrutiny it becomes clearer that the concern is with an improper understanding of the Law.

Biblical law is quite specific about prohibiting marriage with idolaters. Commandments to that effect appear frequently in the text of the Torah. Should this have been the problem, the letter most likely would have stated so explicitly. Most certainly, it would have also quoted some of those ordinances directly.

Rather, we are told that the people and some priests are mingling their seed sexually and thereby violating the law of *sh'atnez*, the mixture of wool and flax, and the law of *kela'im*, sowing a field or vineyard with mixed seed. What is more, emphasis is placed on the fact that Israel is a holy people and that the priests are the holiest of the people.

The logic here is that God has instituted commandments that prohibit the mixing of two things that are distinct from one another. Wool is a material derived from an animal, while flax is derived from a plant. Though both are made into fabrics and can be interwoven, they are both very different in nature and that integrity must not be violated by admixture.

It would seem that the dispute here has to do with sexual liaison, rather than intermarriage. Intermarriage is specifically and emphatically prohibited. Yet it seems probable that since there is no direct commandment forbidding sexual relations per se, it may well be that the prevailing view at the time was that sexual liaisons were permissible, providing that they did not result in marriage. This was definitely not the position of the authors of the MMT letter.

There is an additional possible component. A segment of the priesthood is taken to task along with the people. This may simply mean that there were some priests guilty of this type of sexual misconduct whose behavior would only legitimatize a wanton violation of the Law, in the opinion of the Sectarians. However, it could have further implications.

A priest was forbidden to marry harlots, widows, or divorced women. Yet this is another instance where, by omission, it could be interpreted that although marriage is strictly forbidden in these cases, sexual liaison would not be. In either case, the logic would be that by transgressing the boundaries of sexual propriety, both the people, in general, and the priests, specifically, have profaned their status, rendered themselves unclean, and violated the Law. They have mixed together that which was to remain apart. The vision of the Hebrew prophets was that eventually all the nations of the earth would recognize the sovereignty of God, worship at His Holy mountain, and be one. One builds by respecting boundaries and honoring natural bounds, not by violating or obliterating them.

It is the hope of the Sectarians that all Israel will understand the Law correctly and refrain from those practices which violate the Sinai Covenant and thereby bring disaster and suffering to the entire people. The Dominion of Evil continually seeks to break down the boundaries between the holy and the profane, between the appropriate and the inappropriate, by misleading the people into abandoning or transgressing the commandments. For when the Law is not fulfilled and not kept properly, the Curse is activated and the nation is reduced to great suffering and impotency. This weakness fuels the Dominion of Evil.

This brings us to the third destructive lure of the Age of Darkness, the profanation of the Temple. The Damascus Scroll suggests that the Temple is the individual in particular. It defines profanation of the Temple in two ways. First—in the physical sense—the Temple, the physical body, is profaned when one does not strictly observe the laws distinguishing between clean and unclean.

Mankind's purpose is to serve God. By violating the laws of ritual purity and of cleanliness, one renders oneself temporarily unfit to connect with God on the highest level. By not distinguishing between the holy and the profane, by doing what God has expressly forbid, one violates the very purpose of being. One disconnects from God's service and pursues his own will, distancing himself from the Creator.

Spiritually, according to the scroll, one defiles his or her soul by blaspheming and rejecting the laws of the Covenant.

> Moreover, they have defiled their holy spirit with a tongue of blasphemies. They have opened their mouth against the laws of the Covenant of God saying, "They are not truly clear" [i.e., They are not truly established. They have no foundation.] and they speak abominations about them. They are all those, who ignite fires and cause sparks to burn [becoming fires]. Their webs are spiders' webs and their eggs are those of vipers. Whoever is close to them will not be cleansed. As one draws closer he will incur guilt, for it follows inevitably. For God remembers their deeds and His anger will be kindled because of their exploits. For they are not a people of understanding. They are a people of destructive advice, in that they have no understanding. (CD5:11–16)

The task of the righteous man, as depicted in the Sectarian literature, is to free himself from the influence of the deceivers—"the Men of the Pit," as they are called. Those who seek to survive the last days of Dominion of Evil are asked to hold fast to the Law as interpreted to their forebears by the Teacher of Righteousness.

They are to refrain from and distance themselves from the three traps of Evil—profiting from injustice, breaking down the boundaries between the holy and profane, and doubting the importance and supremacy of the Law of God, by word or by deed.

How this was to be accomplished was in the context of the Covenant Community. As is characteristic of Jewish thinking in general, so, too, among the Sectarians and Essenes. Salvation was not seen as an individual issue but, rather, in broader terms as the salvation, first, of the people of the Community, then of Israel, and finally, of humanity as a whole.

The Covenant Community, be they Essenes or Dead Sea Sectarians, developed a specific communal organization to express their aspirations and facilitate the Way of Life prescribed by the constitution, set down by the founders of the Community, and delineated by the Interpretation of the Law that was presented to them by the Teacher of Righteousness. To better understand this, we need to examine the structure and the organization of the Community as it was set up by the Damascus Covenanters.

5

FORM EXPRESSING CONTENT: UNDERSTANDING THE STRUCTURE AND REGULATION OF THE SECTARIAN COMMUNITY

Form is the outward manifestation of inner essence expressing itself in material form. How an individual organizes and conducts his or her life, and the physical characteristics it takes on as a result, communicate to the world something of the essence of the individual.

For example, the style of dress one adopts, one's manner of deportment, one's patterns of speech, and general personality traits all communicate something very specific about the individual. The broader patterns of our lives, the careers we choose, the roles we play in family and community, and the interests we pursue are external expressions of our inner being.

The same holds true for a community. To understand its inner core, the essence of a community, it is wise to focus on its structure. The way a group organizes itself reflects the principles upon which it is built. The principles upon which the community's life turns illustrate its aspirations and the underlying beliefs the group holds about the world and their relationship to it.

The Organization of the Community

The community portrayed in the Sectarian literature had a very clearly delineated internal organization. Through an examination and analysis of the tight, formal structure of the Covenant Community, we have an opportunity to gain considerable insight into the spiritual beliefs and worldview of a significant segment of first century Israel. If the literature does indeed reflect the organization and beliefs of the Essenes, then we are being given a window to a sizable and influential segment of Jewry.

Both the Damascus Covenant and the Community Rule speak on the structure of the Community and the rules that were to govern its regulation. The structure of the Community can best be approached from the general to the specific. I would prefer to start with what the scrolls say regarding the general organization of the Community and move systematically through the divisions within the Community to the responsibilities and obligations of the individual members.

The scope and organization of the Community can largely be reconstructed from the information found in three of the Sectarian scrolls: the Community Rule (1QS), the Damascus Covenant (CD), and the Messianic Rule (1QSa). For the sake of simplicity, in portraying the structure of Community I will organize the materials by subject matter. In annotating the sources of the information, I will refer to each of the documents by code letters: CD for Damascus Covenant, CR for Community Rule, and MR for Messianic Rule. The following, then, is a brief outline of the Community's overall structure.

The Community was originally formed by priests who traced their lineage back to Zadok, the High Priest under King David, and who separated themselves from the Temple in Jerusalem, forming a new Covenant Community in Damascus. At its core, the Community remained centered around the priesthood. Authority was vested in the priests, the Sons of Zadok. It was they who were to determine doctrine, coordinate property use and distribution, and administer justice (CR).

One chose to join the Community as a matter of free will. When one did so, one had to swear an oath to return to the Law of Moses and to abide by the teachings of the Sons of Zadok. The Community was also referred to as "The Congregation" and "The House of Truth" (CR).

The Community was ruled by priests, who had to be well-versed in the Law and in the *Sefer Haguy*, the Book of Meditations. Were any priest insufficiently trained and not knowledgeable enough—while, at the same time, a Levite met these qualifications—the latter's decisions and instructions were to be followed instead. The Community was, in turn, organized into groups of ten, fifty, one hundred, and one thousand. This replicated the organizational principle used by Moses to group the people for purposes of administration during the forty years of wandering in the desert (CD).

The entire social structure of the Community was that of a well-thought-out and comprehensive hierarchy. Upon formal acceptance into the Community, one was examined carefully regarding one's knowledge of the Law, one's understanding of the precepts of the Community, and one's level of religious observance. The individual was then ranked according his level of attainment. This fixed his position within the Community and affected everything from where he sat during the Meal to when his opinion was asked for during meetings. This process was repeated yearly and one was ranked anew. One could be advanced or moved back, depending on the level of spiritual achievement demonstrated by one's knowledge and observance (CR).

The Community ate, prayed, and deliberated in common. The Pure Meal and Pure Drink were communal events. Participation in them indicated full membership within the Community. Prayer and study, as well as general debate and discussion, were also communal in nature. When the Congregation assembled, the priests sat first, the elders second, and third, the people sat by rank. All were asked to speak in turn by rank and could not interrupt one another while speaking. Moreover, subordinates always had to defer to those superior in standing, in all matters pertaining to work and in all issues concerning money (CR).

Although matters of doctrine, property, and justice were decided by the priests, they were done so apparently in conjunction with the Council of the Community. The Council was summoned by the priests, the Sons of Zadok; and those eligible to serve on the Council were the elders, the judges, the officers of the Community, the chiefs of the tribes, the chiefs of the divisions, and the Levites (MR).

The Council consisted of twelve men and three priests. If the Council was truncated and had only ten men, one of the ten had to be a priest. Anyone serving on the Council had to be perfectly versed in the Law and had to be just, honest, and righteous in all his actions. In all his dealings he was to be truthful, just and honest, kind and gracious, and humble (CR).

What is more, one individual among the Council was designated to study the Law day and night—presumably to be a permanent, living resource to the Council in its deliberations and advice. Among those deliberating, each Council member was asked for counsel, opinion, and advice, in order of superiority (CR). According to the Messianic Rule, the order followed was that of the priests, then the Levites, chiefs, judges, and the people. In the Damascus Covenant, proselytes were added to the end of the list.

A person nominated to the Council went through a two-year probationary cycle before being confirmed. If a Council member transgressed the Law advertently at any time, he was removed from the Council and expelled from the Community. If the trespass was inadvertent, the offender was suspended from the Council and excluded from the Meal for a two-year period. If, after that point, he became whole again, he could be reinstated (CR).

The Council was called the House of Holiness. Its function was to atone for the Land and to pave the way for the punishment of the wicked. It was to be set apart as holy, and he who interpreted the Law should not hide anything he had learned or uncovered regarding the Law from the Council. Living by the rules set down for the Community and the Council established a spirit of holiness, which in turn atoned for the sins of unfaithfulness and the guilt of rebellion (CR).

The holiness of the Council lay in its function of regulating the Community and keeping it focused on the observance of the Law and on the correct performance of the Commandments. By so doing, God's Grace was gained, which resulted in a flow of blessing to the Land on all levels, without the need for the flesh of burnt offerings or the fat of animal sacrifices (CR).

The Damascus Covenant informs us that the Community had an administrator, referred to as the *Mevakair*. The term itself is rather interesting. The verb from which the word comes, *bekair*, in its technical sense, means "to critique, review, audit, control." That seems to be its primary connotation in this context.

On a secondary level, the term may also refer to close personal interaction, attending to the needs of the Community. The verb, *bekair*, in its most common sense, means "to visit, to attend to."

The *Mevakair*, the administrator, was to instruct the Congregation in the works of God. In all likelihood, this meant the day-to-day regulation of the Community, which was doing God's work. It may also be alluding to instructing the Community in the Law, its ordinances, and in the interpretation of the Law set down by the Teacher of Righteousness. Either way, the *Mevakair* was instructed to love the people as one loves children and to guide them as one tends to a flock (DC).

On the practical side of the coin, the *Mevakair* as administrator was to be solely responsible for all buying and selling. He alone was responsible for limiting transactions with the Sons of the Pit, the wicked, to the receipt of payment. It was also the job of the *Mevakair* to examine every person entering the Community. He registered their property. It was he who was to examine each entrant on his knowledge level of the Law, his observance level, his conduct, his strength and abilities, and then assign him a rank in the Community.

Only the *Mevakair* could admit one into the Community. It was his decision. Whoever entered the Community was bound to act in accordance with his word. All suits and judgements were to be brought before the *Mevakair*. We are told also that in the case of leprosy, if a priest was not knowledgeable or experienced enough to handle the determination, the quarantine, and the cleansing processes that needed to be done, he was to be instructed by the *Mevakair*. So instructed, the priest was to follow the procedures outlined strictly (CD).

In summary, there are several important observations that can be made regarding the significance of the Community's structure. First, it is of particular importance that the Community broke from Jerusalem and, under the auspices of a number of Zadokite priests, formed a new way of life.

A Nation of Priests and a Holy People

The communal nature of the Community derives from the very nature of the priesthood itself. The organization of the Temple ritual and the priestly participation in it were communal by nature. The priests operated as a coherent class, with a specific hierarchy of functions. This commonality and sense of structured existence was carried over into the new Covenant Community, established originally in Damascus.

The meals, the prayers, study, and deliberation, all done in common, were, in essence, structural carry-overs from the Temple organization. This, and the involvement of the priests in all levels of the Community's life, strongly suggests that the overall objective of the

Covenant Community was to prepare first themselves, then ultimately the entire people of Israel, to fulfill their role as a nation of priests and a holy people, as expressed in the Law.

That the priests who founded the Community removed themselves from Jerusalem and termed themselves the "Sons of Zadok" points to the belief that the official Temple priesthood was tainted and not capable of fulfilling the Laws of Moses properly. It is entirely possible that, to some degree, the Jerusalem priesthood was blamed for a severe failure of leadership and for facilitating and encouraging the downfall of the people.

The Scoffer, or Man of Lies, that is portrayed in the literature as the chief antagonist and persecutor of the Teacher of Righteousness, is said to have deceived the people and to have led them into rebellion against the Law. The implication seems to be that this Deceiver was a priest, very possibly the High Priest.

As we will see, a number of the legal disputes the Community had with the authorities in Jerusalem revolved around differing views of what constituted the correct interpretation and application of specific laws. Incorrect application of the commandments meant, to the Covenant Community, a gross violation of the laws and, subsequently, the incurring of divine anger and suffering.

The impetus behind the Community was one of social renewal and spiritual regeneration. The Community was based on the leadership of the priests as ordained in the Torah, in the Law of Moses, and was established with the understanding that its members freely chose to enter a renewed and revitalized Covenant, reaffirming their allegiance to the Law and submitting themselves to God's will.

Such submission required surrendering their dependency on material goods and no longer putting their trust in material security. All property within the Community was communally held, dispensed, and utilized. Personal possession ceased to exist upon acceptance into the Community. The slavery of material concern was negated by entering into the Community of the Covenant.

Submission to God also involved devotion to the Law. It required the structuring of one's life in accordance with the Interpretation set down by the Teacher of Righteousness. This living interpretation of the Law was continually amplified by the Interpreter, who studied the Law, and by the Guardian and Council members who meditated on it, taught it, and acted in accordance with it.

Within the Community, there was great emphasis placed on learning and observance, as well as on consistent moral growth. Although the Community had an organizational hierarchy, one's position within it was dependent on one's level of knowledge and one's consistency of religious observance. Understanding, ethical behavior, and the observance of the commandments were the hallmarks of the individual and the basis of his or her standing within the Community.

Preparing the Way

Before going into the process of entry and the personal obligations undertaken by one seeking membership in the Community, let me make a few observations regarding the inner significance of the way the Community was structured.

One of the most noteworthy features of the Community's organization is illustrated in the division of the members of the Community into tribes and into subsequent divisions of tens, fifties, hundreds, and thousands. This particular form of organization parallels the structure of the Israelite camp, established under Moses when the people were in the deserts of Sinai.

There was obviously a conscious application of an older paradigm and a deliberate replication of the organizational principle of the desert community of pristine Israel used in the structure of the Covenant Community. The objective seemed to be to create a community based on the experience of Sinai. That would express a desire to duplicate the physical and spiritual reality of the Sinai experience, on a day-to-day basis, through the life of the Community.

This leads us to consider a couple of important questions whose answers should indeed shed considerable light on the intentions and spiritual objectives of the Community. What, then, is the deeper significance of the desert in terms of religious symbolism and spiritual reality? What is implied in harkening back to the desert experience? What was so important about this model of existence and why strive to duplicate it?

At first glance, these questions could appear a bit puzzling and the answers elusive. It is only when one comes to understand what the desert experience represented in the development and evolution of the People of Israel that it becomes clear why the Sectarians sought to emulate it when structuring their community.

A strong indication of the significance of the desert, per se, can be found in the words of the prophet Isaiah. "A voice rings out, 'Clear in the desert a road for Adonai [God]. Level in the wilderness a highway for our God! Let every valley be raised, every hill and mountain be made low. Let the rugged terrain be made level and the ridges become a plain. The Presence of Adonai [God] shall appear and all flesh as one shall behold, for Adonai Himself has spoken.'"

A key element in the thinking of the Covenant Community was the belief that their way of life was to lead to and prepare for the End of Days. At that time, God Himself would come and establish His Kingdom on earth, after the way had been paved by a messianic presence. The forces of Darkness would be permanently vanquished and God would hold all of humanity accountable in the Final Judgement.

As we will see in the messianic literature, redemption is ultimately to come to all of humanity. God will reveal a new Torah, a new Law, at that time. In doing so, the whole cosmic drama and the entire process of the Revelation, the Sinai experience, would be repeated. God would appear with His might fully revealed, once again to interact directly with the Sons of Man, establishing a new Covenant and a new Law. Thereafter, the living Word of God would flow continually from Mount Zion to the benefit of all humanity.

The Covenant Community harkened back to the desert because it was the scene of the Revelation, that singular event in which God appeared and confronted the people directly. It was here in the desert, in the Sinai experience, that God issued the Covenant with Israel and established them as a nation. It was here that the New Covenant, the New Law, would be promulgated as well. It was the desert that symbolized the road to the new reality. By traveling the road of the desert, they were to open a way. The Community was to lay the foundation for the Second Revelation, the renewal of the people, the emergence of the New Law, and the salvation of mankind.

How then, was the way to become opened?

The way was to be opened through a community of people who freely organized themselves along the lines of Israel's pristine social formation and rededicated themselves to living their lives in strict and proper adherence to the Law of Moses.

Logically, since the Law was given to the people in the desert and the Torah set up the structure for the observance of the Law along lines which were ultimately to be carried over when they settled in the Promised Land, then it stood to reason that to fully observe the Laws and properly fulfill the Commandments of God, it would be necessary to replicate the original social and religious structure as first outlined by God through Moses.

The core of the Community, like the core of the desert community, was the priesthood. The priests were the intercessors who channeled the divine energies of good and of blessing to the people. They facilitated the sacrifices that regulated the day-to-day interplay between the congregation and the Divine. The Levites assisted them by leading the prayers and facilitating the supplications of the people. Working together, the priests and Levites continually focused the life of the community on service to God.

In the Community, the priests had three sets of functions: to regulate doctrine, to administer property, and to dispense justice. Translated into common practical terms, this meant that the priests were to teach and lead by example. They were to take responsibility for handling the material needs of the community. They were to be the core of the court system, regulating the conduct of the community members. This was all to be done in strict accordance with the commandments laid out in the Covenant.

This suggests that the strict hierarchy required in the life of the Community reflected, on a practical level, the operational principle of the primacy of the Law. The Torah, the Law, was the living word of God. Living the Law properly and fully observing the commandments meant that the Community was fulfilling Israel's obligation under the Covenant. In the short term, fulfillment of the Covenant would bring blessing. In the long run, it would eventually lead first to the salvation of Israel and, subsequently, to that of mankind.

One of the chief Levitical functions of the priests was that of rectification. The sacrifices of the sin and guilt offerings performed by the priests were designed to atone for the direct transgressions and the inadvertent errors of the people. Through atonement, correction was achieved spiritually and Israel's relationship to God and to His Covenant was kept in balance.

The function of the priest's work and the Levitical ritual was, in essence, that of maintaining close and constant communion with God. Atonement meant acknowledging one's sin, repenting of it, asking forgiveness for it, and determining to permanently foreswear any repetition of the transgression.

Each individual act of repentance acknowledged sin. Each offering the priest made sought to reestablish the connection between the individual and God. Moreover, by the individual acts of rectification accomplished by the sacrifices and the accompanying priestly intercession was atonement continually made for the Land and for the people as a whole.

In the Covenant Community, sacrifice was replaced by a way of life that emphasized morality, communal focus, and strict observance of the Law. The Hebrew word for "sacrifice," *korbanut*, derives from the verb root *karev*, which means "to draw near," "to approach and come close." The ritual functions of the Temple priests were those of sacrifice. In metaphysical terms, the work of the priests was to draw close to God and to bring the people into direct and immediate communion with Him.

Within the Covenant Community, the centrality of the priests and the hierarchy of which they were the core reflected the strong desire on the part of the Community to be organized in a fashion that would permit and facilitate continual communion with the Divine.

The View of the Camp and the Tabernacle

For the vast majority of the Jewish world, the role of the Camp as described in the Torah was transferred from the desert dwellings of the migrant Israelites to Jerusalem. The Camp was seen originally as the desert encampment. During the era of the settlement and the period of the Judges, the Camp was probably seen as the territory settled by the Israelites or the City of Shiloh, where the Ark of the Covenant was housed. Eventually, the term "The Camp" came to be seen as the Holy City, Jerusalem.

The Tabernacle of early Israel was replaced by the Temple in Jerusalem. The Temple stood at the heart of the City—the central essence of the Temple being the Holy of Holies at its core. The very center of Israel's relationship with God as a people was bound up in the Temple and Temple service. The priests brought blessing and harmony to the Land through their work and through their intercession. The sacrifices maintained the intimate connection between man and God. The High Priest would enter the Holy of Holies on the Day of Atonement and seek to atone for the sins of the people and pray for the welfare of the Land and the people.

The view of the Covenant Community was very different. The people of Community saw themselves as the Camp, rather than Jerusalem proper. They considered themselves to be the microcosm of the people of Israel. Central to the Community was not the Temple, but rather the Law. As the Holy of Holies was the core of the Temple, the Council was the core of the Law that governed the Community. As the sacrifices were designed to atone for the Land and the people, the Covenant Community believed that their way of life—of adhering faithfully and completely to the Law, meditating on its innermost meaning, and performing the commandments in the light of the revealed interpretations—achieved that universal atonement.

Moreover, the Holy of Holies in the First Temple originally served as a focus for the revelation of God's will. The Divine Presence was felt to reside there and, through it, divine inspiration manifested and blessing was channeled. Harkening back to the desert model of the Tabernacle and to the First Temple, the Covenant Community looked to the Council as the Holy of Holies and the Interpreter of the Law as the Holy Spirit who revealed the Divine Will.

Like the *Urim* and *Thummim* of old, the *Sefer Haguy*, or Book Meditation, served as a source of divine inspiration and guidance, a continual link to God. The Council of the Community was required to be proficient in it. The Guardian of the Community, the *Mevakair*, was to be guided by it continually. It was incumbent on all members of the community to study it.

Hence, two structural forms influenced the organization of the Covenant Community. One was the form and function of the Temple. The other was the ideal of the desert. The Community wanted to replicate, on a daily basis, the experience of the desert and, at the same time, sought to take on the spiritual functions of the Temple.

The relationship here is one of form and function reflecting each other. The Community had a hierarchy that symbolized submission to God. The supremacy of the Law of Moses served as the basis of that submission.

The Significance of the Desert Experience

The Community had within it divisions of ten, fifty, one hundred, and one thousand, each headed by a leader. The leaders and the judges served under the priests. The regulation of the entire Community was controlled, in turn, by the *Mevakair*, the Guardian, whose role as Administrator, Teacher, and Shepherd of the Faithful seems to parallel that of Moses. The role may well have been modeled after the example of the Teacher of Righteousness.

After all, it is not at all improbable that the *Mevakair*, the Guardian of the Community, was also the Interpreter of the Law mentioned in the Sectarian literature. In fact, it would stand to reason that if one is duplicating the experience of Sinai, one would need a Moses figure as being central to the stability and operation of the Community.

There are several reasons why this harkening back to the desert experience, as a way of life, is significant and important to understand. The desert experience represented the beginning of the Jewish people, the pristine years of their existence. As such, it was a time of emancipation, of hope, and of formation.

The years of the desert experience brought the Israelites to Mount Sinai, provided them with their internal organization, and established them as a people; and through the Covenant made with God, they were forged into a holy people. Having gained their freedom from Egypt, the Israelites chose to accept a relationship to God that immediately constituted their identity, both spiritually and nationally.

The desert experience was one of salvation. Not only was Israel freed from bondage, but also over time it was purified from the sins of the fathers. A new generation emerged in the forty years of wandering. The old pattern of servitude and fear was shed for one that had faith in God, one which was prepared to serve and to obey the Covenant and honor the Will of God.

God fed the people manna for all those many years. He guided them through all their travails with a pillar of cloud by day and a pillar of fire by night. God personally provided for the Israelites. He sustained them physically, organized their social and religious structures, enunciated the Laws, and spoke directly to them through Moses. This was a time of great intimacy between the people and God. It was a time of intense interaction and communion.

The presence of God rested on the Holy Ark and on the Tabernacle and was the source of Divine guidance, blessing, and protection. The priests were appointed by God to minister to the Tabernacle and to serve as the connective link between God's immanence and the lives of the people. Communion was, in fact, a day-by-day reality.

The Covenant Community accepted on itself the structure of the desert experience and the spiritual reality of the Tabernacle/Temple by embracing the first and becoming the second. The Community sought to fulfill the biblical objective of becoming a nation of priests and a holy people.

They sought to achieve intimacy and communion with God through a way of life. Submission to the Law, focusing on moral behavior, ethical interaction with one's fellow man, and devotional practice all replaced the sacrifices. Sacrifices were now acts of self-control and moral development, not animal offerings.

The Communal Meals and the Congregational Assemblies, in deliberating doctrine and policy, transformed the community as a whole into a priestly society. The Community became the Temple. The Council of the Community served as the Holy of Holies, maintaining close contact with God by study and meditation, guidance and example.

A closer connection was made within the Community between external organization, religious practice, and inner spirituality because the forms of outer expression were transferred from institutions to the collective of individuals that comprised the Community.

In order to have an intimate relationship with God, service to God had to be internalized. The connection could not be made indirectly through an established priesthood in a physical Temple. Rather, communion became possible when one became part of a community that became the Temple, adhered to the Laws of God, and made their offerings through moral conduct and mutual respect for one another.

The statement the Community made by replicating the organization of the desert was profound indeed. It sought to purge itself of the past, to purge away the sins of fathers and the sins of its own generation—those of rebellion and worship of the material. A return to the desert is a return to a pristine existence, a rebirth as a people covenanted to God.

The way opened in the desert is one of dependence on God, social leveling, justice and humility, atonement and rectification. Moral development and spiritual evolution, rather than physical survival and material attachments, become the central focus of existence.

The Way of the Desert is a Way of Life. It is one of truth and justice. It is one of humility and submission. It leads past the slavery of idolatry and material dependency to true freedom. It leads one back to oneself. It is a path freely chosen, for only a free people can choose to covenant with God. Only a free people can serve God unafraid. Only the emancipated can create a structured way of life, which fosters human harmony within a divinely ordained and consciously accepted organizational pattern. Such a way of life seeks constant rectification and direct communion with God. This, indeed, is the model for salvation. It is the paradigm to which the Covenant Community adhered.

6

TO BE A NATION OF PRIESTS AND A HOLY PEOPLE

To fully appreciate the true purpose of the Covenant Community and its spiritual values, one must gain a full view of the life of the Community. This is reflected in the rules by which the Community was governed, the principles by which the members lived their lives, and the behavioral norms expected from those who chose to be part of it.

It should be pointed out here that if we are to take the ancient sources seriously, Josephus and Philo in particular, then it is inappropriate to picture the Community as singular or limited to one geographic location. Philo places the Essenes in both Syria and Judea. He states that they live in villages, tilling the soil, tending flocks and herds, or working as craftsmen. Josephus writes that the Essenes dwell in cities and villages, and that everywhere their communal organization is the same. When traveling on journeys, Essene travelers are warmly received by their fellows. They treat each other as long-standing friends.

In describing the Covenant Community, we are reconstructing not merely a picture of a way of life common to the Essene communities in general, but also a set of spiritual beliefs and values that the Community is meant to exemplify. Their specific mode of life has very clear assumptions about what the Community saw as the true nature of service to God. These inner assumptions are in some ways implied and, in others, expressed within the framework of the communal norms and regulations.

Particularly revealing are the rules that governed an individual's acceptance into the Community and regulated his or her behavior once within it. The values a society, a community, or an association hold are frequently most visible and comprehensible in the guidelines they set down for their members. This was certainly true of the Covenant Community.

Anyone entering the Community did so as a matter of free will. The initiate to the Community vowed his or her allegiance to a new way of life. They determined to relinquish their former lifestyle and voluntarily adopt the set norms that governed the Community. They also agreed to share the convictions expressed in this new mode of living.

According to the Community Rule, one joined the Community by personal choice, devoting oneself freely to the observance of God's precepts. Individuals were expected to hold fast to the Commandments and not to abandon them during the reign of Evil, with its terror and affliction. They had to separate themselves from the Wicked and no longer associate with corrupt individuals. An entrant to the Community had to swear a binding oath to observe the Law of Moses and the Interpretation as given to the Sons of Zadok.

As part of the initiation ceremony, the priests recited all of God's favors and all the goodness that God had shown toward Israel. Then the Levites recited all of the transgressions and sins of the people. The initiate, at this point, had to admit publicly that he or she and his or her ancestors had strayed from the Law. They also had to acknowledge God's infinite mercy. This acknowledgment resulted in the priests blessing the initiates, while the Levites cursed the Sons of Darkness.

This dramatic ceremony points strongly toward the concept of free choice. One could choose to remain within the community of the wicked, to reject the Law, and to live one's life along the lines of delusion, arrogance, and rebellion. Or one could choose to admit one's failings. One could acknowledge the errors of the past, both personal and communal. Then, one was in a position to readjust one's life, by reaffirming commitment to the Law of Moses. One could choose to live one's life in accordance with it, in a community formed specifically for that purpose.

It is not one's personal merit that warrants forgiveness from God for departing from His ways, from the Torah. Rather, it is God's compassion and mercy, that are the operative factors. When people admit their errors, grieve over the stubbornness and rebellion of their forbearers, and make repentance for their breach of the Covenant by breaking with the realm of the Wicked, then are those individuals redeemed by the grace of God.

We are told that no one is to walk in the stubbornness of his own heart. This imperative reflects back on the biblical view that the people were stiffnecked and stubborn, constantly testing God and rebelling against His instructions and against the Law. This is a constant theme, both in the Five Books of Moses—the Torah—and in the Books of the Prophets. Here, stubbornness of heart is defined by the Community Rule as following one's inclination toward evil. We are told to circumcise our hearts, ridding them of the evil urge and purging them of stubbornness and arrogance.

Those wishing to enter the Community were examined by the *Mevakair*, the Guardian of the Community. An individual was scrutinized carefully. The *Mevakair* first, and later the Council, examined the applicant's deeds and level of observance of the Law. His or her knowledge of the Law and level of understanding were looked at very closely. These two areas were considered to be indicators of the individual's spiritual development. These areas of spiritual competency were examined, not only upon admission to the Community but also on a yearly basis.

Once deemed suitable for prospective entry into the Community, one went into a two-year probationary cycle. For the first year, one lived within the Community as an outsider. One was neither allowed to partake of the communal food or drink, nor share in the use of the communal property. At the end of the first year, the Council deliberated on the individual's understanding and level of observance of the Law. During this time, the initiate was taught the rules of the Community.

At the beginning of the second year, if the Council approved, the initiate turned over his or her property to the bursar. It was registered, but not touched by the Community. At the end of the year, the candidate was reexamined and, if found worthy, was admitted to the Community. He or she was then inscribed in the roles and given a certain rank within the Community. The individual was now a full member of the Community and so was allowed to participate in the

Meal and Drink of the Community, to participate in its deliberations, to appeal to the communal courts, to share in the communal property, and to offer council and judgment, as appropriate.

The Messianic Rule (1QSa) informs us that everyone in the Community—men, women, and children—was obligated to hear the precepts of the Covenant and the exposition of the Law. Every man from his youth was instructed in the precepts of the Covenant and in the *Sefer Hagui*, the Book of Meditation, for a period of ten years. Each was to learn according to his age level and level of understanding.

On the Status of Women in the Community

Let me digress for a moment to deal with the issue of the place of women in the Community. Regrettably, there is not an abundance of information addressing women specifically in the literature. However, the lack of sufficient information should not lead one automatically to conclude that the Community was monastic or celibate. Careful reading of the scrolls can lead one to the realization that women were an important part of the Community.

There is certainly abundant testimony to illustrate that the Community was dominated by men, in terms of the leadership. The Community was founded by priests and the priests were the organizational and ideological core of their way of life. The Chiefs and Judges were subordinate to the priests and the Levites in all matters. The War Scroll, which clearly belongs to the corpus of Sectarian literature, indicates that the Community believed that it would have to play a major role at the End of Days to insure the victory of the forces of Light. The Community believed that its composition and leadership reflected that understanding. All of this points to a male-dominated leadership.

However, that does not mean that women were not a very important element within the Community. In talking about the people of the Community, the Messianic Rule subordinates them to the Chiefs and Judges. The people, however, are the majority. True, the officials of the Community were men. Yet it is a big leap to then assume that the entire Community was therefore solely constituted of males. Since the officials of the Community only constituted a small percentage of the population, the term "people" may very well refer to both men and women.

As mentioned above, the Messianic Rule placed the obligation of the Law on everyone equally. Every man, woman, and child was to be taught the precepts of the Covenant and was to hear the exposition of the Law. In a subsequent reference to being taught the precepts of the Covenant, it says that every man, according to age and level of comprehension, was to be schooled in the *Sefer Haguy* for ten years.

It seems probable that if, in the first reference, it stipulates that everyone in the Community was included in the injunction, then in the parallel reference all men, women, and children in the Community were also meant. This seems to be reinforced by the concept that people were to be schooled in the *Sefer Haguy* from their youth and in terms that were age-appropriate.

One should not be trapped by a narrow reading of terminology. In the MMT, the only letter to be discovered among the Dead Sea literature, the principle is spelled out specifically that just because the Commandments are phrased in the masculine, it is not correct to assume they are meant for, or binding on, only men. The letter states that the wording is merely adhering to convention. The *mitzvot*, the laws and commandments, are binding on everyone.

The MMT also touches on the issues of priestly marriage, monogamy, the laws of incest, and the appropriateness of divorce, if there is an issue of marital incompatibility. All of these issues are related to family and proper sexual relationships. It would seem strange to focus so much attention on these issues if Sectarian life were primarily monastic and celibate. Why bring up issues related to women if women were not a major force within the Community?

As we shall see in dealing with the legal materials, the Sectarian Community emphasizes and places signal importance on monogamy. Polygamy is condemned as incest. In validating its argument, the literature draws on examples from the Book of Genesis. It argues that God made only one mate for Adam. He had a helpmate, not multiple wives. It points out that life on earth was saved through the procreation of animals, which were brought onto the Ark two by two. Moreover, the Community interpreted the biblical prohibition in Deuteronomy against multiplying wives for oneself as a condemnation of polygamy.

The Sectarian Community looked for examples of appropriate sexual behavior in the Law. Examples both in Genesis and Deuteronomy were taken as having the force of moral law. Does it not seem likely, this being so, that like the Jewish world as a whole, the Community would also strongly adhere to the very first commandment God issued—that is, to be fruitful and to multiply? If observance of the Law was paramount in their way of life and sexual morality such an enormously important issue to them, how could it be that they would deliberately exclude women from the Community?

True, Pliny the Elder, in his writings, portrays the Essenes as a small celibate community living by the shores of the Dead Sea, who largely attract followers from the outside who are attracted to their way of life. However, Pliny was writing in 77 c.e., after Jerusalem was destroyed and the State fell. This was a postwar period. This does not reflect the reality of life in Israel during our period.

Josephus describes some of the Essenes, in similar terms, as not always marrying. However, Josephus also makes a point of saying that there are other Essene communities that do foster marriage and children.

Both writers are describing the Essene community shortly before, and not long after, the devastating War with Rome from 66 to 73 c.e. This picture does not necessarily represent what the Essene and Sectarian communities may well have been like over the prior two centuries.

More accurately, the picture is likely to have been one in which women were a vital part of the Community and its life. This was a community which, in very large measure, was bound to the Law and to its observance. The Law deals heavily with women and family. It is far from inconceivable that the status of women within the Community and within the Essene movement was much the same as that of men who were not holding positions of authority in the Community.

The Reasons for the Community's Regimen

Let us return to the organizational structure of the Community. The Messianic Rule elaborates on the role of the Community member over time. At the age of twenty, a man could be enrolled in the Community. At that juncture he could begin to have an intimate relationship with a woman, but at no time prior to that point.

At age twenty-five, he could become an official, serving the Congregation. And at age thirty, he could commence participating in lawsuits and could act as a judge or chief, if he had the understanding and the ability to effectively perform these services. Anyone serving as an official would go through a three-day period of sanctification and ritual purification before performing any duties related to the Assembly of Judgement, the Council of the Community, the War Council, et cetera. Leadership was a sacred obligation and had a sacred status.

The regimen set down for the member of the Community paralleled, and no doubt strengthened, the hierarchical structure of the Sectarian social framework. Great importance was placed on structure, rank, and obedience. The impetus for this emphasis on authority and order can better be understood by looking at the exposition of Hosea 5:10 that appears in the Damascus Covenant.

The verse reads, " Princes of Judah have become like those who remove the boundary. Wrath shall be poured upon them." The context of the quote refers to the prominent and powerful, those who should be leaders of the people, having become examples of lawlessness instead of virtue. As a result, God ultimately will punish them in His wrath.

The sins of the leaders, presumably the Sons of Darkness, are the accumulation of illicit wealth, bearing malice, taking revenge on one's fellow, and indulging in hatred and sexual misconduct. These are acts of rebellion against God and His Law, done out of arrogance by those who, in the stubbornness of their hearts, persist in doing only what appears right in their own eyes.

The invective here is directed against those who refuse to bend to the Law of God, setting their own standards, justifying their own transgressions, and rejecting the Covenant. The tearing down of the boundaries is a direct reference to defying the terms of Covenant with God, in word and in deed—then, having the arrogance to turn around and justify such action. This behavior is seen as an outrage to God, which produces divine wrath. In the short term, that anger is manifested as Israel's suffering and degradation. In the long term, it will be manifested, at the End Time, as the complete destruction of the Sons of Darkness.

Within the Community, the rules that bind its members together reinforce proper observance of the Commandments. Proper observance of the Law, in turn, fosters a way of life that atones for the sins of the people and will lead to ultimate redemption.

The structure and order maintained by the Community's organization was a vehicle for maintaining the boundaries of the Law and for insuring the fulfillment of the Covenant obligations incumbent on all Israel. The Law is a discipline. It is a spiritual model. It is the basis of man's relation to God and Israel's future as a people. To break the yoke of the Law, to reject its teachings and wantonly violate its precepts was seen to be tantamount to spiritual and national suicide. The Community was determined to prevent that possibility by creating a communal way of life whose very structure and organization reflected a strict adherence to the Covenant and thereby a gateway to salvation.

The issue was so serious that no compromise with the wicked was even possible. The Damascus Covenant is very clear. Those who reject the Law shall have no place in the House of the Law, in the Community. Ultimately, they will have no place in the reconstituted Israel. The Community Rule states forthrightly that if a man enters the Covenant, hears its words and still clings to the idols of his heart, walking in the stubbornness of his own way, he will be destroyed. All the curses of the Covenant will cling to him.

"He shall not be justified by what his stubborn heart declares lawful" (CR). Such conduct cannot be rectified by atonement, ablution, or ritual purification. It is willful rebellion against God. As such, it is far more than sin, than transgressing the boundary. It is the destruction of the boundary, the annihilation of the framework that set Israel up as a holy people and a model for the nations. Such a heinous act God will not tolerate.

In joining the Community, great emphasis was laid on separating oneself from falsehood. In biblical law, one separated from something because it was considered to be unclean. The implication is clear. Falsehood and deception were seen as morally unclean and unholy. Hence, one had to distance oneself from it completely or be contaminated by it. Exposure to falsehood rendered one unfit for divine service or direct contact with God.

Distinguishing between clean and unclean underlies much of the Law. The distinction of cleanliness is one in which someone, something, or some activity is pure. That is, it befits God's service rather than being impure. For impurity renders things unfit to be associated with the holy or with divine service. Since contact between the two produces contamination, the holy must be kept separate from the impure or be rendered unclean. The very word "holiness"—in Hebrew, *kodesh*—has the root meaning of "being separate," "apart from the mundane."

Understanding Ritual Cleanliness

There are several categories of cleanliness in the Torah. One is connected to food. Certain types of animals were considered unfit for human consumption and thereby would render a person unclean. One was not to eat carrion, carcasses, insects, reptiles, scavengers, et cetera. The reason was straightforward. Man, being created in God's image, reflected the divine, so it was important not to defile oneself by eating the unseemly.

A second category of uncleanliness revolved around another form of contamination— namely, idolatry. Serving other gods, giving credence or allegiance to anything other than God Himself, was considered to be an abomination. So much so that the commandment not to have any other gods was extended in biblical law to encompass a wide range of prohibitions aimed at obliterating any practices associated with idolatry.

Biblical law prohibited tattooing the body, shaving oneself bald as a sign of mourning, speaking with familiar spirits, soothsaying, lacerating the body, sacrificing blemished animals, and eating meat with blood in it, just to name a few, because of the close association of these activities with pagan worship and practice. Everything connected with idolatry and pagan worship was considered unclean and unfit human behavior. It was unbecoming to the human being, whose spirit was fashioned in God's own image. If one was to have a close relationship to God, drawing near to God implied being godlike, holy, separate from that which was vile or degrading.

The third type of impurity was ritual uncleanliness. The biblical laws of *tum'ah*, "ritual uncleanliness," were concerned with a state of corruption or defilement that rendered an object impure and therefore unacceptable and prohibited for use in divine service. It also characterized a person who, because of bodily dysfunction, was temporarily unfit to be in the Temple or in Jerusalem.

Ritual purity was a very serious matter, in that it affected the priests and the divine services. The functions of the priesthood were varied and all of great importance for the well-being of the nation. Among the many crucial tasks that the priests were to fulfill, some were paramount. The priests were to serve in the Temple, handling the ritual and the sacrifices, to assist the prayers, and to intercede for the people. They were to serve as a link between God and Israel and make offerings to atone for the sins of the nation.

If the priests came into direct physical contact with objects or people who were in an impure state, they became impure and unable to perform the functions of the priesthood. That this would have serious implications on the welfare of the people and the Land is obvious.

People in an impure state were not considered to be completely whole and were therefore temporarily blemished. As such, it was deemed inappropriate for them to be making offerings to God. Objects that were impure, such as blemished animals or animals deemed by God to be unfit for human consumption, were not to be presented to God. God, as Creator, was to have the best of offerings. Only the choicest was fit to be presented before God, in thanksgiving for His mercy and for the bounty He provided.

Uncleanliness was seen as a temporary state as far as an individual was concerned. One suffering from a bodily dysfunction, one that biblically was stipulated to be a state of ritual impurity, remained impure for the length of the affliction and for a specified period of time following recovery. After that point, he or she went through a purification ritual, and at the coming of dark, became ritually clean once again. The individual was often obliged to make a specific sacrifice, now that it was again possible to enter the Temple and approach the priests and stand in God's Presence in the holy precincts. As part of the cleansing process, one had to bring sin or guilt offerings for certain types of ritual uncleanliness.

The imperative of ritual purification is that it cleanses the person and brings the individual back into a rectified state of grace with God. Not only could an Israelite become impure, but the Land itself could become impure, cutting off or restricting God's grace on that level also. Serious transgressions, particularly idolatry, caused the Land of Israel to be defiled. Sexual immorality was another major pollution that could corrupt the Land (Leviticus 18:27–28), as was violence and lawlessness. The prophets Isaiah and Ezekiel both state that idolatry and bloodshed brought uncleanliness to the Land.

Morality as Ritual Purity

Biblically, the purity rituals were originally directed toward the priesthood. They were the preparatory mechanism for repentance and atonement. The priests handled the intercession with God on behalf of the people and had to be in a state of ritual purity in order to stand in front of God.

The trend among the Jews in general, by the Roman period, was to extend the priestly laws to the general population as whole. Philo's statement that it was customary for a couple to bathe and immerse themselves ritually after sexual intercourse, the *Mishnah*'s regulations regarding the washing of the hands, and the rabbinic rulings that even common foods are to be handled in ritual purity (*Tosephta Berakhot* 6:2–4) should be seen in this light.

This tendency was pronounced among the Qumran Community. The Community Rule states that those entering the Community had to separate themselves from the wicked, because he who transgresses the Law is unclean. One was not to have any social interaction with such a person. One was not to eat or drink with the wicked. It was forbidden either to buy from them or to sell anything to them. The wicked were unclean morally. Therefore, anything they touched was contaminated. The wicked and anything associated with them had to be avoided. A distance had to be kept, in order to avoid moral corruption.

The determination that violation of the Law renders one unclean is a highly significant statement. In a sense, it creates yet another class of contamination, that of the spirit. Although a lot of the law in the Torah is expressed as ritual, very large sections of it also deal with social, civil, and criminal law. Regardless of classification, the central focus of most of the Law is on moral behavior. To assert that violation of the Law renders one unclean and impure is to emphasize that moral conduct in human affairs renders one fit to be in God's Presence and immoral behavior violates the Covenant, the core agreement with God. Immorality both forces a withdrawal of divine grace and mercy, on one hand, and opens the door for divine wrath and punishment, on the other. Such a stance is very reminiscent of the spirit of prophetic literature.

This view of the centrality of moral behavior in the Law of God is certainly in line with the message of the biblical prophets. We know that the Community was heavily influenced by the prophetic books. A number of important commentaries on sections of prophetic writings were found in the Dead Sea caves. Many of these commentaries play a very important role in the apocalyptic literature, much of which was central to Sectarian thinking. As far as the literature is concerned, sin and evil are moral corruption, which render anyone in contact with them ritually unclean.

An interesting commentary on a verse from Amos lets us know that the Community, which exiled itself to Damascus, looked to the prophetic writings as a basis for helping to understand and to implement the Law. The Damascus Scroll, in interpreting the verses from Amos 5:26–27 "I will exile the tabernacle of your king and the bases of your statues from My tent to Damascus," states that the Tabernacle symbolizes the Books of the Law and the bases of the statues are considered to represent the Books of the Prophets.

This means that the words of the Prophets uphold the Law. According to the Sectarians, the Torah stands on the foundation of the Prophets. How is that? The implication seems to be that the words of the Prophets, the way they saw and understood the Law, reveal the true nature of all the commandments. The conceptual framework of the prophetic literature is taken as the central basis for understanding the Law as a whole. The prophetic conception of the centrality of morality to all of Mosaic Law was accepted as the fundamental truth behind the entire Covenant and all of the commandments. In short, the Sectarian viewpoint may well have been that all of the commandments of the Law represent moral principles and hold moral imperatives.

The view that the Prophets had revealed, that the entire Law was really moral law regardless of the external forms it took, would account for such a discernable shift in emphasis regarding sin, the effects of sin, and atonement for it within the structure of the Community and in its way of life. Sin is no longer just transgression of the laws. In its broader sense, it is rebellion against God and repudiation of the Law. The sins of the nation are the moral violations that are polluting the Land and rendering it impure. The consequences of immorality are the withdrawal of divine favor, the cessation of divine protection, and the imposition of suffering on the Land and on the people, by God, for noncompliance with the terms of the Covenant.

The Community Rule states that the Community, by living the Law and through the Interpretation, establishes the spirit of holiness. The spirit of holiness manifest in the Community, in turn, atones for the guilt of rebellion and the sin of unfaithfulness, which have brought so much suffering and destruction. The perfection of the way is personified in the living example of the Community. Their way of life, obedient to the Law and crafted through the eyes of the prophets, was understood as a free will offering—one that draws down God's love and grace without the need for actual physical sacrifices. Moral behavior and mutual respect are the true offerings to God. That is the way to grace and to salvation. That is the real, core connection between the people and God.

The opposite is wickedness and sin, the way of Darkness. Immorality is rebellion against the Law. Those who walk in its path are the Sons of Darkness. They will eventually have to face God's full fury for so doing, if they do not repent and return to Him and to His Law. Wickedness is equated with falsehood and the members of the Community are obligated to separate themselves from it, as it is unclean, contaminating one's very relationship with God and making it impossible to stand in His Presence.

Separating from Falsehood

Within the Community, separating from falsehood, from the ways of the wicked, takes four forms. First, one was to distance oneself physically and psychologically from the wicked. One joined the Community and was immediately isolated for a probationary period of two years. During this time, one was taught the ways of the Community and was continually tested regarding one's knowledge of the Law and one's level of observance.

Second, one was separated from one's possessions, a source of evil and impurity, being both the fruits of the drive for acquisition and the object of false security. Acquisition leads to greed and violence. Reliance needs to be centered on God, not on material things.

At the beginning of year two of the probationary period, all of one's possessions were registered, and at the point of acceptance within the Community, one's property was merged with the Common Property. All material goods were communal and were administered by the Guardian of the Community. What we see here is, first, a gradual and then a permanent weaning away of the individual from acquisition and ownership.

A member was obligated to obey a superior in all matters pertaining to work and to money. What is more, the true value of work and money is illustrated by a provision in the Damascus Covenant. There it stipulates that every member must turn over two days' earnings per month to the Guardian, to be distributed to the poor, the homeless, the widows, orphans, and women who have no fathers or spouses. One was to be attached to working toward social justice and not to materialism.

Third, one was also segregated socially from the wicked. There was no social intercourse with them. Eating and drinking with the wicked were strictly prohibited. Commercial interchange with them was forbidden as well. Only the Guardian of the Community had any interaction with them at all. Social contact revolved around the Community itself. All eating, drinking, prayer, study, and deliberation were done in common. No member could seek justice in a court, other than the Council of the Community.

Lastly, the Community member was cut off intellectually from the wicked. No discussion of doctrine, no arguing or debating with the wicked was permitted. One was to separate oneself from any false or incomplete interpretation of the Law. Rather, one was to inquire of God regarding the true nature and meaning of the Law. By inquiring of God, one would come to understand the hidden meanings of the commandments and know where exactly they had sinned.

The process of separation was the road to repentance, as well as the guarantee of redemption. One had to return to God by returning to His commandments, which epitomized the moral codes and ethical principles they embodied. Such repentance, such a return to the Way, could only be accomplished by making a break with the past and admitting one's transgressions and sins. Separation was that break—the requisite physical and psychological shift.

To prevent relapse, separation from temptation and from evil influence was essential. The dominion of Evil still held sway in the world. Vindication of the righteous would only come at the End of Days with the coming of Divine Judgement. One was obliged to remain separate in order to remain holy. Separateness, then, was the key to insuring piety, to achieving adherence to God, and eventually, to reaching salvation and national redemption. A great deal was at stake.

The Rules of the Community

The rules that governed the conduct of the Community's members are important to understand from two interrelated standpoints. On the one hand, they represent the tangible expression of the philosophy of life that was the underpinning of the Community. It is through their practical regulations, their rules, that we glimpse the workings of this community and understand the ramifications of their beliefs on day-to-day reality. Beliefs are only hollow phrases and empty abstractions if they have no concrete form of affirmation or any real effect on everyday life. A community enunciates its true beliefs clearly when its sentiments are accurately embodied in a way of life.

On the other hand, it is also important to remember that we are dealing with a Covenant Community, whose primary objective was to establish and maintain a lifestyle in strict accordance with its understanding of the Torah, the Law of Moses. It was a Torah-driven community, so it is necessary to pay close attention to the connections between the rules set down and the commandments from which they may well have been abstracted.

The members of the Community lived and worked together as an organic whole. They ate, drank, and deliberated in common. Each member had to obey his or her superior in all matters of work or money. Each was responsible for his fellow. One was obliged never to address a fellow in anger, stubbornness, or envy. If one saw a fellow transgressing, it was imperative to rebuke him or her that same day or else incur guilt on oneself. Such rebuke had to be done truthfully, humbly, and with charity. Moreover, the admonition had to take place in front of witnesses. Only afterwards could one accuse the individual involved before the Assembly of the Congregation.

What we see here is a sense of mutual responsibility. The implication is that we are indeed are our brother's keeper. The philosophy is that if we see another transgressing and make no effort to admonish him or correct him, then we are guilty of contributory negligence. We become guilty of the same transgression because we had the power to prevent it, at the time, and did nothing. The principle being espoused here is that of mutual responsibility. Not to counteract a transgression or to refrain from intervening is, in fact, to participate in it.

The biblical basis for this approach lies in Leviticus 19:17–18, which reads, "You shall not hate your kinsman in your heart. Reprove your neighbor and incur no guilt on his account. You shall not take vengeance nor bear a grudge against your kinfolk. Love your neighbor as yourself. I am the Lord."

The implication of the biblical injunction is that not rebuking and not admonishing a fellow when he has sinned or transgressed is an act of hatred. You are depriving the individual of the chance to repent. You are condemning the person involved to make the same mistake in the future and to be punished again for his transgression, when you had the opportunity of helping him break the cycle.

Moreover, by not taking responsibility for aiding the person to understand what the transgression is and to be purified through repentance and forgiveness, you take on responsibility for the sin instead. This is not how one is to treat a family member, a fellow, or a neighbor. Admonition and intervention, when a person is seen going astray, is an act of love and acceptance. That is the commandment.

The Covenant Community obviously saw itself as a brotherhood, as a society. All were viewed as neighbors and kin. Therefore, one had to take care of one's fellows. It was necessary to show love by accepting the responsibility of correcting others and teaching them. Everyone and his neighbor were not only equal, the two were viewed as one. If one loved and respected his neighbor, then one took the time to help him walk a straight path. One's neighbor was expected to do the same, reciprocally. Inasmuch as a person was held equally culpable for the punishment of a transgression ignored, so, too, was an individual equally blessed by the grace granted to those who acknowledged their error and repented.

The various communal regulations set out in the Community Rule can be grouped together into several larger categories, which often have a biblical background. One of the most important categories was that of rebellion. A person was considered to be taking the law into his own hands by disobeying a superior or answering a fellow member rudely or stubbornly. Rebellion, per se, encompassed speaking against a priest in anger, betraying the truth (the Law and the Interpretation), walking in the stubbornness of one's own heart, and murmuring against the authority of the Congregation. The latter two offenses were considered so serious that if convicted of them, a person risked the possibility of outright expulsion from the Community.

Here, too, there is a biblical basis for the emphasis placed on rebellion as violation of Law. Deuteronomy 6:16–19 enjoins the people not to try or to test God, as they did in the desert. Only by doing what God has commanded is Israel to rest peacefully on the Land. Deuteronomy 13:1 forbids any alteration or modification of the Law. One is not free to follow the inclinations and impulses of one's own whims and fancy. One is not free to disregard or rationalize away the Law. It is Divine Law, not human law. There is a considerable difference.

Not only can one not abrogate, change, or alter God's Law at one's caprice, but in dealing with the interpretation and application of the laws, one cannot rebel against the authority or rulings of those transmitting the Law. According to Deuteronomy 17:8–13,

> If a case is too baffling to decide . . . you shall promptly repair to the place which the Lord, your God has chosen, appear before the Levitical priests, or the magistrates in charge at the time, and present your problem. When they have announced to you the verdict in the case, you shall carry out the verdict that is announced . . . scrupulously observing all their instructions to you. You shall act in accord with the instructions given you. . . . You must not deviate from the verdict that they announce to you either to the right nor to the left.

A second category of illicit behavior that carried grave consequences—very heavy penance, exclusion from the Community, and in some cases, expulsion—was that of malice. Those forms of malice that effected the entire Community, such as pronouncing the Name of God, slandering the Congregation, or betraying the Community, all meant expulsion and excommunication. This was a permanent disbarment from the Community. One was consigned to a place outside the confines of the community of the righteous. No member of the Community could have any contact or intercourse with this individual from that time forward.

Other forms of malice—lying about property matters, insulting or humiliating a fellow member, bearing a grudge, taking revenge or slandering someone—all carried a penalty of a one-year penance and exclusion from the Community for the duration of that time. Under careful scrutiny and review by the Council, over time, one could eventually reestablish oneself within the Community.

In order to gain a broader perspective of the importance of the moral laws stressed within the working framework of the Community, it should be noted that much of the impetus, much of the legal background, stems from the Holiness Code of Leviticus 19. Shaming a person, hating someone, bearing a grudge or extracting revenge are all prohibited in Leviticus 19:16–18. Stealing and defrauding, as well as blasphemy, are similarly forbidden by direct commandments from God (Leviticus 19:11–13, 35).

It would seem that in consonance with the Holiness Code, a core of regulating principles for the Community was abstracted to establish an operating structure, which would clearly express its goal of ensuring a way of life based on a behavioral norm consistent with the Law, its statutes, and its spirit. More regarding this interrelationship between adherence to the Law and the Community's way of life will become apparent in the upcoming chapter on the legal materials.

Before passing on to an examination of how the Sectarian literature reflects a specific view of the laws, how they were seen and
applied, I want to digress for a moment and touch on the question of
free will, as viewed by the Sectarians.

The Matter of Free Will

The question of free will is most important to consider, in light of the
enormous emphasis placed by the Community on the importance of
understanding correctly, implementing fully, and observing properly
the commandments of the Torah, the Law.

The Torah is the Law of God, as far as the Jewish people are
concerned. The objective of the Law is to instruct one regarding what
God expects from the individual and from the people. It constitutes
the basis of the interaction between the nation and God. God and Israel
formed a Covenant, an agreement to work together as partners, at
Mount Sinai. This arrangement was not one of coercion. Rather, it
was freely undertaken by both sides. It was offered by God and was
accepted by Israel.

At Mount Sinai, after God reveals the Ten Commandments to
the people directly and Moses subsequently repeats all of the laws that
God directed him to issue to Israel (Exodus 20:1–23:32), we read the
following: "Moses went and repeated to the people all the commandments of the Lord and all the norms. And all the people answered with
one voice saying, 'All the things which the Lord has commanded we
will do!' Moses then wrote down all the commandments of the Lord"
(Exodus 24:3–4).

In preparation for the finalization of the Covenant, Moses makes
a special sacrifice. Next, "Moses took one part of the blood and put it
in basins and the other part of the blood he dashed against the altar.
Then, he took the record of the Covenant and read it aloud to the
people. And they said, 'All that the Lord has spoken we will faithfully
do.' Moses took the blood and dashed it on the people and said, 'This
is the blood of the Covenant, which the Lord now makes with you
concerning all these commands'" (Exodus 24:6–8).

The people of Israel freely and voluntarily undertook the commitment of the Covenant at Mount Sinai. It was an act of choice and
of free will. The Covenant was solidified only upon the acceptance of
both parties involved. The Covenant is a contractual arrangement.

This presupposes an agreement made between two parties freely and voluntarily. An obligation imposed by one side on the other against his will is not a covenant, but rather slavery. God went to great lengths to extract Israel from slavery. It would make no sense to view the Covenant at Sinai as an attempt to reimpose servitude on the people in a different form.

That choice is the basis of Israel's relationship to God. This point is restated often not only within the Torah, but also in the prophetic writings as well. One of the clearest expressions of this reality is enunciated in Deuteronomy 30. God sets out before the people the Choice, the Blessing, and the Curse. They are admonished to choose observance of the Law and thrive, or reject the teachings of God and suffer for violating the terms of the Covenant.

It should be clearly understood that free will does not always equate, necessarily, to total freedom of action. Once the people of Israel accepted the terms of the Covenant, they became bound to uphold the provisions of it, the commandments. Choice no longer constituted one of acceptance or rejection of the Covenant, but rather one of complying with and honoring one's obligations under the agreement, or violating the terms of the Covenant. That was the post-Sinai choice option.

Moreover, if one breaks the terms of a contract, one has to suffer the penalties that were stipulated at the time the agreement was implemented and went into effect. From the standpoint of the Covenant Community, those were the parameters within which the entire people of Israel had to work. To reject the Law was not an option. It was rebellion against God, by deliberately violating the terms of the agreement and by repudiating the entire Covenant.

In essence, the Covenant could not be repudiated, only violated. Such violation, in the view of the Law and the Prophets, brought uncleanliness and pollution to the Land and triggered the Curse, the expression of God's wrath stipulated in the Covenant. God's grace was then alienated from Israel and from the Land. The Land, in turn, separated itself from the people by becoming barren, unproductive, and unsafe. In the minds of the Covenant Community, the only option and hope for the Land and the people was to separate from those who polluted the Land by rejecting and violating the Law and by repudiating it through word and deed.

As the Covenanters saw it, the answer was quite simple. To restore Israel's proper relationship to God and to be saved as a nation, receiving His blessing and protection, it was necessary to return to the Covenant. To do so required swearing allegiance to it, coming to understand the true meaning of the commandments, and observing them faithfully as individuals, as a community, and as a people.

This process began with an act of free will. A person sought to join the Community, voluntarily, and to undergo a two-year training and probationary period. This was undertaken in order to freely surrender the past, learn what God expected of him, and develop a way of life that met the obligations set down at Mount Sinai. That way of life was reflected in the structure and norms of the Community.

With regard to free will, the Community sought to attract people back to the Covenant voluntarily and of their own volition. No one was solicited for membership. Rather, people sought the Community out. Their resolve was tested carefully. The individual's level of learning, adaptability, and observance were closely scrutinized, both before entry into the Community, and as long as he remained a part of it. Choice existed on both sides. The individual seeking admission did so voluntarily, and the Guardian and Council of the Community were free to accept him or her or could reject the person, barring him or her from entry.

Once a member of the Covenant Community, choice was redefined. Having reaffirmed the Covenant with God, swearing an oath to fulfill the Law of Moses and to abide by the regulations of the Community and the Interpretation of the Law, one could either live in accordance with the Law or transgress it. Choice now revolved around honoring one's spiritual and communal commitments, or choosing not to. Those who chose not to were subject to penalty, penance, and exclusion while going through a process of repentance and probation. In the case of very serious behavioral and/or moral breaches, one's position within the Community could be threatened, either through grave reduction in rank or with outright expulsion.

Since one was reviewed regularly regarding one's knowledge, obedience, and observance, the level of choice within the Community meant that one chose between spiritual development, with increased communal authority and responsibility, on the one hand, or regression and loss of status, on the other. On a broader level, one's actions meant the difference between being encompassed by the Community or being permanently excluded from it. That was the choice.

The paramount importance of free will and personal choice is also clearly pictured in the Community Rule's exposition on the subject of human nature and the two spirits within man. According to the scroll, a person's nature is determined and fixed by God prior to birth. This is not to say that a person is predetermined to be good or bad—rather, as the scroll points out, that God has a specific concern for each individual soul.

Prior to birth, God fashions the individual and his overall nature. God has a glorious design and specific task for each soul. He provides for the soul and all its needs in advance of its earthly travail. To put this in more modern terms, what the Rule seems to be saying is that God establishes an individual's personality, capabilities, and inner uniqueness prior to birth. He has a special role, or life purpose, designed for each person. If the individual acts in accordance with God's plan and purpose, all his needs will be taken care of, for they are already provided for.

The scroll continues by stating that a person has two spirits within him, either of which can come to rule the individual. One is the spirit of light and the other is the spirit of darkness. Those who choose to walk in the Way of Light are the Children of Righteousness. They are guided, or ruled, by the Prince of Light. Conversely, those who choose to walk in darkness are the Children of Falsehood and are ruled by the Angel of Darkness.

The Angel of Darkness is said to be determined to lead the Children of Light astray. This may be accomplished by afflicting them with distress, chastisement, and persecution. The implication in the scroll is that the Sons of Light are most vulnerable to being misled and seduced into darkness when they are undergoing these conditions.

The Rule states that every deed and action of man is based on these two spirits within him. "The nature of all the Children of Man is ruled by these two spirits. During their lives, all the hosts of mankind have a portion of their division and walk in both their ways."

Man is viewed as having within himself both natures. As he lives his life, the admixture of the two and their influence on him changes proportionally. No action taken is necessarily outside the interplay of these two forces. Man, in fact, is free to act in accordance with either spirit, and as he does, he alters the balance of forces within himself. Either the light or the dark will gain ascendancy.

If a person walks in the Spirit of Truth, he or she manifests and cultivates humility, charity, patience, and understanding. Such a person will have complete trust in God and will rely on God's infinite goodness and mercy. He or she will develop a spiritual capacity which discerns the inner purposes of everything. Such individuals will gain the ability to perceive the mysteries of truth and to conceal them from the undeserving. Developing a Spirit of Truth leads to healing, great inner peace, everlasting joy, and blessing.

If, conversely, one walks in the Spirit of Falsehood, what emerges is greed, arrogance, pride, deceit, lies, and violence. One becomes unclean, estranged from God, and cut off. This leads to a heavy heart and an ill temper. Ultimately, it will lead to illness and plague, eternal torment, endless disgrace, and possibly to extinction. The Choice lies within the soul of every individual. The struggle is fierce and constant—a raging conflict (CR).

What is the purpose of this continual struggle? We are told that the Ways of Light and Dark, and the interplay between them, are designed to enlighten man. The struggle between the two spirits actually allows for the paths of true righteousness to be made straight within the individual. With the strengthening of true righteousness, the laws of God are instilled in one's heart.

The view being expressed here is very profound. The individual soul is created by God with a specific destiny and purpose to fulfill that accords with the divine plan. One is equipped for life with a soul of a singularly unique and individual nature, as well as a set personality. Should the individual soul determine to live its life in accordance with God's Will and in harmony with its true inner nature as established by God, then the soul will be able to access the ample sustenance God has set aside for it in its earthly sojourn.

God's laws are eternal. They are meant to be instilled within the heart and thereby bind man to God through inner understanding and righteous action. In order to accomplish this, man is given two opposing spirits of light and dark. They are continually at odds with one another and struggle for supremacy.

A soul can harken to and act in accordance with either. That is a personal choice. Every decision one makes is made in accordance with the interplay of the two spirits. Each action, once decided upon and completed, strengthens one side or the other. One is steeled by the eternal struggle within. If one can overcome the temptation to succumb to despair, distress, persecution, and suffering, the way of light opens up and becomes triumphant. A path is made straight out of the wilderness. The Law of God becomes internalized, inscribed in the heart, and one comes to know the Way of God from the inside, rather than from without.

We are informed that "God established both spirits in equal measure until the final age and has set an everlasting hatred between their divisions." The eternal reward of each person is in accordance with the divisions between light and dark, great and small, within himself.

Each individual soul is eternal. In life, the soul wrestles with the conflict of two contending elements within. Should one adhere to the light in one's choices, light triumphs. If not, darkness does. The balance can always be changed in the course of one's lifetime. One's eternal reward, however, is based on the proportion of light over dark as it stands at the culminating stage of one's earthly travail.

The scroll tells us that throughout the current age of darkness, the struggle between truth and falsehood is fierce. But this is not an eternal conflict. At the time of the Visitation, the End of Days, falsehood will be utterly destroyed. As part of the Judgement process, God will purify every person. They will be measured by the yardstick of the truth. Those who survive will be taught the knowledge of the Everlasting Covenant, the Glory of Adam being theirs. At the time of the Final Judgement, everyone's individual destiny will be set. Their lot will be established in accordance with the soul's spirit at the time.

What is being conveyed here is the belief that the reign of evil, ignorance, and despair are not to be forever. A new era in human civilization and human life will emerge. The Day of Judgement, the time of God's direct intercession in human affairs, will change reality permanently. Falsehood, the reign of the forces of darkness, will be destroyed and humanity in its entirety shall be judged. With falsehood and deception gone, the souls of mankind will be exposed directly to the Truth and it shall be the measuring stick of salvation.

Those found worthy, presumably those who have lived their lives in accordance with the design God had set out for them and who have clung to the light, will be assigned a portion according to the state of their souls, their level of spiritual development at the End Time.

It appears that this concept is to be understood on two levels. One is purely individual; that is, when a person dies and passes to the next world, the level to which his soul has progressed or regressed, depending on the ratio of light to dark within, determines his position within the structure of that reality. On the other hand, a similar process is to take place at the time when God terminates the current age and intervenes directly to judge mankind.

Then, God will establish a new world order in which each living soul that survives the Judgement will be purified. Each soul will be weighed according to its internal apportionment of light and dark elements. On that basis, God will determine every individual's position in the new order.

It seems clear that within the current age of confusion and conflict, in an era of tremendous struggle between good and evil, the operation of free will and choice is absolutely vital. It is an integral part of man's shaping of his own destiny on several different levels. What the nature of free will and choice will be like and how they will function in the coming age is not clear from the literature.

A logical assumption, based on what we have already come to understand, may be inferred in order to answer this question. As has been noted already, free will and the range of personal choice changed in form and in scope when a person moved from the outside world into the sphere of influence of the Community. It changed yet again when he went from being an outsider and an initiate to a full member of the Community. Free will and free choice altered in scope, but did not cease to exist.

Presumably, both in the shift from the current age to the next one on a global level, and from life on earth to eternal life on the personal one, the reality is the same—namely, that choice, personal decision making, and the assumption of responsibility for oneself and one's actions will still be principles of life, but in a different context and with different forms of expression.

The post-Judgement Age will be characterized by the knowledge of Adam. Mankind will again live in the same close intimate relationship with God in which Adam and Eve did originally. The Glory of Adam and Eve was their deep communion with God and their state of innocence, unmarred by the existence of Good and Evil. What seems implied is that prior to eating of the Tree of Knowledge, human existence transcended the dichotomy of good and evil and the turbulent struggle their emergence brought into the world.

The Glory of Adam involves a new, or possibly reinstated, knowledge. The Knowledge of Good and Evil is to be replaced by the Knowledge of the Most High, characterized by an Everlasting Covenant. The new world is to have a new knowledge. That new knowledge is to be embodied in a new Covenant. A new Law will emerge, one written into the hearts of all people. A new contract will be engraved within the soul—one in which the choices made are neither in reference to compliance with God's Will nor acceptance or rejection of the Law, but rather decisions about its implementation, observance, and actualization.

Just as the Law of God will be transformed in the Coming Age, so, too, will there be a transformation of free will and choice.

7

THE LEGAL MATERIAL: TOWARD A CORRECT UNDERSTANDING OF THE LAW

During the first two centuries before the Common Era, the second and first centuries B.C.E., there was a considerable battle raging in Israel between those Jews who were traditional, pious, and observant of the Law and the hellenizers, those in Israel who sought to emulate Greek ways and often sought escape from traditional Jewish values and practices. They wanted to assimilate into the new, cosmopolitan culture, the hellenistic way of life.

This confrontation is well attested to in the Books of the Maccabees, in the writings of Josephus, and in a number of the apocryphal and pseudoepigraphal books from this time period. By the first century of the Common Era, the primacy of the Law had triumphed universally among the Jews both in Israel and in the Diaspora. The threat of hellenization evaporated, disappearing over time with the victory of the Hasmoneans.

During the period of Jewish independence under the Hasmonean dynasty, and certainly by the Roman era, the burning question among the Jews was no longer whether the Law was still binding, but rather how was it to be interpreted properly. A prerequisite for fulfilling the Law was to understand it correctly. Only by a proper understanding of the Law could it be properly observed. The Jews' first and primary obligation was to honor the commandments and to fulfill God's Will by keeping the Covenant faithfully. The central issue, therefore, was how that was to be done correctly.

In order to understand the depth of this question, several factors must be taken into account. The first is the ambiguity of many of the commandments as they are stated in the Torah, the Law of Moses. Take, for instance, the commandment to observe the Sabbath. Very few specifics regarding Sabbath observance are actually stated in the Law, although it is one of the Ten Commandments and of extreme importance.

Regarding the Sabbath, the Torah lays down the following injunctions and commandments:

> The Sabbath is to be remembered and observed (Exodus 20:8, Deuteronomy 5:12). No one, man, woman, child, servant or slave, nor any animal is to work on the Sabbath. It is to be a day of rest (Exodus 20:9–11, Deuteronomy 5:13–15) and a day of holiness (Exodus 16:23, 31:15).
>
> No fires are to be kindled on the Sabbath (Exodus 35:3) nor is one to go forth from his domain on that day (Exodus 16:29). Food is to be gathered and prepared on the sixth day of the week to cover that day and the Sabbath as well (Exodus 16:23–26).

The laws are clear and concise. Yet when one starts to consider them carefully, in terms of their implementation, more questions are raised than answered.

For example, the difference between remembering and observing is not clarified. The prohibition against working on the Sabbath is central to its observance. Yet what exactly constitutes work? That is left largely undefined. The requirement of not leaving one's place is rather bewildering, leaving more than one possibility open for interpretation. Having no fire on the Sabbath, particularly if one is not to leave one's place, seems contrary to logic. It would almost appear to be a punishment rather than a blessing. This in no way accords with the reality of the Sabbath being holy.

The commandment to keep the Sabbath holy would seem to imply setting aside the day for prayer and meditation, contemplation and devotion. This can be inferred from the special sacrifices ordained for the Sabbath (Numbers 28:9–10). Yet this is not explicitly stated or elaborated in the Law.

The various religious groups in Israel during this period approached these types of questions about the Law rather differently. The Sadducees took a more or less strict and literal interpretation of the laws. They chose to accept the principle that if something is articulated in the Law, then it is to be strictly observed. Conversely, if something is not stated in the Law, then it is not an issue. References to the disputes between the Pharisees and the Sadducees that appear in the *Mishnah* do tend to suggest that the Sadducees did, in fact, discuss and interpret the Law. However, they did not necessarily abstract any new, auxiliary practices from them.

The Pharisees, scribes, and other related groups did interpret the Law, as well as abstract new legal principles and practical applications from it. This process was known as the Oral Law. It utilized the oral traditions surrounding the practice of the Law that the Pharisees believed went back generations, in order to define how to observe the Commandments. It also employed specific principles of logic to extrapolate ever clearer guidelines for observance. The Oral Law sought to interpret the Torah, the Mosaic Law, and refine its practical application based on tradition, on the use of precedent, and through legal exegesis.

For example, the Sadducees, centered at home on the Sabbath, allowed no fire to be present and no food to be cooked. The commandment not to kindle fire on the Sabbath was taken to mean that there was to be no fire at all present in the house. This approach relies strictly on a minimalist view derived from the written commandments.

The Pharisees, on the other hand, using precedent and exegesis, derived several auxiliary practices. They derived them from principles based on a different viewpoint. Pharisaic practice allowed for warming the house on the Sabbath by keeping a fire burning that was lit the preceding day.

The Pharisees argued that one could not kindle a fire or cook on the Sabbath but that nothing in the Law explicitly forbade a continuing fire from being present. That is, a fire lit on Friday during the day, which had enough mass to it, could be allowed to continue to burn, uninterrupted, through the Sabbath. Hence, light and heat would be available for Sabbath comfort, without work being involved or the Sabbath being desecrated.

The inference for this approach can be made by taking the example of the Israelite experience under Moses in the desert of Sinai.

When manna fell during a weekday, one could only gather enough for one day's rations. However, on Friday, one was to gather enough for two days. The manna would last two days, to cover the Sabbath, when no manna would fall.

Since only kindling a fire was prohibited, this would not necessarily preclude the possibility of having a fire continue to burn. Kindling and burning are not the same. Kindling is work, an act of creation and of labor. Burning is a state. Once initiated, it continues to exist.

No Jews questioned the inappropriateness of cooking on the Sabbath. For the Sadducees, who did not have a fire present or burning on the Sabbath to begin with, the warming of food on the Sabbath was not an issue. For the Pharisees, the question did arise. They extended the same principle of continuity. If something was initiated before the Sabbath and required no maintenance, it could be allowed to continue into the Sabbath and be benefited from.

A fire that was kindled Friday could remain burning through the Sabbath to provide heat and light. In turn, the sustained fire allowed food cooked the day before to be kept warm over the Sabbath. These practices were established and justified through reliance on tradition and through the methodology of exegesis imparted by the Oral Law.

The Pharisees shared with the Essenes, the Sectarians, and other similar groups a tradition that gave great weight to the prophets and their writings. Among the Sectarians, the Essenes, the Pharisees, and later the Rabbis, the practice of prohibiting commercial transactions as a form of work, and the practice of forbidding the carrying or lifting things on the Sabbath, were both taken from examples found in the prophetic books of the Bible.

> "If you refrain from trampling the Sabbath, from pursuing your affairs on My holy day; if you call the Sabbath 'a delight,' the Lord's holy day is honored. And if you honor it and do not go your ways, nor look to your affairs, nor strike any bargains, then you can seek the favor of the Lord. I will set you astride the heights of the earth and let you enjoy the heritage of your father Jacob. The mouth of the Lord has spoken" (Isaiah 58:13–14).

Interpreting the Law through the use of examples drawn from the prophets was widespread within Jewry at this time. The practices mentioned in the prophetic writings were reinstituted under Ezra and Nehemiah, when the Jews first returned to the Land from the Babylonian exile. Nehemiah prohibits any commercial activity from taking place in Jerusalem on the Sabbath. Neither is anyone allowed to load or carry merchandise on the Sabbath (Nehemiah 13:16–22).

These remained important principles. These practices were in force and subject to further refinement throughout the period. Issues related to carrying things, to transportation, to the loading of animals, and to engaging in commerce on the Sabbath are all discussed prominently in the *Mishnah*. The Pharisees and their successors, the Rabbis, made extensive use of the traditions and methodology of the Oral Law to clarify and expand the scope of observance. They relied on example, as well as on logic, as the basis of interpreting and actualizing the Law in practice.

The approach of the Essenes and the Sectarians was somewhat different. The Essenes were also indebted to the prophetic works. They thoroughly studied and revered the writings of the Prophets, but with a different view and purpose. For them, these writings shed valuable light on the Law, in general, and on the Will of God specifically. Prophecy was understood to be direct communication from God. Because of that, the Sectarian literature speaks of "the Law of Moses and the Prophets." The Mosaic Law and the prophetic writings are often spoken of in the same breath, so to speak.

The injunctions relating to the Law found in the prophetic writings were considered to be as authoritative and binding as the Commandments themselves in terms of practical observance. This was no doubt true of the Pharisees and the Rabbis as well. Yet there is an important difference in approach between the Pharisees and the Essenes.

The Essenes' relationship to the Law involved a several-pronged approach. On the one hand, the Teacher of Righteousness, when ordering the Community, set down a specific interpretation of the Law that was to be their rule and their guide to observance. Thus there was a definitive Interpretation that formed the foundation of the Community. The Interpretation became its norm for observance.

Yet we also know that within the Council of the Community, there was an Interpreter of the Law who studied the Law and was duty-bound to reveal to the Council everything he discovered regarding the inner secrets and the hidden meanings of the Torah. Moreover, the Council members and the *Mevakair*, the Guardian of the Community, were to be well-versed in the Book of Meditations and be guided by it continually.

All of this would suggest that some sort of direct divine guidance regarding the application of the Law was also sought through the Holy Spirit. It was occasioned by study and meditation. The Sectarian Community sought to understand the Commandments and the Will of God, not only through the writings of the Prophets and their interpretation, but also through prophecy and divine inspiration directly.

Later we will focus specifically on the prophetic literature and the Sectarian commentaries on it. For the time being, it is sufficient to emphasize the point that a dynamic relationship was established by the Essenes between the interpretation and observance of the Law and the example of the Prophets. Whereas the Pharisaic approach to observance was through tradition and exegesis, the Essenes relied on the interpretation of the Teacher of Righteousness, in-depth study, and divine inspiration.

Most of the legal materials discovered among the Dead Sea literature tend to be Sectarian in nature. These materials most likely reflect Essene thinking and practice primarily. Comparison with contemporaneous Jewish literature can tell us a great deal about the legal views and approaches to the observance of the Law that were characteristic throughout Israel during these three centuries. This is very valuable in that such a comparison allows us to gain a much fuller perspective on the scroll material and the views it is expressing.

However, the primary objective throughout this work is to tap into the message of the scrolls and to elucidate the spiritual views that are reflected in the material. That is as true with the legal material of Qumran as it is of the other types of literature that will be examined. In order to do this effectively, it would be wise to present first the relationship of some of the legal material found in the scrolls to biblical law, then to touch on the significance of the textual material, and finally, to illustrate its connection to contemporaneous sources and rabbinic literature.

Sabbath Observance

We have seen how biblical law mandated the observance of the Sabbath. We have seen how prophetic tradition interpreted biblical law and expanded it. How, then, did the Sectarians and Essenes view it?

The Damascus Covenant deals fairly extensively with the laws relating to the Sabbath and its observance. The various regulations set down fall into several different categories that relate to the biblical injunctions. These categories include types of work forbidden on the Sabbath, the issues of lifting and carrying, and keeping the Sabbath holy. Some of the ordinances mentioned have parallels in mishnaic literature and others do not.

The concern over what constitutes work is of paramount importance because the Sabbath is the counterpoint to the work week. Working on the Sabbath profanes it. Any such profanation is extremely serious because the Sabbath is the paradigm for holiness. Six days are for completing all of one's work. The seventh day, the Sabbath, is holy. It is a day of rest, dedicated to God. As God rested on the seventh day, so, too, is Israel commanded to emulate God and to rest on the Sabbath.

The Sabbath is the reality of holiness. The people of Israel are called a holy nation. They are to rest on the seventh day. The Land of Israel is termed holy. The Land is to rest on the seventh year, the Sabbatical Year. On the Jubilee Year, which is at the end of seven cycles of seven years each, the Land is to rest. At that time, all debts are to be canceled. All property is to revert to its original owners. All slaves are to be freed. On the Sabbath of Yearly Sabbaths, the Jubilee Year, everything considered to be holy, the people and the Land, are to be restored to their pure, original status. Moreover, it is noteworthy that states of ritual impurity last either seven or fourteen days. Holiness, the Sabbath, and ritual purity are all connected realities.

The principle of seven is one of transcendence, of purity, of dedication to God, and of rest. In short, it is one of holiness. Not only is the seventh day separate from the rest of the week, but it is the counterpoint. It is equal in weight to the other six days. The week is cut into two, the six workdays and the Sabbath. The Sabbath is both the culmination of the week and the countervailing force.

Rest encompasses holiness. Rest marks the culmination of the process of work. Holiness is completion and rejuvenation, on the one hand, and it is quietude, reflection, and transcendence, on the other. The Sabbath is the time of rest. As such, it is holy. The people are to be holy, by living out the holiness of the Sabbath. By keeping the Sabbath, they make it holy. By maintaining Sabbath holiness, they become connected intimately to God, for God is holy.

Work and rest/holiness are to be kept separate from one another. To mix the two would be profanation of the Sabbath. This would impair or negate the whole process and purpose of Sabbath observance.

To create the proper separation necessary for holiness to be expressed, the Damascus Covenant states that all work is to cease on Fridays. Sabbath commences when the sun is within one orb of the horizon. In a similar vein, the *Mishnah* indicates that the Sabbath candles, marking the cessation of work, are to be lit while there is still daylight, Friday before dusk (*Shabbat* 2:7).

Technically, in Jewish law, a day starts only at sunset. If labor must cease before sunset on Friday, the work week is being terminated before the Sabbath actually begins. The Sabbath does not then mark the completion of the week, but rather is a separate reality, the work week having culminated and closed before the Sabbath began. Here, the fourth commandment is being fulfilled: to remember the Sabbath and to keep it holy.

This concept of preserving the holiness of the Sabbath by distinguishing it from the work week is also reflected in several other ordinances of different types. The Damascus Covenant states that one was neither to freely mingle with other people nor engage in mere idle chatter or common discourse with others on the Sabbath. The wearing of soiled clothes on the Sabbath was proscribed as well. Soiled clothes or clothes taken out of storage had to be washed in water or rubbed in incense before they could be used on the Sabbath (CD).

That which had been touched by the activity of the work week had to be purified so as to make it acceptable for use on the holy Sabbath. The emphasis in these laws is placed on separating the mundane from the holy, on keeping the Sabbath sacred, by refraining from carrying the routine of the week into the Sabbath. On the Sabbath, one was to direct attention to God and to God's service. The routine and the mundane were to be strictly avoided, as a breach of the sanctity of the day.

The *Mishnah*, in elaborating the 39 forbidden types of work prohibited on the Sabbath, lists largely activities associated with working the land. Work itself was understood to mean agricultural labor, first and foremost. The Essenes and the Sectarians understood it the same way, as the Sadducees no doubt did also. The Torah and the commandments address an agrarian society.

In response to the changes that took place in society over time, both the Pharisees and the Essenes, honoring the prophetic tradition and the practices established by Nehemiah, extended the concept of work to include commerce and skilled labor. In reference to commerce, the Damascus Covenant (column 10) says, "No man shall go about doing business on the Sabbath."

The *Mishnah* does not state that doing business on the Sabbath is forbidden. Rather, it takes the prohibition for granted and expands on the concept. "A tailor should not go out with his needle close to nightfall [on Fridays] lest he go forth and forget [and have the needle with him on the Sabbath], nor a scribe with his pen" (*Shabbat* 1:3).

In the *Mishnah*, in chapters 3 and 4 of Tractate *Shabbat*, the concept of *Muktzeh* is discussed. Objects are allowed to be moved from their resting place and utilized on the Sabbath only if the use to which they are put is not related to work that would normally be done with them. A hammer, for instance, could be used to crack nuts open—but it could not even be picked up if the intention was to hammer a nail. Not only was work on the Sabbath to be avoided, but any activity which might lead to work was to be eschewed as well.

In rabbinic law, as reflected in the *Mishnah* (and presumably among the legal rulings of the Rabbis' predecessors, the Pharisees), activities related to commerce and business, such as lifting, carrying, loading or unloading an animal, moving things out of storage, writing, et cetera, were all prohibited and discussed at length. Picking up clues from prophetic literature and from biblical example, the Pharisees and the Rabbis proscribed commerce and business on the Sabbath, classifying them as work. The Sectarians and Essenes, as we shall see, took a similar view.

In chapter 31 of the Book of Exodus, God's designation of Bezalel as a master craftsman and his commission to build both the Ark and the Tabernacle are juxtaposed with the commandment to observe and keep holy the Sabbath. It was logical, then, for Jewish authorities to assume that there was a connection between the two. Since the two commands were joined together when God spoke, and the common element between them is doing work, they were seen to be logically related.

Therefore, what is referred to as work regarding the Tabernacle's construction would then reflect work that is forbidden on the Sabbath. Exodus 35:33, in discussing the work of Bezalel, refers to it as *melechet machashevet*—that is, skilled labor. Hence, skilled labor, as well as commercial transactions, were deemed work and proscribed on the Sabbath.

As noted above, the classifications of work prohibited on the Sabbath included the prohibition against lifting and carrying. This innovation was already taking shape during the biblical period. On one hand, the prohibition seems related to the injunction that one is not to leave one's place. If an individual is not to leave his place on the Sabbath, neither should anything be made to leave its place.

Both mishnaic law and the Damascus Covenant forbade moving anything to or from one's house on the Sabbath. The *Mishnah* deals at considerable length with the issue of moving things from one domain to another on the Sabbath. Lifting or carrying would be related issues, inasmuch as those activities would be involved in the movement. Moreover, the movement of things, which often involves lifting and carrying, is often related to business or commerce.

The implications of all these concerns are clear. The concept of work was extended during the period of the Prophets to include commercial activity and skilled labor. Hence, lifting and carrying were forbidden because they facilitated those activities. During the Greco-Roman period, the Pharisees and the Essenes extended the prohibition to include taking anything in or out of a house. The Rabbis prohibited removing anything from storage on the Sabbath (*Shabbat* 7:3). They also forbid moving anything from a private domain to a public one on the Sabbath and vice versa.

Aside from their relationship to commerce, lifting and carrying were, in and of themselves, considered a form of work. The Essenes, like the Rabbis, forbid one to assist an animal giving birth, although the latter permitted intervention so that the newborn did not hit the ground (see *Mishnah*, *Shabbat* 18:3, and CD, col. 11).

The Damascus Covenant forbids lifting a fallen animal out of a pit on Sabbath. Even though the animal may be trapped or injured, it was not considered sufficient reason to violate the prohibition against work by lifting the beast from its position.

In the case of a life-threatening situation, the approach was somewhat different. The Damascus Covenant (CD, col. 11) allows one to save a man who has fallen into water or fire by pulling him out using an instrument of some sort—a ladder, rope, et cetera. The need to save human life is to take precedence over avoiding work on the Sabbath. Yet to avoid violating the injunction not to lift anything on the Sabbath, the appropriate response was seen to be pulling someone out by means of an intermediary tool. That way, one was not doing it directly.

Although the Pharisees, in all likelihood, allowed picking up and carrying a child on the Sabbath (*Shabbat* 21:1), the Essenes, however, did not. They went as far as prohibiting the carrying of perfume and the lifting of sand or dust (CD, col. 11).

What we see here is a dual concern over the activities of lifting and carrying anything on the Sabbath. They are seen as part and parcel of commercial activity and, in and of themselves, forms of work. The message conveyed here is that once something is identified with work, it is to be avoided in all its various forms and nuances, even down to the seemingly insignificant.

Work is prohibited on the Sabbath because the Sabbath is holy and God expects its holiness to be maintained. Work is antithetical to the rest and holiness of the Sabbath. Maintaining the complete separation between the holy and the mundane is of crucial importance.

There can be no equivocation in obeying God. The violation of holiness renders it null and void. Holiness is a pure state. It cannot, by definition and by nature, be an admixture of anything. Work on the Sabbath destroys its sanctity. Therefore, how work is defined determines the guidelines for preserving the sacredness of the Sabbath and allows for the fulfillment of one of the most primary commandments.

To go one step further, let us consider the relationship between not moving something from one place to another on the Sabbath and the commandment to remain in one's place on that day. Both the Pharisees and the Essenes understood the commandment "not to move from one's place on Sabbath" to mean that one did not travel beyond the village or city one was in at the time the Sabbath began.

Remaining in place, be it a person staying in his or her locale for Sabbath or not moving things from place to place, symbolizes another key concept connected with the Sabbath and with holiness. Holiness and spiritual transcendence involve respecting boundaries. To be at rest, to be in a transcendent state, a state of holiness, is to let yourself and the things around you be at peace.

To as great an extent as possible, one is asked to work within set personal boundaries and to distance oneself from the concerns of survival, of change, and of material well-being. The boundaries of those around you and even of the things around you, animate and inanimate, have to be respected and left in peace if holiness is to be made manifest.

Interaction and interchange involve a dynamic with others. By involving oneself with others, one is forced beyond one's own center of gravity. Interaction is a process by which the people involved are linked together. A group dynamic takes place that drives the evolution of events and is experienced jointly by those participating. This is a process of creation and development. It is appropriate during the work week, but it is contrary to experiencing holiness if focused on something other than service to God.

The Essenes saw the Sabbath as a time for centering within oneself, honoring one's own boundaries, and experiencing one's own holiness through the sanctity of the Sabbath. One was not to work, not to do business, not to move things about, not to indulge in idle conversation. One was to remain where one was. One was to reflect, to be focused within oneself, and to serve God by so doing.

According to the Damascus Covenant, the Sectarians went even further in their thinking. They forbid not only forms of work, such as commerce and skilled labor, but extended the prohibitions to cover actions that would lead to or be connected with work. They did not feel it was appropriate to do anything on the Sabbath, which (though it was not in and of itself work) could entail labor or could effect some profit and benefit in the future.

The Essenes did not want to do anything on the Sabbath that would begin a process that would involve work in the future. Neither talk of work, nor the making of any loans were permissible on the Sabbath. One could neither discuss money matters nor make any decisions regarding money or financial matters. One could not even chide a servant on the Sabbath. Nothing could be done or even initiated on the Sabbath that would in any way, directly or indirectly, create work or work-related benefit in the future. Inclusive in the principle of work were even the elements of planning and initiation.

Holiness is a complete reality, totally separated from the day-to-day processes of everyday survival. Whereas on six days of the week we are focused on the exigencies of physical life, satisfying our bodily and psychological needs, the Sabbath is a day of rest and holiness. It is a day of timelessness, during which nothing is done or even contemplated that relates to the mundane world. Rather, we are commanded to remain in our places, to serve God, and thereby have our spiritual needs met. That is how we truly become holy, by experiencing holiness through a centering within our own personal boundaries and by respecting the right of everyone and everything around us to do the same.

The View of Idolatry

In biblical law, there are a great number of commandments that center on the prohibition of idolatry and on the practices connected with the worship of foreign gods. "You shall have no other gods beside Me" and "You shall not make for yourself a sculpted image . . . You shall not bow down to them or serve them" (Exodus 20:3–4) are the first and second commandments.

Many other commandments prohibited specific practices that were commonly associated with pagan cults and idolatrous worship. The prohibitions against necromancy, speaking with familiar spirits, tattooing the body, lacerating oneself with razors, and sacred prostitution, for example, all fall into this category, as they were all cult practices.

In general, there were commandments outlawing the worship of idols and prohibiting any acknowledgment of other gods. One was forbidden to make sacrifices to other gods or even mention their names. The definition of idolatry included the incorporation of any idolatrous practices into the pure worship of God. There were commandments prohibiting any worship of God through the use of pagan rites. There was concern, as well, that the people not get enticed into idolatry by personal, intimate contact with idolaters. This accounts for the prohibitions against intermarriage and covenanting with pagans.

In biblical literature, there are primary grounds on which idolatry is attacked. There are very cogent reasons why idolatry was so thoroughly assaulted in biblical law. First and foremost, idolatry is a direct and primal violation of the Covenant. The Law, the Torah, is the very basis of the Covenant, the eternal contract between God and Israel. The commandments are the contractual terms that bind Israel to God's service and God to Israel. To violate the First Commandment and worship another god is to repudiate God Himself and thereby invalidate the bonds of Covenant.

Biblical law emphasized a complete and total separation from idolatry—its beliefs, forms, and practices. It sought to keep the Israelites away from idolatry's influence entirely. Idolatry was the antithesis of service to God. It was ranked with murder and bloodshed as the prime source of pollution that destroyed the Land both morally and physically. Idolatry and its practice brought corruption and human degradation. This reality invoked God's wrath, leaving the Land cursed and barren.

For centuries, the message of the Prophets had been that unless idolatry was completely uprooted from Israel, the Temple and the State would be destroyed by God's consuming anger. That message was taken to heart by many Jews during the horror that accompanied the destruction of the country by the Babylonians. It was reinforced during the many years of the Exile that followed.

This realization—that idolatry by its very nature threatened the existence of Judaism by striking at the heart of Israel's relationship to God—was not lost on Ezra and Nehemiah when the Second Jewish Commonwealth was established. Alongside measures to enforce the prohibition against doing business on the Sabbath, Nehemiah forced a wholesale divorce of pagan wives upon the entire returning Jewish community.

The disappearance of idolatry in Israel is attributed to the Persian period in talmudic literature. Both the *Song of Songs Rabbah* (7:8) and Tractate *Yoma* (69b) state that idolatry had long been totally uprooted in Israel. The discussions found there center around whether this took place during the time of Esther or the time of Daniel. Either way would place the change, the complete disappearance of idol worship in Israel, some time in the Persian period.

The issue of the reinfection of Israel with the plague of idolatry no doubt loomed large during the struggle with Hellenism. The cultural conquest of the Near East by Greek civilization reignited the conflict with paganism, although the shape and content of the struggle were different. The resistance to hellenization by most of Judea was epitomized in the refusal to yield to idolatry.

The repudiation of idolatry became a central act of faith. As such, the practice of fighting and dying to preserve the Jewish faith was firmly established in Israel as a result of the Maccabean struggle. During the royal persecutions under Antiochus IV, which preceded the revolt, many Jews preferred to die rather than violate the Covenant with God. This determined resistance to the pressures of paganism would remain a constant during the Greco-Roman period. The Jews' steadfast refusal to abandon God and the Covenant would manifest itself just as strongly during the Hadrianic persecutions (which followed the Bar Kochba Revolt—the Second War against Rome), as it had three centuries earlier under the Maccabees.

By the time of the emergence of the Sectarian Community, the question of idolatry had shifted. The danger was no longer so much a matter of practice. The worship of other gods had passed away from Israel during the Persian period. Rather, contact with idolatry or idolaters was viewed as morally contaminating. In the *Mishnah* (*Berakhot* 9:1), one is clearly instructed to say a prayer thanking God for uprooting idolatry from the Land every time one passes a place idol worship used to occur.

Jewish practice became so intent on keeping distant from idolatry and idolatrous practices that even indirect contact was proscribed. Much of Tractate *Avodah Zarah* deals with the various levels of indirect contact with idolatry that one is to avoid. Mishnaic law prohibits selling anything to Gentiles that could conceivably be used in idolatrous worship or in its cult. Hence, one was forbidden to sell certain types of animals commonly used in cultic ceremony to idolaters. Neither could one buy wine from them because of the close association between wine and many of the pagan rituals.

During the Greco-Roman period, separation from idolatry involved two distinct, but related, concerns. First, there was a growing consensus that in order to completely fulfill the commandment not to serve other gods, one had to avoid doing anything that would support or encourage idol worship in any way, even indirectly. Second, there was the belief that contact with idolaters led to ethical, social, and moral decline. It is common in rabbinic literature to have a serious moral transgression characterized as being akin to idol worship. A grave breach of moral law was equated with idolatry.

The Dead Sea literature strongly indicates that the Community saw idolatry as moral corruption. The Community took ethical deterioration, and the resulting moral decay, as very serious threats to having a true relationship to God.

In much the same way as rabbinic literature sought to isolate Jews from idolaters and the moral problems such contact was seen to generate, so, too, does the Sectarian literature go to great lengths to separate the Community members from the People of the Pit. Numerous regulations, injunctions, and admonitions in the literature are directed specifically against the People of Corruption, the Sons of Darkness. The Sons of Light and the Sons of Darkness are inimical to each other. Therefore, the two have to be kept far apart from one another.

The Damascus Covenant states that members of the New Covenant, formed in the Land of Damascus, were to separate from the Sons of Darkness. They were to do so by living their lives in strict accordance with an exact interpretation of the Law. Emphasis is drawn to Deuteronomy 7:9, which says that grace will be bestowed by God to the thousandth generation of those who keep the commandments.

The reign of Evil is said to hold sway until the completion of the present Age, the one that mankind is currently going through.

During the reign of Evil, man is lured into corruption by three snares: fornication, riches, and profanation of the Temple. These snares all involve moral transgression.

Idolatry is seen to be all that is morally corrupting. Moral corruption, then, becomes the agent for negating the entire Covenant, casting the people deep into sin and incurring the wrath of God. To prevent this, the Community set up a way of life in harmony with the principles laid down by the first covenanters and by the Teacher of Righteousness. At the completion of the present Age of Darkness, it is the Community that will be justified and forgiven of its sins. The sins of their forefathers, which included idolatry, subsequently will be washed away as well.

The literature repeatedly identifies the Sons of Darkness as those who remove the boundaries set by the Law. They not only violate the Law, they repudiate it. In fact, they have abandoned the Law entirely. Separation from them, and all they represent, stems from the same two concerns that required a separation from anything idolatrous: violation of the Covenant and fear of moral degeneration. According to the Damascus Scroll, all who reject the Law are setting up idols in their hearts.

Abandoning the Covenant and the Commandments is to destroy one's inner, emotional connection to God. Something else is at one's spiritual core, something other than God, and whatever that idol is, it is disrupting any true relationship to the Divine. To deny the Covenant leads to setting up something other than God as the supreme force in the universe. That, in turn, leads to moral decay and evil. The evil then plays itself out by bringing destruction and devastation.

It is both significant and poignant that along with the practical prohibitions against selling to heathens any animals or vessels that could be used in pagan sacrificial rites or sacrificing animals bought from them, there is yet another prohibition that addresses the heart of the issue.

One is instructed to put to death any prophet or dreamer whose predictions came true and who then preached idolatry. Idolatry is equated in the Damascus Covenant Scroll with rebellion against God. Rebellion against God is often associated, in the literature, with abandonment of the Law. We are told that this type of phenomenon—a prophet preaching idolatry and the abandonment of the Law—is a test by God. Presumably, the prophet's integrity, ego, and ability to withstand self-aggrandizement are put to the test. If, after God grants him clear vision, the prophet succumbs to self-delusion and the will to power, then he cuts himself off from God. He becomes corrupt and, hence, forfeits his life. Moreover, if rebellion and moral disintegration manifest and those exposed to it do not destroy it, it will destroy them. That is an even greater test.

Idolatry, the great evil that displaces God from one's heart and from one's life, cannot be fought. It must be disengaged from. Its symptoms are moral decay and spiritual degeneration. Only an adherence to the Law of God will protect one from losing the divine connection. Through faithfulness to the Law and observance of the commandments does one remain connected to God. Ultimately, it is God personally who will vanquish evil, ending the Age of Darkness, the reign of idolatry. Until then, mankind must keep far from evil. For the Jews, that means observance of the Torah, the Law of God, and adherence to the Covenant. That is the message of the scroll.

Two of the three great snares of Evil are the accumulation of riches and the profanation of the Temple. Both of these evils are not only connected to idolatry, but also to ritual impurity—another major concern of the literature.

The accumulation of riches is defined by the Damascus Scroll as ill-gotten gain, that which was accumulated by vow or anathema, by defrauding the Temple, by robbing the poor, or by victimizing the widow. Profaning the Temple was defined as not observing a distinction between the clean and the unclean, in accordance with the Law.

Profaning the Temple was also the catchall phrase for breaking with the Law. "They defile their holy spirit by blaspheming against the laws of the Covenant, by saying, 'They are not certain.'" (CD)

Fornication, the accumulation of ill-gotten wealth, blaspheming the Law, and desecrating the Community were all seen in the same light. On one hand, they are all major breaches of moral law, which have widespread ramifications. On the other hand, just like sleeping with a woman during menstruation, these sinful tendencies were considered violations of the laws separating the clean from the unclean. Hence, an equation is made between morality and purity and between immorality and ritual uncleanliness. The laws separating clean from unclean are usually referred to as the "Laws of Ritual Purity." They form a very important part of biblical law and were of great importance to all groups within Judaism during this time period.

In order to more fully understand what the importance of the equation of immorality to uncleanliness was, and what implications it held for Jews at that time, it would be wise to examine the laws of ritual impurity and, particularly, to explore how they were understood by the Sectarian Community.

Purity and Impurity

In order to understand the importance of ritual purity and the overwhelming concern in the Law regarding ritual uncleanliness, it is important to gain insight into the nature of the Temple and the priesthood. What function did they play in the life of the People of Israel?

In the Sinai experience, the forty years in the desert, Israel served God through prayer, ritual, and sacrifice centered in the Tabernacle. The Tabernacle was a portable Sanctuary. Within it was a movable altar, specific ritual furnishings, and areas for prayer and sacrifice. The center of the Tabernacle was the Holy of Holies, an enclosed area that housed the Ark of the Covenant.

It was in the desert that Aaron, Moses' brother, was made High Priest at God's command and his descendants were designated to become the priesthood in perpetuity. Under King David, Jerusalem became the capital of Israel and when Solomon built the Temple there, it became the Holy City. At this juncture, Jerusalem came to represent the sacred focal point for all of Israel. The Temple replaced the Tabernacle as the focus of worship.

The function of the priests was to maintain the ritual, to accept and offer the sacrifices of the people, and to bring down divine blessing onto the people and onto the Land. The sacrifices and offerings were meant to atone for sins, to express thanksgiving for God's protection and blessings, and to acknowledge God's complete sovereignty. The priests interceded for the people. The High Priest sought atonement for the Land.

The Temple was seen as the center for divine service. The Holy of Holies was the throne of God. It was within the Temple that intimate contact took place with the Divine on a constant basis. The life of the people and the well-being of the Land hinged on the ceaseless activities of the Temple and the priesthood.

In essence, fulfilling the Covenant with God required two different focuses. Many of the commandments spelled out the moral and social laws that were to govern society, as God wanted it structured. These laws regulated social interaction and assured a high ethical standard of interpersonal conduct. Violation of any of these norms disrupted relations with God, in terms of both the nation and the individual.

Rectification came in the wake of the acknowledgment of mistakes and as a result of the process of repentance and sacrifice. Blessing came as result of the recognition of God's protection and providence and of the process of thanksgiving and offering. It was the priesthood that acted as the conduits, first, by which the energy of people was channeled toward God, and subsequently, by which the flow of Divine Grace was directed toward the people and the Land.

Intimacy and the constant readjustment of life experience were the objectives and the reality of the Temple service. The Temple was the link between Heaven and Earth. The priests were the guardians and the technicians of the Temple, the intercessors for the people, and the channels for God. The Temple and the priests were a unified whole. Their role in fulfilling the Covenant was to maintain the link of intimacy and to protect the welfare of the nation.

In order to accomplish this, both the priests and the Temple had to remain pure and uncorrupted at all times. Therefore, the issue of ritual purity was of paramount importance to all Jews. That is not only evidenced by the extent to which the priestly laws in the Bible are explicitly enumerated and recounted, but also by the great amount of attention the issue receives in the Jewish literature of the Greco-Roman age.

In biblical law, ritual impurity was a form of uncleanliness that rendered a person, animal, or object unfit for sacred service. If something became ritually unfit, it could not be brought to the Temple. It could not be used. Neither could a priest touch it. It could have no contact with the Temple or the priesthood, for it was ritually unclean.

The three primary sources of ritual uncleanliness were leprosy, the involuntary discharge of bodily fluid, and contact with a corpse. Leprosy referred to a whole range of skin diseases and disorders. Involuntary discharge included fluid eruptions, menstruation, nocturnal emissions, cohabitation, and childbirth.

Contact with a corpse involved not only touching a human corpse, but also being in a building that housed a corpse. Both rendered a person ritually unclean. Ritual uncleanliness was transferable, based on physical contact. So, for example, if a leper touched something, it became ritually unclean and anyone touching it would, in turn, be contaminated.

Ritual impurity, however, was not a permanent state. It could be corrected. In many cases, the impurity lasted a specific period of time. For example, a menstruant was ritually unclean for seven days. In some cases, determination had to be made regarding status. A leper was quarantined for two weeks. If his condition did not deteriorate, he was declared clean. If he was declared unclean, he remained in that state until the condition passed and until the passing of the unclean state was verified by a priest.

Though not always stated explicitly, the purification ritual generally involved ritual immersion in an active body of water or in a ritual bath, fed by "living water." Most purification rituals also required the bringing of a specified sacrifice or offering as the concluding part of the process.

Within the Jewish world at this time, there was a great deal of discussion regarding the contracting of ritual impurity, the degrees of uncleanliness imparted, and the rites of purification. Many practices were clarified. Some were even extended beyond the biblical purview.

The Rabbis enunciated the concept of overshadowing—that is, the extent by which one becomes ritually unclean due to falling under the shadow of an area contaminated by corpse impurity. If one came within proximity of the shadow of a grave, a tomb, or a house with a body still in it, one became ritually unclean as a result.

According to the Mishnah (Nega'im 13:6–8), if a leper's head and the better part of his body enters a house or a swatch of his garment is carried into a house, the house becomes ritually impure and, by extension, so does everything in it.

There is considerable rabbinic discussion regarding the susceptibility of certain grains and food to ritual contamination by contact with water and related fluids.

The Pharisees and the Sadducees argued extensively over what type of contact rendered the hands ritually impure and therefore required washing. This issue appears prominently in the Gospels as well.

Questions of ritual impurity, its extent, and the means for rectification are extensively discussed in the literature of the times. These questions take up twelve tractates in the Mishnah and Tosefta. They are focused on, at great length, in the Temple Scroll and other legal materials from the Dead Sea literature.

Ritual uncleanliness had to be handled very carefully. If not watched properly, it could contaminate the Temple and the priesthood. This would then impair communion with God and interrupt the flow of blessing to the Land.

The Temple Scroll, which is not a specifically Sectarian work, centers much of its attention on laws and ordinances related to ritual purity. It very likely reflects the strong tendency within the Jewish world, as a whole, toward strict safeguard of the Temple and the priesthood.

For example, whereas biblical law indicates that after cohabitation, both husband and wife remain impure until evening and become clean after bathing (Leviticus 15:16–18), the Temple Scroll states that no man after having sexual relations with his wife can even enter Jerusalem, let alone the Temple, for three days.

The evidence in all of the literature from our period points clearly in the direction of overriding concern for the proper handling of ritual impurity. What needs to be asked at this point then is, what was the significance of these laws for the Sectarian Community? How was their thinking impacted by them? What was the relationship of the impurity laws to their way of life?

As was mentioned earlier, to the Sectarians their community was seen as the Temple. To them, the Council of the Community was the Holy of Holies. They felt that their way of life substituted for the prayers and sacrifices of the Temple. Their organization was the new Temple and they were representative of a nation of priests.

Their view of ritual impurity would be the same as that of other Jews: namely, that anything that induced a state of uncleanliness impaired communion with God and brought about disruption in the flow of divine blessing. Ritual impurity would therefore preclude a person from active involvement in the Community. If the Community was the Temple, a person who was ritually unclean would have to be totally excluded.

The Sectarians seemed to have understood ritual impurity as encompassing two different levels of existence. On the one hand, like other Jews, they took the purity laws quite seriously on a practical, physical level. The Damascus Covenant goes as far as saying that one in need of washing is akin to one in a state of ritual impurity and, therefore, may not even enter a synagogue. The logic is that just as a ritually unclean person is prohibited from entering the Temple, so, too, an unwashed person is not fit to enter a synagogue and stand in prayer before God.

On the other hand, the Sectarians also saw ritual purity on a metaphysical level. It is stated that the process of advancing the rank of members of the Community according to the level of their deeds and the degree of their understanding of the Law is the equivalent of washing one's hands. This implies that the act of promotion within the ranks of the faithful is based on moral and intellectual development, and that it is recognition of one being freed from yet another degree of defilement.

Dealing with the process of ritual purity cut practically, in both directions. Being in a state of ritual uncleanliness, as defined in the Bible and as outlined in the Temple Scroll, would serve to isolate one temporarily from the life of the Community. This was a temporary, physical state. By being ever more diligent in pursuance of the commandments and in knowledge of the Law, one rose in rank in the Community, became more holy, and was moved further away from defilement spiritually. This condition was of a more permanent nature.

According to the Community Rule, having any contact with the Sons of the Pit, the Sons of Darkness, rendered one unclean. The Sons of Darkness are ruled to be ritually impure, because they are morally corrupt. Therefore, like anything that is ritually unclean, any contact with it renders one as unclean. Hence, moral uncleanliness is equated with ritual uncleanliness. The practical effects of both are seen to be the same legally.

This Sectarian ruling parallels the rabbinic rulings, which declare that idolatry, and anything related to it, causes ritual impurity. The *Mishnah* states that idolatrous offerings impart the same degree of ritual uncleanliness, as would corpse contamination (*Avodah Zarah* 3:8). Moreover, biblical literature itself suggests a relationship between ritual uncleanliness and moral corruption. The Bible stresses that idolatry and bloodshed bring uncleanliness to the Land (Ezekiel 36:25, Psalms 51:4).

By its ruling, the Community is affirming that contact with corrupt people renders one defiled, temporarily corrupted, and no longer in a position to serve God. The effect would be exclusion and isolation from the Community. Repentance and atonement would have to be made.

The reference to the Sons of the Pit, specifically, is to those who willfully and deliberately reject God's law and who consciously live immoral lives. Contact and interaction with such individuals is seen as contaminating. One is thrown off-center and temporarily separated from full service to God, one's highest duty.

Such contact is seen as unproductive, since contact with corruption, physical or moral, renders the clean, unclean. The base, unclean person, however, is not purified by contact with the righteous. Only confession, contrition, and repentance on the part of the individual can render the Son of the Pit truly clean. Hence, separation, moral vigilance, and adherence to the Law of Moses are all necessary components to remaining in a pure state, enabling one to serve God.

The Community Rule defines ritual uncleanliness as transgressing the Word of God, on one hand, and violating your own personal word, on the other. This speaks of integrity. When a person gives his word to someone, he is creating a personal obligation. When he affirms something as the truth, he is placing his entire reputation behind it. To violate one's word is to break trust with others, to circumvent one's obligations, and to destroy one's integrity. By not upholding his word, a person transgresses against others and violates his own nature, damaging the soul.

By transgressing the Word of God, the Law, people cut themselves off from service to God. The possibility of communion with God is eclipsed. A person becomes unclean, unfit to stand before God. He is excluded from God's Presence. Deep connection to God is not possible as long as this state of impurity continues and remains in force. The scrolls describe the Sons of Darkness as being those who remove the boundaries. Wishing to free themselves from moral constraints, they break the bounds of discipline and ethics. As they break the bounds of the God's Law, they are simultaneously erecting barriers to God. They have become impure and, therefore, they have become isolated and cut off as a consequence.

Accepting God's Will means submission to God. Following in the Way, in the knowledge, understanding, and observance of the Law is the act of being the Temple, of becoming the Holy of Holies. Adherence to God's Law is to stand in His holy place. Observance of the commandments places one in a position to receive the Holy Spirit. The result is to bring blessing to others and to be forgiven for one's sins. Biblical law reflects the belief that in purity and in communion with God, atonement is achieved. In holiness, the priests receive the Presence of God, the sins of the people being forgiven.

In a similar vein, the Community Rule affirms that sins are cleansed by the spirit of holiness. To the Community, cleanliness was adherence to the Law. Adherence to the Law was submission to God. Submission to God involved becoming the Temple, the receptacle for receiving the spirit of holiness. Upon receipt of the spirit, one was then cleansed of sin and subsequently became a channel for the flow of God's Grace.

8

THE TEMPLE AND THE TEMPLE SCROLL: PART ONE

One of the largest, most complete scrolls discovered among the Dead Sea literature is that referred to as the Temple Scroll. This book is, arguably, one of the most important scrolls ever found. Its importance stems from two major factors. First, the scroll is written in the form of a direct revelation of the Law, a dialogue between Moses and God. Its format is that of the Torah. Indeed, the Temple Scroll claims to be Torah, the Word of God, as given to Moses at Mount Sinai. Here we have, in essence, a second, possibly alternate, version of the Law.

Second, it is clear that this scroll is not a Sectarian document. Much of the scroll focuses on the physical structure of the Temple, the actual sacrifices, the Temple rituals, and the priestly regulations. These are concerns central to all of Israel. The core of Jewish life on the physical, emotional, and spiritual levels were governed by these very realities. The life of the people as a whole was dominated, regulated, and given spiritual meaning by the Temple, the ritual, the sacrifices, and the festival observances.

Moreover, we know from the Sectarian literature that the Community saw itself as the embodiment of the true Temple and that they viewed their way of life as a substitute for the sacrifices and rituals. It is not very likely, therefore, that they would have composed a document of this type, which centers on the physical details of the Temple and on the sacrificial rites.

In point of fact, the Covenanters established a social organization and a distinct way of life based on a strict observance of the details of the Law of Moses. Their way of life was governed by the Interpretation of the Law handed down by the Teacher of Righteousness. It is highly unlikely that they would dare to presume to tamper with the Law itself. It would have been unthinkable for the Community to have endeavored to author anything that purported to be a version of the Torah.

This is not to say that the Community did not hold the Temple Scroll to be holy. On the contrary, their objective was to live as purely, and as directly in line with the truest interpretation of the Law of Moses, as possible. It stands to reason, then, that their interest and reverence for the Temple Scroll would be very great. The scroll is a document that was believed to come directly from God to Moses, on Mount Sinai. Logically, this would be held to be most sacred and of paramount importance to their entire way of life.

In order to explore the impact of Temple Scroll on the thinking of the times and on its spiritual message, one needs first gain a sense of what the scroll actually is. There would seem to be two distinct ways of viewing the nature of the Temple Scroll. One approach was articulated by the late Yigal Yadin, who published the Temple Scroll, and the other by Ben Zion Wacholder, in his book *The Dawn of Qumran*.

Yadin's view of the Temple Scroll is that it represents an interpretation of the Torah. He argues that the scroll focuses on the Temple and the Temple Service. The laws that dominate the text involve the Temple itself, the priesthood, the sacrifices, and issues of ritual cleanliness. He stresses that the Temple Scroll is an integrated text, suggesting that it was edited from traditional biblical material and that it postdates the Torah.

All of the laws in the Temple Scroll are grouped together quite neatly. They are harmonized as well. There is a logical correlation and order between the laws as they are presented in the scroll. This would suggest that the scroll material was compiled and edited from an earlier source. Yadin believes, therefore, that the scroll represents a summary of Mosaic Law. To support this position, Yadin points out that aside from the precision and tight organization of the text within the Temple Scroll, there is no repetition or any duplication of the laws, as is so commonly found in the text of the Torah. This would suggest that the Torah is the source material and the Temple Scroll, a redaction of it.

With regard to the new material found in the scroll—that is, laws that do not have any parallel in the Torah itself—Yadin views it as supplementary material added by the author or editor of the scroll. He points out that it is not uncommon in Jewish religious literature to have old traditions, not previously recorded, brought up in legal discussions to illustrate or clarify a point of law or practice.

In rabbinic literature, in the *Mishnah* and in the *Midrash*, certain *halakhot* (legal practices not mentioned in the Torah but based on long-recognized legal precedent) are often brought up in the course of discussion for purposes of elucidation. In short, Yadin sees the Temple Scroll as an extension of the Torah, in the form of a summary and an interpretation of the Law.

On the other hand, Wacholder views the scroll as an alternative Torah. He argues that by the post-Exilic period, the period of the Second Temple (after the return of the Jews from Babylonia), the Torah, as we have inherited it, was already canonized. By the Second Temple period, the Torah was already fixed in its present form and universally accepted by the Jewish people. The Samaritan version of the Law of Moses and the Septuagint, the Greek translation of the Bible, transcribed during the Hellenistic period, confirm this fact.

Wacholder points out that the Temple Scroll itself asserts that it is of Divine authorship. God speaks in the first person, as "I," continually. God is never referred to in the Temple Scroll in the third person, as "He." When speaking to Moses, God addresses him as "You." What is being portrayed in the scroll is a direct dialogue between God and Moses. The only things referred to in the third person are the laws themselves, the terms of the Covenant. This implies that the Temple Scroll is of Divine authorship and is a direct revelation from God. This Torah is to be considered equal to, or even possibly superior to, the recognized Torah.

Hence, we are very likely dealing with an alternate Torah, not a supplement to it. This is not a commentary of Torah or an elucidation of the laws. Rather, the Temple Scroll is a separate, equally binding, revelation of the Law, handed down by God to Moses at Mount Sinai. As such, the material contained in the scroll would be of great importance for the whole people of Israel. As a second Torah, it would stand as confirmation of the sacred and enduring nature of the Sinai

Covenant, emphasizing the centrality of the Temple and the services, and reaffirming the holy nature of Israel's mission.

For the Covenant Community, the scrolls would have an additional significance. The Temple Scroll, as an equal to the Torah, would have been as important a source for the proper understanding of the Law and its true application as the Torah itself. Since the Community was determined to fulfill the Law completely and uphold it in as pure a form as possible, considerable attention would have to be paid to the laws being emphasized in the text, as well as to the laws being enunciated here for the first time.

Is there any precedent for the concept that there could be two equally valid Torahs? Actually, there is. Professor Wacholder points out that the eighteenth verse of Deuteronomy 17, in referring to the king, states, "When he is seated on his royal throne, he shall have a *Mishneh Torah*' written for him by the Levitical priests." Technically, the term *Mishneh Torah* means a "Teaching of the Law." The *Targum*, the ancient Aramaic translation of the Torah, interprets the term to mean a copy of the Law. However, the Septuagint, the ancient Greek translation, renders the term "a Second Torah."

In the Temple Scroll, the Royal charter is expanded beyond the provisions mentioned in the canonical Torah. Whereas in the Torah, the king is commanded to have a *Mishneh Torah* written for him by the Levitical priests, he is also commanded to learn and observe faithfully every word of this Torah. Moreover, he is not to deviate from the Instruction at all.

The Temple Scroll goes somewhat further. Explaining that the kings of old did not faithfully observe the Covenant and despised the Law, particular mention is given to the Covenant made with Jacob at Beth El. The reference to the Beth El Covenant is significant. At that time, God promised Jacob that his descendants would be brought back to the Land of Israel. They would become numerous and inherit the Land of Israel, becoming a blessing to all the nations of the earth. God was to be with Jacob and his descendants always, and He was to protect them. A failure on the part of the biblical kings of old to uphold and maintain the Covenant brought the reverse consequences and actually led to untold suffering and national ruin.

The scroll goes on to say that this Torah is the only one valid for use by the Levites when instructing the king in the Law and in his obligations under the terms of the Covenant. The implications here are very important. This second Torah is that of the kings. It was given at Mount Sinai along with the canonical Torah. The king is being made responsible for the guidance and welfare of the people on all levels. Not only is the king supposed to be the ruler and physical guardian of the nation, he is also to be very well-versed in the precise application of all the laws affecting the Temple, the sacrifices, and the ritual upon which the welfare of the entire people depends.

Although the king does not officiate in the Temple in any manner, he is still viewed as the guardian of the truest traditions regarding the application and practice of the Temple Service. This sets the king up as both a partner in the divine guidance of the people and as a control factor as well. His knowledge and his power are to ensure proper service to God through the maintenance of those rituals that lead to repentance and atonement and to national salvation and blessing.

The scroll emphasizes the Covenant with Jacob and reiterates the curses set down in Deuteronomy, which become operative as punishment for violating the Covenant. This would suggest that the Covenant at Mount Sinai was an extension or renewal of the original Covenant made at Beth El. It was there that Jacob became Israel. At Beth El, the altar of idolatry was removed and it was replaced by an altar to God. It was at this holy place that God established the Covenant as eternal.

The symbolism here is profound, indeed. The concept that is emphasized is that the Covenant with Israel is eternal. Though violated, it is renewed by God after the people are punished by the terms of the curse and after they have turned back in repentance. Submission to God leads to a revival of the Covenant and opens the road for fulfillment of its terms.

The purified nation is permanently established in the Land of Israel. A basis for constant communication with God is established in the form of the Temple. God's blessing and protection ensue as a result of Israel's submission to the Divine Will, and that blessing, in turn, flows out to the benefit of all humanity.

The implication of the king's position, as laid out in the Temple Scroll, would have meant to the Community, if not to all of Israel, that the desperate situation the Jews found themselves in was the result of the direction the kings of old had taken—the effects of which were still being felt.

The kings of Israel and Judah did not obey the terms of the Covenant faithfully. Rather, they led the people astray and despised the Law. They were, in actuality, directly responsible for the people and they betrayed that responsibility by misleading the nation into moving away from the Law. The result of the kings' course of action was that the people followed their lead and sinned against God, violating the Covenant. Hence, the curse placed on those that violate the Law by rebelling against it was activated against the whole nation.

This being the case, the laws as enunciated in the scroll are of paramount importance. They represent the full interpretation of the priestly and ritual laws that were designed to keep Israel's relationship to God rectified and in balance. They represent the true relationship and the close partnership required between the monarchy and the priesthood, to ensure the flow of Divine Grace to the nation and to the world.

To Jews in general, this document (in all likelihood the Royal Torah) would be very sacred but not functionally usable until the advent of the Messiah. Without independence and without the reestablishment of the monarchy, full application of this Second Torah would not necessarily be possible. Thus, to many this Torah would be sacred as the coming Torah, the Torah to be implemented after the emergence of the Messiah and the subsequent restoration of the state. This Second Torah would be the blueprint for the Third Temple and for the New Order that would follow the advent of the messianic era.

To the Essenes, in general, and to the Community, in particular, the significance of the Temple Scroll would be somewhat different. Since the Community believed that there was no need for a physical Temple or for actual animal sacrifices, the importance of the Temple Scroll for them comes from another direction.

The Community believed, as did the biblical Prophets, that ultimately the Law is written in one's heart. Understanding the Law is to internalize it and to own it from within. The structure of the Temple —which was to house the holy spirit, allowing God to dwell on earth— was replaced by the structure and way of life of the Community. Their way of life sought to materialize and make manifest the Law of God. Righteousness and justice, moral behavior and submission to the Will of God were the replacement for the sacrifices and for the ritual.

The Community held that the coming of the Messiah was the precursory event leading to a repetition of the Sinai experience. At that time, God would again reveal Himself directly to the people and reestablish a new Covenant, issue a new Torah, and reconstitute His relationship with Israel and with the world.

It is unlikely that the Community saw the scroll as a blueprint for the reintroduction of a physical Temple and animal sacrifices. Rather, the Community was looking forward to a whole new Law—a complete, new, revitalized relationship to God—as the core of a national and global revival.

It is most likely that the Community saw the Temple Scroll as a second revelation given at Sinai, which further clarified the priestly rites and Levitical rituals that were to be observed as part of the existing Law. Hence, the use of this material would be twofold. First of all, it would have to be studied carefully by the Community, in order to ensure that the laws were understood and fulfilled as completely, and as properly, as possible.

One of the primary objectives of the Community's way of life was to emulate priestly experience and extend the priestly laws to the Community as part of their way of life. By so doing, they would become a truly holy people and nation of priests. By living a priestly life, they would pave the way for the coming of the End of Days, the Divine Judgement, and the New Covenant. Toward that end, study and implementation of the Temple Scroll, with its emphasis on ritual purity, Levitical laws, and sacred service would be of vital, practical importance.

Second, the Community believed there was great, deep, inner meaning within the Commandments of the Law. The Law and the Commandments were studied carefully daily. The Interpreter of the Law was responsible for sharing the secret insights he had into the Law with the Council of the Community. The Council based all their decisions, judicial and theological, on the interpretations learned from the Law. One's very position in the Community, in fact, depended on the level of one's knowledge and observance of the Law. This would imply an ever-growing understanding into deeper and deeper levels of the Commandments, their inner meaning and their practical relevance.

So, whether one views the scroll as a Second Torah or as a Summary and Commentary on the Levitical laws, the Temple Scroll and the laws it detailed were of tremendous practical importance. This would be true for the entire people of Israel, regardless of how the scroll would be viewed by any particular group. This is so because there is a set of underlying beliefs about the Temple, the ritual, the Commandments, and the relationship between God and Israel that are deeply rooted in the biblical experience.

The reality of the Temple symbolized the epitome of God's relationship with Israel. The Temple restored, whether interpreted as a purified Temple, as a Third Temple, or as a holy community, meant national salvation and the establishment of the true working relationship God intended for Himself and His people. Restoration of the Temple, the purification of the priesthood, and the reestablishment of the monarchy meant nothing short of the reconstruction of the true relationship to God, whether that restoration was interpreted literally or symbolically.

To understand precisely what the Temple represented, why it was of such enormous importance, and what the God–Israel relationship was truly supposed to be, we need to hear what the Holy Scripture tells us.

The Mishkan *and the* Mikdash

The first direct contact and communication between God and the People of Israel as a whole took place on Mount Sinai. From that point on, it was God's intention that His Presence and His influence be ever present among the people. God wished to guide His people, supervise them, provide for them, and interact with them. There was to be a perpetual, two-way communication between man and God.

Since the people could not remain indefinitely at Mount Sinai, some form of facilitating communication had to be created. The answer was the creation of the Ark of the Covenant, the Tabernacle, and the Tent of Meeting. The Tabernacle, which surrounded and sequestered the Ark of the Covenant, was the dwelling place of God's Presence among the community of Israel. Surrounding the Tabernacle and the altars set in front of it was the Tent of Meeting. The enclosure produced by the Tent of Meeting encompassed the Tabernacle and the area where the sacrifices, rituals, and prayers were offered. Within the confines of this sacred space, God spoke to man and the people submitted to God. The theophany of Mount Sinai became a perpetual reality, characterizing the deepest levels of connection between God and the people.

For forty years during the desert experience, the Sanctuary was the core and center of the life of the Israelites. There, Moses spoke with God. There, all the sacrifices and prayers were done. The Sanctuary always stood in the middle of the camp. The Levites encamped by clans around it on the west, the south, and the north. Moses and Aaron and their families camped on the east. A pillar of cloud covered the Sanctuary by day and one of fire by night. When the cloud was resting over the Sanctuary, the people remained encamped. When it rose and moved, they broke and followed where it led them.

During the early centuries of the Settlement in the Land of Israel, the Sanctuary remained at the city of Shiloh and served as the center of national focus. After King David's capture of Jerusalem, the Sanctuary was moved there. With the completion of the Temple under King Solomon, the Ark was installed in the Holy of Holies. The furniture was installed in the sacred precincts and the remaining paraphernalia was stored.

The Temple in Jerusalem became the permanent Sanctuary, the *Mikdash*. Its design and function matched that of the portable Sanctuary, the *Mishkan* of the desert experience. The First Temple, that built by Solomon, was to last four centuries, functioning as the spiritual center of a people.

With the return of the Jews from the Babylonian exile, the Temple was rebuilt under Ezra, Nehemiah, and Zerubavel. The Second Temple followed the pattern, design, and function of the First Temple, with the exception of the Ark. The Ark of the Covenant was missing from the Holy of Holies in the Second Temple. This was so because prior to the destruction of Jerusalem by the Babylonians, on God's instructions, the prophet Jeremiah removed the Ark from the Temple. God required that the Ark be hidden away until the day He Himself chose to reveal it.

For five and one-half centuries, the Second Temple stood as the religious, political, and economic core of the Jewish Commonwealth throughout the Persian, Greek, Hasmonean, and Roman periods, until its destruction in 70 C.E. As was the case in biblical times, all Jewish life revolved around the holy Temple and Jerusalem, the Holy City. The Temple was the spiritual center at the heart of Judaism. It was the basis of Jewish spiritual identity.

Biblical References to the Temple and Its Meaning

The biblical record reveals several central realities regarding the nature and function of the Temple that are crucial in understanding its enormous importance. By fully grasping these realities, it becomes possible to adjust our ears to the words of the Temple Scroll and hear its message in the same context, as did the Jews of the Greco-Roman era.

First is the fact that the initiative, the design, and the imperative to establish a dwelling place for God's Presence within the nation came directly from God. God commands at Mount Sinai that the *Mishkan*, the Tabernacle, be built. God gives exact specifications for its design, construction, and use. God even goes as far as designating Bezalel, specifically, to act as His agent in designing and constructing the Ark, the *Mishkan*, and all the Vessels and Furniture.

Most of the Book of Exodus deals first with the emancipation from Egypt and then with the acceptance of the Covenant and the Giving of the Law at Mount Sinai. The concluding chapters, Exodus 35 through 40, focus on the building, the erection, and the activation of the *Mishkan*, the Tabernacle or Sanctuary. The three major events that come to constitute the birth of the Jewish People are becoming a free people, accepting the Covenant with God, and instituting the operation of Sanctuary. Freedom, the Law, and Divine Service are all integral to the constitution of Israel as a nation and as a Holy People. All that remains is to be brought to the Land of Israel, to settle there and have a permanent base for the nation, so they can fulfill the Law as a free people.

Once the Israelites had settled in the Land and peace finally came, King David transmitted to Solomon the plans he received from God for the Temple. The Temple in Jerusalem was to be the successor of the *Mishkan*. The portable Sanctuary was to be replaced by a permanent Sanctuary.

> And you, my son Solomon, know the God of your father, and serve Him with single mind and fervent heart, for Adonai searches all minds and discerns the pattern of every thought. If you seek Him, He will be available to you. If you forsake Him, He will abandon you forever. See then, that Adonai chose you to build a Temple as a Sanctuary. Be strong and do it.
>
> David gave his son Solomon the plan of the porch and its houses, its storerooms, its upper chambers, its inner chambers, and the place for the Ark. And the plan of all this, he had by the spirit. (1 Chronicles 28:9–12)

God is again commanding that the Sanctuary be built. Once more, He is specifying exactly how it should be done and designating who specifically is responsible for seeing that it is completed.

The plans are transmitted by God to David. The task of getting the Temple built and in operation falls on Solomon. There is an intimate connection between the King and the Temple from the very beginning. The command and the design come to King David, the construction and activation are the responsibility of Solomon once he becomes king himself.

Also intimately connected to the Temple from the very beginning is the High Priest. "He [the priest who is highest among his brethren, upon whose head the anointing oil has been poured and who has been ordained to wear the vestments, i.e, the High Priest] shall not go outside the Sanctuary, and profane the Sanctuary, for upon him is the distinction of the anointing oil of God" (Leviticus 21:12).

The welfare of the entire nation depended upon the King and upon the High Priest. They, in turn, depended upon the close connection they had with the Temple, the Sanctuary.

The priests offered sacrifices daily on the altar to make expiation for the sins of the people. The High Priest made offerings for the expiation of the priests. On the Day of Atonement, the High Priest interceded with God in the Temple's Holy of Holies on behalf of the entire People of Israel. "He [the High Priest] shall purge the innermost shrine, the Tent of Meeting, and the altar. Moreover, he shall make expiation for the priests and for all the people of the congregation" (Leviticus 16:33).

The King would seek God's word directly, through the use of the *Urim* and *Thummim*. When the King sought direction from God, he would consult the *Urim* and *Thummim*, a device that was implanted into the High Priest's Breastplate. This was done in the Temple, under the direction of the High Priest.

The function of the priests was to sacrifice the sin and guilt offerings and to receive the produce offerings, the thanksgiving offerings, and the peace offerings. They were to keep the balance maintained between God's grace and Israel's obligations. Israel was to serve God with devotion and live by the moral imperatives of the Law. In return, God would bless the people and the Land would prosper. The role of the priests was to maintain the equilibrium through the Temple service, by expiating sin and by returning to God the prayers and offerings of the people.

The fact that in the Book of Deuteronomy, God commands every King to have a Torah, a copy of the Law written for his own personal use, tells us that the King's role was, in large part, Keeper of the Covenant. The King was to protect the people. Protection did not only mean providing physical security for the nation. It also meant overseeing the implementation of the Law, seeing that the commandments of God were being upheld.

As the High Priest was Keeper of the Divine Service, the King was to be the Protector of the People. That involved making sure that the Covenant was observed and the commandments fulfilled. Submission to the Divine Will meant harmony and blessing under the terms of the Covenant. Rebellion triggered the curse and then both the Land and the People would suffer. The role of the King was to be the exemplar of obedience to God. He was to seek direction and guidance from God. He was to ensure the safety of the nation and protect the Temple and the services. He was to lead by physical and moral example.

This was to be accomplished by harkening to the living Word, as well as the written Word, of God. God's living Word was transmitted to the King and to the people through the Prophets. As God spoke to the Israelites in the desert through Moses, so, too, did He speak to the people of Israel through prophecy. Prophecy, too, was often linked with the Temple. There was a class of prophets who were directly connected to the Temple. Some of the classical Prophets, like Jeremiah and Ezekiel, were priests.

Prophetic interaction with the King and the court is frequently attested to in the Bible. Saul is counted among the Prophets, which is part of the reason that he is chosen to be the first King of Israel. The Prophet Nathan is a member of King David's Court. The Prophet Elijah confronts Ahab and his court several times. King Hezekiah seeks the advice and assistance of Isaiah, as Zedekiah does with the Prophet Jeremiah.

The Temple served as the nexus, the focal point, for God's sovereignty over Israel. Through the Temple, God maintained a Presence among His People. His Presence was felt in the Holy of Holies, the innermost Sanctuary of the Temple. There the people served God with prayer and sacrifice, through the agency of the priesthood. There, the King came to oversee the nation and to ask for divine guidance. In the precincts of the Temple, the Word of the living God was heard through the mouths of the prophets. The King, the priesthood, and the Prophets all shared roles in maintaining the linkage between God and his People.

When the Temple existed, God's very Presence could be felt there. God's power and His concern for His people were recognized as being intimately connected with the Temple, the sacred dwelling place. The people understood God's rule, supervision, and protection to be linked with the intimacy of the Sanctuary. "Our foes have trampled Your Sanctuary, which Your people possessed. We have become like a people You never ruled, to which Your Name was never attached" (Isaiah 63:18–19).

According to Leviticus 19:30 and 26:2, veneration of the Sanctuary is equivalent to the keeping of the Sabbath. The observance of the Sabbath is the paradigm for the power and sanctity of the Temple.

The Sabbath is the experience of tranquility and serenity. It is the day of rest that allows one through prayer, contemplation, and devotion to commune with God. Sabbath is a time of peace. So, too, is the Temple. David's injunction to Solomon is that the time has come to build the Temple and to focus on the worship and service of God now that there is finally peace.

According to Psalm 68, God is awesome in His Holy Precincts, thereby giving power and strength to His people. From peace and communion comes vitality, strength, and purpose. The people are to come and submit to God's Will. The King, the priests, and the Prophets are to receive their direction from God and instruct the people in His ways.

The biblical record preserves the reality that this was not always the case. The arrogance of the Kings, the ignorance of the Prophets, and the complicity of the priests destroyed the Sanctuary and the kingdom. The sins of the leaders were emulated by the people. They ignored and violated the moral imperatives of the Covenant. They worshiped other gods. They venerated power, position, and wealth. The result was devastation.

"... Because you have outdone the nations around you, having not obeyed My laws nor complied with My statutes, having not even observed the rules of the nations around you," says the LORD God, firmly, "I, in turn, will deal with you and I will execute judgements in your midst, in the sight of all the nations." (Ezekiel 5:7–8)

He has stripped the Tent of Meeting like a garden. He has destroyed His Tabernacle. Adonai has ended in Zion the Festivals and the Sabbath. In His raging anger, He has spurned King and Priest. Her gates have sunk into the ground. He has smashed her bars to bits. Her King and leaders are in exile; instruction is no more. Her prophets, too, receive no vision from the LORD. (Lamentations 2:6, 9)

Horror comes and they shall seek safety, but there shall be none. They shall seek vision from the prophet in vain. Instruction shall per-

ish from the priest, and counsel from the elders. The king shall mourn
and the prince shall clothe himself with desolation. (Ezekiel 7:27)

"Mortal, do you see what they are doing, the terrible abominations
the House of Israel is practicing here, driving Me far from My Sanctuary?" (Ezekiel 8:6)

The Bible equates rebellion against the Covenant with lawlessness, immorality, violence, and idolatry. These themes are echoed very
clearly in the Temple Scroll, in the general literature of the Dead Sea
materials, and in the Sectarian writings from Qumran, as well. The
responsibility for the downfall of the nation is placed primarily on
the leadership. The monarchy, the priesthood, and the Prophets followed the path of their own hearts, not the way of God. In their arrogance and stupidity, they led the people astray. Society became corrupted. The Covenant was breached and the result was devastation
and ruin.

The generations that authored the scrolls and the generations
that preserved and studied them viewed their situation as perilously
close to that of their forefathers. They were determined not to make
the same tragic mistakes. How was tragedy to be averted? How is the
true relationship between Israel and God to be reestablished? They
saw some of the answers in the sacred Temple Scroll. What was it
that they came to understand?

In order to understand the significance the Temple Scroll, its
psychology and its messages, it would be wise to isolate and explore
individual sections and themes as they appear in the scroll. It would
be of benefit, for example, to compare some of the laws and regulations as they appear in the Torah with their parallels in the Temple
Scroll and also to discuss those topics that the scrolls lay particular
emphasis on. Finally, it is important to gain a sense of how the Jewish community may have viewed and interpreted them, both practically and metaphysically.

It should be noted that a comparative analysis of the laws and
statutes, as found in the Torah and in the Temple Scroll, is an objective process. Assessing how they may have been translated into daily
religious life is a far more subjective process. Here, one can draw
inferences from the text and extrapolate its impact on communal
behavior. Yet this is a process of creative extension, based on what
we do know of biblical precedent, Judaism in the Greco-Roman period,
and the Jewish community's norms and organization.

Reading the Temple Scroll on a symbolic level to attempt to abstract and define the possible theological and metaphysical messages that may be drawn from it is a purely subjective process. Understand that when so doing, we are engaging in what could be called reconstructive *midrash*. We are attempting to move back into the mindset and viewpoint of the Jewish experience in the Greco-Roman world, interpreting the material symbolically from that standpoint.

Such a process is *midrash*. It is an exposition of the sacred texts of the Dead Sea caves. There are limitless possibilities in *midrash*. The objective here is to express what can personally be felt and understood of underlying assumptions and messages, with which the literature of the Dead Sea is replete. Hopefully, our understanding bears some relationship to the ancient understanding held by the community of Israel some twenty centuries ago.

The Emphasis Placed on the Holidays and the Festivals

Following a brief prologue, the Temple Scroll immediately focuses its attention on the holidays and on their ritual observance. This is highly significant, in view of the fact that approximately 40 percent of the Temple Scroll is dedicated to describing the proper times, the proper observance, and the nature of the sacrifices connected with each of the holidays of the biblical calendar.

Paralleling the Torah, the Temple Scroll outlines each of the holidays in sequence, beginning with Passover, the spring festival, and ending with Sukkot, the harvest festival. The laws relating to the holidays, and their respective observance, are laid out in clear order. They are presented in a cohesive form and in an unobstructed flow. The great importance attached to them is illustrated by the very facts that they are the first major subject area covered in the scroll and that such a high percentage of the scroll deals with them directly or in connection with the descriptions of the Temple itself.

Like day-to-day worship, the holidays involved sacrifice and supplication. The Sanctuary, be it the *Mishkan* or later the Temple, was the facility through which the sacrifices were accomplished. The festivals were high points of the ritual year and, therefore, focal points of great spiritual importance for the entire nation. The sacrifices and services were the raison d'etre for the Temple.

What makes the festival cycle so vitally important can best be understood by examining what is said about them in the Torah, in the Temple Scroll, and in the Book of Jubilees, which is closely connected theologically with the Temple Scroll. These three ancient sources compliment each other, providing us with a broad view of the nature and significance of the biblical festivals and seasons. By comparing and correlating the information found in these sources, it is possible to gain a deeper insight into the spiritual significance of the biblical holidays and the festival cycle. The best place to begin is with the Sabbath.

The Sabbath is the most important of any holiday in the Jewish year. The Sabbath is the only holiday mentioned in the Ten Commandments. It is the commandment that is situated directly between the three commandments related to belief in God and the six succeeding ones, which relate specifically to mankind. The first group of commandments deal with belief in God and with worship. The last six commandments relate to human interaction and responsibility. The connective element is the fourth commandment. The intercessor between man and God, between the heavens and earth, is the Sabbath. The Sabbath is the great link.

The Sabbath is also the great paradigm for all of the holidays. All of the festivals outlined in the Bible are modeled on the observance of the Sabbath. The Bible and the Temple Scroll both refer to several holidays by calling them each a Sabbath. Yom Kippur, the Day of Atonement, is actually called the Great Sabbath.

If the Sabbath is the great model for all of the holidays and festivals, then its position in the Ten Commandments is quite significant. The implication would be that the Sabbath and the festivals, with all of the ritual observances that accompany them, serve as a bridge between God and Israel. Hence, the Temple, the Sanctuary where God's Presence dwells and where Israel comes to worship and to serve, is the physical link between the two. The festivals, then, are the organic connection between them.

Leviticus 19:30 equates keeping the Sabbath and venerating the Sanctuary. The observance of the Sabbath and the holy days strengthens the Indwelling of God's Presence within Israel. It fortifies the connection between man and God by validating the Temple through worship and service.

The Sabbath reflects the abundance of God's goodness and grace. Six days a week the Israelites in the desert collected manna. The sixth day always provided enough to sustain the people over the Sabbath (Exodus 16). In the Sanctuary and in the Temple, the priests were instructed to put out the shewbread, the loaves symbolizing provision and prosperity, every Sabbath. At the same time, the loaves from the preceding week were distributed to the priests for consumption (Leviticus 24:5–9).

The underlying concept here is reliance on God. Six days, one can work. Six days, one can gather and prepare. Six days, it is necessary to strive to have one's needs met. But the seventh day is God's. There is a cessation of work and of effort. Survival is not an issue. Enough has been provided for everyone for the Sabbath. It is a time to rest, to worship, to be silent, and to reconnect with God and with the world God created. The Sabbath is to be kept holy. It is a day of rest, in honor of Creation (Exodus 20:8–11).

There is to be no work, no striving, no seeking provision, because one is to reconnect with God through rest, worship, and quiet. One is to rely solely on God and on His providence. To work, to prepare, to go out and gather is to refuse to rely on God's word and on His providence. The commandments prohibiting the use of fire, gathering, and working can be understood in this light.

The observance of the Sabbath is one of complete rest, because it is most holy. It is a perpetual sign that God has consecrated the people who observe it. The observance of the Sabbath is a perpetual sign of the Covenant. The essence of what the Covenant represents is symbolized in the Sabbath and its observance. That would also be true, by extension, of the holidays and festivals. The Sabbath is among the very first commandments issued and is also the last one mentioned on Mount Sinai, before Moses descends the Mountain with the finished tablets of the Law (Exodus 31:16–17).

The first twenty-eight of the fifty-five columns of the Temple Scroll (11 Q 19) deal specifically with the holiday cycle and with the attending sacrificial offerings. The holidays and the Temple service appearing in such a prominent place would indicate the prime importance assigned to the cycle of the sacred seasons in the Temple Scroll.

In the Torah itself, God gives instructions for the building of the Ark and of the Sanctuary, in Exodus 25 through 31. Chapters 35 to 40 describe the building of the Sanctuary and its installation and dedication. It is in the beginning chapters of Leviticus that follow (Leviticus 1–7) that the various sacrifices are commanded and described carefully by God. In chapter 8, Aaron and his sons are ordained as the culmination of the entire process.

In contradistinction to the priority set in the Torah, the Temple Scroll lays emphasis on the holidays and the sacrificial ritual by beginning with them, rather than with the description of the building and structure of the Sanctuary. That subject is dealt with second in the order of priority in the Temple Scroll. The order of importance appears to be reversed. The reason for the difference in emphasis may be seen by hearing what the Book of Jubilees says about the Sabbath, the paradigm for all holidays.

> And he said to us [the angels of the presence and the angels of sanctification], "Behold, I shall separate for Myself a people from among all the nations. And they shall also keep the Sabbath. And I will sanctify them for Myself and thus shall I bless them. And they will be My people and I will be their God. And I have chosen the seed of Jacob from among all that I have seen. And I have recorded him as My firstborn son, and have sanctified him for Myself forever and ever. And I will make known to them the Sabbath day, so that they might observe therein a Sabbath from all work."
>
> And thus He created therein a sign by which they might keep the Sabbath day with us on the seventh day, to eat and drink and bless the One who created all things, just as He blessed and sanctified for Himself a people who appeared from all the nations, so that they might keep the Sabbath together with us. And He caused their desires to go up as a pleasing fragrance, which is acceptable before Him always. (Book of Jubilees 2:19–22, Charlesworth)

The Sabbath is being defined here as a transcendent reality. It exists in the Heavens as the basis of both God's Presence in the universe and the principle of sanctification. Through Israel, the Sabbath is brought down to the world. Through its observance, both Israel and all of Creation are sanctified. The Keeping of the Sabbath connects the two realms of Heaven and Earth together.

On one hand, the Sabbath affirms the sanctity of Creation itself. On the other, it sanctifies those who observe it. This act draws mankind close to God and establishes the holiness of Creation, by affirming both God's role as the Creator and the transcendent nature of God's Will that is reflected in Creation. Moreover, just as the Presence of God in the higher realms is acknowledged by the angels, God's Presence and sovereignty in the earthly realm is fully recognized by Israel.

Both acts are accomplished through the same means—namely, the observance of the Sabbath.

The very basis of the Covenant is the Sabbath. God is made known and is acknowledged as the Creator and Sustainer of the universe through the observance of the Sabbath. It is through the Sabbath that His Presence is felt. That very connection unites the upper and lower worlds. Rest, worship, contemplation, and prayer, the core of the Sabbath observance, create the experience of transcendence. That state of transcendence connects Heaven and Earth. It affirms God as Creator and sanctifies Creation through Israel's observance.

The keeping of the Sabbath is the core of the Covenant between Israel and God. The reality of the Sabbath observance is the very basis for the entire Covenant. The connection is clear. The state of transcendence that the keeping of the Sabbath creates is maintained and extended through observance of the Commandments, through the Covenant as a whole. This transcendental experiencing of reality through the Sabbath and through the Covenant makes God's Presence in the world real.

God's Presence has to be acknowledged experientially in order to be effective on earth. We need to know God. Such knowing comes from the experience of transcendence, the essence of the Sabbath. This transcendent state facilitates experiencing God's immediacy in the world. The experience of God's immediacy, in turn, sanctifies Creation and those involved in the process. Israel, the people who sanctify the Sabbath, are sanctified themselves by being drawn to God.

Transcendence leads to a merging of wills. Through the Sabbath observance, the Covenant is to be kept. Through the Covenant, Israel is blessed because the keeping of the Covenant produces and maintains the state of transcendence. That transcendence unifies all worlds and brings us into communion with God. It is for that reason that Israel's desires are a pleasing fragrance and are always acceptable to God. As long as people keep the Sabbath, they are maintaining the state of transcendence that is the underlying principle behind the Covenant, behind man's true relationship to God.

This being the case, it is not surprising that the Temple Scroll places observance of the holiday cycle first and foremost. The holidays are all extensions of the Sabbath. The Sabbath is the model for all the holidays, as well as for the entire structure of the holiday cycle. The holiday and festival cycle is given first priority, because it represents the principle of the Sabbath, the core of the Covenant, in its fullest form.

All of the holy days, like the Sabbath, demand rest, prayer, and communion with God. Their observance leads to the state of transcendence. Through that level of experience, the people are sanctified, the days are sanctified, Creation is made holy, and God is acknowledged through the experience of His immediacy.

It is also important to note that during these holy seasons, through the medium of transcendence, the opportunity to rectify one's relationship to God and to recalibrate the soul to resonate more clearly with the Will of God is most present. It is during the major holidays within the ritual year that the people are commanded to offer sin offerings for atonement, along with the festival sacrifices.

Transcendence opens the way to communion with God. Experientially, it allows room for the deepening of our awareness of our connection and relationship to God. That level of intimate consciousness provides the opportunity to be forgiven for our trespasses and to realign our will with the Will of God—hence, the ever-present requirement of a sin offering during these sacred times.

In order to understand the supreme importance attributed to the observance of the holidays and festivals more clearly, it is wise to examine the great core principle of the Sabbath from an additional perspective. The Sabbath is not only a most holy day and paradigm for the holidays in general, it is also the principle of seven. As such, it serves as the very foundation of the calendar and the yearly ritual cycle.

The Sabbath Principle: The Emphasis Placed on the Holidays and the Festivals

Biblical law clearly specifies that an important part of the ritual and festival cycle is that of marking the New Moon. Aside from the Sabbath, it is the only recurring holiday within the sacred cycle. The Sabbath marks the week as a sacred unit. The New Moon signals the beginning of a new month and marks it as a sacred block of time as well.

The holidays and festivals are all referenced to the months of the year. Hence, when the months occur is of utmost importance, since they regulate the timing and the subsequent observance of all of the festivals. The observance of the festivals, in turn, is a cardinal element in the observance of the Covenant and therefore one of the foundations of Israel's relationship to God.

It is obvious from the biblical commandments that the festivals and holy days are intimately connected to the agricultural cycle and to the solar seasons. Passover is the Spring Festival. Shavuot is the Festival of the First Fruits. Sukkot is the Harvest Festival.

These two realities, the sacred year being tied to the solar year and the regulation of the months being determined by the cycle of the moon, produce an ancient paradox. The solar year has 365 full days and the lunar year has a full 354 days. A discrepancy of eleven days per year exists. If the festivals were observed strictly according to the regulation of the lunar calendar, they would be seriously out of synchronization with the seasons of the year much of time. Passover, for example, would slip periodically out of spring into the summer and the winter seasons. Such an event is incongruous and inappropriate for the sacred spring holiday.

A great deal rides on the correctness of the calendar. If the calendar is in error, one would end up celebrating an ordained festival on the wrong day, violating the instructions of God. This would be tantamount to a violation of the Covenant. Festivals and holidays are holy occasions and sacred periods of time. If observed in error, the efficacy of the holiday is destroyed. One would be celebrating a sacred occasion on a profane day. A holy celebration done on a profane, unclean day would conceivably render it unclean, an abomination to God.

In order to avoid this dilemma, there are alternate possible solutions. One approach is to reconcile the two calendars by a process of intercalation. That is the approach taken by the ancient Babylonians, and it seems to have been the norm in Israel, at least during the Second Temple period (*Mishnah Arachin* 2:2).

The biblical ordinance specifies the month of *Aviv*, Spring, as the first month of the year. Days are counted from sunset to sunset and months are reckoned from New Moon to New Moon. This parallels the practices of the ancient Babylonians. In the Babylonian system, each of the twelve lunar months contained either twenty-nine or thirty days, bringing the yearly total to 354. This meant that a full month was lost, in relationship to the solar year, every three years. Thus, every three years a thirteenth month was added to the calendar.

Eventually, in 380 B.C.E., the Babylonians adopted the Metonic
cycle discovered by the Greeks and intercalated a full month into the
calendar seven times within every nineteen-year cycle. The Jewish
calendar still uses this system of calculation to this day.

There is clear indication from various ancient Hebrew sources
that intercalation as the means of maintaining an integrated lunar–
solar calendar was the prominent method in Israel during the Second
Temple period. References to the months of the year made in the
Apocrypha literature, for instance, use the Aramaic names of the various months, which were derived from the Babylonian calendar. *Tosefta
Sanhedrin* 2:2 indicates that in the days of the Second Temple, the
decision to insert the thirteenth month in a given year was based on
agricultural considerations at the time.

The assumption being made in the lunar–solar calendar is that
the cycle of time itself, as well as the sacred seasons of the year, are
all regulated by the month—the month being the most definitive element of the calendar. The Sectarian materials among the Dead Sea
literature, however, seem to present a very different view.

According to the Damascus Covenant, the Sectarian community
was to observe all holidays and festivals based on the calendrical considerations that are found in the Book of Jubilees. The Community
seems to have shared the same view regarding the sacred nature of
the festival observances, as did the author of the Book of Jubilees. The
concern is very straightforward.

> . . . Command the children of Israel so that they shall guard the years
> in this number, three hundred and sixty-four days, and it shall be a
> complete year. And no one shall corrupt its [appointed] time from its
> days or from its feasts, because all [of the appointed times] will arrive
> in them according to their testimony, and they will not pass over a day
> and they will not corrupt a feast. But if they are transgressed and they
> do not observe them according to His commandment, then they will
> corrupt all of their [fixed] times, and the years will be moved from
> within this [order] and they will transgress their ordinances. And all
> of the sons of Israel will forget, and they will not find the way of the
> years. And they will forget the New Moons, and [appointed] times and
> Sabbaths. And they will set awry all the ordinances of the years. . . .
> [A]nd there will be those who examine the moon diligently, because it
> will corrupt the appointed times, and it will advance from year to year
> ten days. Therefore, the years will come to them corrupt and make a
> day of testimony a reproach and a profane day a festival, and they will

mix everything up, a holy day as profaned, and a profane one for a holy day, because they will set awry the months and Sabbaths and feasts and jubilees. (Book of Jubilees 6:32–37, Charlesworth)

The author of the Book of Jubilees states that it is God's intention that the holidays, Sabbaths, and festivals are to be observed according to the fixed cycle of a 364-day year—the reason being that the lunar year has a total of 354 days, and that means a loss of ten days every year in relation to the solar year. The Book of Jubilees is expressing the widely held concern that the holy days of the year, so fundamentally important to Israel's relationship to God, will be desecrated by improper observance caused by the calendrical discrepancy between the lunar and solar years.

However, the author's solution is not one of intercalating an additional month into the year periodically. No suggestion is made to continually readjust the balance, to bring the sacred lunar year into alignment with the solar year. Rather, the Book of Jubilees assaults the concept of a lunar calendar altogether. How can that be? Aren't the months ordained biblically to be lunar? Don't the holy days depend on the lunar year? So how can the lunar calendar be abandoned?

The author of the Book of Jubilees is looking at the sacred year in a different light. He is assuming that since the festivals and holy days are linked to the yearly agricultural cycle, their rightful place is within the solar year. That would guarantee consistency.

To observe the holidays in the context of a lunar year means so much natural slippage that the regularity of the festivals becomes very tenuous at best. The sanctity of the holidays and festivals is desecrated through this perpetual malalignment. To intercalate is to assume the primacy of the lunar year.

The view of the Book of Jubilees is that the holidays belong within the context of a solar year and not a lunar year. The New Moons and the lunar months, then, are the only holy days that float through the calendrical year. The advantage of a 364-day solar year is that it is consistent with the agricultural year and, even more importantly, the holidays become permanently fixed calendrically.

In a solar year of 364 days, each of the twelve months has exactly thirty days. Four days in the year are not considered to be belong to any given month—the two solstices and the two equinoxes. The calendar becomes one of exactly fifty-two weeks of seven days each. If the months are solar and the holidays are referenced to them, then the sacred calendar becomes fixed, permanent, and consistent. Connecting the holidays to the solar months would allow them to fall on the exact same day of the year regularly.

The only exception to this principle would be the New Moons. They would move around from one year to another. The advantage here is that the holy days would be stabilized. There would be no chance that the correspondence between an ordained festival and the appropriate time of holiness would be broken or disturbed. The Sabbaths of the year, the holy days, and the festivals would all remain synchronized with the flow of divine energy and blessing. All would be in fixed accordance with the Will of God. Israel would be honoring its sacred commitments to God under the Covenant, and God would bless His people and pardon their transgressions in accordance with the Law given at Sinai, at the appropriate times.

If, in the eyes of the Community, the New Moon's true significance does not lie in it being the arbiter of the calendar, what is its spiritual import? Moreover, if it is not the lunar month that is at the core of the ritual year, what is?

The Hebrew Word for "month," hodesh, is derived from the verb root meaning "to renew." The reappearance of the moon marked renewal. On one level, that referred to the beginning of a new lunar cycle. The moon reemerged and was commencing its cycle of waxing, waning, disappearing, and reappearing. On another level, the cycle of the moon inaugurated on the appearance of the New Moon marked the process of spiritual renewal.

The light of the moon is reflected light. Whereas sunlight is direct and constant, the light of the moon is indirect, refracted, and in process. According to the Book of Enoch (Ethiopic Version, Enoch 78:6–8, Charlesworth), as the moon waxes it does so by 1/14 of the reflected sunlight per day, reaching full illumination on the 14th and holding it on the 15th of the month. When the moon wanes, the decrease in light follows the exact same pattern, diminishing by 1/14ths.

Here the principle of seven, the moon waxing in fourteen-day intervals and waning in fourteen days, is connected to the process of the revelation of light and the withdrawal or hiding of the light, as characterized by the movement of the moon.

By insisting on the sanctity of a 364-day solar year, emphasis is being put on the sanctity of the Sabbath, the holy principle of seven. A 364-day year is exactly fifty-two weeks of seven days each. The twenty-eight days of light in the lunar cycle also reflect the sanctity of the principle of seven. Both direct, constant light and cyclical, revealed light are considered to be holy—the holiness reflected in the connection to the principle of the sabbath, the cycle of seven.

Light is seen here as having two manifested realities—that of sustenance and blessing, the light of the sun, and that of revelation and concealment, the cycle of the moon. Both are considered holy. In the general Hebrew calendar, the holy days are determined by the lunar months. In the Jubilee calendar, the holy days are associated with the solar months.

The assumption of the Hebrew calendar, connecting the festivals with the movement of the moon, is that the spiritual nature of the holy days and festivals is primarily that of revelation. God reveals aspects of His plans for humanity and for Israel through the sacred holidays and festivals. They are portals of light, gateways through which dimensions of our relationship to God is periodically revealed. We have the opportunity of connecting with these divine realities, through the observance of the festivals, through the proper use of these portals of opportunity.

The assumption of the Book of Jubilees, and the groups that adhered to its calendar, is somewhat different in emphasis. Here, the holidays are tied to the solar cycle. This implies that the light behind the holy days and festivals is that of the sun, that of sustenance, warmth, growth, and abundance. This approach sees the holidays as sources of blessing. This would connect the holidays to the reality of the Covenant.

The biblical emphasis is on observing the commandments, the terms of the Covenant. The efficient result of so doing is that God blesses Israel on all levels, physically, emotionally, spiritually. Israel is blessed on the national level, on the personal level, and serves as a source of blessing for all nations. The connection of the holidays to the solar calendar reflects this emphasis on the holidays as being a prime element in the fulfillment of the Covenant with God.

The festivals of the New Moon, in the Jubilee calendar, become the only really mobile elements. The flow of the cycle of light floats through the year. It represents the continual flow of the revelation and concealment of the Divine Will, as it ebbs and flows through the year. A distinction is made between two realities. The festivals represent the manifestation of God's grace, compassion, and supervision of the world He created. The New Moons take on the added meaning of the deeper levels of reality that God makes available through the process of revelation and assimilation. This process is made available to us periodically. Its commencement is heralded by the appearance of the New Moon. It transcends the holy days and does not need to be linked to them.

When all is said and done, the real core principle underlying the entire calendrical and festival structure is not the principle of the months or seasons, but rather the principle of the Sabbath. The principle of the Sabbath is reflected in the principle of seven. The Sabbath and its observance is the model and underpinning for all of the holy days and festivals. Moreover, it is reflected and reinforced by the extension of the structural use of seven in the calendar cycle.

The Book of Jubilees and the Book of Enoch both insist on the use of a 364-day solar year. Three hundred and sixty-four days break down into exactly fifty-two weeks of seven days each. So, the year is automatically structured to have the Sabbath as the determinative feature of the entire calendrical year. The ritual and calendrical emphasis lies squarely on the Sabbath.

It is significant that the calendrical fragments found in Qumran speak of the holidays in reference to the holiday cycle, by referencing them to the specific week of the year that they would fall on. The frame of reference used is that of the week, not of the month. Each week of the year actually bears its own name, based on the name of the priestly family that would officiate in the Temple at that time. For example, "The Tuesday of *Abiyah*, the Passover. The Sunday of *Shekanyah*, the Waving of the Sheaf. The Thursday of *Yakim*, the second Passover. The Sunday of *Chazir*, [the Feast of Weeks (Shavuot)]" (4Q321, frag. 4, col. 4, ll. 7–10).

In contrast to the Torah, the War Scroll states that there are to be twenty-six courses, or divisions of priests and Levites, to serve the altar over the course of the year. This would mean a fifty-two-week year, during which the priestly divisions rotate and each serves the Temple at two junctures during the year. The emphasis is being laid on the week, not the month, as the basis of the calendar and the ritual.

In the biblical laws, the holiday cycle and the sacrificial cycle are spelled out very clearly. The concept of the primacy of the Sabbath and the underlying spiritual principle of seven is very apparent. Several festivals are referred to as Sabbaths, the Day of Remembrance and the Day of Atonement being prime examples. The three major festivals, Passover, Sukkot, and Shavuot, are all connected with the principle of seven.

Passover is seven days. Sukkot is seven days, the eighth day being Atzeret. There are seven weeks (seven times seven) separating Passover from the Shavuot. The holidays mentioned in the biblical festival cycle—Passover, Shavuot (the Feast of Weeks), the Day of Remembrance, the Day of Atonement, Sukkot (the Feast of Booths), Atzeret, and the Sabbath (Numbers 23)—total seven.

In the Temple Scroll, when outlining the sequence of the holy days and their accompanying sacrificial ritual, a couple of festivals are mentioned that have no counterpart in the Mosaic Torah. The Temple Scroll details the festivals of the New Wine and the New Oil. Like Shavuot, these holy days are separated by a cycle of seven weeks. It also mentions a six-day festival that consecrates the wood used in the Temple for building. It follows right after the Festival of the New Oil.

The order of the holidays, as outlined in the Temple Scroll, follows the biblical pattern and extends it. Passover falls in the middle of the first month of the year. It is followed seven weeks later by Shavuot, which in turn is succeeded seven weeks later by the New Wine festival. After another interval of seven weeks, the Festival of the New Oil is celebrated. Then, the Festival of the Wood is observed.

There is an organic connection between the holidays. The first festival, that of Passover, celebrates the Exodus from Egypt. The Exodus represents the emergence of Israel as a people and the commencement of God's fulfillment of the Covenant made with Jacob. It is followed, after seven weeks, by Shavuot, which commemorates the Giving of the Torah, the extended Covenant and also the Festival of the New Grain, which is connected with the Land of Israel.

The Festivals of the New Grain, the New Wine, and the New Oil have intrinsic links to each other. They are all separated from one another by periods of seven weeks. They are all agricultural holidays, which binds them to the Land of Israel. These festivals are also all connected to the Temple service. The New Grain is connected with the sanctification of the grain. This harkens to the shewbread and to the meal offerings. The New Wine Festival sanctifies the wine. Wine is used for the libations that accompany the sacrifices. The New Oil Festival establishes the sanctity of the sacred oil used for anointing, used for mixing with the meal offerings, and used for lighting the *Menorah* and the lamps of the Temple.

The cycle of the Festivals moves first from Passover, from emphasis on freedom and peoplehood, to the extension of the Covenant, the commemoration of the Sinai Covenant on Shavuot. Then the holiday cycle proceeds to focus on the maintenance of the Covenant through the Temple and its ritual, which epitomize the continual interaction between Israel and God. This is symbolized by the Festivals of the New Oil and the New Wine. Finally, the Festival cycle concludes with Sukkot, the Harvest Festival, which centers on the fulfillment of the Covenant with Jacob—namely, the secure settlement of Israel within the Land of Israel, under God's protection and blessing.

There is a deep interconnection portrayed here between the holiness of the Covenant, the sanctity of the Land of Israel, and the centrality of the Temple to both. This conception is in close harmony with the biblical view. All three realities are interlocked. The intimate relationship between God and Israel is the Covenant. God and Israel are to work together in the Land. That is the fulfillment of the Covenant with Jacob and the foundation for the expanded Covenant established at Sinai. The people are to live by the commandments in the Land. God's Presence will manifest in the Temple and the Word of the LORD will go out to all peoples from there.

The sanctity of the relationship between Israel and God is underscored by the fact that the festivals connected directly with the Land—those of the New Grain, the New Wine, and the New Oil—are all referred to in the Temple Scroll as festivals of the First Fruits.

The Temple Scroll tells us that the bread of the First Fruits are for the priests, and the cereal offering of the New Grain is to be eaten with the bread on Shavuot (Wacholder, frag. Remains of 11Q Torah, col.19:5). Reference to the Festivals of New Wine and New Oil as also being Festivals of the First Fruits is made subsequently. The people are to celebrate before God, eating the fresh grapes and drinking the New Wine, at the time the atonement is made for the wine (Wacholder, 21:4–10). We are further informed, "And they shall sacrifice the first of the New Oil, on the altar of the burnt offerings, the First Fruits before Adonai" (Wacholder, col. 21:16). Column 38:4–7 states, "And they shall eat them in the days of the First Fruits of the grain, of the wine and of the oil. . . ."

According to biblical law, the first born of everything, be it plant, animal, or male child, belongs to God. It has sacred significance. By declaring that what first emerges from the ground is sacred, the Bible affirms that everything the Land yields is to be revered, for it represents God's grace and blessing. God's grace and blessing stem from His Presence in the Land, which is facilitated by the Temple service and is maintained by observance of the Covenant.

The core of the Festival cycle, as delineated in the Temple Scroll, is comprised of holy days that celebrate the First Fruits. This centrality of First Fruit Festivals within the space of the sacred months of the year emphasizes the sanctity of the Land. The Land and the people are blessed by God directly. These blessings are the result of the full observance of the Covenant, both through righteousness and justice, and through the proper maintenance of the sacrifices and offerings—the objective of the festival rituals being the revelation of God's Presence continually to the people.

God's Presence is centered in the Holy of Holies. The ability of the people to connect with God's Presence is through the sacrificial services. "And the entire altar of burnt offerings and all its vessels will be of pure bronze. And the . . . which is above it, and the washbasin and its stand, and its . . . are of bronze. . . . *to see My Face within My Sanctuary.* . . ." (Wacholder, col. 3:14–17).

Beginning with Passover and building a crescendo over the succeeding months, the sacral calendar crests with the Festival of the New Oil and the sanctification of the wood. The flow of spiritual energy pinnacles and then embarks upon a month-long climax.

At this point, 177 days have passed—divided by 30 days, that is 5.9 months. With the commencement of the seventh month, the climax of the ritual year occurs. The seventh month commences with the Day of Holy Convocation, the Day of Remembrance, and crests with the Day of Atonement, the Great Sabbath. The month culminates with the Sukkot, the harvest festival, and concludes at the end of Sukkot with Atzeret, marking the terminus point of the sacred year.

What the Temple Scroll is presenting us with is a detailed picture of the sacred year, in the context of the full solar year. This sacred year is the first seven months of the calendrical year. It represents sacred time. What we are shown is a pattern, whereby the holy days do not constitute islands of sacred time and space scattered throughout the calendar. Rather, there is one long, sacred season that encompasses the first seven months of the year. The flow of energy is continuous from one holy day to the next. The holy flow is synonymous with the agricultural year, from planting to harvest.

The calendrical year is effectively divided into two distinct parts. First comes the intense, continuous, sacred season of seven months. Then, the Sabbath of the year, the dormant months corresponding to fall and winter occur, allowing for rest and regeneration. These two interrelated realities are carefully delineated and separated from each other by the seventh month. The seventh month concludes the sacred year and initiates the Sabbath of the year.

With an intense period of introspection, atonement, and harvesting, the seventh month brings closure to the sacred season of growth, development, and plenty, and inaugurates the remaining part of the year as the Sabbath. For five months, the people are to enjoy the fruits of their labors and the great beneficence of God. As God provided manna for the people in the deserts of Sinai, now He provides abundance through the sacred season. Just as the people were to live off of the manna collected on Friday through the Sabbath, so, too, were the people to enjoy the abundance harvested at the end of the sacred season through the Sabbath of the year.

The spiritually intense, and ritually full, sacred season dominates the first half of the year. This is evident from the flow of uninterrupted energy that is begun by the Passover, sustained by the presence of the Festivals of the New Grain (Shavuot), the New Wine, the New Oil, and the Wood, and is climaxed by the Day of Atonement and the Sukkot Festival. All of the festivals serve as landmarks and as way stations along a river of sacred time that flows through the first seven months of the year. After reaching its zenith, the flow of time moves into several months of rest, tranquility, transcendence, and peace.

The seventh month is the climatic period of fulfillment. It commences with the Day of Holy Convocation, the Day of Remembrance, which prepares the people for the future by harkening back over what has already transpired. That part of the year during which everything is nurtured draws to a close. Physically and spiritually, everything has blossomed and grown to maturity. During this holy season of growth and development, there is a constant effort made to remain aligned to God's Will. All of the holy festivals atone for the Land. Now, on the Day of Atonement, focus is placed intently and squarely on atoning for the sins of the people.

The spiritual welfare and the physical welfare of the nation are intimately intertwined. First the Land is judged, then the people are. This is the high point emotionally and spiritually of the year. With forgiveness comes salvation. The blessing is celebrated by the harvest festival, Sukkot. As the sacred year began with a festival of seven days, so it ends with one. As the very first day of the year is a day of holiness, so, too, Atzeret, as a distinct and separate holy day, marks the last day of the sacred year. With salvation comes peace, the quiet months of fall and winter.

EXCURSUS
The Temple Service and Ritual

Before exploring the Temple Scroll further, it is important to gain a clear, firm understanding of the nature of the sacrifices, the functions of the priests and the Levites, and the regulations surrounding the Temple service.

The Nature of the Priesthood

In the days at Sinai, the tribe of Levi was designated by God to be reserved specifically for service to God. One family from that tribe—that of Aaron, Moses' brother—was designated to be the priesthood. The priests were anointed upon their ordination. The process of anointing the priests was done by pouring the sacred oil on their garments. The High Priest was anointed by having the oil poured on his head. This same procedure was performed when anointing the King. In Leviticus, chapters 4 and 6, the High Priest is referred to as the "Anointed Priest."

This process of anointment consecrated the priests to the Temple service. They shared a common bond ritually. The Ark, the Holy of Holies, the Tabernacle, the Altar, the *Menorah*, and the Temple furniture were all anointed when they were first put into divine service.

157

The priests were also outfitted with special garments when in the Temple and, in some instances, were required to change garments while performing divine service. The priests alone were authorized to handle the ritual. The Levites were forbidden to approach the altar or the holy vessels (see Exodus 28, 30, and 40).

Levites could not become priests. Priests could not be elevated to the position of High Priest. One's status was determined by birth. One had to be a descendant of Aaron to be a priest. One had to be a descendant of Zadok, who had been High Priest under King David, to be High Priest.

The High Priest paralleled the rank and stature of the King. Like the royal garments, the priestly garments contained gold and purple. The King wore a crown and the High Priest wore a miter. Both the crown (*atarah*, in Hebrew) and the miter (*mitznefet*) are also periodically called a *netzer*. The same term is used to refer to the sanctity of both (Exodus 29:6, 39:30, 2 Samuel 1:10, Psalms 89:40, etc.).

The Temple service centered on the sacrifices and the sacrificial ritual. This was the exclusive domain of the priests. The *kohanim*, the priests, did the sacrifices and interceded with God on behalf of the people. The Levites handled the singing and the prayers during the services and served as the general custodians of the Temple.

In order to officiate in the Temple, a priest had to be whole. He could not serve at all, doing the sacrifices, if he were in any way physically impaired—that is, blind, deaf, crippled, et cetera. During the Second Temple period, in practice, blemished priests were allowed to serve with their *mishmar*, performing secondary functions, and they could partake of the eating of the sacrificial portions. They were also allowed to bless the people.

Whether this was true during the First Temple period is not clear. Leviticus 21 forbids a blemished priest from even entering the Temple. No priest, however, could serve at all, under any circumstances, if he were in a state of ritual impurity. Only after the affliction passed was he purified and allowed to resume contact with the sacred realm of the Temple.

The priests were divided into *mishmarot*—that is "shifts" or "divisions of duty." A *mishmar* handled all of the services and priestly functions during their tour of duty. The *mishmarot* rotated on a weekly basis. There were twenty-four *mishmarot* according to the Torah, twenty-six according to the Book of Jubilees. Each week of the year was assigned to a specific *mishmar*. Priests from outside of Israel could come and join their *mishmar*, so long as they were not associated in any way with the Temple of Onias in Egypt.

It was the priests who were responsible for slaughtering the sacrificial animals, maintaining the altar, interceding for the people, and carrying out the offerings on the altar. Chosen by lot, twenty priests from the *mishmar* would serve by doing the *Tamid*, the daily sacrifice. The remainder of the priests would serve by doing the other sacrifices for individual supplicants. A portion of all the sacrifices was ordained to go the priests. Certain sacrifices could only be eaten by the priests and, then, only within the sacred precincts of the Temple.

Aside from partaking of their part of the offerings, the officiating priests were allowed to keep the skins of the sacrificial animals they offered. They were the recipients of the bread offerings at the end of the week and they were able to make use of donations made to the Temple. Once something was vowed to or donated to the Temple, it became consecrated. As such, only the priests could touch or make any use of it.

Certain parts of the service were to be conducted exclusively by the High Priest. It was the High Priest alone who went into the Holy of Holies on the Day of Atonement and interceded on behalf of the entire people. The High Priest also seems to have served as an advisor to the King during the days of the First Temple. Since the priests also functioned as court judges, it is most likely that the High Priest officiated as the head of the court system.

During the Second Temple period (in the absence of a monarchy), the Temple and the priesthood stood at the heart of the nation. The national life centered around the Temple spiritually, economically, socially, and, to a large extent, politically. The Great Sanhedrin in Jerusalem was the High Court and would make definitive decisions regarding ritual practice and religious observance.

The Nature of Ritual Purity

In order to be involved in the Temple service, either officiating at the altar as a priest, maintaining the Temple as a Levite, or participating as an Israelite bringing an offering to the Temple, one had to be in a state of ritual purity. Ritual impurity was a temporary state of uncleanliness, which prevented one from coming into contact with the Temple, the priests, or the holy realm of sacrifice.

The state of ritual impurity was unacceptable to God. One must be careful not to approach the holy service in such a state, so as not to be excluded from the Divine Presence (Leviticus 11:43–47).

The three main causes of ritual contamination were leprosy, issue from the sexual organs, and contact with dead bodies. Ritual impurity occurred through affliction by certain physical maladies, such as plague, leprosy, and open sores or wounds. It occurred through secretion of bodily fluids, such as nocturnal emissions, sexual emissions, menstruation, afterbirth, et cetera. Ritual uncleanliness occurred also through direct contact with carcasses, reptiles, dead bodies, bones, burial sites, et cetera.

The quarantine period lasted until evening for the lesser degrees of uncleanliness and seven days for the greater degrees. In the case of leprosy, it lasted until recovery was effected. Ritual immersion was almost always involved in the purification process. In the greater degrees of impurity, the washing of the clothes was also involved. In the most serious cases, sacrifices were required as well. To purify the leper after recovery, a priest sprinkled a mixture of water and blood on the individual. In the case of corpse contamination, the mixture was of water and the ashes of the Red Heifer. In both cases, the priest who sprinkled the mixture became unclean in the process.

The laws governing the priests' relations to family also bear witness to the need to remain ritually pure. Priests could not marry prostitutes or divorcees. In addition to those restrictions, the High Priest could not marry a widow either. Moreover, he specifically had to marry a virgin. Priests could not defile themselves by coming into contact with a dead body altogether, unless it was the remains of a parent. The High Priest could have no contact at all with a corpse.

The state of uncleanliness, of ritual impurity, was a purely physical one. It was a temporary state that rendered one ineligible to be involved in the sacred realm of the Temple until the condition was healed.

The Sacrificial Services

The sacrificial service was the core of the daily worship. It was the key element marking the ritual observance of the holidays. The *Tamid*, the eternal sacrifice, was done daily—once in the morning and once in the afternoon.

The *Tamid* began right after dawn. The priests gathered in their work positions. The Levites collected on their watch and the Israelites serving that day in the Temple assembled at their posts. The function of the Levites was to sing the liturgy and to stand guard. The Israelites serving in the *Maamad* assisted the Levites by directing the movement of the worshipers.

The process began with a ritual ablution. Afterwards, the priests divided into two groups and inspected the Temple to see that all was in order. Then, led by a priest who had been chosen by lot to remove the ashes from the preceding day's sacrifices, the priests ascended the altar. The designated priest removed the ashes and arranged the firewood for the day's sacrifices, as well as the coals for the incense offerings.

In preparation for the actual sacrifices, the officiating priests washed their hands and feet. At full light, the inner altar and the *Menorah*, the candelabra, were prepared for use. Then, the *shofarot*, the trumpets, were sounded to signal the opening of the gates.

The *Menorah* was lit. The lambs were slaughtered and prepared for offering. The priests gathered with the people in the Chamber of Hewn Stones to read the Ten Commandments, and the prescribed biblical verses (Deuteronomy 6:4–9, 11:13–21, and Exodus 13:1–10, 13:11–16). At that point, the priests who had no role to perform in that day's services removed their vestments and left.

A musical instrument called a *magreyfah* was played to signal the beginning of the burning of the incense. At this juncture, the Levites took their positions on the choir platform. At the same time, the head of the *Maamad* led those who were to undergo ritual purification to the Nicanor Gate of the Temple.

As the service reached a climax, the incense offering was done and the people were blessed. This was followed by the sacrificial offering, then the meal offering, and finally, the libation of wine. As the finale, a flag was raised and the liturgy was sung by the Levites.

During the interval between the end of the Morning *Tamid* and the beginning of Afternoon *Tamid*, all of the private sacrifices on behalf of individuals were done. The private sacrifices concluded between the eighth and ninth hours of the day. Regardless of the length of the day, each day was divided into twelve segments, ("hours,") of daylight, and twelve of night. The private sacrifices concluded at segment 8.5 of the daylight.

The Afternoon *Tamid* followed the exact same pattern as the morning one, with two exceptions. The logs were not arranged on the altar and there was no priestly benediction. After the *Tamid* in the evening, two logs were placed on the altar to keep the altar fires burning all night. Oil was placed in the *Menorah* to replenish it and all seven candles were relit. Around sunset, following the *Tamid*, the Gates of the Sanctuary were shut. As evening approached, the priests gathered in the sacred precincts and partook of their meal of sacrificial meat and bread.

On the Sabbath, no individual sacrifices were offered. For the Sabbath, there was a second additional sacrificial offering of two sheep and the shewbread. The hymn sung to accompany the *Musaf*, the additional Sabbath offering, was the 32nd chapter of Deuteronomy. According to the Talmud, the chapter was divided into six sections. One section was read each Sabbath. This would correspond to the rotation of the twenty-four *mishmarot*. Each priestly rotation would read one-sixth of the chapter on their respective Sabbath. Hence, four full cycles of the chapter would equal twenty-four Sabbaths.

The *mishmarot*, the priestly rotations, would change for the week at the end of the *Musaf* service on the Sabbath. The *mishmar* would arrive in the morning before the services and take over from the outgoing *mishmar* after services were concluded. The second *mishmar* brought in the new loaves of the shewbread. There were two sets of loaves, six loaves per set, twelve altogether. The old bread and the old accompanying incense from the preceding week were removed. The old incense was offered up and then the old bread was distributed to the officiating priests and eaten.

The holy days, the Festivals, and holidays also had *Musaf* services. These were special sacrificial offerings that were done in conjunction with the Festival. Like the Sabbath, they were done in addition to the regular daily sacrifices. In this manner, as in the abstaining from work and the focus on rest, prayer, and contemplation, the Festivals shared the nature and spiritual tenor of the Sabbath.

The Passover sacrifice consisted of a burnt offering of two bulls, one ram, and seven unblemished, yearling lambs. It included a meal offering of choice flour and required a sin offering of a goat. The same was true for the Shavuot sacrifice and for the sacrifice of the Atzeret at the culmination of the sacred portion of the year, although on the Shavuot Festival a peace offering of two additional lambs was added.

During the seven days of Sukkot, the climax of the sacred year, the *Musaf* offering for the holiday was two rams and fourteen lambs per day and a decreasing number of bulls per diem. That is, thirteen bulls on the first day, descending daily to seven bulls on the seventh day.

In the Torah, the Sabbath laws are outlined first, then the laws of Passover, Shavuot, the Day of Remembrance, the Day of Atonement, Sukkot, and Atzeret. What ties them all together is the pattern of the Sabbath. There was to be no work, only service to God on these days. The daily sacrifices and services were augmented by additional sacrifices and ritual, built on that of the Sabbath. Although the holidays each add additional observances, which are characteristic of their unique significance, the underlying observance, both personally and ritually, was that of the Sabbath.

Each Festival had its own special observances. Passover marked the Exodus from Egypt and liberation. Hence, Passover required the additional sacrifice of one unblemished yearling lamb per family, to be slaughtered, roasted, and eaten before midnight of the first night with bitter herbs and unleavened bread. For the seven days of the festival, no one was to eat or even possess any leavened food. And the story of the Exodus was to be related to the entire family during the holiday.

On Shavuot, the Grain Harvest Festival, the first sheaves of the new grain were brought to the priest and waved before God, to be accepted on the family's behalf. No bread, parched grain, or fresh ears of a new crop can be eaten until the waving takes place. The law commanding that the corners of the field be left uncut during the harvest and the fallen, dropped sheaves be left where they fell, for the poor, was to be observed meticulously.

Sukkot, celebrating the full harvest, involved the ceremony of the waving of the *lulav*, symbolizing all species and varieties of vegetation. During these seven days, the harvest was to be celebrated and the people lived in temporary booths in the fields.

Connected with the Passover is the celebration of freedom as a people. On Shavuot and on Sukkot, the rich plentitude of the earth is to be acknowledged and God's love and compassion, which sustains it, is to be recognized and praised. The earth's plenty is to be enjoyed and shared with the less fortunate, for God's bounty was meant to provide for all people.

Linking all of the holy days and festivals together are several concepts. The first is that of holiness. These days are separate realities from the experience of the mundane week. Normally, one's focus and attention is on work and on production. On the higher level, that focus manifests as creativity, accomplishment, and efforts at self-realization. On the lower level, effort focuses on survival, fulfilling duties, and handling obligations.

On the Sabbath and holy days, one is required to rest, to return to a state of total dependence on God. One is expected to refocus on God, on one's relationship to God, and on the divine order in the universe. Not working involves rest, not just as a cessation from labor but also as a quietude allowing for the realignment of self with God through prayer, meditation, and contemplation.

The Sabbath and the holy festival days all involve additional sacrifices. The term *korban* not only means "a sacrifice." It also means "a drawing near," "an approach," "a closeness." We are asked to sacrifice our own concerns and to release the intent singular attention we pay to day-to-day life. We are called upon to transcend it. We offer up our desires, our concerns, our interests, and our fears, dissolving our connection temporarily to this world. By redirecting our attention and our energy on the Sabbath and festivals to inner quiet and to reconnection with God, we bring to the world a state of holiness and a reality of true peace.

The Sabbath and the holy days are times of intensified access and increased closeness to God. One can connect with God on a daily basis, through work and through creative effort—hence, the *Tamid* Offering. Yet there is an additional accelerated path open on the Sabbath and holidays. This is achieved through external quiet and internal attunement. This is symbolized by the *Musaf*, the Additional Offering.

It is also very significant that the Sabbath and the holy days all include a sin offering. The sin offering is one of atonement. It is an act that purifies the people and brings them back into full synchronization with God's Will and with His purpose. True holiness involves centering back on the divine purpose that underlies all of existence.

Observance of the Sabbath and Festivals involves atonement. Atonement is the process of acknowledging one's mistakes and taking responsibility for one's transgressions. It involves surrendering the desires and the distortions of one's own will that allowed this pattern of behavior, unacceptable to God, to be manifest in one's life. It is the pattern of immoral behavior, as well as the drives and motivations that sustain it, which are to be burned up as the sacrifice.

Once acknowledged, repented of, suffered through, and released, personal rectification is made, and one is again at one with God. The process of sacrifice, the process of rectification and atonement, is not

a singular event. It is a periodic one. Cleansed of one fault, one negative or destructive pattern, another may be exposed, which, in turn,
needs to be addressed as well. The holy times are opportunities for
rectification. During these periods, sins can be repented of and forgiven. During the Sabbath and holy days, the course of the nation can
be kept on track by the constant realignment with the Will of God.
This process is the ritual core of the Covenant.

The reason for the sacrifices, according to Leviticus 17:10, was,
specifically, atonement. Atonement was effected because the blood
of the animal was shed. Blood is physical life force. The blood of the
sacrificial animal symbolized the life of the individual bringing the
offering. When presenting the sin offering, the individual making
the sacrifice had to place his hands on the head of the animal, identifying himself with the animal.

The ritual here suggests the concept that because the supplicant
had sinned, his life was forfeited to God. He therefore had to be willing to sacrifice his life to achieve reconciliation with God. As is affirmed in the Torah, God does not desire the death of the sinner but
rather that he repent of his evil and change his life direction. In order
to accomplish that, the penitent sacrifices his life symbolically through
a surrogate, through the sacrificial animal.

Leviticus 17:11 states that it is forbidden for anyone to eat the
blood of an animal. The blood is life. Only God, as the giver of life,
has the right to receive it. The blood of the sacrificial animal was
sprinkled on the altar and then the remaining blood was poured into
a container at the base of the altar, to be taken to a sacred place and
poured into the ground.

The sin offering of the holy days was done on behalf of the entire community. Individuals were required to bring sin offerings as
part of the repentance process. The sin offerings, which were part of
the holiday sacrifices, were designed to make atonement for the entire
people. The welfare of the nation is the concern of the High Priest in
particular, and of the Festival observances, in general.

The offering of the pascal lamb on Passover marked the redemption of the people. A special offering of well-being was added to the
Shavuot ritual. On Sukkot, the *lulav* ceremony was done to acknowledge God's grace, as expressed in the fertility of the land. All of these
rituals center on a concern for the welfare of the entire people.

So did the ritual of the Day of Atonement. The High Priest had
to sacrifice a bull in atonement for his own sins and for the sins of his

entire household. Then he had to sacrifice a bull received from the tribes, to make atonement for the entire people. Two goats are also offered. One was slaughtered, its blood to be used in the cleansing ritual. The blood of the sacrificial animals was carried into the Holy of Holies by the High Priest and sprinkled on the curtain and before it, seven times. The High Priest stood totally alone in the Holy of Holies, asking for God's forgiveness and making expiation for the people.

This ceremony purified the shrine of the transgressions of the nation. The sins of the Israelites were seen as defiling the shrine. No nation composed of numerous individuals is totally righteous in action over the course of a year and therefore totally blameless. Actions contrary to the statutes of the Law, even if done unintentionally, marred the interaction between God and Israel. The blood of repentance was the agent that cleansed the shrine of the impurities of sin.

The sins of the nation were placed on the head of the second goat, the scapegoat, by the High Priest, through laying on of his hands. By so doing, the sins of the people were removed from them and transmitted to the carrier goat. Thus transferred, the sins were transported into the wilderness by the release of the goat, never to be seen again.

The sins of the entire people affected the welfare of the nation. They had to be atoned for and expiated, or the Covenant would be violated and the people would suffer the consequences. Some sins, such as violence, idolatry, and sexual transgressions were such severe sins that their presence would pollute the Land, violate the heart of the Covenant, and bring the curse of God's wrath (Leviticus 18:27–28, Ezekiel 36:25, Psalms 51:4). Stopping evil, repenting of it, rectifying the damage, and abandoning destructive practices were essential components in maintaining Israel's Covenant commitment.

Sin offerings were offerings of purification. They were done on behalf of the entire people of Israel on every Rosh Hodesh, on every day of the Passover Festival, on Shavuot, on the Day of Remembrance, on the Day of Atonement, and all through Sukkot. If the priests incurred guilt or the people as a whole did, the sin offering was done. The welfare of the entire nation depended on keeping the relationship with God pure and the Covenant observed fully.

The sin offering was also utilized by individuals in the process of becoming ritually pure after a defilement of some sort. Hence, sin offerings accompany the purification rituals involving the recovery from such things as leprosy, childbirth, hemorrhages, et cetera. Standing before God and serving God were not compatible with being in an impure state. Sin caused impurity. Natural impurities created the same condition as sin-induced ones—namely, one was not whole. Therefore, not being whole, one could not fully give of oneself and serve God. This temporary barrier to service had to be rectified physically—through healing, through sacrifice, or through both.

The holy days were times of rectification, release, and purification. They were times of introspection, spiritual intensity, and of drawing close to God. God's Presence, supervision, and grace were acknowledged. The bounty of God's love was celebrated. The people took responsibility, under the Law, for their behavior. The intense interaction between God and the people spanned over one half of the year. Moreover, on a weekly basis, the door to deep connection with God was open every Sabbath.

The welfare of the individual was connected to the welfare of the people. Through this process of total connection with God and total involvement in divine service, the Covenant between Israel and God was physically energized, symbolically expressed, and ritually fulfilled.

9

THE TEMPLE AND THE TEMPLE SCROLL: PART TWO

The Structure of the Sanctuary

God's Presence came down from above and manifested. The Divine Immanence rested upon the Community of Israel for the first time at Mount Sinai. It was there that the relationship between God and the people of Israel was formalized and set. Once that was accomplished, it became necessary to establish a permanent place for God's Presence to dwell in the midst of the Community. If God was to guide and protect His people, and the Israelites were to be God's active representatives, then a continual dialogue between them had to take place. In order for that to occur, a permanent dwelling or contact point had to exist. This was the reason for the creation of the *Mishkan*, the Dwelling Place.

The original *Mishkan* was the core of the Tabernacle constructed at Sinai. The Tabernacle and *Mishkan* were designed and executed at God's command and built according to His specifications. The Tabernacle and the *Mishkan* were carried through the desert for forty years. Eventually, they were set up in the city of Shiloh, after the settlement of the Israelites in the Land.

The structure of the Tabernacle was very simple and quite straightforward. At its center was the *Mishkan* itself. Completely covered, this enclosure marked the sacred space where the priesthood confronted God directly. Its interior was subdivided into two parts: the *Kodesh*, the Holy Place, and the *Kodesh HaKedoshim*, the Holy of Holies. The *Mishkan* was sectioned off inside by a curtain. The Holy of Holies comprised one-third of the inner area of the *Mishkan*. The other two-thirds made up the Holy Place.

It was in the Holy of Holies that the Ark of the Covenant resided. It was placed upon its platform, called the *Kaporet*—the "Mercy seat." The *Kaporet* was a large slab of gold, with two cherubs flanking it, one on each side. This constituted the Throne of God. The Presence of God, the cloud, hovered over the Ark and the Throne. Sometimes, it hovered over the entire *Mishkan*. This was the symbol of God's constant contact and supervision. God's Providence was immediate and visible.

The sacrifices took place on a high, movable altar that stood inside the Tabernacle, in front of the *Mishkan*. The altar for the sacrifices, as well as the altar for the incense, were always before the Presence. Thus, the visible links between Israel and God—that is, the worship and the sacrifices, as well as the Divine Presence—were continual and ever-present. The Providence of God and His protection of Israel were physically apparent at all times.

Surrounding the *Mishkan* was a much larger structure made up of interlocking frames and curtains, which made up the *Ohel Moed*, the Tent of Meeting. The enclosed area was also subdivided. The *Parokhet*—a large, very detailed, free-standing curtain—stood right in front of the entrance to the *Mishkan*. This not only protected the access to the Sanctuary, it effectively divided the area within the *Ohel Moed* into two distinct sections. In front of the *Parokhet* stood the Great Laver, for washing, and some of the other furniture. In front of the Laver was the Sacrificial Altar and the ramp leading up to it.

Several observations can be made regarding the Tabernacle's design and function. First, the presence of a 2:1 ratio is evident in the physical construction of the Tabernacle. The *Ohel Moed* surrounding the *Miskhan* is twice as large as the *Mishkan* itself. The *Mishkan* is divided into the *Kodesh*, the Holy Place, and the *Kodesh HaKedoshim*, the Holy of Holies. The Holy Place is twice the size of the Holy of Holies.

Second, access became more restricted the closer one came to the Divine Presence. The Holy of Holies was half the size of the Holy Place within the *Mishkan*. The *Mishkan* was half the size of the Tent of Meeting around it. The Tribe of Levi surrounded the Sanctuary. The camp of the Israelites, in turn, encircled the Levites guarding the Sanctuary.

Third, holiness increased the closer one came to the Divine Presence. The Camp of the Israelites was considered holy. People who were in a state of ritual uncleanness, such as lepers, dwelt outside of the Camp altogether. The dead were buried outside of the Camp as well. Within the Camp, the Tribes were positioned around the Tribe of Levi. The Tribe of Levi was holier than the other tribes, being specifically dedicated to God's service. Even more holy were the priests, who were responsible for the ritual and for the services.

Priests who were not clean, or not on duty, could neither approach the holy vessels nor officiate at the altar. Most holy was the *Mishkan*, and even that was divided into the Holy Place and the Holy of Holies. Israelites could only enter the court. They could not enter the *Mishkan*. Only the priests could do that, and not at all times. Even they could not enter the Holy of Holies. That privilege was reserved for the High Priest on Yom Kippur.

The reality being demonstrated here, in the structure of the Tabernacle and the Camp, is one of approaching God. First, one must be clean or no approach is possible. Then, one embarks on the path of holiness that leads to an encounter with God. At each stage of the way, with each step on the Path of Holiness, there is a progressive condensing of space. There is an intensification of energy and focus the closer one comes to facing and experiencing the Divine Presence.

The approach to God is gradual. There is a series of stages one must go through. The first stage is becoming clean, healed, and whole. The second step is encamping and dedicating the focus of daily life to God. One must recognize the holy and acknowledge it in day-to-day life. Third, one must wash, then light the lamp and the altar of incense, awakening the inner light and the emotions.

Washing in the Great Laver symbolizes introspection and inner cleansing. Lighting the *Menorah*, the seven-branched candelabra, represents increasing the light within oneself to the point of seven, to the level of transcendence and peace. Igniting the incense is symbolic of awakening the emotions, so intimately connected to the sense of smell. By opening the emotions from within, one is exalted by them. They become an offering. They become carriers of the spirit to higher realms of consciousness.

What is being portrayed is a process of purification, a process which encompasses increased awareness and leads to the refining of the emotions. By going through these processes, one becomes transformed. As one moves forward, the functions being performed are increasingly elevated in status and reality. The priests all wash at the Great Laver. Only the priests who are part of the *mishmar*, the weekly rotation, officiate at the sacrificial altar. Then, only designated priests from the *mishmar* do the daily communal offerings or enter the Holy Place. The High Priest alone is allowed to enter the Holy of Holies.

The sacrifices symbolize what one gives up in approaching God. That which is brought from the physical world, the best it has to offer, is sacrificed. One must relinquish the ties to the material world. The choicest of the material world is transformed by fire, evaporating in smoke. The daily offerings are made on behalf of the community. They are followed by the private sacrifices: the guilt offerings, the peace offerings, the thanksgiving offerings. Again, the focus narrows from communal to personal concerns.

The intercessory prayers on behalf of the people are said by the priests in the Holy Place. Movement now goes within. A few priests address God in the enclosure of the Holy Place. Here, the focus is even more intense. The approach to God moves to the internal realm of sacred space. Here, prayer becomes meditation. Worship becomes communion with God from deep within the self.

Finally, only the High Priest stands in the Holy of Holies, face-to-face with the Presence of God. In the confines of the most compact physical space, the High Priest alone encounters the greatest majesty of all—direct contact with the Divine. That which is the most vast is to be found concentrated in the smallest space. One encounters God in the Holy of Holies, the heart of hearts, the center of the core.

The physical, emotional, psychological, and spiritual approach to God was one of gradual stages. One entered the Holy City and made one's way to the Holy Temple. In the Temple, one sang and prayed with the Levites. The priests washed and ascended the altar for the sacrifices. Some of the priests entered the *Mishkan*, to pray for the people and to entreat God on their behalf. During the Day of Atonement, the High Priest entered the Holy of Holies and faced God alone asking for His forgiveness. He sought God's mercy in pardoning the transgressions of the nation.

The paradigm here is clear. The closer the movement toward God, the more condensed is the space, until one reaches, first, sacred space, and ultimately, most sacred space, the encounter with God. As the movement progresses, more and more is relinquished until one is deep within the sacred precincts, standing alone. The farther the process goes, the more transformation takes place. The movement is initiated by the Israelite, assisted by the Levite, brought to fruition by the Priests, and ultimately climaxed by the High Priest.

In the days of the First and the Second Temple, the Temple in Jerusalem emulated the general structure of the Tabernacle. As in the case of the Tabernacle, form followed function and meaning. Hence, it is important to pay some attention to the general structure of the Temple, since its form, content, and spiritual significance were all closely inter-related. Form reflected meaning. Each function had a spiritual import.

The First and Second Temple were divided into three distinct sections. First came the Forecourt, the Court of the Women and the Strangers. It was followed by the Middle Court, the Court of the Isra-elites. Then came the *Mishkan*. The *Mishkan* was itself subdivided into three sections: the *Ulam*, the *Heikhal*, and the *Devir*.

The *Ulam*, the Entrance Hall, served as a porch. Its function was to initiate the sacred precinct, thus separating the sacred from the profane. The entrance to the *Ulam* was marked by two free-standing pillars, named Jachin and Boaz. According to the Septuagint's rendi-tion of Ezekiel 40:49, ten steps lead up to the *Ulam*. Beyond the *Ulam* was the *Heikhal*. The *Heikhal* was the Main Hall. Here is where the sacrificial altar and the ritual furniture were to be found. The *Heikhal* was the center for worship and sacrifice.

During the Second Temple period, the *Heikhal* was subdivided into two separate divisions. One section, the Court of the Priests, was created around the altar. This area served as the platform for the priests. The Court of the Priests was raised. This kept the altar and the sacrificial area sacred and inviolate. A second area was designed to confine those who came to bring offerings. This partitioning of the Main Hall prevented the Israelites from mixing with the priests and from getting too close to the Altar.

The third element of the Temple was the *Devir*, the Holy of Holies. The *Devir* housed the Ark of the Covenant during the days of First Temple. Jeremiah removed the Ark from the Holy of Holies right before the Babylonian assault on Jerusalem, which led to its destruc-tion in 586 B.C.E. Since the secret of where it was buried died with the prophet, the Second Temple had the Throne enclosed in the *Devir*, but the Ark was not upon it.

The *Ulam* measured twenty cubits wide by ten cubits long. The *Heikhal*'s measurements were forty cubits in length and twenty cubits in width. Both halls of the Temple, therefore, were built on a ratio of 2:1. The *Devir*, the Holy of Holies, however, measured twenty by twenty cubits, a 1:1 ratio.

Each of the four corners of the *Ulam* and each of the corners of the *Heikhal* had a chamber. That is, each corner of both halls housed a specially designed, large, enclosed room. Each Chamber had a different purpose. On the corners of the *Ulam* were the Chamber of the Nazirites (Southeast), the Chamber of the Lepers (Northwest), the Chamber of the Oil (Southwest), and the Chamber of the Wood (Northeast). On the four corners of the *Heikhal* were the Chamber of the Shewbread Makers (Southeast); the Chamber of the *Mikveh*, the Ritual Bath (Northwest); the Chamber of the Sacrifices (Southwest); and the Chamber of the Defiled Altar (Northeast).

Surrounding the Temple on three sides was a second building, called the *Yatzi'a*. This edifice was three stories high and housed all of the priestly vestments, utensils and paraphernalia, and Temple treasures. It encompassed the Temple building on all sides except the front.

The structure of the Temple was linear. One passed through the Pillars of Jachin and Boaz, entering the sacred precinct of the Temple. In the *Ulam*, people gathered to pray. Beyond the *Ulam*, in the *Heikhal*, the sacrifices and the divine services were performed. At the back of the Temple was the completely self-contained *Devir*, the Holy of Holies, the place of God's Presence or Indwelling. The Temple building itself was contained within the confines of the *Yatzi'a*. Access to the Temple was possible only from the front.

One progressed from the midst of the Holy City to the sacred precincts of the Temple. Within the Temple, holiness and sanctity increased with greater and greater intensification as one moved more deeply into the sacred divisions. The place of gathering and prayer led to the place of sacrifice. The epitome of this place was the altar itself. Beyond the altar was the *Mishkan*, the Place of God's Indwelling. That itself had two dimensions, one concealed but accessible to the priesthood and one most hidden, sacrosanct, and only accessible to the High Priest.

The symbolism of the Temple structure was that of singular direction. The path to God's Presence was straightforward. The approach to God was gradual and it involved an intensification of holiness as one progressed. Only the clean in body and spirit could approach. The laws of ritual cleanliness and the underlying purpose of the personal sacrifices was purification of body and soul. The sacrifices were done in a state of purity.

Purification brought rectification. The personal offerings were the renewal of one's obligation to remain connected to God and committed to the Covenant. The communal sacrifices brought atonement, realignment with God and with God's purpose. Maintaining an intimate relationship with God through sacrifice and devotion, in turn, led to introspection and inward communication with God. Beyond the sacrificial altar stood the *Devir*, totally closed and concealed. The priests disappeared inside. They offered the incense but nothing more. To stand in His Holy Place, one had to move within.

The penetration into the heart of the *Devir*, into the Holy of Holies, was done by the High Priest alone. Facing God's Presence and hearing His Voice comes at the deepest level of self, through an internal step into the core of being. In the innermost depths of the soul, in the hidden of the hidden, alone and with nothing, one encounters God.

Purification led to prayer. Prayer led to sacrifice. Sacrifice opened the way to atonement, and atonement to introspection and soul searching. The path of holiness culminated in meeting God within. Through the external stages of the process—seeking, being purified, praying, acknowledging, and making the sacrifice—there is still a duality. Connection is sought between the individual and/or the nation, on one hand, and God, on the other. The ratio of the dimensions of the *Ulam* and of the *Heikhal* are both 2:1. Only when one turns within and moves into oneself does one experience the unity and face the Presence of God. The dimension ratio of the Holy of Holies was 1:1.

The enclosed Holy of Holies was a perfect cube, dimensionally. It measured ten by ten by ten cubits—a ratio of 1:1:1. In view of the position of the Holy of Holies within the Temple structure, there is an important metaphysical truth that is being stated architecturally. One moves through the sacred path of the Temple from prayer to sacrifice to transcendence. One progresses from external reality to closeness to God and then to the experiencing of God's Presence. The 2:1 ratio becomes 1:1. A perfect cube is formed. Hence, when one reaches the innermost level of being, the soul, the soul's approach toward God, and the Indwelling Presence of God are all manifest as equal parts of the same process and the same reality.

The Architecture Outlined in the Temple Scroll

In the Temple Scroll, we encounter a pattern of design that is not exactly the same as that of the First and Second Temples. Like the Temple in Jerusalem, there are three courts. However, instead of a linear pattern, where one court leads to another, the Temple of the Scroll is built of three concentric courts. There is an Outer Court, a Middle Court, and then, the Inner Court.

The Outer Court was the court for women and for foreigners. The wall surrounding this court had twelve gates, one for each of the tribes of Israel. Each wall had three gates. The distance between each of the gates was exactly 360 cubits. The gates themselves were fourteen cubits wide. They each extended seven cubits outward and thirty-six cubits inward (11Q19a, col. 41).

Each gate was three stories high. On their roofs, columns eight cubits high and connected by beams formed a place for the annual building of Festival Booths on the holiday of Sukkot, the Feast of Tabernacles. During the Festival, this was to be the dwelling place for the elders of the congregation, the princes, the chiefs of hundreds, and the chiefs of thousands (11Q19a, col. 42).

Between each gate, eighteen rooms and storerooms were to be built. Each group of rooms was assigned to a specific tribe (11Q19a, col. 44).

The Middle Court was the Court of the Israelites. Here, too, the walls had twelve gates, each one named for a different tribe. Only men over the age of twenty, and who were paying the annual one-half shekel Temple Tax, were allowed to enter. There is reference to the wearing of specific garments in relationship to this gate. It is not clear whether this referred to the priests or to the people (Yadin, Temple Scroll, col. 38).

In lines 1 through 3 of column 40, the phrases, "to wear the garments," "to be serving," and "the Children of Israel, that they do not die" appear, according to Yadin's reconstruction. This may refer to the wearing of white garments. According to Josephus, it was customary among many Jews to wear only white when entering the Temple.

The description of the Inner Court is the most extensive. It begins on column 30 and runs through column 36. The Inner Court has only four gates, one per wall. At each side of the four corners were areas designated as "cooking places." Along the walls within this court were porticoes that housed tables and chairs. This would be the sacred precincts in which the priests would eat their consecrated portions of the sacrifices.

The Temple Scroll (11Q19, col. 37) states that a place had to be made for the priests with tables and chairs for their sacrifices, first fruits, tithes, and peace offerings. Since all of these offerings were partaken of by the priests, that would account for the need for tables and chairs sequestered in porticoes. Each of the four walls contained a portico with the tables and chairs inside. Presumably, each portico was for the eating of one of the four types of offerings mentioned.

The prohibition against mixing the peace offerings of the priests with those of the people is quite explicit. Logically, if one were not to mix different peace offerings, how much more so the other different types of offerings. Hence, it would seem that the place for the priestly eating of the offerings would also be carefully segregated. That would also explain the need for four different cooking areas.

Yadin argues that there was an encasing wall within the Inner Court that separated the sacred area reserved for the priests from that of the Israelites who were bringing offerings. Within the retaining wall stood the *Mishkan*, the Altar, and the area for the slaughtering of the animals. He bases his concept on 1 Kings 8:64 and on Josephus' description of a similar barricade erected by King Solomon. Josephus does mention that Alexander Jannai erected a wooden fence around the altar and the *Mikdash* (Antiquities XIII:373) and that eventually there was a one-cubit-high stone partition that surrounded the Altar and *Mikdash*, beyond which only the priests could go (Wars 5:226).

Within this fenced-in sacred area stood, first and foremost, the *Mishkan* (referred to here as the *Mikdash*, the Place of Holiness). To its southeast were the Enclosure of Laver and the Enclosure of the Vessels. In front of *Mikdash*, to the south, was the Sacrificial Altar, and to the north, the Ceiling of the Twelve Pillars. From the Ceiling of the Twelve Pillars hung chains.

Through a system of chains, rings, and moving wheels, the sacrificial animals were held for slaughter. To the northwest of the *Mikdash* was the House of Stairs, which led up to the roof of the *Mishkan* and then connected to the rooms of the *Yatzi'a*, giving the priests direct access from the sacred chambers.

Prior to the sacrifice, the Columned Porch west of the Sanctuary served as a holding area for the sin and guilt offerings. The Columned Porch was divided into four sections. One was for the sin offerings of the priests, one for the guilt offerings of the priests, one for the people's sin offerings, and the last one for their guilt offerings. All four groups of offerings had to be strictly segregated from one another and not intermingled (11Q19, col. 35).

The concept of the holiness of the sacrificial service to God seems to embrace the notion that there is separation between the holy and the holy. Different types of offerings, even though they are both holy, cannot be intermingled without contamination. Neither can the offerings of the people be mixed with those of the priests.

According to column 45, lines 3 and 4, when the priestly *mishmarot* change watches, they are to remain apart from one another. The *mishmar* that arrives enters from the left side, and the departing *mishmar* exits through the right. They are not to intermingle with each other. Not even their vessels are to come in contact with one other. Neither the priestly concourse, nor the equipment they use was to interact with one another.

What is very noticeable in the Temple Scroll is the extreme care taken to maintain not just holiness, per se, but also to differentiate and to delineate the various degrees of holiness. Great precaution was taken not only to separate the holy from the profane, but also to distinguish one degree of holiness from another.

Jerusalem, the Holy City, takes on the same role as the Camp of the Israelites did in the forty-year sojourn in the Sinai under Moses. The City itself is sacred and must be kept undefiled. Several interesting requirements are set down in the Temple Scroll, which emphasize this fact.

For three days after sexual intercourse with his wife, a man is forbidden not only to appear in the Temple but even to enter the Holy City at all. He must go through the period of ritual impurity and then cleanse himself, or he may not approach the city, let alone the Temple. The scroll makes similar statements regarding other forms of ritual impurity as well. They are not to defile the Holy City by entering it in an impure state, "because I, Adonai, dwell within it, because I, Adonai, dwell among the Children of Israel forever" (Wacholder, frag. rem. 11Q Torah, col. 45:13–14).

In column 46, the requirement is set forth that latrines, outhouses, the lepers' colony, and colonies for those suffering from fluxes be established as separate camps, each a distance of three thousand cubits outside of the City. They were to be placed not only away from the city to avoid contact and contamination, but also to be placed out of sight. No unclean person or unclean animal was allowed to desecrate the Holy City.

The food and drink and the vessels used within the city were to be pure as well. This is where God has caused His Name and Presence to dwell. "Everything that there is in it shall be pure, and everything that goes into it shall be pure: wine, oil, all food, and all drink shall be pure" (Yadin, Temple Scroll, 47:7).

Hence, not even the skin of a clean animal, sacrificed in another city, was to be brought into the Holy City. Neither as a skin nor in the form of a vessel could a clean skin be brought into the city, if it were not the one of an animal sacrificed in the Temple. Only the skins of ritually clean sacrificial animals that had been consecrated by being offered on the Temple Altar could be present in Jerusalem in any shape or form (Yadin, Temple Scroll, column 47).

The City was holy because the Presence of God dwelt there, which was a result of the Temple being there. Therefore, considerable effort was made to distinguish between the holiness of the City and the greater holiness of the Temple. A platform was to be erected around the Outer Court of the Temple, according to the scroll. Twelve steps would lead up to it. Around the Outer Court, a trench or moat was to be dug, one hundred cubits wide. This was done to separate the two from one another, as being different degrees of holiness. The express purpose of the trench was to prevent one from entering the Temple suddenly and thereby defiling it.

As mentioned earlier, the Temple envisioned here is itself subdivided into three distinct courts. The concentric courts each signify a different level of holiness, the Inner Court housing both the Altar and the *Mikdash*. The *Mikdash* itself is divided into three chambers of increasing holiness: the *Ulam*, the *Heikhal*, and the *Devir*.

On one hand, the nature of the City and the nature of the Temple are the same. Holiness pervades both because God has established His Indwelling, His Presence there. People in the City and in the Temple have to be holy and must be in a state of purity. They are a holy people, functioning within the Holy City and the Holy Temple. On the other hand, substantial concern is expressed for maintaining the differences.

What distinguishes people is their state of holiness. Either one is ritually prepared to move toward God, or one is, temporarily, not. One also must rely on the priesthood to carry out the sacrifices. What separates the City from other cities, and, in turn, separates it from the Temple, are the degrees of holiness. The Land of Israel is holy.

Jerusalem is the holy center. The Temple is even holier, because here God's Presence dwells and guides the Land, making it holy. The core of the Temple, the Holy of Holies, is the most sacred, being the contact point with God.

Within the Temple Scroll, the sense of the sacred is closely tied to the reality that contact with God, directly and on an ongoing basis, is not only possible, but necessary and imperative. What makes the people of Israel a holy nation, the Land of Israel a holy land, and Jerusalem the Holy City is the Indwelling of God and the constant contact between man and God that this represents.

All of the institutions—the Sanctuary, the Temple, Jerusalem, the priesthood, and the monarchy—are all vessels. They are sacred because they facilitate direct contact and communication with God. Without the Indwelling of God, without His immediate Presence, all of the outward manifestations would be meaningless. The people were consecrated, the Land was settled, and the Temple was established solely in order for God to rule over His people.

God's kingdom on earth is established when God rules directly. When God alone is the guiding force and protecting power, when God speaks directly to us and is accessible at all times, then holiness emerges fully. The sacred is the result of Presence of God being manifest. God being present creates holiness and that holiness sanctifies human life. Sacredness is the effect of God's nearness.

Holiness is a state created by God's interaction with man. God makes His Presence known in order to communicate with, to guide, to sustain, and to protect His people. Without that interchange, there is no holiness in the world of mankind. There is no place for God.

God's Presence is made manifest through vehicles of receptivity. The People of Israel had to receive both God's Presence and God's Law at Mount Sinai in order to become holy. Fulfilling the Law of God, abiding by the commandments, is the prime vehicle for facilitating the interaction with God and thus for maintaining holiness.

The acceptance of God's sovereignty and service to God are manifest ritually in multiple forms and dimensions. One approaches God in a state of ritual purity. It is of utmost importance to preserve the sanctity of Jerusalem, scrupulously observing the Temple ritual and the sacrifices. The core of worship centers on the very existence and presence of the *Mishkan*. All of these factors help establish and insure the Indwelling of God's Presence. In turn, maintaining ritual purity, reciting prayer, and the bringing of offerings keep an individual holy, facilitating worship and ritual. On a parallel track, the priestly work of handling the sacrifices facilitated atonement and drew one closer to God.

The purity of Jerusalem and of the activity that took place there served to enhance the Name of God and to demonstrate what God expects. This perpetuates holiness. God wants His Presence to shine forth from the Holy City and from the Temple. "They shall sanctify My Temple and they shall be in awe of My Temple" (Wacholder, frag. rem. 11Q Torah 46:11). The purpose of the Altar was "to make My Face appear in My Sanctuary" (Wacholder, 3:14).

The sacred is that which is created by the Presence of God. The holy is that which is prepared to receive the Indwelling of God. In the view of the Temple Scroll, a nation becomes holy by submitting to the living Word and to the guiding hand of God. That is the Kingdom of God. This echoes and amplifies the perspective of the Torah and is expounded by the Sectarian literature.

The revelation of God's Presence creates holiness. Direct human interaction with the Divine Presence of God maintains the state of holiness. The emphasis placed on purity, on the sacrificial services, on the structure of the Temple, on man's moral duty, and on the functions of priesthood and king is done because all of these forms are the vessels for and the methods by which the Divine Presence is received.

To approach God, one must become holy. To connect with God's Presence, one must share in the state of holiness. To come face-to-face with God involves a process of accepting and refining one's own state of holiness. This is accomplished in stages and is a very gradual and reverential process. It involves constant devotion, concentrating focus, releasing one's hold on the past and on material things, accepting increasing separation, and being able to stand alone.

In external form Israel, Jerusalem, the Temple, and the ritual all symbolized this process of establishing the Kingdom of God. If acted out fully and correctly, transformation took place, holiness was achieved and maintained, and a constant interaction with God was established. In the perspective of the Temple Scroll, this process would lead to personal fulfillment and national well-being. In the view of the scroll and the Sectarian literature, by reconstructing the Temple, by observing the rituals correctly, by maintaining personal purity, physically and morally, and by reinstating true kingship, the true state of holiness, inwardly and outwardly, would be reestablished in Israel, and God would rule on earth. This transformation would ultimately lead first to national salvation and then to the redemption of all of humanity.

The Symbolism of the Temple Structure: The Recurrence of Twelve

One of the first structural elements of the Temple, as portrayed in the Temple Scroll, to strike one's attention is the recurrence of the number twelve. The concept of twelve appears a number of times, both structurally within the design of the Temple and functionally in the context of the Temple ritual.

Twelve is a highly significant number because it relates to the entirety of Israel. Twelve is the number of the tribes. The twelve tribes of Israel represent the totality of the nation. Twelve, in the context of biblical numbers, suggests the peoplehood of Israel. Since the biblical emphasis is on Israel as a holy nation, twelve constitutes the number of holiness in the functional sense.

The twelve tribes represent the holy people. The framework through which the Covenant is to be observed is as a nation of priests. Israel was consecrated at Mount Sinai as a whole people. Hence, twelve symbolizes Israel as a people through which the Covenant is to be preserved, adhered to, and maintained. The dimensions and aspects of Israel's mission are thus represented collectively as the twelve tribes.

The wall of the Outer Court and the wall of the Middle Court both contain exactly twelve gates. In both cases, each of the gates bears the name of one of the twelve tribes. As one crosses the moat, the sacred boundary from the Holy City to the Holy Temple, one confronts twelve gates leading into the Temple. What divides the sacred from the more sacred is Israel.

The tripartite structure of the Temple reflects the three degrees of holiness that are represented physically by the Land of Israel as the Holy Land, by Jerusalem as the Holy City, and by the Temple as the Holy Place. The Outer Court represents the Land of Israel. The Middle Court symbolizes the Holy City of Jerusalem. The Inner Court represents the *Mikdash*, the Holy Place of the Divine Indwelling.

The Outer Court is the Women's Court. It is also that of the stranger, the foreigner, and the resident alien. Lineage as a Jew comes through being born of a Jewish woman. So the Women's Court represents Israel as a people. That peoplehood is collective, yet it is through the gates of the various tribes that one enters into the realm of the holy.

The Outer Court is also the Court of the Foreigner. The foreign visitor and the alien resident represent the nations of the world. Both Israel and the nations reach the first stage of holiness through the physical reality of the Holy Land and through the interaction with each other. One crosses through the Gates of the Tribes to reach the Outer Court, and once inside, there is a unity created between the people of Israel and the nations of the world. The first stage of movement toward facing God is the solidification of Israel and the convergence together of Israel and all the nations of the earth.

When one proceeds into the Middle Court, the same path must be taken through the Gates of the Twelve Tribes. Israel is the portal to the second degree of approach to God. Now, one enters the Court of the Israelites. The second stage of approach is movement into the realm of mediation. Israel is designated as a nation of priests, a holy people. This means that at a certain point in the process, the people of Israel have to function as a conduit of divine energy for the world at large.

As Moses was an intermediary, a leader, a prophet, and a teacher channeling God's instructions to the Israelites, so, too, Israel is to serve as a similar vehicle for the nations of the world. The nations of the world having joined together with Israel, now receive instruction, blessing, and divine grace through Israel. That is the second stage of interaction with God.

As one moves into the Inner Court, one passes through one of four gates. Four times three has been reduced to four times one. Now, entrance is still possible from any direction. However, once a direction of approach has been determined, there is only one point of entry. One's focus is narrowed to a singular path.

The four doors can be seen as the four corners of the earth. As one progresses to the Inner Realm of Holiness, one reaches it from a specific direction and enters into it as a sole individual. Those Israelites who enter the inner realm, the third level of holiness, are doing so as a flow of single individuals. Those entering constitute a representative body. These worshipers are Israelites representing the people of Israel, much as in the previous stage Israel represented the nations.

Within the Inner Court, there is a subdivision. The core of the Inner Court is the Court of the Priests. Here, the priests serve as intermediaries for Israel. As the nations receive the divine influx, God's grace and God's instructions, through Israel, Israel receives it through the work of the priesthood and the sacred services they perform.

The work of the priests culminates in the work of the High Priest. It is the High Priest alone who stands before God directly and interacts face-to-face with the Divine Presence. It is through the High Priest that the priests receive the divine influx of grace and the living instructions of God.

What is interesting about the way the Temple is described in the Temple Scroll is that these three interlocking, concentric courts are portrayed as a process of inner to outer. The Inner Court is described first, then the Middle Court, and finally the Outer Court. Hence, the implication is that holiness emanates from God's contact with the individual soul that has penetrated to the core of holiness, having gone through a process of refinement.

God's Will and God's blessing are transmitted to the High Priest—that is, to any soul that has progressed through all the levels of holiness and is able to face God directly. The flux of the divine grace and blessing then flows to the priests. It moves from those individuals who have achieved unification with God, to those who have reached the level of continual service to God. From there, the flow of divine energy is transmitted to those who bring sacrifices and offerings. That is, to those individuals who in the context of their daily lives, periodically separate themselves from the external and the mundane, enter the inner realm of consciousness, and serve God by personal sacrifice and by acts of love and thanksgiving.

The priests and the Israelites, making sacrifices at the Altar of God, are operating on the innermost levels of holiness. The result of their devotion radiates the divine energy outward to the four corners of the earth, through the four gates. They facilitate the flux of divine grace to the People of Israel as a whole, represented symbolically by the Middle Court. It is transmitted through Israel, through the twelve gates, via the twelve tribes of Israel—first to those nations drawn to Israel, represented in the Outer Court, and then to the world at large, the Holy City beyond the sacred confines.

Within the concentric courts of the Temple, the structural recurrence of twelve plays an important and consistent role. Twelve steps lead across the divide to the Temple. Entry into the Outer Court is through twelve gates. Each gate is a self contained unit. There is a space of 360 cubits between each gate, reflecting the 360 degrees of a circle. Each gate has a full compliment of storehouses assigned to it. Both of these features conceptually harken back to the ideas of completion, self-containment, and fulfillment. The first reference structurally to the tribes of Israel is one of independent, individual identities, which are materially blessed and spiritually complete.

One can enter into the Temple through any of the gateways. Each is unique and individual. Yet they are all tribes of Israel. The twelve tribes also constitute the access points through to the Middle Court. The walls of the Outer and Middle Courts are approach barriers. These courts serve as protective rings around the Sacred Precinct, the Inner Court. One approaches God gradually, having to penetrate barriers to do so, and only by entering through one of the tribes of Israel.

When one reaches the Inner Court, one is in the Holy Precinct. Here, sacred subdivisions appear. Here, one finds the House of the Laver, the Altar of Incense, the Altar of the Sacrifices, and the Sanctuary itself. Within the Holy Precinct, one also finds the Chamber of the Twelve Pillars. In this chamber, the sacrificial animals were to be prepared for the offering. No longer are the twelve tribes represented as independent and self-contained. No longer are they portals within a wall. They have become pillars within a sacred enclosure. Their function has changed from facilitating passage to facilitating service and worship. At the level of sacrifice, at the point of direct service to God, the twelve tribes have become melded into one unit.

At the level of the Outer Court, where the movement of God's Presence radiates toward the outside, from the internalness of the Temple to the external Holy City, abundance is bestowed upon the tribes. At the level of the Inner Court, where man reaches inward into the realm of interaction with the divine, sacrifice, thanksgiving, and offering initiate the sacred dialogue. At this level of holy service, the tribes are an integral whole. The many have become one.

The structural shift that occurs within the Inner Court, unifying the twelve tribes into a collective whole, represents the outward manifestation of a spiritual metamorphosis. To serve God, the tribes become a consolidated people, melded together and dedicated to actively and fully maintaining the Covenant.

Maintaining the sacrifices and observing the Festivals and holy days was a central, core element in fulfilling the terms of the Sinai Covenant. Observance of the Covenant established and maintained the working relationship between God and Israel. The Temple Scroll symbolically places the People of Israel at the heart of this paradigm of divine–human interaction. Individual Israelites come and make personal offerings. Individual priests make the daily communal offerings and the festival sacrifices. Yet it is the people as a whole who are always at the center. It is the people as a nation that is blessed.

The Temple Scroll describes the Chamber of the Twelve Pillars as the place for preparation of the sacrifices. By so doing, the scroll is symbolically asserting that the oneness of the people, brought about by devotion and service to God, is the basis for the interaction between God and man.

Devotion brings oneness. It solidifies the many into the one. The oneness of the people reflects the oneness of God. A parity of one to one has been struck. The result is that when such parity is created through a clear focus on the observance of the Covenant, a direct relationship and interactive dialogue takes place between God and Israel, between the divine and the human realms. Through the sacrifices and the worship, the tribes become one. The people merge with the priesthood during the holy services. The priesthood itself is encompassed by the High Priest and his functions. The High Priest ultimately stands in the Holy of Holies alone, on behalf of the entire nation.

The entire structural sequence of the Temple leads to this point of culmination. The approach to God continually produces condensation and unification, until ultimately there is only a relationship of pure unity remaining. It is God and His people, each facing the other, one on one.

Some Insights Regarding the Festivals

The Festival Cycle from Passover through the Festival of the New Wood, as outlined in the Temple Scroll, also has a close relationship to the symbolism of the unity of the twelve tribes as the people of Israel. Ritually, the twelve tribes are interwoven into the very core of the festival observance. Intimately involved in the celebration of these particular festivals are the concepts of the twelve divisions of Israel being equally represented and the importance of the people of Israel in maintaining the connection between God and the world.

During the Festival of the New Wine, twelve lambs were sacrificed—one for each of the tribes. In addition, twelve rams were sacrificed. This was accompanied by a libation offering of four hins of wine. According to the scroll, one-third of a hin was poured out for each of the twelve tribes (Wacholder, Frag. Remains of 11Q Torah, col. 19:14–16, 20:1, 21:2).

The ritual during the Festival of the New Oil was similar in nature. A half of a hin of oil per tribe was offered during the festival, as well as one ram and one lamb for each of the twelve tribes (Wacholder, col. 21:14–15). During the celebration of the New Wood Festival, the sacrifices were made and accompanied by the offering of the wood. This was done over a six-day period. Two tribes per day officiated (Wacholder, col. 23 and 4Q para. Torah, frag. 2–3).

From Shavuot through the offering of the New Wood, those things being consecrated—the grain, the wine, the oil, and the wood—are all elements of primary importance in the Temple ritual. The ritual year begins with the release from bondage and the wave offering of barley. Then it proceeds through the consecration of the primary commodities required to conduct the Temple ritual.

Symbolically, we begin with emancipation and the emergence of the peoplehood of Israel during Passover. Then, responsibility for observing the Law and the Commandments is taken on during Shavuot, the Festival of Weeks. It is at this point that the sanctification of the Land and the dedication of the holy produce commences. The consecration of the grain, the wine, the oil, and the wood signify both the sanctification of God's abundance and that of the commodities necessary for the maintenance of the Temple ritual. Grain represents the food crops, and wine, the drink. The oil and the wood symbolize both the harvests of the trees and the sources of warmth, light, and shelter.

These four items specifically also represent the necessary ingredients for the worship services. Grain is the shewbread. Wine is the libation. Oil and flour were required for the sacrifices. Wood symbolized not only the fires of the altar, but according to 4Q para. Torah (frag. 2–3), the consecrated New Wood was used exclusively for any construction done in the Temple.

One of the primary underlying conceptions here is the central importance of worship and service in the continual fulfillment of the Covenant. During Passover, Israel becomes a free people in a position to serve God. The terms of the service to God are restated, renewed, and strengthened during Shavuot. The commitment to the Covenant is reaffirmed at this time. During this same festival, the yearly consecration of the emerging, holy produce—so integral to the Temple service—takes place as well.

The observance of the Covenant, the sanctity of the Temple service, and the centrality of the people of Israel are all closely interlocked. The culmination of the Passover brings a period of seven weeks leading to the Shavuot. Shavuot, in turn, initiates seven-week cycles that lead to the New Wine and the New Oil Festivals, which conclude with the New Wood Offering. The Acceptance of the Covenant leads to Israel's observance of the Temple service.

There is another organic connection between Shavuot, the Festival of the First Grain, and the Festivals of the New Wine, the New Oil, and the New Wood. In the Temple Scroll, they are all called Festivals of the First Fruits. Column 19:5 states that the bread of the First Fruits are for the priests. They are to eat the cereal offering of the new grain during Shavuot. Column 21:4–10 indicates that during the Festival of the New Wine, the people are to eat the grapes, the fresh fruit of the vine, and drink the wine before God. In column 21:16, the New Oil is referred to as first fruits. Column 38, lines 4 through 7, speak of the eating of the sacrifices during the days of the first fruits of the grain, of the wine, and of the oil.

In biblical law, the First Fruits belong specifically to God and, as such, are extremely holy. They are to be used only within the precincts of the Temple and they are not redeemable. The consecration of the First Fruits returns in thanksgiving the initial part of God's bounty. It acknowledges God's grace and sanctifies both the produce and the Land.

The freedom to serve God, the acceptance of the Covenant, the Temple ritual, and acknowledgment of God as the source of everything are all essential components necessary in the service of God. Service to God is central to the observance of the Covenant. The Covenant is at the heart of Israel's connection to God. Through the festival cycle, the people of Israel, the Covenant, the Land of Israel, the Temple worship, and God's Presence and His Grace are all intrinsically intertwined.

From the Shavuot and the New Wood segment of the festival cycle, one passes to the period of the Day of Remembrance and the Day of Atonement. The high point of the ritual year is reached with the emphasis being on placed on atonement. Atonement is another bridge that connects the holy days into a yearly cycle. This is natural enough for several reasons.

First, atonement is rectification. The core of Israel's relationship to God is through observance of the Covenant, and that is done by following faithfully all of the moral, social, and ritual laws that make up the terms of the agreement. The expectation is not that all the people are going to be able to properly fulfill all the 613 commandments, consistently and at all times. Rather, they are to strive continually to live within this framework. As within any legal system, transgressions, oversights, mistakes, and omissions are bound to occur. Since the Torah, the Law, is a divine imperative and the basis of the covenantal relationship, punishments for breach of the Law are not sufficient, in and of themselves. Awareness of the gravity of the mistakes, regret, and the determination to learn and improve are all elements necessary in rectifying transgression and keeping the Covenant a dynamic relationship. Hence, the process of atonement underlies the entirety of the sacred year and the holy days.

Second, the Temple Scroll states that the festival sacrifices are to atone for the Land, and its holy bounty, the grain, wine, and oil. These festivals not only acknowledge God's sovereignty and grace, but also bring that which is to serve God directly into alignment with God's Will. The sanctification and dedication of anything to God is predicated on atonement. The grain, the wine, the oil, and the wood are all being sanctified, not only to thank God for His love and abundance, but also to dedicate them to God so as to make the Temple services and the ritual observance of the Covenant possible. In turn, the maintenance of the Temple service brings atonement, which keeps the relationship with God focused and pure, dynamic and interactive.

As the festivals atone for the Land and its yield, the Day of Atonement, Yom Kippur, atones for the people. The Land is holy. The People of Israel are holy. Both are holy because God's Presence dwells within both. This Indwelling is the basis of the living, evolving relationship between Israel and God. In order to maintain that holiness, atonement is necessary. Climaxing the sacred year, Yom Kippur focuses exclusively on repentance, rectification, and atonement. The atonement of the people, and of each and every individual within Israel, stands at the emotional apex of the holy year. Whereas during the festivals atonement is the underlying, unifying element, during Yom Kippur atonement is the only objective, the sole focal point.

The festivals celebrate the Land. Their focus is on rejoicing in God's mercy and goodness. The festivals center on the continual acknowledgment of God's fulfillment of His Covenant. Atonement is made for the Land through Israel's observance of the festivals. The result of this recurring rectification of Israel's behavior with God's Will is the vitalization and strengthening of the Covenant, which then brings divine blessing and peace. On Yom Kippur, the focus shifts and intensifies. On the Day of Atonement, the covenantal emphasis is placed squarely on Israel's obligations and responsibilities to God. Israel is to confess its sins, to admit its errors and transgressions in order to return to the path of the Law with a pure heart. It is Israel's relationship to the Covenant that marks the zenith of the religious and sacred year.

The theme of return, rectification, and harmonization with the Divine Will builds to a crescendo during the festivals and climaxes with the intense solemnity of Yom Kippur. The atonement theme in the holidays yields to the work of repentance and atonement on the part of the people on Yom Kippur. God's role in the Covenant is stressed in the observance of the holidays and festivals. At the apex of the sacred year, the emphasis is laid on Israel's faithfulness to its mission and its relationship to God. At this juncture in the flow of holy time, great scrutiny and attention are paid to Israel's consistency in living up to the role it assumed when undertaking the terms and obligations of the Covenant at Mount Sinai. This process of being held accountable climaxes the sacred year because it stands at the very heart of the Covenant, at the very core of Israel's mission.

The Covenant is a dynamic, living, and evolving relationship between Israel and God. It involves serving God, at all times and in all aspects of life: social, civil, familial, and ritual. God is served through consistency, devotion, righteousness, and justice. That is the underlying message behind the Law and the biblical record. That is the dominant message behind much of the Dead Sea literature.

Atonement keeps everything in balance and in harmony. Life is the river. Morality, justice, and service to God are the navigational process. Repentance, rectification, and atonement are the course corrections, the navigational tools.

At the end of the sacred year is the Festival of Booths, Sukkot. Sukkot marks the harvest holiday, the festival that celebrates God's abundance. The harvest is the outward manifestation of His supervision of the world, a direct result of His great love and compassion for creation. Within the context of the Torah, God's abundance at this time also bears a specific meaning in terms of the relationship between Israel and God. The rich bounty of Sukkot marks the reward for fulfilling the Covenant. It is the holiday of the Covenant's blessing.

In Exodus and in Deuteronomy, when God speaks of fulfilling the Covenant, He stresses both the blessing and the curse. In fulfilling the terms of the Covenant, the people are rewarded with God's blessing, which includes physical protection, peace in the Land, and a bountiful harvest. To violate the Law and breach the Covenant would bring divine wrath, destruction, and starvation.

The atonement process, which stretches from Shavuot through to Yom Kippur, serves to maintain, protect, and strengthen the Covenant. The reward for faithfulness to the Covenant is the abundant harvest of the Sukkot festival, which concludes the sacred section of the calendrical year. The message here is quite clear. The Covenant is a living dialogue between God and Israel. The relationship that it embodies is played out continually. The importance of fulfilling the Covenant is vividly illustrated annually as the drama of the sacred year plays itself out.

The sacred year consists of a long series of festivals and holy days that begin by celebrating the ability of Israel, as a free people, to serve God willingly and faithfully. Much of the sacred year, comprising the first seven months of the calendar year, emphasizes Israel's service to God and its mission to the world under the terms of the Sinai Covenant. The festivals emphasize God's fulfillment of His part of the covenantal agreement, through His bestowing of blessing, abundance, protection, and peace. Moreover, the festival celebrations stress Israel's continual observance of the Law as fulfillment of its obligation under the terms of the Covenant. Israel's covenantal obligations on a ritual level are met through its worship and through the processes of introspection, repentance, and atonement.

The culmination of the sacred year comes with the celebration of the Sukkot festival. The rich harvest that Sukkot gives thanks for is the concrete result of Israel's active participation in upholding, observing, and strengthening the Covenant. By maintaining its commitment to God and to fulfilling the terms of the Covenant, God's blessing, the Blessing of the Covenant, is earned and activated on an annual basis. The yearly sacred cycle then has a consistent and poignant message.

Beginning with Shavuot and ending with Sukkot, a dynamic relationship is played out between Israel and God. The Covenant is observed and its obligations are fulfilled. Constant awareness and vigilance are maintained. Mistakes and transgressions are acknowledged and rectified. The result is the emergence of reward. God blesses Israel with the Blessing of the Covenant. Both the Land and the people are blessed with divine inspiration and guidance, as well as with material prosperity. This comes as a direct consequence of the correct functioning of the Covenant, as a living interplay between Israel and God.

Passover, Shavuot, and Sukkot in the Book of Jubilees

At several junctures the Book of Jubilees speaks of the three major festivals. It is important to touch on some of this information in order to round out our understanding of the significance of the festivals, as understood by the Jewish world of the Greco-Roman era.

The Book of Jubilees refers to Passover as "a memorial." This term is also used in the Dead Sea material, as well as in later rabbinic literature, to describe Rosh Hashanah, which precedes Yom Kippur by ten days. As we have seen, the scrolls term this holiday a day of memorial, a day of the sounding of the *shofar*.

The term "memorial," *zikaron* in Hebrew, also has the meaning of actively reconnecting with something or someone. Take the following examples from Jewish liturgy: *Zecher Tzaddik LeV'rachah*, *Zecher LeYitziat Mitzrayim*, and *Zecher LeMikdash*.

The first phrase, "the memory of the righteous person is for a blessing," is an active principle. The implication is that by reconnecting with the reality of a righteous person who has passed on, through the memory of his or her life and deeds, one activates the same level of blessing that their actions did when they lived.

The second phrase, "the memory of the Exodus from Egypt," is connected with the observance of the Sabbath. It is equated, in the prayer over the Sabbath wine, with the Creation of the World. The Exodus from Egypt was a new creation, the emergence of the Jewish people. Observing the Sabbath leads to a renewal of Creation, in general, and a renewal of the Jewish people as well. The observance of the Sabbath prepares the way for revival and rebirth on a weekly basis. That is made possible, in part, by its active connection with the reality of the Creation itself and the events that led to the emergence of Israel as a people.

The concept of "remembering the Temple" is also not merely a passive process of recollection. Many of the prayers in the traditional liturgy recount in detail all of the sacrificial rituals. These prayers are meant to reconnect the individual with the reality of the sacrifices and the Temple service. Even though we cannot physically perform these services, they can be activated and participated in, through the mind and heart.

Memorial, or remembering in Jewish tradition, is a participatory process of connection and activation. It is an active endeavor, designed to maintain continuity and connection with past realities, thereby reactivating them. By so doing, they come to life and have a direct impact on our lives. This principle is quite operative in the Book of Jubilees and sheds great light on the emphasis placed on the festivals in the Dead Sea literature.

According to the Book of Jubilees, it is not sufficient merely to be ritually clean and purified for the festival of Passover and, presumably, for the other festivals and holy days as well. One must also be scrupulous in observing the festival at the appropriate time. Failure to do so would result in being permanently cut off from the Jewish people. One has to be in total harmony with the memorial of the Festival, both physically and spiritually.

If the Festival is kept properly and on time, for the coming year all plagues are averted. The Pascal offering is to be roasted in fire, but no bones are to be broken. If none of the bones of the Pascal offering are broken, none of Israel's bones will be broken in the coming year. That is, they will be free from war, disease, and oppression. Reconnection with the reality of the first Passover and its experiences reproduces the same concrete effects in the future if done properly and in a state of purity.

The Pascal offering was to be eaten in the Sanctuary, facing inward into the depths of the Sanctuary. This requirement, outlined in the Book of Jubilees, suggests that one of the deepest reasons for the eating of the Pascal offering was to assimilate the original experience of interacting directly with God and being led to freedom. That experience was one of being turned inward. Reconnection was to be made with God, God's Presence, and His Covenant.

The Book of Jubilees makes the observation that at the time when the first Passover was being observed, the people were in a state of great anxiety. Anxious they remained from that first night up to the point when they successfully crossed the Red Sea. This suggests that reenacting, remembering the events of the Exodus through the Passover ritual, brings those participating in the process through their current fears. Proper observance of the ritual recreates the original experience and reactivates it in the present. Those partaking of the ceremony are led from their current fears to emotional salvation and to physical security.

The second festival, that of Shavuot, connects heavily with the Covenant. What is interesting about the connection, as it is made in the Book of Jubilees, is that the emphasis is placed on the Covenant with Abraham. The implication here is that the Sinai Covenant is an extension of the one initiated through Abraham. The Book of Jubilees asserts that the Festival of Shavuot is the yearly renewal of the Covenant. This statement is an obvious reference to the Sinai Covenant. The full Covenant is actively renewed annually at this time. Yet its importance is derived from the connection it has with the patriarchal Covenant.

It was with Abraham that the Covenant was established. All of the terms of the Covenant with Abraham are seen by the Book of Jubilees as being directly associated with the Shavuot festival. God announces Himself as *El Shaddai*. He becomes Abraham's God and will be the God of all his descendants. Abraham's seed is to inherit the Land perpetually. As a sign of the covenant, Abraham and all of his offspring are to be circumcised from one generation to the next. As a sign of the transformation that takes place as result of the Covenant, Abram's and Sarai's names are changed to Abraham and Sarah.

Yearly, on Shavuot, the Covenant is renewed. The Jews participate in an eternal event of the utmost significance. What is being reaffirmed annually are not only the extensive terms of the Covenant, manifested in the Commandments and given by God at Mount Sinai, but more importantly, it is the reiteration and reenforcement of the original bond, binding Israel to God and vice versa.

It is the unique relationship between God and Israel that is being stressed here. This close relationship, originally established with Abraham, is seen as the underlying foundation for the broader Covenant spelled out at Sinai. The true importance of the Covenant is the bond it creates and affirms between God and the people of Israel, the descendants of Abraham. The Sinai revelation is an important extension of the Covenant. But its basis in the intimate interconnection with God is what is of core value.

Abraham initiated the Festival of Shavuot to celebrate the first fruits and to honor, and affirm, the Covenant. With the Covenant, a new relationship between man and God emerged in the world. Abraham and his descendants are the first fruits of this evolutionary step of God revealing Himself within the context of Creation. God asks Abraham to follow Him and to become perfected. The Covenant is the vehicle for intimacy with God, and that intimacy leads to being perfected.

The Book of Jubilees gives two interlocking meanings to the name "Shavuot." On one hand, "Shavuot" means "weeks." It refers to the seven weeks of the first agricultural cycle. The festival celebrates, then, the cycles of the Land and God's supervision and guidance in maintaining the regularity of growth and abundance. On the other hand, "Shavuot" is also the plural of *Shevu'ah*, meaning "oaths." Hence, "Shavuot" refers back to the various covenants God made with Noah, with Abraham, and with Israel. This festival emphasizes the continuity of the Covenant, rejoices in the intimacy between God and Israel, and celebrates the guiding hand of God over the Land He designated as His own.

The sacred year ends with the Sukkot Festival, which, like Shavuot, was initiated by Abraham, according to the Book of Jubilees. Abraham called this day "the Festival of the Lord." Abraham is said to have built booths and invented the *lulav*, the four species of vegetation that are waved during the worship service and in the booths. Abraham made offerings of thanksgiving to celebrate the bountiful harvest, the reward of the Covenant. The festival was the occasion for the expression of great joy.

Abraham is said to have sacrificed an offering of seven rams, seven sheep, seven lambs, and seven goats, with their meal offerings and libations, as an expression of pure joy and thanksgiving. He is said to have prayed seven times during the day. This information suggests a strong emphasis being placed on the Sabbath principle, in reference to the nature of Sukkot. Sukkot, being the last festival of the sacred year, is not only one of thanksgiving and joy but also a celebration marking conclusion, transcendence, and rest. The seven-month sacred cycle is brought to a conclusion with the celebration of Sukkot. The Land comes to the point of rest, and the great Sabbath of the year commences. The people who have interacted so intensely with God, who have gone through a long process of service, repentance, and atonement, have earned a rest. They have come to a point of transcendence and tranquility. They have achieved a Sabbath of the Soul, their relationship to God reaffirmed and revitalized, in the pursuit of perfection, wholeness, and holiness. Next year, the work will start again.

10

VIEWING THE SCROLLS' LEGAL MATERIAL

Considering the enormous importance placed on the Covenant in the Dead Sea literature as a whole, it is rather noteworthy that only a couple of scrolls actually discuss any of the laws or commandments, per se. This point is worthy of particular attention, when one remembers that the commandments and their observance lie at the very heart of the Covenant. The Law is the articulation of the Covenant.

Legal issues are mentioned in the Damascus Covenant, the Temple Scroll, the MMT letter, and in the fragmentary Ordinance and Purification texts. Admittedly, these texts are major ones. Yet in terms of the scope of the literature itself, the total percentage of texts dealing with any legal issues at all is surprisingly small. Moreover, as will be seen, the issues that actually are addressed are very specific in content.

The laws that are enumerated in the literature fall into several classifications. These classifications allow us to correlate the commandments and to perceive their emphasis, the focal points of concern that the literature has. It is important to point out that there seems to be an underlying organic connection between them. A large proportion of the laws mentioned are those that concern ritual purity. It is this issue, purity, the prerequisite of holiness, that is the unifying thread connecting the laws articulated and stressed in the literature.

First, there are the various purity laws enunciated. Connected to them is a second group of commandments, which deal with oaths and vows. Both sets of laws are related directly to the Temple. Ritual purity relates to accessing the Temple, participation in the Temple ritual, and the handling and eating of the sacrifices. Vows and oaths relate to the sanctity of gifts and donations made to the Temple, as well as the sanctification of one's actions and deeds.

We find, among the scrolls, laws involving idolatry, laws concerning the perversion of justice, as well as those concerning false prophets. These laws, too, are related to purity and holiness but from a slightly different direction. Corruption, idolatry, and false prophecy are phenomena that constitute rebellion against God and pollution of the Land. They attack the heart of the Covenant, by denying God and repudiating God's Law.

Ritual impurity erects a temporary barrier to serving God. It is a brief state of ineligibility, disallowing one to stand in God's Presence or to touch that which is sacred, when one is not whole. That which is impure, is incomplete and therefore is not to be associated with the holy. Yet impurity is also viewed as a process of being healed. It leads to purification. Its regularity is noted, and prescribed rituals exist to render a person clean when the process completes its course.

Idolatry, false prophecy, and corruption also create impurity, but are of a far more damaging nature. They serve to violate the intimacy between man and God, and as such, they create a level of impurity that is unholy, not merely unclean. Whereas ritual uncleanliness is seen as part of the flow of life, idolatry and corruption are rebellion. While the former is capable of purification and no evil is imputed to it, in the case of the latter, the end result is destruction. Either the evil is destroyed and rooted out, or the phenomena brings destruction in its wake.

There is in biblical literature and in Second Temple literature considerable emphasis placed on this point. The practices of idolatry are a prime source of contamination and destruction. They are a contamination of the spirit. They constitute pollution of the Land and lead to a destructive corrosion of the relationship to God. These practices lead away from God and deny the fundamental relationship established between God and Israel. The result is the violation of the Covenant and the arousal of Divine retribution.

Hence, the laws dealt with in the Dead Sea literature are very specific in focus and are closely interrelated. The laws and practices enunciated center on the issues of purity and service to God. This specific focus is not hard to understand when one realizes that the core of the Dead Sea legal literature centers on Levitical law—that is, laws dealing with the Temple and the Temple service. One obvious reason for this would seem to be that the Sectarians and/or the Essenes were a priest-led community that broke off from the Jerusalem Temple. Emphasizing the differences that led to the formation and maintenance of these groups would be quite natural.

What is of note is that within the entire complex system of laws encompassed by the Torah, by Mosaic Law, only these issues of purity appear in the legal corpus of the Dead Sea material. Central to the Covenant are the laws and commandments. The commandments cover a vast range of ritual, civil, criminal, familial, and moral laws. Yet within the large corpus of Qumranic literature, only a few areas connected with purity and holiness are touched upon in the legal materials. There are a couple of ways of interpreting this paradox.

The first is to assume that this literature is predominantly a collection of materials put together by the Sectarians of Qumran or by another Essene group. Since they were a priestly community who were at odds with the Jerusalem priesthood and broke off to form an independent approach, the emphasis in the documents would logically revolve around the Levitical issues that set them apart from Jerusalem and the Temple.

A second view would be that this literature encompasses a broad spectrum of opinions, representing a wide array of approaches to Judaism from all over Israel. Since the legal literature is very consistent in viewpoint and deals specifically with issues relating to purity and holiness, a couple of conclusions may be drawn.

One would be that the issues of ritual purity, idolatry, and corruption were the central concerns of much of the Jewish world during the Greco-Roman period. There is confirmation of this view in Josephus, in Philo, and in tannaitic literature, in the *Mishnah* and *Tosefta*. In his narratives, Josephus frequently mentions examples of greed, intolerance, perversion of justice, violence, and sexual immorality as the manifestations of the corruption that led to Israel's plight and downfall. Philo dedicates considerable space to discussions of ritual purity in his treatises on the commandments. One complete order of the *Mishnah*, consisting of twelve tractates, deals exclusively with matters revolving around ritual purity, as do the parallel tractates in the *Tosefta*. A thirteenth tractate, *Avodah Zarah*, is dedicated exclusively to issues revolving around association with anything that is contaminated by contact with pagan worship.

A second conclusion could be that the absence of mention of other laws and commandments would strongly suggest that apart from certain important issues revolving around purity and service to God, there was a general consensus within Israel regarding the observance of the majority of the commandments, at least during this period of time. This argument is much more tenuous.

One should bear in mind the wide range of legal questions and concerns that are raised and debated in the *Mishnah*. The *Mishnah* was compiled not that long after the Roman period reached its zenith. A logical assumption would be, then, that many of these issues must have been debated over a long period of time. Hence, the mishnaic discussions are characteristic of concerns that traverse the Greco-Roman period, before any consensus emerged.

It is very possible that there existed at one time a far more extensive legal literature than has survived or has been discovered. That does not mean that the concerns about purity, ritual cleanliness, and the state of holiness were not central issues to the Jewish people as a whole during this period of time. Rather, the singularity of the legal literature found at Qumran represents a unique perspective on an important and extensive subject of interest during the Second Temple period. What has been preserved for us are the clearly defined views held on this subject by a specific community within Israel.

How the Purity Laws Are Stated and What They Tell Us

According to the Temple Scroll, separate areas were set up or were to be set up outside of Jerusalem for segregating various groups of people with different impurities. There were to be separate areas set aside for those suffering from leprosy, from plague, from skin disruptions, from the flux of sexual emissions, from menstruation, and from the aftermath of a birth.

Therefore, we are to understand that it was not sufficient merely to separate a person in a ritually impure state from the general population; such individuals were to be separated from each other as well. This suggests the idea that ritual impurity was not considered to be a single, undifferentiated category. Rather, there were degrees of impurity. Different conditions rendered one ritually impure. Ritual impurities were distinct realities from one another and although the effect of the uncleanliness was the same, the nature and causes of the impurities were not universally identical. Neither were the means by which they were purified after the impurity had passed and healing had taken place. Just as there were degrees of holiness, there were degrees of uncleanliness. Each had to be considered and treated independently from the others.

Not only was the affected individual barred from contact with the holy Temple, he or she was kept at a distance from the Holy City of Jerusalem, as well. We are told that only a person in a pure physical state can enter Jerusalem. Entrance by one not in a state of wholeness and holiness would profane the City. This is a logical enough precaution. Since contact with a person who was ritually unclean, or contact with a dead body, which is necessarily unclean, would render whatever it touched unclean in turn, the Law (as elaborated in the Temple Scroll) is protecting the continual operation of the Covenant.

Should a person who is ritually unclean enter the Temple, the Temple and everything in it would become unfit for divine service, de facto. As a result of being ritually contaminated, the Temple would render impure all who came in contact with it, until the time of impurity passed and the purification rites were completed. As such, for a period of time ranging from days to months, the entire Temple service—so important in maintaining the Covenant and the service to God—would grind to an abrupt halt. This would be, from the spiritual standpoint, absolutely catastrophic. The flow of divine energy, which sustains Israel and the world, would be cut off. There would be no functioning receptacle to contain and to handle it. Moreover, it would constitute a grave disruption in Israel's ability to fulfill her covenantal obligations. That alone could trigger off divine wrath.

In order to preclude this dire possibility, the scrolls prescribe certain precautionary measures to be taken. Some of these precautions are more extensive than in biblical law itself. As we have seen, the impure were segregated from each other. This was to make sure that a person's impurity was identifiable and uncomplicated by a second form of uncleanliness. This way, there was a clear way of tracking the purification process and of being assured that the person, when purified, was completely clean and free from any other potential contaminant.

The impure person was excluded not only from the Temple, but from Jerusalem as well. This accords with the biblical injunction about moving the unclean outside the Camp. The logic remains the same as in the case of excluding the impure from the Temple. If a person in a state of ritual impurity entered Jerusalem, it would convey secondary impurity on the Temple. Though the length of time and the degree of impurity involved would not be quite as extensive, the repercussions would remain just as severe.

Within the Temple Scroll and the Damascus Covenant, there is a tendency to extend the purity laws to areas not explicitly covered by biblical law. In the Temple Scroll, the period of impurity for a man having nocturnal emissions is extended from one day to three days. Moreover, there is an inclusion into the category of uncleanliness caused by nocturnal emissions, of one who has had sexual intercourse with his wife. No such equation is made in biblical literature between nocturnal emission and sexual emission. Another extension relates to impurity conveyed by contact with a corpse. The corpse impurity, normally contracted by exposure to a dead body, is extended to include coming into contact with a slain person, the bone of a dead person in the field, or the blood of a deceased individual.

The Damascus Covenant renders impure anything of wood, stone, or dirt that has been exposed to a man's impurity. Not just the walls, ceiling, doors, and vessels of a dead man's house are rendered impure by the corpse, but according the Damascus Covenant, the impurity extends to nails, pegs, and tools as well. The tendency is to be very careful to protect the welfare of the people. The enormous concern placed on ritual cleanliness and on avoiding ritual contamination is because it is not just a matter of personal suffering and the need for healing.

Rather, ritual impurity can adversely affect the Temple service as a whole and thereby interfere with the flow of energy between man and God. These laws, as expressed, all reflect the same sense of extreme caution being exercised when the issue is the holy services and the fulfillment of the Covenant. Every precaution must be taken to prevent the contamination of and the interruption of Israel's covenantal obligation of service to God.

This would also account for what could be called, "the three-day rule." One impure from a seminal emission and one having sexual intercourse were barred by the MMT and the Temple Scroll from entering Jerusalem and the Temple for three days. The Temple Scroll stipulates that no clean animal could be slaughtered within a three-day journey of Jerusalem. Scroll 11QT 43:12–15 sets the exact same three-day boundary for tithes. One could exchange tithes for money and use the money to buy substitute produce in Jerusalem to fulfill one's obligation only if one lived beyond a three-day journey to the Temple.

Professor Lawrence Schiffman observes (*Revue de Qumran*, January 1990) that the concept of three-days' separation is based on the Sinai model. The people of Israel were required to prepare for three days in advance of the Revelation at Mount Sinai. The Revelation, the face-to-face meeting with God that produced the Covenant, could only take place at the appropriate time, at the appropriate place, and with proper preparation. The MMT and Temple Scroll assume the same conditions need be present to serve God.

Facing God meant a combination of proper preparation, clear timing, and appropriate distance. As Professor Schiffman points out, the rabbinic attitude was that the slaughter of an animal at the wrong time rendered it ritually impure. Whereas, the Temple Scroll stresses that ritual impurity can be created by a spatial violation—that is, if an animal is sacrificed in the wrong location.

According to the Temple Scroll, column 52, if a clean animal were slaughtered within the three-mile radius of Jerusalem, even though it was slaughtered in a legal manner, its meat is *piggul*, "unfit for consumption," because the process took place in the wrong location. It took place in an area in which only sacrificial slaughter was permitted and then only within the Temple according to prescribed ritual. The concept being emphasized is that fulfillment of the ritual obligations of the Covenant require a state of purity. That state of purity is predicated on proper preparation and the performance of the holy work at the appropriate time and the appropriate place.

Fulfillment of the Covenant was not possible in a state of impurity. God's relationship to Israel is a pure one. Israel's service to God has to be pure as well. The state of impurity, on one hand, comes about via contamination. As it is being interpreted by the scrolls, impurity is also the direct result of adulteration.

In the MMT letter, lines 48 and 49 instruct Israel to revere the Sanctuary and to avoid the sin of forbidden unions. The forbidden unions mentioned are the biblical prohibitions against marrying or having intimate relations with an Ammonite, a Moabite, one born out of an incestuous relationship, one with crushed testicles, or one who has been castrated. Prohibited unions also included those liaisons forbidden by biblical law to the priests, such as marrying a prostitute or a divorcee.

In the view of the authors of the MMT, priests who married illegally or had illicit relations polluted the holy seed of the priesthood. By so doing, the potential existed for the pollution of Temple services, the priesthood being contaminated and unfit to serve. Moreover, from the standpoint of the MMT, priests marrying illegally or involving themselves with forbidden liaisons were not only violating the direct biblical commandments to that effect, but were also transgressing the commandments to keep separate that which should not be mixed.

The psychology here is of interest in understanding the thinking of the Sectarian Community. To involve oneself, as a priest, in an illicit relationship is a grave sin, in and of itself. By so doing, one's ability to function as a priest was destroyed. The moral responsibility for these actions was enormous. Yet the MMT stresses that there is an even deeper dimension to this transgression—that of abomination. The MMT quotes the biblical injunction "not to bring abomination into your house." It interprets this to mean that when a priest violates the legal perimeters of priestly marriage, he is mixing seed and defiling the priesthood through adulteration.

The legal literature of Qumran emphasizes not only ritual impurity as a contaminant that cripples service to God and prevents fulfillment of the Covenant, but it also regards adulteration in the exact same light. A clear example of this comes from the MMT letter. The MMT equates an illicit priestly marriage, say the marriage of a priest to a harlot, with the violation of the various biblical laws prohibiting admixture. There are important biblical laws prohibiting the sowing of a field with mixed species of seed, the making of clothing with mixed fibers, the cross-breeding of animals, and the plowing of a field with two different animals yoked together. The implication of all these various laws is that mixing two different things together produces adulteration.

Such adulteration creates impurity, renders things unfit for divine service, and is a potential contaminant, capable of interfering with the observance of one's obligations to God. This concept has strong biblical roots. Consider the case of a person being cleared of leprosy. A priest declared a person clean if either the leprosy completely healed or, conversely, if it completely covered the entire body and turned the skin consistently white. Either way, the person was considered whole and therefore clean, because there was no admixture in the skin's condition. That is, there was no adulteration.

The concept here seems to be that any kind of admixture occurring in an otherwise consistent state created a changed reality. That changed reality was one of corruption through adulteration. Adulteration produced a state similar in effect to ritual impurity, which moved one beyond the state of holiness. Ritual impurity often came about through normal physical function and could be cleansed and pronounced whole after it had run its course. Adulteration, however, had to be avoided to begin with, because it was not a natural occurrence; it was the result of a conscious choice. It was a sin and had to be handled as such. It could have irreparable consequences. If this were true of actions that created adulteration, how much more so would this be true for immoral behavior?

Purity as Moral Behavior

An underlying premise that is spelled out clearly in the Qumran literature is that separation from impurity also means separation from an impure moral life. As discussed earlier, the Damascus Covenant outlines three major moral snares that trap an individual, pervert his soul, hold him in darkness, and render him impure. These are the lures of the Sons of Darkness, the People of the Pit, who rebel against God, corrupt those around them, and destroy the Covenant.

The three snares are labeled "fornication," "riches," and "profanation of the Temple." Both fornication and profanation of the Temple are closely related. They are described in related terms. Fornication is defined as polygamy. Profanation of the Temple encompasses sleeping with a woman during menstruation and any form of incestuous relationship. Both evils involve sexual relations.

As discussed earlier, Profanation of the Temple is also seen as rejection of the Law. The Damascus Covenant states that anyone who says that the laws are uncertain—that is, they repudiate the law and exempt themselves from it—is guilty of blasphemy. Blasphemy is a deliberate rebellion against God and under biblical law is punishable by death.

A repudiation of the Law is a break with the Covenant. It is not merely a rejection of some laws. It is a rejection of the entire Law. Since the Law has at its very basis morality and moral behavior, a rejection of the Law is a positive affirmation of evil. For a Jew to repudiate the Law of Moses is not only to violate the Covenant, it is to rebel against God, to reject the moral imperative upon which the Law is founded, and to imperil both the nation and one's own soul.

Two of the snares of evil deal with violating personal intimacy. The issues of polygamy and illicit sexual relations center on the relationship between man and woman. The most intimate human relationship is between a husband and wife. A violation of that deep personal intimacy renders one unclean and impure, thereby destroying the intimacy between the individual and God.

Another form of intimacy is judicial honesty and public trust. A judge holds another person's life in his hand, both literally and figuratively. Those involved in a court case are placing their trust in the judge, his honesty, integrity, and sense of justice. The judge's decision impacts heavily on the lives of all concerned. This is why the Temple Scroll not only reiterates the biblical prohibitions against accepting bribes, showing partiality, and perverting judgement, but goes one step further. It also stipulates that those who accept bribes and render unjust verdicts are to be executed. Such behavior perverts justice, the result being pollution of the Land.

This principle is enunciated further in the Damascus Covenant. Here, one is forbidden to denounce another in anger or to haul someone to court merely to humiliate him. No member of the Sectarian Community can accuse someone without having first rebuked him and undertaken the responsibility of helping his neighbor avoid sin. No judge is to pass a death sentence based on any testimony by such a non-God-fearing individual, and no person who willfully transgresses the Law can serve as a witness until he has gone through the entire repentance process and has been purified.

Moral purity and ritual purity are conceptually interconnected in the Qumran literature. There are continual exhortations in the scrolls to distance oneself from the moral corruption of the Sons of Darkness, who hold the Covenant and the Law in contempt. There is a conceptual link made between moral corruption and the deliberate violation or abrogation of the Law. That moral corruption is the counterpart to ritual impurity on an inner level.

The term *anshei hashahat*, which the scrolls use as an alternative description of the Sons of Darkness, can be translated in two ways. If you read the word strictly as a noun, the phrase would mean "People of the Pit." The pit implies degradation and death. Garbage is cast into a pit. In biblical times, and presumably in later centuries as well, prisoners were cast into pits. Both the patriarch Joseph and the Prophet Jeremiah are famous examples of individuals being despised by contemporaries and cast into a pit, to be left to die.

Someone being described as a "Person of the Pit" would imply, on one level, having an unsavory life style so pernicious as to warrant death. One could look at the term from the vantage point of Deuteronomy as well. Being a "Person of the Pit" could also refer to the idea that instead of choosing life—that is, the path of the commandments and service to God—these individuals chose death. That is, they chose the path of rebellion against the Covenant.

The Pit also alludes to falling into a trap or setting a trap. The term "People of the Pit" stresses the concept that not only are these people corrupt themselves, but they actively seek to corrupt others. They have fallen into the trap of corruption and seek to ensnare others. This idea of moral corruption as the source of spiritual impurity is reinforced, if you read the word *shahat* as a verb root. The verb root *Sh-H-T* means "to corrupt or become corrupt." The term refers to decay and putrefaction. Both of these phenomena are the aftermath of death. Contact with death brings on a state of impurity.

Proper observance of the Torah and the Commandments involves full compliance with the Law of God. On a physical level, this is only possible in a state of ritual purity. Yet purity also has a nonphysical dimension. The strictures of biblical law encompass all aspects of life—personal, familial, social, and cultic. Just as one must be ritually pure to observe the cultic requirements of the Law, so, too, one must be morally pure to fulfill all the commandments, the substance of the Covenant with God.

Avoidance of rebellion and of evil, on one hand, and faithful adherence to the Law and the Covenant, on the other, constitute the moral purity necessary for maintaining intimacy with God. Observance of the Law is adherence to the strong moral imperative that is the basis of the Covenant and is the foundation of all the commandments. The laws are the form. The moral basis of the laws constitutes their content and meaning. This is the cornerstone of the message of the scrolls.

The Laws Concerning Idolatry and Spiritual Corruption

As has been pointed out earlier, immoral behavior and spiritual impurity are linked together, in the Dead Sea Literature, with the issue of idolatry. In the Qumran documents, idolatry personifies moral corruption. Idolatry embodies the repudiation and the violation of the Covenant. Abandonment of the Covenant involves movement away from the commandments and the moral law upon which they are based. Immorality then takes on the mantle of respectability and the result is the pollution of the Land. In his writings, Josephus decries the pollution of the Land. Josephus identifies pollution of the Land with the rise and prevalence of lawlessness, bloodshed, and violence. Hence, idolatry is linked with moral degeneration and social breakdown.

As such, idolatry was a complete anathema. In the Temple Scroll, a number of biblical laws are restated, which are prohibitions of practices common in pagan worship. They include the prohibitions against graven images, using sacred trees or pillars for purposes of worship, the prohibition of gashing of the skin, of tattooing of the body, and of eating meat with the blood remaining in it. Israelites are instructed neither to cut their hair during the process of mourning, nor to follow the pagan practice of burying the dead everywhere. Since a dead body conveyed ritual uncleanliness, it was to be buried only in designated areas, not in basements, homes, or fields.

The Damascus Covenant forbids the selling of anything to idolaters that could in any way be used as an offering or in their ritual worship. This concept is the subject of lengthy legal debate in both the *Mishnah* and the *Tosefta*. Not only was one to refrain from imitating idolatrous practice, one was not to defile oneself by even indirectly participating in idolatrous worship, even inadvertently. During the Second Temple period, the involvement of Jews in idolatry per se was not an issue. However, idolatrous practice was seen to be a source of corruption and immorality. As such, it was a moral contaminant that could pollute the Land and incur divine wrath.

Hence, anything connected with idolatry was considered a source of moral impurity and ethical corruption. As one had to stay away from the "People of the Pit," who deliberately violate the Covenant and trigger the Curse, so, too, did one have to stay far from idolatry, both directly and indirectly. Worship of God could not be polluted by the inclusion of pagan practices and no validation could be given to idolatry, even inadvertently, by supplying anything to those who could, in turn, use what they had received to honor other gods.

In the Dead Sea literature, idolatry is used as a metaphor for rebellion against God and the moral turpitude that is the inevitable result of breaching the Covenant and the relationship with God. The

Damascus Covenant labels "riches" as one of the three great snares of the forces of rebellion. They define this evil as both the unlawful accumulation of wealth by immoral means and the worship of gold and silver. Idolatry is equated both with greed and with placing one's faith in wealth and power instead of in God.

The worship of power and wealth leads to an overpowering drive to accumulate riches and retain control. Such a drive is all-consuming. Ambition, greed, and self-aggrandizement take over. One is pushed to forge ahead at all costs. Such behavior justifies evil and corruption as necessary and good. The results of this devotion to power are oppression, violence, bloodshed, death, and destruction. Idolatry is seen as a moral sickness, a source of spiritual pollution that leads to physical catastrophe.

Idolatry is the great evil. It is the force opposing God. A person can follow only one path at a time. People can put their full faith in only one place. Either it is in God or it is in Mammon (wealth). Those are the options. In discussing a false prophet—that is, one who performs signs, makes predictions that come true, and then turns around and advocates serving other gods—the Temple Scroll points out that this is rebellion against God. Consequently, this "prophet" must be put to death. This evil must be eradicated from the Land.

According to the Temple Scroll, God allows prophets like this to arise as a test. In essence, this is the supreme test. Are the people going to accept this call to apostasy and abandon God, or are they going to repudiate, in the strongest possible terms, this evil and its contagion?

The Damascus Covenant states that anyone preaching apostasy is to be judged by the law of familiar spirits. This statement connects false prophecy directly to idolatry and condemns it in the most severe terms. Necromancy was commonly associated with pagan religious practice. An important component of idolatrous experience was communicating with the dead and with familiar spirits. No doubt precisely for that reason, Biblical law prescribes the death penalty for anyone invoking familiar spirits. Moreover, the law regarding false prophets appears together in the Temple Scroll with the laws pertaining to both an individual and a city found to be worshiping other gods.

By emphasizing idolatry, the scrolls are coming back to the issue of rebellion against God. Idolatry is being used as the symbol for rebellion and for the desertion of the Law. The assertion in the literature is clear. There is a primal choice to be made. Place your faith and trust in God or in earthly power. Placing your allegiance in gold and silver, in power and money is to withdraw faith from God and from the Covenant. This leads not only to a primal violation of the God–Israel relationship; such an apostasy produces, as a result, moral degeneration and the disintegration of the social fabric. Thus, the life of the nation is physically and spiritually polluted, and this corruption produces a state of impurity that makes it impossible for God's Presence to dwell in the midst of the people.

The Laws Regarding Vows and Oaths

In both the Temple Scroll and the Damascus Covenant, the biblical laws regarding making vows and taking oaths are repeated and, occasionally, restated. One apparent reason for their appearance in the literature is that the Dead Sea materials tend to focus on laws that revolve around the Temple. Vows and oaths were issues that involved God and the Temple.

When one made a vow, something was dedicated to God. It was transferred to the Temple by the action of vowing, which was an act of dedication. That which was vowed became sacrosanct and the sole legitimate province of the priests. One could vow a field, for instance, to the Temple. By so doing, the field technically became the property of the Temple. As such, no one other than the priests could touch it or make any use of it, because it was now consecrated to God and thus holy.

Effectively, what this meant was that when a person vowed something, he or she was voluntarily giving something up, forgoing something that otherwise would be permissible. This could range from the tangible to the intangible. In the case of a field, the access to and the use of the field were given up. On the other side of the coin, one could give up contact with a relative. By declaring that any contact with "so and so" was *korban* (that is, it was of the same status as a sacrificial offering), any possible relationship or interaction with that person would be cut off permanently.

A voluntary oath was a statement sworn in God's name whereby the person swearing was promising to do something or refrain from doing something, under pain of a curse. When making an oath, a person swore to do something and also invoked a specific curse that was to be brought upon himself, if he failed to fulfill the terms of the oath. Fulfillment of an oath was required, even if it resulted in harm or damage coming to the person undertaking it. In biblical literature, the terms *alah* ("curse") and *shevu'ah* ("oath") are often used concurrently and are sometimes used interchangeably.

Oaths were also used to confirm the truth of one's words. In a court case, if either no witnesses or only one witness were present at the time of an event in question, the plaintiff could require an exculpatory oath from the defendant. By taking the oath, the defendant backed the veracity of his statement by swearing in God's Name to its truth and calling a curse upon himself, if this were not the case in fact.

Vows and Oaths in the Temple Scroll and the Damascus Covenant

Before exploring the question of why the laws of vows and oaths are part of the legal corpus of the Dead Sea Scrolls at all, it is important to discuss briefly the laws themselves, their relationship to biblical law, and the light they shed on the evolution of Jewish law during the Second Temple period.

The biblical laws regarding vows, found in Numbers 30:3–16 and in Deuteronomy 23:22–24, can be summarized as follows:

1. When a man vows or binds an oath to God, he is obligated to fulfill it as it was articulated. Not to fulfill it is to profane his word.
2. Whatever a person vows with his lips must be fulfilled exactly as it was vowed. It is to be considered like a freewill offering, because it was freely committed to.
3. God will require fulfillment of the vowed obligation and it must be fulfilled promptly. Failure to do so is a deliberate sin.
4. It is certainly no sin if one refrains from making a vow in the first place. Vowing is not obligatory on anyone.
5. If a young woman still living in her father's house makes a vow and her father hears it and yet remains silent, he is acquiescing to the vow. Therefore, the vow stands.
6. If, on the day that the father hears it, he annuls the vow, it is canceled and God will not hold the young woman responsible.

7. The same rules apply to a husband. If he hears his wife's vow and annuls it on the day he heard it, it is canceled and there is no blame. If he remains silent, the vow remains valid.
8. If a husband remains silent, allowing the vows to remain valid and then later annuls them, he becomes responsible for the violation of the vows. The guilt is on his head.
9. The vow of a widow or divorcée stands valid in any case.

In the Damascus Covenant, which parallels the Temple Scroll in its rendition of these laws, a commentary is made on some of these provisions. The shift in emphasis is noteworthy.

Column 16, line 7 of the Damascus Covenant defines "fulfilling one's vows" as carrying them out. The phrase in Deuteronomy 23:24 "what comes forth out of your mouth" is equated with "a binding oath." The Damascus Covenant is equating the biblical laws regarding vows with oaths. The same laws and provisions are seen to cover both. This correspondence is even more explicitly stated in the Temple Scroll. "A man who makes a vow to Me or promises under oath, binding himself with a formal pledge, shall not break his word. . . . [A] woman who makes a vow or binds herself with a formal pledge in the house of her father, with an oath . . . (11Q19, col. 13, ll. 14–16). The biblical laws regarding vows are expanded in the Dead Sea literature to cover oaths as well. Hence, any verbal commitment made to God is seen to be the same and therefore bound by the same laws. The emphasis is shifted from the issue of dedication of something to God, to the issue of honoring one's voluntary commitment to God.

After making it clear that one must fulfill by action one's vow or oath, the Damascus Covenant goes on to say that if one has vowed to fulfill a commandment, it must be done even at the cost of one's life. Conversely, if one has vowed to violate a commandment, it must be annulled and cannot be fulfilled even at the cost of one's life (11Q19, col. 16, ll. 8–9).

What seems to be detailed here is one of the main criteria to be considered in determining whether or not a vow should be held valid or should be annulled. The implication of this restatement of the law is that any vow connected with the Law itself, with any of the commandments, is absolutely valid precisely because it involves the Law and the Covenant. The vow reinforces by oral commitment the imperative of fulfilling the commandment. Under no circumstances can the commandment involved be left unfulfilled or left undone.

Moreover, any attempt at committing to an abrogation of a law is automatically null and void. The vow accepting the Covenant, taken at Mount Sinai by the entire Jewish people, and the vow taken by the Sectarians to bind their lives permanently to the Covenant and faithfully observe all its provisions take precedence over any subsequent vow regarding obedience to the Law. Because the Law is binding on all Jews permanently, one cannot choose whether or not to be bound by the Law or to observe the Commandments.

Therefore, an oath only reinforces one's commitment. Since a vow is sacred and one is bound to make good on it, a vow to observe a commandment is an act of voluntary devotion. A vow to violate a commandment would be an act of rebellion. The latter, therefore, is null and void by nature. Failing to observe a commandment, particularly after having given one's word and having dedicated such an action to God, would be a willful and deliberate violation of the Law. So, too, would be upholding a negative vow and transgressing a commandment after having deliberately stated your intention to do so. Both courses of action constitute a capital offense.

In reality, a great many issues connected with vows would touch on the commandments, either directly or indirectly. Since vowing itself involved the act of consecrating something to God, this paradigm serves as a very clear guideline for determining whether or not a vow is valid. The principle being stated is that if a vow supports the Law, if it is in harmony with it, then the vow is incontrovertibly valid. If, on the other hand, the vow would violate the Law, it is absolutely invalid. The former must be fulfilled at all costs. The latter has to be annulled and its fulfillment avoided at all costs.

This criterion clarifies the position of a man making a vow. Since there are no provisions made in the Torah for the abrogation of a vow, this principle serves to establish what is truly a vow and what is not. Moreover, a father or husband can be put into a position of having to decide whether or not to let the vow of his daughter or wife stand. Since no criteria for making that decision is included in biblical law, a criterion is being established here. This principle not only provides a guideline for the man involved, it would prevent the father or husband from making an arbitrary decision regarding his daughter's or wife's wishes.

In Scroll 11Q19, lines 11 and 12 of column 16, it is stated that if a wife's vows are to perform a commandment, the vow is to be upheld. If, on the other hand, her vow is to violate a commandment, the husband is to annul it. If, however, it is not clear whether a vow should be validated or annulled (implying it does not involve a commandment, per se), the vow is to be left standing.

The Damascus Covenant thus sets down the conditions by which vows are to be judged and held valid. It clarifies the criteria for a man regarding his own vows and circumscribes the prerogatives of the father or husband by establishing precise guidelines.

Examining a Root Assumption

In examining the question of why the laws on vows and oaths are included in the restricted legal corpus of the Dead Sea material, we touch on a deeper stratum of meaning. Many of the laws of the Torah are not present in the legal materials found at Qumran. This could simply be a fluke of history. That is, these are the only scrolls of their kind that happened to survive the ravages of time. Doubtless, more legal materials may be found in the future. It is by no means inconceivable to assume that much of this literature was lost over the centuries.

Yet among the materials that have survived, there is a remarkable uniformity of content and style behind them. The assumption could be made, then, that there are organic connections that link them together and that perhaps there is a consistent viewpoint that emerges from them—a connection not just in terms of subject matter and the conclusions drawn, but also in terms of spiritual perspective.

The key to understanding the spiritual concern and the inner, core assumption the legal material makes regarding vows and oaths may be to consider the question of the punishment involved for violating an oath.

Although there are no external, legal sanctions in biblical law for violation of an oath, its violation was seen as bringing down the wrath of God on the violator. Since God's Name was invoked, not only was the violator subject to the curse included in the oath, but more importantly, the taking of a false oath is a violation of the Third Commandment (Exodus 20:7 and Deuteronomy 5:11).

From the standpoint of Jewish belief, in general, punishment for a false oath rests in God's hands. From the viewpoint of the scrolls, the violation of an oath could also be tied to even more serious consequences, to the curse involved in willful disregard of the Covenant.

Deuteronomy 29:18–19 states, "When such a one hears the words of these sanctions, he may fancy himself immune, thinking, 'I shall be safe, though I follow my own willful heart' . . . The Lord will never forgive him. Rather, the Lord's anger and passion will rage against that man, until every sanction recorded in this book comes down upon him and the Lord blots out his name from under heaven."

This injunction refers to a person who seeks to abandon God and the Covenant, preferring to follow the dictates of his or her own will, rather than the Will of God. The worship of one's own desires is viewed in the Qumran literature as akin to the worship of other gods. The laws prohibiting idolatry are, as we have seen, some of the select biblical laws specifically included in the scroll material. It is not a far reach to assume that there are organic links between the various laws mentioned in the scrolls and that certain connections can be made by implication.

The inclusion, in the scroll literature, of the laws relating to vows and oaths along with those directed against idolatry would suggest the possibility that in the view of the authors of the Damascus Covenant and the Temple Scroll, violating a vow or an oath, like idolatry, was a deliberate repudiation of the Covenant on some level. The curses that underlie all oaths, therefore, may have a direct connection to the Curse of the Covenant.

A deliberate repudiation of the Covenant breaks the bond with God. Such a violation incurs God's wrath and brings on the fulfillment of the curse enunciated in Deuteronomy. The scrolls seem to equate a willful disregard for an oath or vow made in the same light. It brings down the curses that were invoked at the time the commitment was undertaken. There is a distinct parallel. Both involve a deliberate break with God. Both result in the fulfillment of the curse.

Moreover, vows and oaths are taken in God's Name. Failure to honor an oath or vow is to take God's Name in vain. Failing to fulfill a vow or an oath made in God's Name is a repudiation of God, in much the same way that serving other gods would be. They both constitute abandonment of God and of one's obligations to Him.

Oaths were sworn in the Name of God (*BaShem*), by the Presence of God (*nefesh HaShem*), and by the living God (*chai HaShem*). These three terms seem synonymous. The Name of God is synonymous with the divine Presence and the power of God. The terms are all, in fact, interchangeable in usage when undertaking an oath. They reflect collectively the concept of God's interactive Presence within Creation. One is swearing an oath by connecting it directly to the divine vitality that pervades the world. To violate a promise made in connection with an affirmation of God's immanence in the universe is to betray God Himself. It is the same type of betrayal of God that a repudiation of the Covenant would entail. The consequences then would be just as dire.

Vows and oaths represent undertaking a commitment, acting truthfully, and validating one's honesty and devotion voluntarily. One is freely giving one's word. One is assuming an obligation, in God's Name, and is dedicating a course of action to God's service. By failing to fulfill such an obligation, one discredits oneself by denying God and the Covenant, by taking God's Name in vain.

The commandment, not to take God's Name in vain, follows immediately after the prohibitions against worshiping other gods. According to Deuteronomy 6:13 and 10:20, swearing by God's Name was equal to revering God's Name. Swearing by the names of other gods was apostasy (Exodus 23:13, Joshua 23:7, Jeremiah 5:7, 12:16). The underlying link between the commandments is the implication that like idolatry, taking God's Name and hence a reflection of His essence, in vain is a repudiation and abandonment of God.

We know from the amount of literature found in the *Mishnah*, *Tosefta*, and the Gospels on vows and oaths that this subject was a source of considerable importance, interest, and debate during the Second Temple period and beyond. Therefore, its inclusion in the legal materials of the Dead Sea Scrolls is quite understandable.

Yet the Dead Sea literature, particularly the Sectarian materials, often has a specific and unique viewpoint. This is certainly true of the laws regarding vows and oaths. On one hand, the inclusion of these laws in the literature is based on their connection to the Temple and the Courts. Vows were statements of dedication and sanctification. Vows were voluntary gifts to God; they were deeply connected to matters of personal commitment and piety. Oaths were tools of validation. They were an indispensable part of court proceedings. There is a very practical basis for their inclusion.

On the other hand, the inclusion of these laws also indicates something else. They are indicative of the deep concern within the Jewish world as a whole, and among the Sectarian communities in particular, about the sanctity and inviolability of the Covenant. Beyond the pragmatic concerns dealt with in these laws, their grouping and their inclusion in the legal framework of the scroll material reveal a deeper and more hidden significance that speaks to the heart and soul of Jewish existence.

The entire relationship between Israel and God is based on a profound mutual trust and on a deep level of commitment, both personally and nationally. Abandoning that trust and commitment, by word and deed, would be the ultimate breach of faith. The message here is that our word is our bond. What we commit to in our lives reflects our very relationship to God. To abandon our commitments to God is to violate God's trust. The consequences of such action are invariably devastating.

11

THE END OF DAYS

Of particular interest, both historically and theologically, are those sections of the Qumran literature that refer specifically to the End Time. That is, they make reference to, or provide information about, the end of the historical cycle as we know it. The End Time being the period of redemption, it is the culmination of human history as mankind has experienced it from the beginning of Creation.

In human experience, one really only gets a clear and full picture of what has happened in one's life when the process has completed itself. We can reflect on our experiences most objectively and find the fullest meaning in them when they are examined at a distance, after the fact. In terms of the totality of human evolution, the Dead Sea literature holds that the same principle applies. An epoch is perceived and understood most completely after the point of its resolution.

In the Dead Sea Scrolls, as well as in the contemporaneous literature of the times, the resolution point of human history is the point of redemption. After mankind is redeemed by God, the full import and significance of the human experience from the beginning of history will be clearly understood. This is the meaning of the term "apocalypse."

The word "apocalypse" comes from the Greek, meaning "a revelation." The term is referring to two interrelated concepts. First, what is being revealed in the apocalyptic literature are the details of the End of Time. That which is being delineated is the course of events that will unfold when the time of redemption actually arrives. Second, the implication is that as the redemption of mankind takes place, what will be revealed are the deeper, ulterior reasons for the direction that the course of human history took from the beginning. As that process of human evolution concludes, the dynamics that drove it and its meaning and purpose are finally exposed to full view and are clarified.

With the culmination of the cycle of human history as we have understood it, a new era of human experience is inaugurated. An evolutionary shift takes place in human consciousness. The fundamental realities of human experience are changed forever. Mankind is redeemed by God, and history, as we have known it, is fulfilled. As a result, a new level of human experience is born and a higher level of human consciousness is opened up. This, too, is a revelation. At the End Time, a new order of human reality will be revealed.

To comprehend the End Time is to gain an understanding of the process of redemption and to sense the implications that the redemption of humanity has for subsequent generations. The End of Days, the End Time, is not the termination of mankind. Rather, it marks the conclusion of the pattern of human existence initiated at the beginning of history. The End of Days is the time of God's redemption of humanity and the pivotal point for the evolutionary shift of human consciousness and experience.

Before delving into the views held by the Qumran literature regarding the End Time and the redemption, it is best to gain a fuller background by examining the biblical origins of the concept. To do this, we begin by taking a careful look at statements made about the End of Days in the writings of some of the later Prophets and in the Book of Daniel.

The Biblical View of "The End of Days"

The concept of the End Time appears to have emerged gradually at the end of the biblical period. Some of the late Prophets make reference to the reality that will emerge at the End of Days. The concept is developed most fully in the Book of Daniel, which was composed long after the Destruction of Jerusalem and the onslaught of the Babylonian captivity.

The prophet Jeremiah frequently returns to the theme of Israel's apostasy and impending punishment. He stresses that because the people of Judah are not repenting of their idolatrous practices and the resulting moral corruption and because they are not returning to the Covenant, the country will be overrun by their enemies and thoroughly destroyed. Jeremiah also expresses the consolation that the captivity and the suffering will last seventy years, at which time the people will return and Jerusalem will be restored.

In speaking about the End of Days, Jeremiah predicts a similar judgement by God and a similar process taking place on a global level. God will redeem the people of Israel and bring them back from the lands to which they were banished. God will raise up a branch from David's line. He will reign as king and establish justice in the Land (Jeremiah 23:5–8).

At the End Time, God's wrath will be unleashed on those who despise Him, who willfully obey only their own hearts. Upon them and upon the false prophets who support them, God will let loose a storm. The anger of God will not abate until it completes itself and God's purpose has been fulfilled (Jeremiah 23:16–20).

God's purpose is to reestablish the Covenant with Israel on a firmer basis. Just as God brought Israel out of Egypt to establish the Covenant with them, God will bring the scattered Israelites out of their exile and dispersion, at the End Time, to reestablish the Covenant.

> "Decidedly, a time is coming," declares the LORD, "when it shall no more be said, 'As the LORD lives, who brought the Israelites out of the Land of Egypt,' but rather, 'As the LORD lives, who brought out and led the offspring of the House of Israel from the lands of the north and from the lands to which I banished them.'" (Jeremiah 23:7–8)

> Lo, the storm of the LORD goes forth in fury, a raging tempest. It shall whirl down upon the head of the wicked. The anger of the LORD shall not turn back, until it has fulfilled and completed His purposes. In the End of Days, you shall perceive it. "At that time," declares the LORD, "I will be God to all the clans of Israel and they shall be My people." (Jeremiah 30:23–31:1)

After the events of the End Time, the rescue of the Jewish people by God directly, from the persecution and dispersion inflicted during the final chaos, will remain an indelible impression in the minds of all peoples. The final redemption of Israel will eclipse what God did for the Israelites when He extracted them from Egyptian slavery.

The fury of God's intervention into human history at the End Time has several purposes. Israel's redemption is the concrete sign of God's reemergence directly into human affairs. Direct interaction between man and God is to be a major element in the new, emerging, post-redemption reality. Moreover, the Jews are rescued from their exile and securely resettled in the Land, so that God's Covenant is reestablished in Israel. The foundation of the Covenant is that Israel accepts and serves God, and God makes His Presence continual and tangible in their midst.

It is not only the Israelites who are to experience Divine interaction during the End Time. According to Ezekiel (38:16–39:16), the Land is invaded by enemies from the north in the course of a broader cataclysmic war, before God and nature intervene and destroy the forces that oppose Him. During this End Time, Israel will turn back to God and be saved. Concomitantly, both Moab and Elam will be destroyed and sent into captivity as well, subsequently to be rescued and restored during the End Time (Jeremiah, chaps. 48 and 49).

In the aftermath of the End Time, the foundation of the new reality is laid. One of its central components is the restoration and permanent establishment of Israel. Another is the direct, continual flow of communication from God to the world, through the Temple in Jerusalem. This direct linkage between man and God will be the cornerstone of the Kingdom of God. God will rule the world. Justice will be permanently established and warfare will become an historical footnote, having permanently passed out of the realm of human experience.

> At the End of Days, the mountain of the LORD's House will stand firm above the mountains and tower above the hills. Hence, all the nations will look upon it with joy, and many peoples will go and say, "Come, let us go up to the mountain of the LORD, to the House of the God of Jacob, that He may instruct us in His ways, so that we may walk in His paths. For instruction shall emerge from Zion, the Word of the LORD from Jerusalem." Thus, He will judge among the nations and arbitrate for many peoples. And they shall beat their swords into plowshares and their spears into pruning hooks. Nation shall not take up sword against

nation. They shall never again know war. (Isaiah 2:2–4) (Also see: Micah, chap. 4)

The process of redemption, which characterizes the End of Days, is spelled out in detail in the Book of Daniel. The Book of Daniel stresses the concept of the Four Kingdoms that precede the establishment of the Kingdom of God. In chapter 2, the King dreams of a statue composed of four sections—a head of gold, a torso of silver, thighs of bronze, and legs and feet of iron or an admixture of clay and iron. In chapter 7, Daniel has the vision of the Four Beasts.

In the King's dream, the elements of the statue become less valuable and less stable as one progresses. In Daniel's vision, the fourth beast is mightier than his predecessors and is far more destructive. This beast devours the earth and overcomes the holy. In his rage, the beast conquers many lands, including the Holy Land, and then assaults heaven itself. He overtakes the Sanctuary, tramples the heavenly host, and forces the abandonment of God's Holy Place. Even the offerings to God are suspended.

Chapter 8 equates the beast with a king who will arise, who is extraordinarily deceitful, cunning, and destructive. This king speaks and acts with great arrogance. The arrogance referred to can be paralleled to that of King Nebuchadnezzar and King Balshazzar, mentioned extensively earlier in the book. Nebuchadnezzar comes to believe that he, not God, built the great empire of Babylon and that he is secure and all-powerful. As a result, God reduces him to being an outcast who, impoverished, lives on an animal level, scavenging and feeding on grass for seven years, until he finally acknowledges God and His ultimate sovereignty.

Nebuchadnezzar is restored to his throne. His son, Belshazzar, is not so fortunate. Belshazzar pits himself against God directly, desecrating the holy vessels, using them in drunken revelry, in debauchery, and in connection with idolatrous worship. As a result of this rebellious arrogance, God has the king's sentence written on the wall of the palace. His kingdom was to be taken from him, and his days were numbered. According to the story in chapter 5, Balshazzar died that night.

The stories of Nebuchadnezzar and Balshazzar seem to foreshadow and explicate the cataclysmic events later associated with the End of Days in Nebuchadnezzar's dream and Daniel's visions. Human arrogance and rebellion against God are seen as the underlying causes that lead to a progressive deterioration of civilization. In the last stage of corruption, civilization self-destructs, feeding on itself, and driven by the uncontrolled drive for wealth and power that are represented by the King or the Beast. The drive for world domination culminates in great conflict, death, and devastation.

Chapters 11 and 12 detail the nature and tenor of the events of the End Time, as revealed by the angel Michael. The King who would conquer the world rages against God and any peoples supporting God. His conquests are extensive, bringing great destruction in their wake. He will invade the Holy Land and, in his arrogance, blaspheme God. He will rage against the Covenant, and some will abandon it. But the people devoted to God will stand firm. The knowledgeable among them will teach others. Some of them will suffer persecution and death in the process.

The final scene of the war, championed by this king, is one of total defeat and utter destruction. In the dream of Nebuchadnezzar, a giant stone emerges, smashes the statue, and crushes it to dust that is blown away and never seen again. In the vision of the Four Beasts, the last, most terrible beast is killed and consigned to the flames. In chapter 12, a last great battle is fought in the Holy Land, between Jerusalem and the coast, during which the King and his forces are totally defeated. The angel Michael appears and sets the stage for the Final Judgement of humanity.

A throne appears upon which the Ancient One, the Most High, sits and receives the kingship forever. God judges all of humanity. The reign of Evil is destroyed once and for all in the process. God then establishes His exclusive rule on earth. All peoples serve God in the post-redemption era. It is a new time—a new spiritual reality emerges on earth where His dominion is permanently and irrevocably established, the dominion of arrogance having fulfilled itself disappeared forever (Daniel, chap. 7).

This is the picture of the End of Days that emerged during the dark days of the Destruction of the Kingdom of Judah, Jerusalem, and the Temple. It is a picture first articulated in detail and elaborated on during the early Second Temple period—that is, during the Persian and early Greek periods. It was with the Book of Daniel that apocalyptic literature was born.

It was with the rising tension that developed between the Greek and Hebrew civilizations that apocalyptic literature mushroomed into an extensive, and emotionally powerful, genre. This highly charged literature and thought profoundly effected the Jews and ultimately unleashed forces that would change the course of history.

The Decline of Prophecy in Israel and the Emergence of Apocalyptic Vision

A core feature of the Covenant was that God was to be ever-present in Israel and was to rule the nation as its sovereign. They were to be His people, and He was to be their God. This was meant in the literal, practical sense. God was to be intimately involved in the lives of the people and the nation. The relationship was to be interactive.

In political terms, this meant that Israel was to be a theocracy. God was the ultimate authority. In social and religious terms, this meant that God was ever-present, at all times. God was accessible through personal worship and through the Temple service.

During the biblical period, from the establishment of the Temple in Jerusalem onward, a tripartite system was established to allow for God to rule over His people. God communicated with and worked through three distinct, but interconnected, vehicles. God guided the King through affairs of state. God spoke to the people through the Prophets. God sustained the Land and the people through the priests.

Political power and the destiny of the nation lay in the hands of the monarchy. The King was seen as acting as a surrogate for God. God was to protect the people and to lead them, according to the terms of the Sinai Covenant. With the establishment of the monarchy, the King took on that role on God's behalf. Ultimately, all blessing and all disaster emanated from God. It devolved upon the King to be in close harmony with God's wishes, if he wished to govern successfully. If a King acted in accordance with the divine guidance, the nation prospered. If not, famine, disease, war, and subjugation to the enemy followed.

As has been mentioned already, the priests fulfilled the Temple functions. The Temple ritual was designed to atone for the mistakes of the people and to keep the connection between God and the people both close and in balance. From that harmony, blessing and prosperity would flow. The priests were conduits through which God's love and concern for His people flowed. It was through the Temple that the people served God and that the divine–human connection was maintained.

God made His Will known to the King and to the people. This
was achieved through the Prophets. The Prophets were imbued directly with God's Words. They spoke directly to the monarchs and to
the people, expressing the Will of God. Jeremiah, for example, was
on close personal terms with King Zedekiah, sometimes remonstrat-
ing and sometimes giving counsel and advice. Jeremiah also prophesied publicly in the marketplace and at the gates of Jerusalem, to
noble and commoner alike. The Words of God were overpowering,
impelling the Prophet to speak and convey the divine Will, even at
great personal peril.

The monarch–priest–prophet triad was the vehicle by which God
maintained His effective Presence among the Israelites. King David
established the kingdom, uniting the tribes, setting up Jerusalem as
the eternal capital and preparing the foundations for the building of
the Temple. Nathan, the Prophet, was closely connected to King
David, as was Zadok, the High Priest. Both were close to his son
Solomon as well.

According to Deuteronomy, the King was to have his own copy
of the Law of Moses and was to be instructed in the Law by the priests.
When the King wished to consult God on important, urgent matters,
he would go to the High Priest, who would consult God and receive
instruction from Him through the use of the priestly breastplate, called
the *Hoshen Mishpat*, the "breastplate of judgement," in conjunction
with an activating device known as the *Urim VeThummim*.

The relationship between King and High Priest was very deep
and interdependent. Both were vessels of God. In different ways, they
were responsible for the welfare of the nation and for being vehicles
for the expression of the Divine Will. God fulfilled His part of the
Covenant through the agency of the King and the Priesthood. That is
symbolized by the fact that the King and the High Priest were the only
two officials who, upon taking office, were anointed. The monarch
and the High Priest were the "anointed ones."

An intimate relationship also existed between the King and the
Prophet. If one takes into account the relationship of both King Saul
and King David to the Prophet Samuel, the relationship of the Prophet
Elijah to King Ahab, that of Isaiah to King Hezekiah, or that of
Jeremiah to King Uriah and to King Zedekiah, not only does one see
the various dynamics and complexities of the relationship between
King and Prophet, but their deep interconnection with each other can
be seen as well.

This triumvirate of king–priest–prophet expressed the divine guidance of the nation throughout the biblical period. With the destruction of Judah, the demise of Jerusalem, and the elimination of the First Temple, a dramatic shift took place. The Babylonians led the Judean monarchs into exile and imprisonment. When the Jews were allowed to reestablish Jerusalem and the Temple under the Persians, it was for the purpose of rebuilding Judea as a province of the empire. The Prophets and the priests were allowed to return. However, the monarchy was effectively extinguished.

There were Prophets who returned to Jerusalem at the beginning of the Persian period. Zachariah, Haggai, and the others were very much involved in the rebuilding of the Temple. However, after that no other prophets are mentioned. Like the monarchy, prophecy passes from the scene. On a ritual and spiritual level, the Ark of the Covenant, the *Urim* and *Thummim*, and the Breastplate of Judgement were gone. On a political level, the monarchy was defunct. The old structure had vanished and could not be restored. Hence, prophecy, too, passed away.

Josephus, in his essay "Against Apion" (1.8), states that prophecy disappeared in Israel at the time of Artaxerxes. That would place it in the time of Ezra and Nehemiah. This coincides with the picture presented in the *Mishnah*. Tractate *Avot* begins by detailing the evolution of the Law, of its interpretation, and of religious authority. "Moses received the Law from Sinai and committed it to Joshua, and Joshua to the elders, and the elders to the Prophets. Then, the Prophets committed it to the men of the Great Assembly" (*Avot* 1:1).

The Great Assembly was an official body established by Ezra to deal with interpreting the Law and implementing it properly. The Great Assembly consisted of priests, Prophets, and Sages. Their goal was to establish a new basis for interpreting the provisions of the Torah and for observing the Covenant. "They said [taught] three things: Be deliberate in judgement, raise up many disciples, and set a fence around the Law."

Understanding what God wanted from the people and pinpointing how the Law was to be obeyed and the Covenant observed changed in form through time. During the biblical period, this was done through prophecy. Now, with the establishment of the Second Temple, study of the Law, the teaching of its interpretation, and the instruction regarding its practical application all passed into the hands of scholars. Sages and scholars were to build a fence around the Law, interpreting the commandments, searching Scripture, and defining its practical application in daily life. That is how the Covenant was to be kept active and vital.

When questions arose, scholars of the Law were to arbitrate and to judge. They were, in turn, to raise disciples competent to do the same and to pass on the traditions. The function of the Prophets as the interpreters of God's Will passed to the Sages.

Not all questions regarding God's Will could be handled in this framework; only questions of the Law could be dealt with in this manner. In 1 Maccabees 9:27, regarding the time of Jonathan, it says that tribulations afflicted the Jews to an extent greater than any that had occurred since prophecy ceased in Israel. In chapter 4, it states that when Judah Maccabee pulled down the altar in the Temple, which had been desecrated by the Greeks, the stones were stored in a separate, isolated room. The reason for so doing was that Judah and the people were not sure what God wanted done with the defiled altar. So they were storing it in quarantine, until a prophet arose who could tell them what was to be done with the stones.

Years later Simeon, one of Judah's brothers, was appointed by the priests and the people to be both their leader and to be High Priest. His lineage was to continue in this role until a "faithful prophet" arose in Israel. That is, the Hasmonean family was established as a High Priestly dynasty designated to rule Israel, until prophecy reemerged and God's rule over His people was reestablished. The Hasmonean model of ruler was, ultimately, to be a temporary one. The true pattern of kingdom and dominion would be that instituted by God Himself at some future point.

The apocalyptic view of the End of Days also emerges during the period of the Restoration under Ezra and Nehemiah. The apocryphal Book of 2 Esdras laments the Destruction of Jerusalem and the Temple. It grieves over the burning of the Law by the Babylonians. When referring to the Law, both the Five Books of Moses as well as the secret apocalyptic writings of Moses are mentioned. Ezra is said to have brought and reestablished both.

Moreover, apocalyptic passages referring to the final war with the forces of evil, their defeat and destruction, the Judgement of humanity, and the establishment of world peace—all associated with the End of Days—are mentioned in the works of Ezekiel (chaps. 38, 39), Joel (chap. 3), Micah (chap. 5), and Zechariah (chaps. 3, 6, and 8).

Over time, prophecy was replaced by apocalypse. Prophetic inspiration was supplanted by scribal tradition and scholarly interpretation.

Apocalyptic literature and scholarly interpretation of the Law have a common basis—that of the Covenant. According to the Sinai Covenant, Israel pledges its obedience to God and God actively intervenes in the affairs of the people. God's promise is both that of intervention and of redemption. Interpretation of the Law provided the framework for fulfilling the terms of the Covenant on a daily basis, in as thorough a manner as possible. Apocalyptic vision served to keep alive the faith in God's Final Redemption, that intervention that would establish God's unchallenged rule on earth. The establishment of God's Kingdom and dominion at the beginning of the new era inaugurates the fullest implementation of the Covenant.

God is to establish Israel as a permanent reality. The people of Israel are to dwell securely in the Land in a general environment of world peace. Israel will be able to fulfill its obligation to live in direct accord with the divine directives. The Covenant, like the people of Israel, will be renewed and reconsecrated by God. The forces of evil will have been destroyed forever, and subsequently, the Word of God will flow continually to all the peoples of the earth from Zion and Jerusalem. This is both the fulfillment of the Covenant made to Jacob at Beth El and expanded at Mount Sinai and the beginning of a new Covenantal relationship between God, Israel, and the World.

During the socio-political upheavals of the Greek period and during times of political domination, cultural conflict, and religious persecution, apocalyptic fervor and expectation among the Jews intensified and accelerated. To understand the emotional and psychological forces that were unleashed and the effects that they had historically, we need to examine carefully the views that emerged during the Greek period regarding the End of Time.

In order to do this, we should compare the various concepts and patterns that emerge from the apocalyptic literature as a whole. This involves discussing the concepts found in the Dead Sea Scrolls in direct connection to contemporaneous material. We need to compare the conceptions in the Dead Sea literature with those found in other Hellenistic Jewish writings of the Apocrypha and Pseudo-Epigrapha. By analyzing the contents of the apocalyptic material from Qumran, in conjunction with similar Jewish material written during the same time period, we should get a clear picture of the view of the End Time and its aftermath, as it was understood by the Jewish world in the Greco-Roman period.

The Extermination of Evil and the Apocalyptic Process

In the view of the Apocalyptic literature, both within the Dead Sea material and in contemporaneous, Hellenistic Jewish literature, one reality is seen as the most prominent in shaping human existence. That reality is the conflict between good and evil. The defining factor that most clearly delineates the age in which man has been living since the expulsion of Adam and Eve from the garden of Eden is the existence of evil.

The Dead Sea literature—particularly the Sectarian works—refer to human history, as mankind has experienced it, as the Age of Wickedness. What has dominated human experience from the beginning of time is the corruptive influence of evil. The existence of evil is seen as the very hallmark of the age of mankind, which began with the expulsion from Eden.

The apocalyptic literature envisions a time when a new age dawns for mankind. As we have seen from the biblical viewpoint, the coming era is to be one of world peace, spiritual harmony, and direct interaction with God. The kingdoms of man, based on power and the supremacy of human values, will be replaced by the Kingdom of God, a world governed by divine guidance and moral values. To achieve this end, the dominion of evil has to be removed from human experience. This does not mean merely the defeat of evil. The literature emphasizes the complete and utter annihilation of evil, the permanent termination of its existence on earth.

The scroll referred to as the "War of the Sons of Light and the Sons of Darkness" represents the clearest exposition of the final confrontation between the forces of Good and the forces of Evil. This scroll portrays the last war, the conflict that will bring the current age of mankind to an end and will open the way for the emergence of a new era of human history. The war between the forces of light and of dark is seen to be the culmination of history as we understand it. This war is the ultimate contest that leads to the complete obliteration of evil. The elimination of evil as a reality on earth is viewed as the most important step in clearing the way for the emergence of God's dominion on earth.

The War Scroll states that there is a divinely ordained time to come, when redemption will be at hand and when God will remove the dominion of evil from the earth permanently.

And in the End, he will come out with great wrath, to fight the kings of the north. His intention is to destroy and to sever the horn of Beliyaal. It will be a time of salvation for the people of God, and the end of the dominion of all the people of his persuasion, the permanent end for all of the persuasion of Beliyaal. There will be great commotion among the children of Yaphet. Asshur will fall, with no one to help him. The rule of the *Kittim* will turn to the defeat of wickedness, leaving no remnant. There will be no refuge for any of the Sons of Darkness. (1QM 1:4–7, *Die Texte aus Qumran*, Koesel)

[You have performed miracle after] miracle with us. From of old, there has never been anything like this. For You have known our appointed time, and on that day, appear to us. [You will demonstrate Your loving-kindness] with us through eternal redemption, removing forever the dominion of evil with a mighty hand and in a war against our enemies of complete extermination. Now, there approaches the day for us to pursue their multitude. For You . . . You will protect the heart of the mighty ones, and no one will be able to take a stand. To You is the might, in Your hand the battle, there is no . . . The moment is predetermined by Your Will. . . . (1QM 18:10–14, *Die Texte aus Qumran*, Koesel)

A similar finality to the existence of evil is expressed in the fragments of the Book of 1 Enoch, found in Qumran (4Q En). "Then after that, in the ninth week, righteous judgement shall be revealed to the whole world. All the deeds of the sinners shall depart from the whole earth, and be written off for eternal destruction, and all people shall direct their sight to the path of righteousness" (1 Enoch 91:14, Charlesworth).

The termination of evil is the end result of the war between light and darkness. It opens the way for the final Judgement of mankind, the culminating event in the process leading to the establishment of God's rule on earth. To understand this more fully, it is important to gain a sense of the basic nature of evil, as the scrolls seem to understand it.

At the core of all evil is rebellion against God. The Damascus Covenant, as we have seen, has a specific view of evil that stresses the concept that at the center of evil is rebellion against God's direct instructions. Some examples are given in the Damascus Covenant of this phenomenon and its consequences. The destruction of Noah's generation came because they disregarded the precepts of God, followed after guilty inclinations and lustful eyes, and did only what they stubbornly clung to in their hearts.

The enslavement of the Israelites was, in part, due to the fact that Jacob's sons, while in Egypt, walked in the stubbornness of their own hearts and did only what was right in their own eyes, plotting against God. At Mount Sinai, after hearing the Word of God directly enunciating the Ten Commandments, the people erected an idol, the Golden Calf, in Moses' absence. Many were to die in the fury God unleashed upon them as a result. At Kadesh, God commanded the Israelites to cross into Canaan and to take possession of the Land. Instead, the Israelites, out of fear, refused to move into the Land, violating a direct order from God. As a result, God condemned the people to forty years of wandering in the desert, effectively imposing a death sentence on that entire generation.

The Damascus Covenant, the Book of Jubilees, and the Book of 1 Enoch all speak about the Fall of the Watchers, the divine beings who deliberately violated God's commandments to them and intermarried with the daughters of men, as is reported in Genesis. In the Damascus Covenant, their fall is the first example of direct rebellion against God. Their offspring were the giants, who, like the Watchers, lusted after their own desires and violated God's precepts intentionally. In His anger, God eventually had them all annihilated. In spite of their renowned prowess, their enormous stature, and their great strength, all trace of their existence was obliterated as if they had never existed.

According to the Book of Jubilees 5:1-11, the angels who rebelled and intermarried with the daughters of men established dominions for themselves on earth. Their behavior on earth was insidious. Their example was so devastating that the fallen divine beings were responsible for the corruption of humanity, which ultimately led to the Flood and to the destruction of Noah's generation.

In punishment, God uprooted the Watchers and cast them all into the depths of the earth, to be held there until the final Judgement of mankind. At that time, they are to be judged for their sins as well. God also consigned the children of the Watchers, the giants, to complete oblivion.

The Book of 1 Enoch, chapters 6–10, explains that the Watchers, having decided to take earthly wives and take sovereignty over the earth, bound themselves to this course of action by oath, knowing that they were deliberately violating God's Law. They not only intermarried with the daughters of men, they committed adultery. They introduced mankind to warfare, to bloodshed, to the eating of animals, to greed, to fatalism, and to superstition. They exposed mankind to violence and oppression. These tendencies were reinforced by the uncontrolled arrogance of the giants, their offspring.

As a result of having taught mankind sin and injustice, the Watchers were forced to witness the total destruction of their children, who, in large part, annihilated themselves. Then the Watchers, the fallen angels, were cast into darkness, to await the final day of Judgement. What they taught mankind is the source for all sin. They are still trapped between heaven and earth and are forced to watch the full ramifications of their actions unfold. Once sin is fulfilled, it is not only the human perpetrators who will be punished, but also the authors of evil.

The core of evil is sin. The origin of sin is rebellion against God. Rebellion against God is a conscious decision and a deliberate act of breaking with God. Nullifying what God expects of each of us by willful indifference or defiance is devastating in its effects. Mankind follows in the path of sin when man in his stubbornness and arrogance chooses to do what he feels he wants to do, knowing that it is in direct opposition to what God has commanded.

In the view of the Dead Sea literature, the violation of the Covenant—that is, the abandoning of the Law of God from Sinai by any Jew—is also a deliberate rebellion against God. Such a course of action is a tremendous source of moral corruption. It breaks the connection between heaven and earth. Such action provokes God's wrath, driving a wedge between God and His people. Such deliberate evil is damaging to such an extent that it contaminates the Land and invokes the devastating biblical curses connected to the violation of the Law.

If God's Kingdom is to be established on earth, if the Word of God is to issue forth to the world from Zion, it cannot be from a place of pollution. Israel has to be purified. The rest of the world must be cleansed of sin as well. Therefore, the termination of evil as a reality on earth and the Judgement of humanity are necessary requisites for the establishment of a world based on justice and peace and one under direct, divine guidance and supervision.

According to the Scroll of Amram and the Damascus Covenant, a characteristic of the Age of Wickedness, the era of the dominion of evil, is that during this age man is given two opposing natures to contend with. Man can evolve or devolve spiritually. God has implanted within each individual a measure of light and of dark. These two forces fight for man's soul. If a person acts righteously, the light gains strength at the expense of the dark force. If he continually sins, the reverse takes place instead. This contest, for the Jew, involves adherence to God's Law as opposed to willful abandonment of it.

What a person does between now and the final Judgement is crucial to the soul in the long term. The time for repentance is now. It is too late when the final hour comes. The struggle is cosmic, as we have seen. It affects not only man, but heavenly beings as well. At the end of time, all will be judged by God directly and that will be the time of the Great Salvation. Evil will be destroyed and righteousness shall become the norm on earth, as it is in the higher realms. Those souls who have held to the light will be vindicated. Those who held to the darkness will be punished, exiled from their places forever.

The Great Evils

Evil is the doing of man. It is a human creation, not a divine one. Humanity has produced it and must live with it. Ultimately, we must all face its consequences. In the words of the Book of Enoch: "I have sworn unto you sinners: As a mountain has never turned into a servant, nor a hill into a woman's maidservant, likewise, neither has sin been exported into the world. It is people who themselves have invented it. And those who commit it shall come under a great curse" (1 Enoch 98:4).

Those who do evil are deluding themselves in thinking that they can act unjustly, oppress others, and not be held accountable for the evil they are generating.

> I swear to you, sinners, by the Holy Great One, that all your evil deeds are revealed in the heavens. None of your deeds of injustice are covered and hidden. Think not in your spirit, nor say in your hearts, that you neither know nor see all our sins being written down every day in

the presence of the Most High. From now on, do know that all your injustices that you have committed unjustly are written down every day until the day of your judgement. (1 Enoch 98:6–8)

The emphasis in the apocalyptic literature centers around the destruction of evil and the elimination of its practitioners. Evil has corrupted human life from the beginning of time. Its presence and strength have interfered with the establishment of God's rule on earth. It is man's own actions, in the form of evil, that have prevented the descendants of Adam and Eve from returning to Eden. Hence, at the End-Time, God will judge all of humanity and will determine the fate of every soul as a prelude to the establishment of His Kingdom.

What are the great evils that still entrap man and fuel the powers of darkness?

The Damascus Covenant, as noted earlier, mentions three great traps, three categories of action that are the bedrock of evil. All of them are tendencies that people fall into which lead them to the darkness and into rebellion against God. The Damascus Covenant lists them as fornication, riches, and the desecration of the Temple. It is important to understand that these terms are general categories of immoral and sinful behavior.

Fornication refers specifically to sexual immorality. This category biblically includes a variety of moral laws, the violation of which is abhorrent to God. Leviticus 18:16–23 forbids adultery, incest, sodomy, bestiality, and sexual relations with a woman in menstruation. Leviticus 20:13–16 goes on to stipulate that they are capital offenses. The implication of a capital punishment is that such a sin is so serious, so heinous, that full repentance and rectification are not really possible on this level. They have invoked the wrath of God. Sins of fornication are abominations in God's eyes and are a level of evil so great that no actual atonement can be made, save giving up one's life.

It is significant that the Dead Sea literature argues persuasively, expressing the legal view, that polygamy is a violation of Mosaic Law, seeing it as something akin to adultery. The scrolls also express the view that sexual relations between an uncle and a niece is incest, even though not expressly stated as such in the Law. In the view of the Sectarians, these practices were fornication, and as such, were some of the worst violations of the Law and the Covenant. They were so serious, they threatened to invoke God's wrath against the people as a whole.

Other forms of sexual misconduct were linked with impurity and pollution. Prostitution, per se, is strictly forbidden in Leviticus (19:29) and priests are forbidden to marry divorcées or harlots (Leviticus 17:2). In the case of the High Priest, even a widow was forbidden as a marriage partner (Leviticus 21:13–14). Impurity prevented one from serving God. These types of relationships were viewed biblically as sources of defilement.

The issue of priestly marriage and appropriate sexual relations comes up strongly in the legal literature of Qumran, as we have seen. The emphasis placed by the scrolls on these issues suggests the view that fornication and sexual pollution damage the relationship between Israel and God by violating the Covenant at the highest level, triggering the wrath of God.

Moreover, the issue of impurity connects these violations of the Law with the second category of sins outlined in the Damascus Covenant—namely, the profanation of the Temple. The profanation of the Temple refers to ritual purity. More specifically, it refers to distinguishing between the clean and the unclean and upholding the laws of ritual purity. In the MMT, the priests are said to be defiling themselves by having sexual relationships with women who they are forbidden to marry. This, too, is seen as a source of pollution that affects the entire country.

Specifically, a state of ritual impurity prevented both a priest or a lay person from serving God within the Temple. On another level, impurity caused by the pollution of immoral behavior or behavior contrary to the Covenant interfered with one's relationship and ability to serve God in more general terms. For example, the behavior of the priests in illicit sexual activity polluted their ability to function as priests, who serve God by interceding for the people. In more general terms, idolatry in any form whatsoever polluted the Land, thereby alienating the people from the very place they were to serve God and observe the commandments.

The literature of the Second Temple period extended the concept of impurity beyond the realm of ritual. "Desecrating the Temple," as the Damascus Covenant puts it, involves deliberately obscuring and/ or failing to observe the laws of purity. The definition of ritual impurity—that is, of not distinguishing between the clean and the unclean— was expanded from contracting physical states of ritual uncleanliness, blemish, or malfunction to include spiritual impurity caused by transgression, sin, and immorality.

There is a precedent for equating uncleanliness with moral transgression. Impurity is indeed related to sin in biblical law. Many of the purification ceremonies in the Bible required the sacrifice of a sin and/or guilt offering as part of the process. An implication of this requirement is that due to contracting an impure state, the link between man and God, the ability and obligation to serve God, was interrupted and therefore could not be fulfilled. A failure had taken place on a primal level between the individual and God. That failure to meet one's obligation to God had to be acknowledged.

The moral form of impurity is stressed in the concept of the Profanation of the Temple. This is a consistent tendency in both the Qumran literature and early rabbinic writings. The *Mekhilta* states that both violence and arrogance render the Land of Israel impure (*Shabbat* 1, *BaHodesh* 9). According to the Talmud (*Yoma* 38b), so does individual transgression.

Who is unclean? The Community Rule answers, all who transgress the Law, all who walk in the stubbornness of their own hearts, and all who do not circumcise evil from their heart. In the Community Rule, transgression is equated with uncleanliness, which, in turn, is equated with falsehood. In its analysis of the component parts, the Rule subsumes the following moral evils under the category of falsehood: greed, indolence, lying, deceit, arrogance, cruelty, lust, blasphemy, uncleanliness, and rebellion.

Moral depravity and immoral behavior are core factors in sin. In the view of the scrolls, they are a source of pollution and corruption that drives a wedge between man and God by placing the individual in a state of impurity. Direct violations of the Law undermine the Covenant. Immoral behavior leads to a state of impurity akin to ritual uncleanliness that makes it impossible to connect with God directly. As long as one remains within the grasp of immorality, one is isolated from God. If not rectified, this behavioral pattern can lead to rebellion, which is an open and deliberate break with God. If one rebels and remains ardent in one's determination to deny God's Law, the extent of one's sins will lead to ultimate destruction.

The last great snare mentioned in the literature is that of riches. The accumulation of great wealth is seen as the third great temptation and source of evil. The Damascus Covenant defines it as a form of idolatry, the worship of gold and silver. The implication is that the accumulation of wealth is a rival source of allegiance, a false god. As such, it is a cardinal sin and following this course would be a violation of the very core of the Covenant. The prohibition against idolatry is at the top of the Ten Commandments. Moreover, idolatry carries a death penalty.

Much of Second Temple literature views both idolatry and idolatrous practice as a source of moral degeneration and depravity. When the scrolls place the accumulation of wealth on the level of idolatry, they are making a very strong statement. Idolatry was the antithesis of the Covenant with God. It represented the opposite of what the Covenant did. The Covenant cemented the relationship between God and Israel. The Law was the bond that united them, making Israel God's people. Idolatry, on the other hand, was a denial of God and a rejection of the moral law that came down from Sinai.

God Himself viewed idolatry as insidious and ordered that it be totally uprooted from Israel. It is viewed in the Bible as the greatest violation of the Covenant. The Prophets continually told the people that if they remained at all connected to idolatry and continually served other gods, then they would be in serious breach of the entire Law, and God in His wrath would destroy the entire state rather than tolerate it.

The worship of gold and silver, money and power replaced the rituals that once served the idols of Baal and Ashtarte. Yet it was only different gods that were being worshiped, according to the Qumran literature. The moral degeneration that accompanied serving other gods still held sway. The danger of provoking God's wrath and unleashing the curses connected with the violation of the Covenant were, in the minds of these pious Jews, just as real. The possible ramifications were just as serious.

One needs only listen to the words of Enoch. "Woe unto you who cause wickedness, who glorify and honor false words! You are lost and have no life of good things. Woe unto you, who alter the words of truth and pervert the eternal Law! They reckon themselves not guilty of sin. They shall be trampled upon the earth" (1 Enoch 99:1–2, Charlesworth).

"Woe unto you, who reject the foundations and the eternal inheritance of your forefathers! Who shall pursue after the wind, [after] the idol; for there shall be no rest for you. Woe unto you, who engage in oppression and give aid to injustice!" (1 Enoch 99:14–15).

Idolatry of the heart—defined by the Damascus Covenant as the worship of gold and silver—like idolatry itself, is the ultimate form of rebellion against God. It is the antithesis of God's Law. As such, it leads to moral degeneration and sin. In Scroll fragments 4Q184 and 4Q185, the evil of rebellion is pictured as a seductress leading the righteous astray into corruption and sin. The idea of rebellion is expanded to include causing others to rebel, to lose virtue, and to turn away from justice. The reader is exhorted, therefore, not to rebel against the Word of God.

The coming of the End of Days is the time when the domain of evil, the age-old era of rebellion against the Law of God and the Word of God, of materialism and its concomitant moral debasement, finally reach their zenith. This leads to a final confrontation between the forces of good and of evil. Ultimately, God's Presence will triumph on earth, but not before good and evil fulfill themselves in a final contest, and heaven and earth conspire to bring down every vestige of the old order. The establishment of God's Kingdom results from the completion of the Age of Wickedness and the Judgement of mankind.

The Birth Pangs of the Messiah

In Jewish literature, the period of upheaval and commotion leading to the establishment of God's Kingdom is seen as one of great turmoil and pain. The great convulsions that eventually bring forth salvation and renewal for humanity are often referred to as "the birth pangs of the Messiah." It is the birthing of a new era of human experience. In a process that encompasses heaven and earth, humanity, and the angelic realms, great sacrifice is made, great pain is endured, and great destruction takes place as the old order, the dominion of evil, is swept away from the face of the earth.

The details of this process of allowing evil to fulfill itself and then be destroyed are well documented in the literature of the period. Beginning with the Book of Daniel and running through many of the apocalyptic writings of the Second Temple period, Jewish literature presents a clear outline of the scope and nature of these events.

The Book of Daniel presents and outlines the concept of the Four Kingdoms. Several times in the book, dreams appear that allude to the idea of four kingdoms prevailing on earth over time. The first and clearest dream, along with its exposition, comes up in chapter 2. In this chapter, King Nebuchadnezzar's vision is revealed to Daniel by God. God bestows upon Daniel the wisdom and the power to make known the deep and the hidden. He makes known to Daniel that this dream refers to the End of Days, the End Time.

It is quite significant that the dream, and Daniel's cognizance of it and of its meaning, all emanate directly from God. Daniel serves as a vehicle for transmitting the Will of God, expressed in this instance as a revelation of the process of history and of the End Time. God, for His own reasons, wants Nebuchadnezzar to understand what will eventually come to pass. Daniel is only the appointed interpreter, a facilitator. The focus is on the Will of God. Attention is paid, primarily, to the Divine intervention into history that will take place at the point when human will plays itself out.

Interestingly, the Four Kingdoms of Man are all seen as component parts of an idol. The suggestion here is that the empire, the drive for human power and control, is idolatry. From the standpoint of the literature of the Second Temple period, including the Dead Sea Scrolls, idolatry is the highest form of rebellion against God. The implication is that the quest for domination by human beings, by one people over others, is the greatest abomination to God. It is the source of moral corruption and evil. It is not surprising, therefore, that the head of the statue was gold and that the breast and arms were silver. The worship of gold and silver have captured the mind, the heart, and the limbs of humanity over the ages.

In Nebuchadnezzar's dream, not only was the head made of gold and the chest of silver, the statue's belly was of bronze and its legs iron. Its feet were an admixture of clay and iron. Daniel interprets the four elements as four kingdoms that will rise over time and dominate the earth. Each will be succeeded by another, which is inferior to it. Each kingdom, in turn, is of less value, less grandeur, and less power. Presumably, each is also of less substance and of less benefit to humanity than its predecessor.

The idol's feet being an admixture of iron and clay suggests two realities to which Daniel alludes. First, although iron is far less valuable than gold, silver, or bronze, it is much stronger by far. The last great empire will be a strong and brutal force. It will outstrip, in terms of power, anything that came before it. It will be cold and unyielding. Yet at its base, the iron is mixed with clay.

The feet of the idol represent the foundation of idolatry. They are a composite of clay and iron. Mankind's subservience to the pursuit of power is composed of incompatible forces that are melded together. The very basis of man's quest for power and dominion, then, is highly unstable. It is composed of two elements that are diametrically opposite to each other. In terms of the last kingdom, it is the strongest and most ruthless, but also the most vulnerable. Ultimately, it cannot hold itself together.

In the end, a rock is quarried that comes and smashes the feet of the statue. Upon doing so, the entire idol is not only crushed to dust, but it is blown away by the wind as well. No remnant remains. No trace is left. Then the rock grows into a great mountain covering the earth and replacing the idol. This is the Kingdom of God. As a rock, the power of God destroys the evil that had ensnared man from the beginning. As a mountain, it dominates the world in a new age, a new era of human existence. For the Word of the Lord shall emanate from the mountain of Zion and sustain the entire world. God's sovereignty will then be established and endure eternally.

In chapters 11 and 12, Daniel concludes with a vision of the End of Days. It is a vision of war and of global conflict. The forces of darkness rage against the Covenant. The ultimate promise of the Covenant is the redemption of Israel and of the world. The forces of evil will try to destroy the Covenant, because its fulfillment means their end. Some will abandon the Covenant and join the forces of dark. However, the people who are devoted to God will stand firm.

Great tribulation will take place. A great conqueror will arise and subjugate many lands and oppress many peoples. His conquest will be extensive and far-reaching. He will blaspheme God and oppose God's Will. The knowledgeable, those who possess spiritual knowledge and stand by God and by moral law, will be resolute. They will teach, even though they suffer persecution and death.

The conqueror will eventually invade the Holy Land, and it is there that he will meet his final end. In a battle between Jerusalem and the coast, he will be ultimately and thoroughly defeated and his armies crushed. The angel Michael will appear first to assist the forces of light and, subsequently, to herald the Judgement of mankind and the establishment of God's Kingdom.

This basic picture of the End Time is not altered, but rather reaffirmed and enhanced, by the literature of the Second Temple period. The End Time will be marked by fear, violence, and a general lack of sympathy and compassion for others. "In those days, the father will be beaten together with his sons in one place, and brothers shall fall together with their friends, until a stream shall flow of their blood. For a man shall not be able to withhold his hands from his sons nor his sons' sons in order to kill them. Nor is it possible for the sinner to withhold his hands from his honored brother" (1 Enoch 100:1–2).

The Book of 2 Baruch (48:33–39) describes the End Time as one that possesses few people who are truly wise in the way of the spirit. It is a time of illusion, rumor, and broken promises. Shame will replace honor, and strength will be humiliated by contempt. Jealousy will flourish and passion will abound uncontrolled, turning into agitation, oppression, and war.

In chapter 70, we are told, nations will hate one another and provoke wars. The despised will rule over the honorable and the many will be delivered to the few. It will be a time of great poverty and impiety. There will be a great loss of life through a chain of upheaval. Many will die in war and tribulation. War will give way to natural disasters and ecological devastation, only to end up in famine and starvation. The earth will devour its inhabitants. (Also see: 2 Esdras chaps. 5, 6, and 9; 1 Enoch 80:2–3.)

The great conqueror, the leader of the forces of darkness (though not specifically termed as such in the literature) represents an anti-Messiah. He is the complete embodiment of evil. In Daniel 7:25, he blasphemes God and persecutes His holy ones. He is portrayed as Belial, the complete personification and embodiment of evil itself, who Israel is to resist and who will eventually be destroyed (Testament of Issachar 6:1, Testament of Dan 5:10, Testament of Judah 25:3, Sibylline Oracle III 63ff).

The Testament of Dan (5:4) states that in the End Time, the tribe of Dan will defect from God and oppose the tribes of Levi and Judah. It will undertake to attack the tribe of Levi, causing them to sin, and will physically assault the tribe of Judah. This would not only place the forces of Dan in the camp of the wicked but at the forefront of the fight to destroy the good. It is out of the tribes of Levi and Judah that salvation and victory will eventually emerge.

This may suggest that the Prince of Darkness will arise from the Tribe of Dan. That is not certain. However, the implication is very clear that there is a force within Israel, an element of the population, which will deliberately depart from the side of God and defect to the enemy when the chips are down. This identification of the tribe of Dan with the side of evil harkens back to the biblical period, when the tribe was heavily involved in and associated with idolatry.

To achieve their goals, the Danites will try to destroy the two mainstays of the Covenant: the tribe of Levi, representing the Temple, the spiritual connection to God, and the tribe of Judah, signifying the Land, the physical connection to God. With no Temple and no State, there is no means of fulfilling the Covenant. Without the fulfillment of the Covenant, the means for establishing the reign of God on earth is blocked. Evil will fight desperately for its survival. For not only the forces of evil, but for evil itself, this is the last battle. Defeat means its complete and permanent annihilation. Evil will fight desperately for its own survival. It may prove of no avail, but it is inevitable.

Evil will fulfill itself; then it will be destroyed forever. War, disaster, fire, and famine will ravage the earth and bring an end to the Age of Wickedness. With its demise comes the Judgement of mankind and the establishment of the Kingdom of God.

12

THE WAR, THE MESSIAHS, AND THE KINGDOM ESTABLISHED

The Literature of Qumran blames the corruption of the nation during the biblical period, and its subsequent destruction, squarely on the monarchy. The Kings of Israel and Judah had not only turned away from the Covenant—even worse, they misled the people into doing so as well. As monarchs empowered by God, they were responsible for leading the people in the path of God's Law. Instead, they followed the ways of their own hearts and emulated the idolatry of the surrounding peoples.

A nation generally follows the example of its kings. The Kings of Israel and Judah led their people on a cataclysmic course that destroyed the country, devastated the land, and resulted in captivity, exile, and dispersion. For that reason, a debt was created. The monarchy, the core of the state, the guarantor of the people's physical security and well-being, had betrayed them and led them to ruin through resistance to God, personal ambition, and the pursuit of power. Their stubborn arrogance and unrighteousness established a precedent, which led to catastrophe. Therefore, in the view of Second Temple Jewry, it was necessary for a righteous descendant of King David to arise at the End of Time, to reestablish the monarchy, physically and morally.

The Davidic Messiah was to lead the people back to God by restoring Israel as an independent kingdom and by leading the forces of Light in a final, triumphant war against the forces of Dark, thus paving the way for the establishment of the Kingdom of God.

The emergence of a Messiah is a reversal of the biblical process as it unfolded historically. For centuries after the settlement in Israel by the Hebrews, the Land was a confederation of tribal territories, bound together by common ancestry and a shared religion. What united the tribes the most, beyond blood ties and beyond common culture, were the belief in one God, the central worship of God, and the Tabernacle.

Under the terms of the Sinai Covenant, God was to be the protector and lawgiver of the people. Their obedience and their loyalty belonged to God directly and exclusively. God was giving them the Land of Israel as a permanent home base, by which the observance of His commandments would be made possible and facilitated. In practice, Israel was to be a theocracy ruled by God Himself, His Will being made known through priests and Prophets.

This is specifically the message that Samuel was conveying to the people when they came and demanded that a king be set up in Israel. The establishment of the monarchy was a compromise that God was willing to make with the people, in view of their insecurity and fear. It represented an expansion of the original terms of the agreement.

For centuries, the divine rule over Israel was centered around the Tabernacle and the Sanctuary. God's Presence focused there and His Will was made known through intercession of the High Priest, the work of the priesthood, and the words of the Prophets. Now, God was willing to add an additional element to that structure. Hence, the monarchy is founded with God's approval.

God was still to be the ultimate sovereign. God was to choose who would be King. The monarch, like the High Priest and the Prophets, was to draw his strength and inspiration from God. He was to find direction through the Word of God and was to act in direct accordance with the living Will of the God of Israel. That was to be the paradigm.

As the first King, God chose Saul, the youngest son of a modest family from the smallest of any of the tribes. The message in this paradigmatic choice is clear. The power behind the monarchy was to be the guiding hand of God alone. It is not the power of the King that protects and rules. Rather, the King, due to his close, intimate relationship to God, expresses the revealed Will of the Divine. As was illustrated by many of the biblical Judges of centuries past, God could save the people by the hand of the few as easily as by the hand of the many. The king, like the priests and Prophets, was to be a vessel for God's direct guidance of the people. He did not have to be strong and powerful, be well-connected, or have vast wealth at his disposal. His power and direction were to come from God. He was to be the hand of God.

It was precisely because Saul failed to take direction from God consistently that he was replaced by David. David, in contrast, characterized the true model for kingship in Israel. He was devout and he was sensitive to his relationship to God. God was often foremost in his mind, as the psalms of David reflect. He was consistent and thorough in carrying out God's instructions. As a result of acting as the agent of God, the country benefited enormously from the subjugation of its enemies and from the political, religious, and social reorganization that was carried out during David's reign.

Unfortunately, later kings did not follow in David's footsteps. The monarchy increasingly became patterned after the typical model of ancient Near-Eastern potentates. Idolatry soon infiltrated the Land as part of this process. Often it was spread, and therefore legitimatized, through royal patronage and with royal sanction. The ensuing struggle between adherence to God's Covenant and the lure of idolatry led to division and a weakening of the social fabric. It led to political divisiveness, moral and social degeneration, and a breaching of the Covenant as well. Eventually, it brought about the complete destruction of the State.

In the view of the Qumran Scrolls, the monarchy had deserted God, had violated the Covenant, and had led the people astray. The kings of old were directly responsible for the catastrophe of the demise of Temple and State. For that reason, they believed that a pious king had to arise to reverse the entire process and bring things back to their intended, pristine state. Since the biblical kings were responsible for destroying the state, a Davidic descendant, therefore, would be responsible for restoring it.

The ruin of the State brought the Destruction of the Temple, the seat of God's Presence, and the dispersion of the Jews. God's plans for the world were thereby, de facto, thwarted. So in the End Time, the Messiah, the descendent of David, was to gather the Jews back together, to restore the State, to rebuild the Temple, to defeat the forces of evil that opposed God, and finally, to bring peace to the world.

The Messiah ben David was to lead the Jews back to God, back to the Covenant. His job was one of spiritual and moral renewal. He was to restore Israel on a sacred, as well as on a physical level. This was to be the prelude to the coming of God's Kingdom. A restored Israel would arise to signal the final confrontation with all the forces worldwide that stood in permanent opposition to God. The resulting victory would put an end to the domain of evil on earth and allow for the final Judgement of mankind and for the establishment of God's direct and unchallenged rule. God alone would rule, the Word of the God emanating from Zion to the entire world. Then would the karmic debt of the Kings of Israel be repaid and the true paradigm of Divine sovereignty would finally become a reality.

It is important to realize that the concept of the Messiah, per se, developed rather late in the Greek period. It is really within the confines of the Dead Sea materials that one first begins to see any sort of clearly articulated doctrine of the Messiah.

In biblical literature, the term *Mashiach*, "anointed one," never refers to the Messiah, as it does in the later literature of the Greco-Roman period. The process of anointing someone with sacred oil was reserved for one who was being called into a special and intimate relationship with God. In the Bible, the term *Mashiach* refers to three different individuals, who traditionally were anointed for a specific, sacred purpose. They were set aside by God for consecration to a precise, set task.

The books of 1 Samuel, chapters 19:21 and 23:1, and Lamentations, chapter 4:10, speak of the anointing of the King. Upon ascending the throne, the King took on the position of ruler of Israel, of God's vessel of power and protection. The King was duly anointed for this sacred task. Similarly, in conjunction with the Temple and the holy service, the High Priest was consecrated in his post by being anointed with oil (Exodus 29:7, Leviticus 8:12, Psalms 133:2). Biblical references also indicate that prophets, who often served the Temple, and the monarchy, were anointed as well (1 Samuel 24:6–10 and 26:16, 2 Samuel 1:14, Psalms 105:5 and 1 Chronicles 16:22).

Within the centuries of pre-exilic biblical experience, no concept of the Messiah ever emerged. Although the concept of the End of Days began to emerge in the late biblical and the early Persian period, the idea of Messiah was to appear only much later. There is extensive reference to the End of Time in Jewish literature during the Greco-Roman period. There is much discussion of the final war between good and evil, the final Judgement of mankind, and the establishment of God's Kingdom. However, no ideal leader is ever mentioned in association with this coming golden age.

The hope of a final redemption is quite present and very forthright in the literature of the Second Temple period. But no Messiah, as such, is actually mentioned in the books of Daniel, First and Second Maccabees, Tobit, the Wisdom of Solomon, Judith, Ben Sira, the Book of Jubilees, and 2 Enoch. Even within the critical chapters of the Book of Enoch (1–36, and 91–104), there is extensive description of the End Time and the coming of God's Kingdom, but no reference to a Messiah, per se.

The reason for this omission is rather clear. The entire purpose of the End of Days is to bring the demise of the old order and the complete obliteration of evil in this world. The structures of human civilization are to be profoundly changed. The spiritual experience and the physical existence of humanity are to be transformed through the apocalyptic process. War, chaos, and geological upheaval will lead to change. In the aftermath, mankind will be judged. Out of the ashes, a new world will emerge, both physically and spiritually. This new world will be the Kingdom of God.

The apocalypse is a means to an end. It is the route that fulfills itself in the triumph of God. The ultimate objective is the reestablishment of a close, personal, working relationship between God and mankind. It is a new world order that is based on God's direct involvement in human civilization and, subsequently, on peace and on universal justice.

In view of this, the job of a Messiah is one of preparation for the coming of God. The Messiah is consecrated to the task of furthering the cause of God during the apocalypse. In the Qumran literature, the Davidic Messiah leads the forces of good in the final conflict, which will bring the coming of the Kingdom. The final objective is the establishment of God's sovereignty; the means to achieving it is the apocalypse. God's vessel during the apocalyptic process is the Messiah—in fact, it is not a Messiah, but rather two Messiahs.

As the Davidic Messiah was to come to rectify the sins of the Kings of Israel and Judah, a second Messiah—one from the tribe of Levi, one who was a High Priest—had to emerge to atone for, and set right, the sins of the priesthood and the corruption of the Temple and its service. The priesthood shared responsibility for the catastrophe that befell Israel and Judah in biblical times. Therefore, a Levitical

Messiah must stand side-by-side with the Davidic Messiah in the End of Days.

In referring to the Return from the Exile at the beginning of the Second Temple period, Scroll 4Q 390 states that God spoke to the generation of the Return and sent them commandments. As a result, the people came to realize what their forefathers had done, to what extent they had wandered away from the Law, and why the State and the First Temple had been destroyed. Before that generation died, however, the Law, the Sabbath, the holy days, and the Covenant were again forgotten.

Even the sons of Aaron, the priests, would not continue to walk in the way of God's Law. People began to do the same evil that was done in the early days of first settlement of the Land. The Covenant would once more be forsaken and be broken. People would oppress each other for material gain and overpower one another in the pursuit of riches. Even the priests would commit violence, rob each other, defile the Temple, and pollute their seed through illicit unions.

During the End of Days, a Levitical Messiah will arise to stand beside the Davidic Messiah. He will purify the priesthood and the Temple. He will teach the Law and its true deeper meaning to the people. As the Davidic Messiah will lead the people through God's direction and supervision, the Levitical Messiah will teach the Law of God and interpret it through divine inspiration. The new era will be ushered in by the "Shoot of David" and by the "Interpreter of the Law." "This one is the Branch of David, who will stand with the Interpreter of the Law, who will rule in Zion in the latter days . . ." (4Q 174 l. 11).

This duality of leadership has biblical precedence. In 1 Chronicles 29:22, Solomon and Zadok are anointed together by the people as King and as High Priest. In Zechariah 6:9–13, the King and the High Priest are commissioned together. Both were permanent positions of divine authority. The covenant of kingship belongs eternally to David and to his seed, according to the Genesis Florilegium from Qumran (4Q 252). There was to be permanent maintenance of the teaching priest (2 Chronicles 15:3) and the priesthood is promised an eternal role alongside the House of David (Jeremiah 33:17–18).

It is important to note that during the messianic uprising against Rome in 132 c.e., alongside Bar Kochba stood the High Priest Eleazar. He collaborated very closely with Bar Kochba, just as the High Priest Joshua had worked in close unison with Zerubabel in rebuilding the

Second Temple and Judea centuries earlier, when the exiled Jews first returned from Babylonia.

During the First Temple period, God's Presence and guidance was felt through King and priest. The sustenance of the people of Israel came through the intercessory work of the priests, led by the High Priest. The protection of the people was the responsibility of the King. The King, High Priest, and the people were all guided by the word of God that came through the Prophets.

The King and High Priest shared the highest level of authority because they were consecrated to these sacred tasks. They interacted directly with God and were responsible for carrying out His Will and the terms of the Covenant. Prophecy supported this process.

God bestowed the gift of prophecy on whomever He deemed worthy. The monarchy and the High Priesthood, on the other hand, were hereditary posts. Therefore, there was no guarantee that direct enlightenment would come upon King or High Priest. So the role of the Prophet was pivotal. The prophetic message was often directed at the monarchy or the priesthood. It was the King who had to lead and to set the example for the whole nation. It was the Levites who were responsible for teaching the people, and the High Priest who was responsible for them. Hence, both King and High Priest had to be amenable to direction from God. This direction came through the medium of the Prophet.

The assumption made in the literature of the Second Temple period is that the road back to Eden, back to mankind's original pristine state, intimately involved the resurrection of Israel. The salvation of mankind came as result of the political resuscitation of Israel and the moral rebirth of the Jewish people, opening the door to the emergence of the Kingdom of God. The reemergence of prophecy, and the reappearance of the monarchy and the High Priesthood were seen as an integral part of this landmark process.

The Davidic Messiah and the Levitical Messiah will not merely be the King and the High Priest of Israel. They are the anointed ones of God, who will lead Israel and the world toward the establishment of an entirely new era in human experience. They are critical components in the establishment of God's Kingdom. As such, it is their enormous short-term role as Messiahs, rather than their long-term status, which is of immediate importance.

Their long-term status will be of true importance more as subsidiaries of God, rather than as centers of power, per se, after the

Kingdom is fully established. In 2 Esdras, the rule of the Messiahs is pictured as being very limited in scope, and possibly in duration as well. Thereafter, the roles of the monarch and High Priest change in accordance with the new world order. The Kingdom of God is largely His.

The Book of Jubilees (chapter 31) declares that the future power of Israel will reside in the hands of the High Priest of Levi. The Testament of Levi (8:14) states that a king will arise out of Judah and will establish a new priesthood, which will be called by a new name. This points to both the continuation of these institutions and their sustained, close interrelationship after the establishment of the Kingdom of God. What the exact nature, function, and extent of this dual vessel will be, after that point, is not spelled out in the literature. However, their existence is clearly asserted. They are to survive and work together, although in a permanently transformed form and with a redefined status.

The Messiahs and the Final War

The pivotal role of the two Messiahs is far more clearly defined in reference to the final confrontation between good and evil. According to the "War Scroll" (1Q M), this final war between the Sons of Light and the Sons of Darkness will be a war to eradicate and exterminate darkness and evil from the earth, once and for all. Many nations will be involved in this global confrontation, but ultimately the victory will be God's alone.

"A time of salvation will follow for the people of God and a period of rule for all the people of His following, and of everlasting destruction for the adherents of Belial. . . . And the sons of justice will shine to all the ends of the earth and shall go on illuminating until the end of the entire period of darkness. Then, in the time of God, His exalted greatness will shine for all times, for peace and blessing, glory and joy, and long days for all the sons of light" (1Q M, col. 1: l. 5,8–9).

The sons of light are referred to in the Hebrew text as God's *goral*. Conversely, the sons of darkness are called the *goral* of Belial, the Prince of Darkness. The use of the term *goral* in the context of the scrolls seems to refer to those whom fate has placed either in the camp of God or in the camp of Belial. The battle lines between good and evil are clearly drawn, based on a predetermination of which souls belong in which camp.

The doctrine of the inner struggle of light and darkness within humanity, as expressed in the Damascus Covenant, states that each human soul must wrestle with this inner conflict until the End of Time. A person must either ally himself with the light or with the dark within his own being during the Age of Darkness. By doing so, the soul will become proportionately more light or more dark, depending on the choice made and the direction taken. At the End Time, the nature of all souls will be fixed. Depending on the course of action one has chosen and pursued, one's soul is now either predominately composed of the light or of darkness. One's status as a Son of Light or Son of Darkness becomes established fact. The emergence of the End Time signals the point beyond which repentance can no longer be done. The time for the Final Judgement has arrived. One's fate is now to be either among the adherents of God or the Sons of Belial.

The term *goral* implies the status one's soul has during the End Time. It is the fate one has chosen for oneself by the life course one has taken during the Age of Wickedness, when the choice between increasing the good or enhancing the evil within the soul was still available. During the End Time, choice is replaced by a predetermined fate, based on the condition one's soul has reached at that time. It is this soul condition, specifically, that is to be tried and judged in the events that will unfold during the End of Days.

The War Scroll refers quite explicitly to the ultimate objective of the complete extermination of evil (1Q M, col. 1 and col. 18 l. 10–12). During the war, the battle lines will shift. At certain points, the Sons of Light have the upper hand, and at times, the Sons of Darkness take the ascendancy. Ultimately, the Sons of Light will have the victory. What the War Scroll is telling us is that the Sons of Light will reign for a period of time, and during this interval, their light will illuminate the entire world. The final stage of the process, however, remains the establishment of God's reign on earth. It is with the coming of His direct rule that peace, joy, and longevity become the norm of human existence.

The role of the Messiahs is tied most heavily to the End Time. Their function centers on the war, on the Final Judgement, and on the reconstruction process. The Davidic Messiah will lead the troops in battle, assisted heavily by the High Priest. It is the priests who will prepare the Sons of Light for battle. No one unclean shall be allowed to enter their camp. All who are fighting for God must be perfect in body and spirit and prepared for the Day of Vengeance. Every soldier in the camp must cleanse and purify himself on the day of battle (1Q M, col. 7).

The battle is directed by the signals being trumpeted by the priests. Trumpet signals are blown on ram's horns to rally the troops. The sounds of the *shofar*, the ram's horn, function as memorials (tactical signals) for alarm, for pursuit, and for reassembly. The priests do not take direct part on the battlefield itself, since that would bring them into direct contact with dead bodies and, hence, render them ritually impure. However, their presence and their effectiveness are indispensable to victory, since they are directing the course of the battle through divine inspiration and guidance. Should they become ritually contaminated, they would be rendered functionally useless (1Q M, col. 7,8).

The function of the High Priest is to exhort the army and to rally it. The High Priest is responsible for assisting in the formulation and direction of the battle strategy. It is the High Priest who speaks to the troops prior to the beginning of the battle, urging them on. During those times, when the army regroups during the battle, again it is the High Priest who is present, taking up a position and addressing the troops. He encourages them to press on. When the battle is done, it is the High Priest who will lead the people in prayer and praise of God (1Q M, col. 15,16,19).

The idea of God's blessings being bestowed upon the Sons of Light during the final battles of the war is reiterated in Scroll 4Q 285. Here, the High Priest is said to address the troops during the final battles and to bless them with the Name of God. They are to be called by God's Name and not just be blessed in the name of the Most High. This means that they are to be imbued with God's Name. The High Priest will invoke the Name of God as he did on the Day of Atonement, and the Sons of Light will be transformed by becoming blessed and empowered by the Name.

This act performed by the High Priest is of enormous importance. The actual Name of God is to be invoked and identified with the Sons of Light at this time. This act will elevate them to a position of great holiness and of great intimacy with God. Their status will become equal to that of the angels. Scroll 4Q 285 states: Blessed are God's actions and blessed are His angels. God and His holy angels will stand in the midst of the Sons of Light, and they, like the angels, will be called by God's sacred Name.

The effect of this blessing will be not only spiritual elevation, but also material blessing. Removed from the Land will be all pestilence and disease, all plagues and obstacles, and all wild beasts. The blessing of the Name aligns the souls of the faithful with the flow of divine energy. They become participants in the process of salvation. They become vessels for the Presence of God on earth, as the angelic host is in heavens. The manifestation of God's power on earth is seen as elevating the souls of the Sons of Light and healing the material reality in which they live and are to serve God.

The work of salvation remains the joint effort of both Messiahs. "The shoot of David will stand with the Interpreter of the Law, who [ ] . . . , in Zion during the End of Days" (4Q 174, col. 1:11).

Scroll 4Q458, fragment 2 suggests that the Davidic Messiah will destroy the Prince of Darkness, and that all the uncircumcised, who follow the way of darkness, will be swallowed up with him. The Sons of Light, on the other hand, will be justified in the end, having followed the one who was anointed with the oil of Kingship and walked according to the Law. It is the seed of David, specifically, who is to maintain and fulfill the Covenant terms of kingship. ". . . [U]ntil the coming of the Righteous Messiah, the Shoot of David. For to him and his seed were given the Covenant of the kingship of His people, for all generations, eternally" (4Q 252, col. 1:3).

The function of the Davidic Messiah is articulated in the blessings of the prince found in Scroll 1Q 5b. The prince of the congregation is blessed because he renews the Covenant, dispenses justice, and protects the oppressed. He stands as guardian of the Sons of Light and establishes the Covenant during the dark days preceding the final triumph of God. During the time of great affliction, he maintains the integrity and observance of the Covenant. Through the fight, he will lead God's people, and eventually, he will succeed in establishing a state for his people permanently, his rule being sanctioned and supported by God. It is up to the Davidic Messiah—with the help of the High Priest, the Levitical Messiah—to destroy the generation of falsehood and to establish a lasting and eternal peace.

War and Triumph

The first enemy to conquer is the one within. Many people have been led astray by the Spouter of Lies (1Q 14). These people have cast off the commandments and ignored the words and teachings of the Prophets. Instead, they revered those who led them astray, as if they were gods. Forsaking God's laws, they walked in the ways of the Gentiles, adopting human law over divine law. Rejecting the Law of God, they sought to follow the customs of the pagan world. At the End of Time, the High Priest will stretch out his hand against Ephraim—that is, against those who defected and became idolaters, rebelling against God and deliberately assimilating into the outside world. They will be ravaged for their rebellion during the End Time (4Q 166, 4Q 167).

The young lion, the Davidic Messiah, will execute judgement upon the rebels. The city of Ephraim will be filled with destruction in the final days, and those who turned the people from the ways of God will stumble because of their guilty counsel. The streets will be filled with the corpses of those who, walking in lies and flourishing by falsehood, perverted the nation. Those who led Ephraim astray with false teaching, lying, and deceit—be they kings, princes, priests, or laymen—shall be brought to destruction because of the route they chose to take (4Q 169).

The Habakkuk Scroll (1Q Habakkuk) and the Commentary on Psalms (4Q 171) both speak of the history of the Sectarian community. Both seem to use those past events to allude to the course of events during the Last Days. In the past, the rebellion against God brought with it corruption, oppression, and violence. Those who followed the Wicked Priest (the Spouter of Lies) came to despise the Law of God and abandoned it. They perverted justice and persecuted the innocent. They pursued and persecuted the Teacher of Righteousness and the Sectarian community with particular vehemence. Similarly, men of violence and breakers of the Covenant will pay no heed to the prophecies. They will disregard the warnings during the End of Days.

The Wicked Priest started out walking in the path of God, in truth. However, he was corrupted by power. He turned from God, associated with men of violent disposition, and used his power to amass great wealth. He led many people astray from the path of God. He deliberately went about vilifying and humiliating those who chose to serve God. He persecuted the simple people and robbed the poor of their possessions.

It is to be surmised that in the End Time, a similar process will occur. The leadership of Israel will emulate the other nations of the world. It will be divided, and those corrupted by power will amass great wealth at the expense of the people and actively persecute the righteous. This pattern is one symbolic of worldwide corruption. Hence, the End Time brings universal punishment and rectification.

Under the leadership of an Anti-Messiah, the *Kittim*, the scourge of God, will arise from afar to devour and devastate civilization. The *Kittim* shall plunder the cities of the earth. They will inspire fear, plot evil, and deal with the nations of the earth in guile and deceit. It is the wealth amassed by the greedy and the corrupt, who lusted after power, which attracts them. They are a scourge sent to punish the cities of the earth for their sins.

The *Kittim* are ruthless and merciless. They murder and plunder indiscriminately. They worship violence, thrive on enriching themselves by plunder and tribute, devastating nations and ravaging the land. The Wicked Priest and his followers, the wicked of Ephraim and Manasseh, who did so much damage and committed such violence, will, in turn, be turned over to the violent *Kittim* for judgement. Their wealth will be confiscated and the Wicked Priest will suffer greatly, being ravaged by disease. He will die a painful death and with great bitterness of soul.

The wicked among God's people will suffer greatly, thereby expiating their guilt through their distress. However, God will not destroy the nation. All who observe the Law in the House of Judah, God will deliver from judgement. On one hand, those who do not turn from evil and fail to return to the Law of God will be cut off. On the other, the congregation of the humble will accept this difficult time as a season of penance and will be delivered. They will be kept alive during the time of famine and humiliation. They will inherit the glory of Adam. The humble shall inherit the earth. The righteous of Israel will possess the Land and enjoy the delights of God's sanctuary.

These two scrolls speak of both a time of great tribulation, when the enemies of God are given a period of brief ascendancy to punish the world for the reign of violence and greed, and also of the final triumph of God, when His Sanctuary is restored and when the honest and the humble take possession of the earth, ending once and for all the age-old reign of arrogance, fear, and tyranny. According to the *midrash* on the Last Days (4Q 174), a new Sanctuary will arise—one built of devoted people who, sensitive to the Will of God, offer up the works of the Law, moral actions, and ethical conduct as the offerings to God. By practicing the precepts of God, they will know God and be strong.

At the End of Days, victory will be assigned to Melchizedek (the Davidic Messiah) and the Sons of Light. All of their iniquities shall be forgiven at that time. Melchizedek will judge the holy ones of God, and he will avenge God by attending to the complete destruction of the camp of the wicked. On the Day of Peace, the Messenger (the Levitical Messiah) will announce the final salvation of mankind and expound fully the interpretation of all the prophetic teachings. All people will then come to understand the deeper meaning of time and the ages of man (11Q Melchizedek).

The Kingdom of God

There are some clues regarding the nature of the post-Judgement world, the coming age of mankind, in the Dead Sea literature. The subject does not appear to be dealt with nearly as extensively as that of the End of Days. There are far fewer references and the details involved are more implicit than explicit. Yet in order to get the full impact of the emotions and the doctrines involved, it is important to examine and to understand some of these allusions.

Many of the allusions to the coming age are connected with things mentioned regarding the Messiah. Scroll 4Q 534–536 refers specifically to the Messiah as the Elect of God. The term "the Elect of God" is used in the Qumran literature in several contexts. This term is often used to refer to the Sons of Light, in general, or to the leaders of the Sectarian community specifically. In this context, it is being used to refer to the Messiah or Messiahs, in particular. However, what it says about the Messiah(s) can be inferred to apply equally to the Sons of Light and their leadership.

This would mean that the allusions to the Messiah, particularly in the Sectarian literature, are meant as broader paradigms. Remember, the Sectarians felt that they were establishing a model of spiritual practice that would ultimately be adopted by the entire purified and reconstructed House of Israel. The idea here would be that the Messiah(s) set the precedent. They set down the new paradigm. It is then established in practice by the elders of Israel. Once established, it becomes the norm for all of Israel.

In these scroll fragments, it is stated that the Messiah will not die during the Days of Wickedness. Moreover, attempts to destroy and defeat him will fail. This same assertion about the protection and survival of the Sons of Light during the dark days of the End Time is also made in a number of the apocalyptic scrolls.

The scrolls state that God will speak to the Elect of God. The reference here seems to have two levels of meaning. On the one hand, God will speak directly with and provide guidance and direction to the Messiah(s) during the End of Days and beyond. Hence, the Davidic Messiah's ability to lead the forces of Good and to defeat the forces of Evil stems directly from God. The Messiah acts only as a physical vessel.

This concept is one that is very characteristic of biblical thought. From Moses through the late Prophets, God's rule was channeled through the leaders of the people. The power and the authority, the good and the blessing that the people received was from God alone. The leaders and rulers of the nation were the agents of God. They were not all-powerful. They were consecrated to God's service. Recognition of the good they were receiving was to go to God, the true source from which all goodness and help flowed.

It was the one isolated occasion in his career, when Moses lost his temper and produced a miracle without making it evident that it was really God who was performing the act, which accounted for his exclusion from the Promised Land. Although Moses was extremely faithful to God and exceedingly humble, one mistake brought this great punishment. Even though he had done so much, when he failed to credit God, even once, with responding to the needs of the people and made it appear, albeit inadvertently, that it was his power that was protecting them and providing for them, he sinned gravely. This action God considered unforgivable. It ended in an irrevocable punishment. Moses would lead the people to the Promised Land, but he would not be able to enter it.

This concept is reiterated in the Prayer of Nabonidus (4Q pr Nab). The king is afflicted with an ulcer for seven years. It is a punishment by God. After the seven years, the Jews of the Exile pardon the king for his sins in God's Name and he recovers from the illness. The Jews do not wish to be thanked. Rather, they tell the king that he must realize that it is God who healed his affliction. He is instructed to write an account of this for future generations to read and understand. In the end, Nabonidus does so. The scroll goes on to say that the conclusion he reached was that the malady lasted seven full years because during that entire time span he was seeking help from gods who he thought were divine but who, in truth, were not.

The message here is that God alone afflicts and heals. All is in the hands of the Creator. To seek salvation anywhere else is not only futile, it only serves to exacerbate the problem. One aggravates and worsens the situation. One only increases the suffering by looking to "other gods," to outside sources for help. Everything flows from God. That is where all eyes should constantly be turned. To look elsewhere is a grave sin. This was the sin of the Kings of Israel. This was their failure. This is where they led the people astray. This course of action brought more than suffering and pain as a result; it eventually brought destruction and devastation.

Scroll 4Q 521 states that both the heavens and the earth will obey the Messiah. Why? Because, he will not turn aside from the commandments of the holy ones. There will be righteous and holy people who will act as vessels for divine communication. This is said specifically of the Teacher of Righteousness in a number of the scrolls. It is mentioned also in connection with the Levites, who are responsible for teaching the people. What is being referred to here is the interpretation of the Law.

During the period after the Judgement of humanity, God will reappear and issue new commandments, as he did originally at Mount Sinai. The Interpreter of the Law, the Levitical Messiah, and the Levites will expound on them afterward. The Davidic Messiah will follow their interpretations very faithfully, and as a result, there will be a harmony of Will affecting heaven and earth.

The paradigm here is that in the coming age, the leadership of the peoples of the world will work in close harmony with the interpretations of God's Words emanating from inspired teachers and prophets. Moreover, this scroll makes it clear that it is not just the leadership who will communicate directly with God. Those who wait patiently in their hearts—that is, they open their hearts up to receive light—will find God. God will visit His spirit upon the *hasidim* ("the pious") and will call the *tzadikim* ("the righteous") by His Name. The *hasidim* will be established on the Throne of the Eternal Kingdom.

The terms *hasidim* and *tzadikim* need to be clearly understood in this context. The word *hasid* comes from the Hebrew root *HSD*. *Hesed* can be translated as "piety," but also means "lovingkindness," "compassion," and "grace." A *hasid*, then, is one who emulates these qualities, and as a result, links his being to God's grace and loving-kindness, thereby manifesting them in the world. A *tzadik* is one who is linked to *tzedek*, "justice" and "righteousness." Through his devotion to morality and to acts of righteousness, the *tzadik* brings justice into the world. The humble ones, the meek who will inherit the earth, are *hasidim* and *tzadikim*. Many will connect with the higher realms of *hesed* and *tzedek*. It is they who will bring down into the world compassion and grace, righteousness and justice, producing balance in the world and the abundance of God's blessing.

The reference to the *hasidim* being established on the Throne of the Eternal Kingdom is another way of saying that the humble and the modest will inherit the earth. They will be the model and the behavioral norm in the coming era of mankind. The Eternal Kingdom refers to the reconstituted reality of earth after the End Time. The Throne represents the center of authority. It is also the link between heaven and earth. The objective of the mysticism prevalent during this period of time in Jewish history was to reach the celestial Throne of God and stand directly in God's Presence. That is, the objective of mystical experience was to achieve intimacy with God in the fullest sense. The Throne was the symbolic image of this intimacy.

The scroll continues to say that God raises up those who are bowed down, opens the eyes of the blind, and releases the captives. Therefore, one should cling to God forever. These phrases are very familiar to Jews. They appear in the morning blessings, recited every day as part of the ancient, traditional liturgy of rabbinic Judaism. Yet here in this context, they seem to be used in a different manner and to have a specific message.

The first three phrases in the text are all in the present tense. The following three, however, unlike the preceding set of phrases, are all cast in the future tense. The sense of the first three phrases is that of immediacy. These are realities that are available to us now, even though we are still enmeshed in the Age of Darkness. They are also realities that will carry over into the next age as well.

The order and conjunction of phrases indicates a clear pattern of experience open to us. If one clings to God first, God will remove the burden of life from one's shoulders. The Hebrew *Zokef Kefufim* is traditionally rendered "to raise up the ones who are bowed down or bent over." The implication is one of lifting a burden off a person's shoulders and allowing him to straighten up. The first stage of the process is relief from the obsessions of life and the regaining of self-esteem.

Next, God opens the eyes of the blind. On a spiritual level, this would be enlightenment. Once the illusions of life are eliminated, once

the burdens that life seems to impose, emotionally and psychologically, are lifted, one's entire perception of life and its meaning change
dramatically. One sees the higher truths, the broader realities.

This leads immediately to "releasing the captive." Enlightenment
gives birth to emancipation. Once a person sees the world as it really
is, he is freed from any attachment to it. That is, the emotional and
intellectual bonds that enslave us to the world are subsequently dis-
solved. Once we can see the world from the higher perspectives of
spiritual reality, the emotional and intellectual investments that we
have, which bind us to the physical plane of existence, are finally
surrendered. The result is that we are emancipated from the bondage
of materialism and illusion.

These stages of the process are stated in the present tense in our
text. The subsequent stages are phrased in the future tense. This suggests that the authors of the text felt that the remaining stages of the
process will only become realities in the next age of mankind, the post-
End Time. In other words, now, clinging to God, devotion to God, is
a three-stage process. In the future, it will be a six-stage process.

The text says that trusting in God's *Hesed*, in God's Loving-
kindness and Grace, will lead to three additional phenomena. God
will heal the *halalim*. He will bring the dead back to life and He will
bring good news (*mevaser*) to the modest. The shift from the present
to the future tense suggests the idea that this is a future, rather than
current, possibility—that these three components of the process of
devotion to God will be accessible realities only after the End Time.

Two of these future concepts do appear in the morning blessings of the traditional liturgy as well. However, there are a couple of
important differences. In the morning blessings found in the Jewish
prayer book, the prayers bless God who heals the sick and revives the
dead. They are in the present tense. The concept of the reviving of
the dead is connected, in the liturgy, with the idea of the daily renewal of Creation by God. The underlying assumption of the liturgy
is that God creates continually. The universe exists on a moment-to-
moment basis, totally dependent on the Will of God. This concept
was most likely shared by the authors of the text. However, it is clear
that the use of the term "will revive the dead" by the Sectarians is
referring to something else, since it is cast into the future.

The theological import of the rabbinic version of this concept is
that just as God resurrects the world in its entirety every day, so,
too, does He restore the souls of the departed to life in the World to

Come, resurrecting them in the future life, beyond the confines of this world. And so, too, is the Next World totally dependent on His Will, continually.

The context of the concept of the revival of the dead in Scroll 4Q 521 points to a very different message. On one hand, it could refer to the resurrection of souls on the physical level as a mark of the new age of mankind. The implication, then, would be that of reincarnation becoming either the norm in the coming age or the awareness of reincarnation as a continuing reality becoming common in post-messianic times. Or it could be read as the fifth stage of the process of spiritual awakening.

In the traditional liturgy, the blessing of healing is phrased "God heals the sick." The term used there, in Hebrew, is *holim*, meaning "those that are sick." In the scroll's version, the term reads *yerafeh halalim*, meaning "He will heal the *halalim*." This term can be translated either as "the sick," or as "the holes," "the voids."

As a logical sequence to the first three terms, the later concept seems more appropriate. That is, that in the post-End Time, devotion to God will be followed by a process of emotional and spiritual connection to God's Grace and Lovingkindness. Trust in God, at that point, having achieved enlightenment and detachment, will bring one to a healing of the voids within. A completion will take place. One will become whole. The inner vacancies, the sense of isolation, of fear, of insecurity and doubt, will all be healed and vanish. Then, the dead will be revived. The individual linked to God's love is truly reborn as a fully functioning, spiritual being. Now he is living on earth as he would live in heaven, on a higher spiritual plane of existence.

The last term mentioned in the text has no parallel in rabbinic literature. It states that God will bring good news to the modest, to the humble. The concept most likely refers to the coming of inspiration and prophetic capacity to the true seeker, the truly humble. It is the humble who are to inherit the earth in the messianic age.

This would represent the final stage in the process of attachment to God in the new age. The soul reborn, brought to a new level of spiritual experience and reality, becomes humble and modest as a result. The Hebrew term *anav* means "humble," "modest." It implies "self effacing," "open and ready to receive." Linguistically, *anav* is a variation of *ani*, meaning "poor."

As a consequence of becoming humble and open, the reborn soul is able to receive "good news," knowledge of the highest spiritual sort, information from higher planes of reality, prophetic inspiration, and great wisdom. In Scroll 4Q 534–536, God calls the Messiah "the Elect of God" and reveals to him the highest mysteries. Would that not also be the case with the elect of God, those who through great devotion and dedication choose to go through the process of spiritual emergence? It is they who in the new age will emerge from their quest humble and open, and thereby inherit the earth. The enlightened ones, the holy ones, will set the model for all people, bridging the gap between heaven and earth by living a fully spiritual existence on this plane of earthly existence.

The new order for humanity will involve a full restoration of Eden. Both the world and humanity are brought back to their original pristine states. The heavens and the earth are to be transformed. Light and blessing will predominate in the new, reconstructed, post-Judgement world. Jerusalem, the center of the new order, will be purified and a new Jerusalem, inhabited by the righteous and the holy, will be ruled over by the Messiah(s). As was the case in the Garden of Eden, no evil will exist in the purified world of the post-End Time.

> And He shall open the gates of Paradise, He shall remove the sword that has threatened [i.e., has barred entrance] since Adam. And He will allow the holy ones to eat of the Tree of Life. The spirit of holiness shall be upon them. (Testament of Levi 18:10–11)
>
> On that day, I shall cause My holy Elect One to dwell among them. I shall transform heaven and make it a blessing of light forever. I shall also transform the earth and make it a blessing, and cause My elect ones to dwell on her. Then, those who have committed sin and crime shall not step foot in her. For in peace, I have looked upon My righteous ones, have given them mercy, and have caused them to dwell before Me. But, sinners have come before Me, so that by judgement, I shall destroy them from before the face of the earth. (1 Enoch 45:4–6)
>
> And you cleanse the earth of all injustice, of all defilement and of all oppression, from all sin and from all iniquity which is being done on earth. Remove them from the earth. And all the children of the people will become righteous, and all nations shall worship and bless Me. They will all prostrate themselves to Me. And the earth shall be cleansed of all pollution, from all sin, and from all plague and suffering. And it shall not happen again that I send these upon the earth from generation to generation and forever. (1 Enoch 10:20–22)

As heaven and earth are reconstituted so as to bring all of Creation and mankind back to their original state of purity, so, too, is

the city of Jerusalem rebuilt as the spiritual capital of the world. From
the reconstructed Jerusalem, God alone will reign eternally. "And the
holy ones shall refresh themselves in Eden. The righteous shall rejoice in the New Jerusalem, which shall be for the eternal glorifica-
tion of God. And Jerusalem shall no longer undergo desolation, nor
shall Israel be led into captivity, because God will be in her midst.
The Holy One of Israel will rule over those [living] in humility and
modesty. He who trusts in Him shall reign in truth in the heavens"
(Testament of Dan 5:12–13).

This is the picture of the coming messianic age of mankind. It is
one of the return to Eden for all of humanity. The relationship between heaven and earth is restored. Both the earth and the human
race are returned to a state of innocence. Evil disappears permanently
from the world and justice, righteousness, and truth become the norm
of civilization. God's Presence reemerges in the world.

Centered in Jerusalem, the living Word of God will flow continually to all the peoples of the earth. God converses directly to
mankind once again. The Temple is rebuilt, and the priesthood is
purified and reconstituted. God's Words, emanating from Zion, are
interpreted by the High Priest and the Prophets, and the King and
rulers faithfully carry out the divine imperatives. The Levites teach
the people, and many people undergo the process of spiritual evolution. They come to understand the deeper levels of truth and to experience greater connection to God and justice and compassion from
their fellow man. "And in those days, the people will begin to search
the Law and to search the commandments, and to return to the way
of righteousness. . . . And they will know that God is the executor of
judgement, but He will show mercy to hundreds and thousands, to
all who love Him" (Book of Jubilees 23:26,31).

Not only is the new order to be one of peace and justice; it is
to be an era of "searching the Law." That is, the coming messianic
age is to be one of spiritual evolution and of soul growth, an age
marked by increased communication between man and God. Hence,
a new level of human understanding and experience is to emerge as
a result. The holy ones willing to go through the process of spiritual transformation will be those who become spiritually elevated.
Their souls will be opened and they will become one with the supernal wisdom. They will come to experience the Word of God directly
from within, as a living dialogue, and thereby come to understand
it intimately.

The Word of God is the Law. The Law is the embodiment of Wisdom. Wisdom is the gateway to intimacy with God. It will be Wisdom, the pursuit of it, its distillation, its assimilation, and its transformative capacity, which will be the hallmark of the messianic age. Man will truly come to know God and to experience holiness by absorbing, assimilating, and becoming one with Wisdom, the deeper paradigms of reality, and the living Word of God.

13

THE SECRETS AND
THE MYSTERIES

Within the Sectarian literature, there is a tacit admission that certain realities have a depth that is beyond the scope of purely intellectual comprehension. The view of the Hebrew Bible is that the levels of man's life that involve direct interaction with God are experiential in essence. These realms of human existence cannot be grasped by thought or by reason alone. They are intense experiences that must be embraced on multiple levels of consciousness.

In the deserts of Sinai, the miracles were the Revelation at Mount Sinai, the pillars of cloud and fire, the voice of God over the Ark, and the wonders and miracles God wrought through Moses and Joshua. In the Land of Israel, it was the Temple, the sacrifices, the rituals, the prayers, and the meditations that were wonders. Interaction with God was the intercession of the High Priest, the leadership of the King, and the Words of God transmitted through the Prophets. These were all dimensions of God's love, protection, and guidance. They were the continuing experience of the Divine Presence.

God's direct involvement in the life of the people was constant, perpetual, and all-inclusive. This multi-leveled reality encompassed a vast spectrum of experience that was designed to keep Israel in close touch with God and to facilitate divine guidance. The interplay between God and Israel took on many experiential forms and constituted the very core of the Covenant. Such experiences as Temple worship, ritual, sacrifice and offering, prophecy, et cetera, encompassed and wove together the realms of physical action, emotional response, intellectual understanding, and spiritual realization.

All of these processes form active parts of the Covenant. In giving Israel the Law, God had revealed the commandments to them. The laws and ordinances became realities because God had commanded them. God instituted all of these realities as elements of observing the Covenant. The emergence of prophecy, the building of the Ark and the Tabernacle, the establishment of the rituals and the priesthood, the settlement in the Land of Israel were all done in connection with the activation of the Covenant sealed at Mount Sinai.

In essence, all of these elements were the manifestations of the Covenant. It was part of the Revelation process. God first revealed Himself. Then He revealed the Law and established the Covenant with Israel. Finally, God created and perpetuated the various means by which the Covenant was to be fulfilled and maintained. All of the details were clearly spelled out and implemented. Although the deeper meanings and intent behind the Covenant and its component parts could only be accessed through experience and comprehended by reflection, the form and general content were clearly delineated for purposes of observance.

In other words, the Covenant between God and Israel was based on the establishment and maintenance of a close working relationship. The Covenant relationship was designed to create an intimacy between God and His people. This intimacy expressed itself continually in the day-to-day life of the people.

Various vehicles were established specifically for this purpose: Settlement in the Land, the Sabbath and the Holy Days, the Temple and the rituals, Priesthood and Kingship, prophecy and the teaching of the Law. Keeping the Covenant meant maintaining the intimacy between God and Israel. The key to maintaining the intimacy was through adherence to God's guidance via observance of the Law, devotion in ritual, and harkening to the direct word of God through King, Priest, and Prophet.

All of the details and requirements for doing so are clearly spelled out in the Torah, in the Law. All is revealed from that perspective. The inner meaning of the Covenant, however, is hidden. By maintaining intimacy and observing the Covenant in all its various dimensions, one can come to experience an interrelationship with the divine. By delving into the experience, by letting it affect one physically, emotionally, psychologically, and spiritually, one can come to a sense of the deeper layers of meaning inherent in the Covenant.

When one reaches to the inner depths of the Law and experiences the deeper meanings and more universal content of the Covenant, one then connects with Wisdom. Wisdom in the biblical view refers to the divine root of things. Wisdom is the core content, the universal essence of Creation. Wisdom is the Supernal Truth. It can only be reached by comprehensive experience, deep reflection, and the awakening of profound realization.

One attains Wisdom through this process of realization. Elements of Wisdom are revealed to the seeker as deep insights and profound realizations. These insights and realizations are points of great enlightenment and are referred to in post-biblical Jewish literature as secrets or mysteries. The message in the literature, both within the Dead Sea Scrolls and in later Jewish mystic literature, is that one must experience a secret or mystery on multiple personal levels, assimilate it, reflect on it, ponder it, and come to know it intimately. Only then does enlightenment overcome the seeker. Only then do profound realizations occur. Direct connection is made to Wisdom, to understanding, at the highest level.

There are two secrets or mysteries that play a significant role in the thought of the Sectarian literature of Qumran: the mystery of sin and the mystery of "what we will become." It is important to explore both of these concepts thoroughly. Aside from being related to each other, they are crucial in understanding the scrolls' view of the End Time and they point to an understanding of the renewed status of mankind in the Kingdom of God to follow.

The Mystery of Sin

The doctrine of the Two Natures, articulated in the Damascus Covenant, stated that God had implanted within mankind two opposing forces, one of light and one of dark. The purpose of this duality was to create conflict and struggle within the human soul. The belief is expressed that without internal struggle there is no spiritual growth—the implication being that mankind required this internal tension in order to evolve to a certain point.

On one hand, the dichotomy of the light and dark forces struggling for control of the soul is a direct result of Adam and Eve's eating from the Tree of Knowledge. Good and evil became concrete realities only after partaking of the knowledge of good and evil. Once good and evil were realized, they became part of human experience. As such, human experience became a conflict. A polarization of energy took place, resulting in inner light and darkness. The forces within the soul were now differentiated from each other. God set them at odds with each other, thereby setting up conditions for inner struggle.

The differentiation of forces left mankind in a state of duality that made it impossible for man to remain in Eden. The eating of the fruit and the rebellion against God created a vast breach within mankind itself. The human soul became imbalanced and separated from communion with God. The expulsion from Eden marked the emergence of a great chasm. Mankind devolved dramatically as a result of the choice made. As a result, humanity would now have to evolve back to its original state of being.

To facilitate this process of return, God set the forces of light and dark against each other. A contest would ensue in which each individual soul would be tested by having to contend with this enormous inner conflict. One could adhere to the light or cling to the dark. The very quality of one's soul and the core of one's being were affected by the decisions made. Adherence to the light increased the proportion of light in one's soul. Clinging to the dark, in thought and action, conversely increased the degree to which one's being was darkened.

This process was to continue for millennia, until such time as God determined to end it. During this End Time, evil would be eliminated from human life and experience forever. The Sons of Light, those souls who at that juncture had evolved and were predominantly light, would be saved, inheriting the new order, the Kingdom of God, the reconstituted Eden. Those who devolved into the Sons of Darkness and refused to repent or give up their evil would be permanently swept away, their souls irrevocably cut off or destroyed.

The concept in the scrolls is that mankind had made the choice of embracing good and evil. Man now had to live out the consequences. Over a predetermined period, God would allow each individual soul to prove itself. In the End Time, souls would be judged as to their nature and the degree to which they had evolved or devolved. The final disposition of their souls would be in the hands of God. Those that were judged to be Sons of Light would inherit the Kingdom of God, the restored Eden. No place would be left for the Sons of Darkness.

The age that ran from the expulsion from Eden to the emergence of God's Kingdom on earth, from the fall of mankind to the final salvation of humanity, was the Age of Wickedness. This age was characterized by the duality of good and evil and the incessant conflict between them. As long as the duality of good and evil held sway, not only could evil develop and flourish, it often had the upper hand. Evil continually sought to perpetuate itself and to grow in strength. The conditions of the Age of Wickedness favored it.

Although it is never stated outright, a major concept here is that evil continually seeks to perpetuate itself and that the wicked among humanity believe they can ultimately triumph over God and over the forces of good. Their objectives and their labors all foster that end. The aims and efforts of the Sons of Darkness are spelled out fairly clearly in Scroll 4Q 184.

This scroll uses the image of a wanton woman as a metaphor for evil and for the workings of the forces of darkness. The Wicked Woman leads the community astray. Her objective is to separate people from God and from salvation. Her foundation is that of darkness itself. Evil emanates from darkness. The forms it takes are manifestations of darkness. The wanton woman sets up her dwelling in gloom. The basis of her appeal is despair and hopelessness.

Her adornments are the various forms the disease of corruption takes on. Evil has many variations, all of them corrupting and debilitating. Corruption is the beginning of all wickedness and all who embrace this path are led to ruin. The paths of evil lead to the guilt of transgression. Its gates open into death. Embracing the wanton is the road to Sheol. All who descend there never return.

The objective of the wicked is to overtake the just. They seek to contort the path of the upright and to divert the righteous from the precepts of God's Law. Their aim is to make the simple rebel against God and turn them from the practice of justice, forcing them to abandon the correct paths of righteousness and truth.

Connection to God means walking in God's Law, obeying the divine precepts, acting righteously, and doing justice. As long as one continues to do so, there is no room for evil. Evil is parasitic. Evil has to continually feed on the good if it is to survive. It has to destroy righteousness, not merely defeat it, in order to foster its own existence. The more good grows, the less room there is for evil to flourish. The stronger the forces allied with God become, the less corruption can exist. There is less and less for evil to sustain itself on.

Evil stands in direct and deliberate opposition to God. It must foster rebellion against God's Will to sustain the very core of its existence. Hence, the forces of evil seek to destroy those who walk with God. Their aim is to sever the link with God, in order to maintain control and dominance on earth. All human action that strengthens God's position in the world does far more than merely threaten the position of evil. Ultimately, it would mean evil's complete and utter extinction.

The implication in the scrolls is that evil stems from the darkness of the soul that resulted from man's decision in Eden to assimilate good and evil. Acting on this decision, God has set up the conflict within mankind as a test and a process of purification. From the standpoint of the forces of good, this struggle is a process of spiritual evolution and of soul growth. If one can overcome the dark forces within and survive the assault of the evil without, one grows spiritually. Victorious, such a soul will eventually become worthy to inherit the Kingdom of God when it is finally established on earth.

From the viewpoint of the forces of evil, the conflict is rather one of sheer survival. Only by destroying the forces of good, and diminishing or eliminating the links between humanity and God on the earth plane, can evil hope to ensure its own survival.

What starts out at the expulsion from Eden as an internal conflict becomes not only an external struggle, but also a universal, final confrontation during the End Time. Either God or the forces of darkness will triumph on this level. The Sectarian literature of the Dead Sea Scrolls makes it abundantly clear that there is absolutely no doubt that God and the forces of light will emerge completely victorious in the end. If this is so, then evil has no future. All who adhere to it will, in the end, perish. Why, then, does man persist in behaving in such a totally self-destructive manner? We are led to consider a great mystery. Why does sin exist at all?

The mystery of sin is addressed in Scroll 1Q 27. All peoples loathe sin. What nation views itself as evil or favors sin, transgression, and corruption? All peoples condemn evil and injustice, yet they all walk in its shadow and are motivated by its influence. All nations praise the truth, yet not one is consistent with it. The truth gets bent, distorted, and often deliberately ignored or overridden. What passes for the truth are often just relative truths, propagated to support illusion, parochial beliefs, and narrow self-interests. What people wishes to be oppressed by another more powerful than they are? What nation wants to be robbed of its heritage? Yet where is there a nation that, at some time, has not looted another of its wealth or taken advantage of its neighbor?

Why is there evil? Why does humanity continue to sin? Why is transgression so ingrained in human civilization? Because people have not come to terms with the ancient mystery, the mystery of sin. The ancient mystery of sin exists solely because humanity does not understand the mystery of the future. They do not understand the ultimate cataclysmic effect of clinging to sin and failing to renounce evil.

The Sons of Darkness do not comprehend the mystery of the future, the mystery of the Day of Judgement. They do not understand what will happen to them. Therefore, they make no attempt to give up evil and save their souls from final destruction. Evil will in the end disappear, as darkness does before the light. Sin will vanish like smoke and no longer exist. Those who are evil and whose souls have been polluted by sin, the unrepentant, will vanish as well. Justice will ultimately be revealed in its fullness. Morality and righteousness will come to regulate the world. Knowledge will pervade the world and there will no longer be any room for evil or those connected with it. The dominion of evil shall have passed away from the earth.

The view of the scrolls is that sin and corruption are perpetuated by ignorance and conceit. Evil, in its drive to justify itself and ensure its survival, seeks vainly to destroy the righteous and to preempt God so as to rule over the earth in His place. The wicked, blindly and persistently, cling to violence and corruption. They strive to debase mankind and pervert justice, because they arrogantly choose to remain oblivious to the ultimate result of their actions: self-destruction and obliteration.

The theme of much of the Sectarian literature and the thrust of their way of life point to the need to move beyond evil and to separate oneself from it entirely. The assumptions made in the literature are that evil is a corrupting force that must be shunned. Confronting evil is of no real value. Those who seek to do evil do not ponder, let alone understand, what their ultimate fate will be. If they remain intransigent and hostile to the Law of God and to the Will of God, they will be lost. Others corrupted by them or tempted by them into a similar rebellion against God will also be destroyed in the end.

Evil is perpetuated by ignorance and by the ensuing arrogance that follows from it. In the End Time, Light will confront Darkness in a final showdown. Until that point, when God ordains the time for salvation, it is not the task of the forces of light to battle evil. Rather, they are to break the chains of oppression, corruption, violence, and rebellion. But how is this to be accomplished?

Breaking the Bonds of Corruption

As we have seen earlier, the Sectarian literature regards riches and wealth as one of the three great snares, one of the three primary causes of evil. The pursuits of wealth and power were seen as prime agents of corruption and evil. These pursuits led to a breakdown of moral behavior, to oppression, and to the perversion of justice. The accumulation of wealth is seen in the scrolls as a road paved by violence, which only fosters abuse and leads inevitably to immorality and injustice. It is the pursuit of power and the accumulation and misuse of wealth that are attacked in the Damascus Covenant.

The question remains open regarding other dimensions of the issue. What of simply being rich? What about wealth in relationship to poverty? Is wealth, in and of itself, bad? What if God blesses a poor man with wealth? These questions are addressed in Scrolls 4Q 416, 4Q 417, and 4Q 418.

These scrolls still view the pursuit of wealth as a pollution of the spirit. The reader is instructed not to demean his or her spirit with any wealth. The human spirit is holy and it has no price. To connect the soul, the holy spirit, with wealth is to embitter it (4Q 416 frag. 2, col. 2, l. 6). The implication of this verse is that emotional and psychological attachment to material security does vast spiritual damage to the individual. Life, in its fullest essence, is beyond dependence on the physical world.

This concept accords with the Sectarian view that one of the most insidious forms of idolatry is the worship of gold and silver. Idolatry is abandonment of God. It is the placing of spiritual, emotional, and intellectual allegiance, the putting of one's full faith, in something other than God. Thereby, one is substituting a god for God. If one places one's faith in wealth, one turns one's heart and soul and fullest efforts in life toward the accumulation of riches and power. One's focal point is salvation through wealth.

Such people are self-serving. They have abandoned God and set up power and influence as gods. They seek salvation in material strength, rather than through the Creator of the Universe. Seeking to escape the fear and uncertainty of physical existence through the work of their own hands, they are often ready to glorify themselves and to take on the role of a god. The point here is that one's ultimate allegiance can be either to God, the ultimate source of being, or to self-glorification, which emanates from fear and attempts to control the conditions of survival. One must choose. One cannot do both.

Line 15 admonishes the reader neither to stay awake for riches, nor to depress the soul with wealth. To do so is to work for the wind. It is to serve an oppressor, for nothing. Moreover, one should not sell one's glory for money or pass it on as an inheritance, leaving oneself impoverished (line 18). Being mentally and emotionally preoccupied with material concerns, either in the process of accumulating wealth or of protecting and retaining it, depresses the soul.

The weight of concern is spiritually debilitating. A person preoccupied with wealth becomes a slave to a ruthless oppressor, and there is no benefit whatsoever in such servitude. He suffers for nothing and is at the mercy of the wind, which has no real substance and is highly changeable and uncertain. If people sell their souls for wealth and power, they are left with nothing real. They are spiritually impoverished, having traded spirit for the illusion of strength and security.

Not only the accumulation of wealth is meant when the scrolls speak of avoiding riches and of demeaning the spirit with wealth. Borrowing money is placed in the same context. To borrow money is based on the same fear of survival. It does not assist a person. In reality it makes one even more impoverished, because it make one more vulnerable. Borrowing money creates debt and increases pressure and vulnerability. One has to pay the money back in a short time. The creditor is in control and the situation favors him. The creditor can take away what little one does have. Moreover, borrowing creates reproach and embarrassment for the borrower. It is a source of bitterness to the soul. It is a prison, not an advantage. Thus, according to Scroll 4Q 417, frag. 1, col. 2, ll. 5–10:

> If one stretches forth one's hand for a loan, one gets burned. The whole of one's being becomes inflamed, presumably by the shame and embarrassment felt. It is no real gain, even materially, for what was borrowed must be returned. What has one ultimately gained, except pain,

humiliation, and lowered self-esteem? As long as one owes money to someone else, one's fate is in the hands of another. One remains vulnerable to circumstances beyond one's control. How is this a good thing? Rather, one is truly happy at the point one is free from the creditor. Why should one put themselves through this and risk corrupting one's spirit? (4Q 418, frag. 9)

One would think that since the Sectarian scrolls teach the avoidance of pursuing wealth, they would glorify and encourage poverty and simplicity as a preferable way of life. Actually, that is not the message. Rather, the scrolls teach us simply to accept what is. They advocate working within the boundaries of one's circumstances. Scroll 4Q 416, frag. 2, col. 2, lines. 19–20 teach that if there is no food, do not seek delicacies. If there are no glasses, do not seek to drink wine. Take only what you need. Use your own inheritance, but only what is necessary for your needs. God's treasure is abundant. Eat what He offers you and do not seek more. Moreover, leave everything else for the sustenance of others (4Q 417, frag. 1, col. 1, ll. 18–21).

The instruction here is that the true path of the spirit is to make do with what God has allotted to each individual. Doing so is an expression of faith. One is to depend on God, not on wealth or riches. For God provides for all and by God's hand are all living things sustained. One must accept that reality and not to seek to change it. If God did not heed our requests and reward us with His mercy and goodness, we would not survive an instant. Our spirits would immediately depart from the flesh (4Q 417, frag. 1, col. 2, ll. 1–4).

If a person is poor, he should desire no more than his portion. This means that the poor person should not be consumed emotionally by the fact that he is in poverty. If he is angry about his condition, or wallows in sorrow about his poverty, then his entire center of balance in life is thrown off. He can no longer function because he is emotionally preoccupied. If he rejoices in sorrow—that is, he gives in to self-pity and to remorse about being poor—life becomes bleak. He loses the will to live. If he lacks bread, he should not fixate on the lack. If poor, he should not despise his life. Rather, he should not derail his life by being consumed over the fact that he is poor (see: 4Q416, frag. 2, col. 3; 4Q 417, frag. 1, col. 1, l.10 and col. 2, ll. 21–end).

The idea is also expressed that one should not "lighten a vessel"—that is, one should not lavish wealth on the humble. If one attempts to radically alter a person's situation from the outside, even with the best of intentions, it can have an enormously detrimental effect. The admonition is not to add wealth to the humble, lest this change from a charitable act into disgrace, causing a modest person to stumble. For the excessive zeal of the benefactor can confuse the heart of the recipient, and thereby do enormous damage (4Q 417, frag. 1, col. 2, ll. 11–15).

What is important is not one's condition, but rather how one handles it. We are told (in Scroll 4Q 417, frag. 2, col. 2) to bless God for all the happiness we have experienced and for the mercy God has shown to us. We are also to praise God for every plague and evil that has befallen us as well. Why? Because God observes all the paths that we walk and judges us according to His understanding, not ours. We are instructed not to be deluded by the evil inclination within our nature, nor by our intellect. Neither the mind nor the emotions are the final arbitrators of reality. They are not the ultimate judge and jury of what is real and what is important. Only God is. Our perceptions are limited and can often be distorted. We are urged to continually investigate the truth. How does one do that? By focusing on the *Raz Nieyeh*, the "Secret of What We Will Become."

Investigating and searching the inner meanings of this great mystery is incumbent on all people. If God restores our fortunes, we are to walk in this new-found path and seek out all the implications of what has happened and what will happen. Among the ramifications we are to search out and understand is this mystery of what we will become. Once we understand it, we will walk on the road of justice and righteousness, and God will exalt our work and our efforts. Others will honor us, and we, in turn, should honor them. We should give thanks to God for being lifted out of poverty and for being given the opportunity to serve. God has bestowed a worthy inheritance. We have been granted a good name and substantial means. It is not an accident that this has occurred. There is a deeper reason for it. It is a divine mystery. So, seek God's Will at all times.

Conversely, the poor should not say that they do not have the means to acquire knowledge. If they bend their shoulder to the task, exercise discipline, and refine their heart and mind in the process, true knowledge will be found. Investigating the "Mystery of What We Will Become" leads to careful consideration of the paths of truth. It leads to thorough examination of the roots of all evil. If a person considers this mystery, he or she will understand the implications and ramifications of salvation and will come to know who will inherit blessing and glory and who will inherit judgement and strict justice.

People should receive the judgements made upon them willingly. The judgements are coming from above. Hence, they should accept the conditions of their life, admit their mistakes, and not try pass over their own failings. Then God will see their sincerity, withdraw His wrath, and pass over their sins. God, in exchange for a person's honesty and repentance, will not let the status quo stand (see: 4Q 416, frag. 2, col. 3; 4Q 417, frag. 1, col. 1, ll. 11–15; 4Q 418, frag. 9).

The message here is that one's condition, one's life situation can be changed by submission to God's Will. Affliction is not meant to be escaped from. Rather, it is to be accepted. This is part of the mystery of being. Why we suffer, what the ultimate root of an individual's or a nation's suffering actually is, is not apparent. The real roots and core remain within the Divine Will, and therefore are hidden from our view.

The assumption in the scrolls is that there is a reason for affliction, suffering, and pain. Since the righteous, those who seek to fulfill God's Will and hold fast to the Law, often suffer, and those who rebel against God and deliberately negate the Law of God often succeed, suffering cannot always be the direct result of abandoning God. It must have another function as well. The scrolls do acknowledge some cause and effect. The people of Israel were led astray in biblical times by corrupt and irresponsible kings. The Wicked Priest, in his own day and age, deceived the people with lies and turned them away from God and God's Law. Therefore, the entire people of Israel suffered, on one level, as a result of this apostasy and the deliberate breach of the Covenant it involved.

On the other hand, the suffering of the righteous and the flourishing of the wicked pose a different reality. The reason behind this apparent contradiction lies buried in the "Secret of What We Will Become." "What we will become" refers to what we will be during the End Time and beyond. We, as individuals and nations, will not be fulfilled until that point in time. Until then, there are certain principles that we must be fully aware of.

The first assumption connected with the mystery of "what we will become" is that many elements of one's suffering and the real reasons for it will not become apparent until the End Time. The second assumption is that one can—through repentance, devotion to God, and careful observance of the Covenant—increase the proportion of light within the soul and evolve spiritually. This is emphasized as being of considerable importance, particularly during the period leading up to the End Time and the Final Judgement of humanity.

The third assumption outlined above is that one must acquiesce to one's suffering and not try to escape it, deny it, or alleviate it. We are told "not to lighten a vessel," that if misfortune strikes, not to hide. Nor are we to run or flee, because if we do so, God will flatten or crush us for attempting it. Resistance is not the answer. Neither is seeking wealth, nor borrowing money, nor, conversely, glorying in poverty and self-pity (see 4Q 417).

Any attempt to avoid suffering leads only to further affliction and pain. Seeking wealth corrupts the soul and increases the proportion of darkness within. Sudden wealth can throw the soul of the righteous into confusion and compromise his essence and integrity. Borrowing money makes one vulnerable and helpless. The debt incurred is a prison. One's life and one's means of sustenance is no longer one's own. One is beholden to others and is under enormous pressure to repay the debt. Wallowing in self-pity or fixating on the misery of poverty only increases the pain. It depresses the soul and one begins to despise life and oneself as well.

The scroll is advocating the acceptance of suffering as a way to work through it. The key to acceptance is to focus on the mystery, the "Secret of What We Will Become," rather than on survival needs and physical desires. Poverty and wealth are both focal points reflecting the purely physical level of survival. That is why both are inappropriate paths for spiritual growth.

Hence, the scrolls advocate acquiescence to whatever one's physical condition is. Material well-being has nothing to do with spirit or spiritual evolution. The scrolls admonish one to consider this element of the mystery carefully. One is neither to rely on the intellect alone, nor make life choices based on what the eyes behold or the heart desires. One should not be deluded or misled by the dark side of one's nature into focusing one's thoughts and attention on the physical side of life or the spirit of the flesh, that which animates our physical desires. That level of human experience is not capable of differentiating between good and evil (4Q 417, frag. 2).

Rather, we are instructed to meditate on and investigate continually the "Secret of What We Will Become." Focus is to be centered on the final outcome of our travail. The emphasis is on the long-term view of our existence. Through meditating on this mystery, we come to know that true prosperity is that of understanding and that true poverty is the poverty of our deeds when seen from the full scope of our complete life experience.

When we walk perfectly in accordance with God's Will in all our deeds and actions, it is as a result of meditating on and investigating this great mystery of being. The inner reality of God's plan becomes far more evident. God's Will becomes so clear, in fact, that it is like crisp black letters on a white page. Things are suddenly so well-defined that it becomes obvious what marks acceptance of God's Will and what constitutes a departure from it. We see the eternal glory of God's mysteries and the might of His deeds in the light of expanded vision and heightened vantage point. That is, we begin to perceive clearly the inner structure and the outer manifestations of God's plan.

Moreover, as a result of focusing our thoughts and attention intensively on this Secret of Becoming, we come to understand the poverty of our deeds in the memory of time. We perceive the lacks and deficits of our life and actions from the timeless vantage point of the End Time. Time, as we understand it, having come to an end leaves the imprint of our lives and their impact clearly imbedded in memory and timelessness.

It is on the sum of our lives that we will be judged. Those who chose the path of Seth, the path of Darkness, will suffer from the decree that was written by God at the Beginning of Time. In the end, those who chose darkness face being cut off from this level of reality. They face punishment, exile, or oblivion. For those who have chosen to keep His word, who have chosen the path of light during the Age of Darkness, their future will be written in the Book of Memorial. In God's very Presence will they be remembered. To those inscribed in the book will God give His spirit as an inheritance—to the holy, as they are a model for mankind to emulate (see: 4Q 417, frag. 2).

Meditate on the secret of becoming and investigate it. That is the prescription for submitting to God's Will and passing through the pain of life's impoverishment. When doing so, one will fully under-stand the Final Judgement and the tribulations that mankind has gone through in the past and will go through during the End Time. God's justice will become apparent.

Meditation and investigation of the "Secret of What We Will Become" lead to Wisdom. Through understanding this deep mystery, one becomes enabled to receive the foundation of Truth. One is pre-pared to differentiate between good and evil from the divine perspective, rather than the limited human one. In the End Time and beyond, the inheritance of this reality will pass to individuals of the spirit. The holy and righteous will serve as models for all people and those who attain to the spirit will distinguish true good from true evil—not from the human standpoint, but according to the law of God's spirit (4Q 418, frags. 43 and 81).

According to Scroll 4Q 525, blessed is the one who speaks the truth with a pure heart and does not slander. One who strives to be holy searches the Torah with pure hands, one's actions being innocent and moral. One attains Wisdom by walking in the Law of the Most High. That entails discipline and constraint. One accepts punishment and does not abandon God in one's hardship. The Law is not discarded in times of anguish and terror, nor loathed in times of distress.

Moreover, the righteous do not renounce their heritage. They do not throw their lot in with the nations nor abandon the ways of God, their inheritance, for an alien culture. Rather, the righteous contemplate God's Law continually throughout their life. They meditate upon it in times of distress and keep it before them always, in order to avoid the error of walking on the paths of evil and darkness. Ultimately, in the final accounting these holy ones, the Sons of Light, will be vindicated, having earned the right to inherit the Kingdom of God, the restored Eden.

Access to true knowledge provides the man of the spirit, the holy one, with a clear vision of God's justice and the integrity of the Divine Plan, as well as with a direct and accurate understanding of Good and Evil from the divine perspective. Thus indicate the scrolls. These elements of direct connection and communication with God by the spirit, clearly seeing Divine Providence and the program of Creation and connecting with Good and Evil from that perspective, all reflect a return to Eden. The End Time reflects a restoration of mankind to its original, primordial state.

In the Kingdom of God following the End Time, God will call the righteous by name. He will observe their deeds and acknowledge them. He will renew their strength and empower them. The spiritual connection, once broken during the expulsion from Eden, will be reestablished on earth. With the restoration of Eden, the renewed direct link between man and God will heal the souls of humanity. Those who still have spiritual impairments to work out will be facilitated in their efforts, their needs being met by God's grace and mercy.

God will free the captives, give sight to the blind, and straighten the twisted. He will heal the wounded, revive the dead, and imbue His spirit on the humble. He will heal humanity on all levels.

In addition to the healing of humanity, Eden, the Kingdom of God, will also have another salient feature. Not only will the true nature of Good and Evil be clearly understood and perceived, but the fruit of one's actions will become immediate realities. In the new order of the restored Eden, true good and evil will be so clearly understood from the divine perspective that no doubt will be possible. Adhering to the good, then, will bring immediate judgement from God and the fruits of one's actions will blossom forth with no further delay. Neither judgement nor reward and punishment will any longer be deferred to the Next World, to the realm of heaven. One will be confronted with the results of one's actions and their consequences, immediately and on this level. To paraphrase the scroll: In His mercy God will judge man and not delay the fruit of good (4Q 521).

The Implications of the Restoration of Eden

The concept of a restoration of mankind to Eden signifies the return of mankind to its pristine state. It represents a new beginning for humanity, based on the original, divine premise regarding human existence and experience. Human life, as we have experienced for millennia, has evolved along the lines of development that were initiated by the expulsion from Eden. Mankind assimilated the knowledge of good and evil and distorted it by making it subservient to human understanding and outlook.

The Dead Sea Scrolls continually cite one of the primary causes of evil as doing what seems right only in one's own eyes and within one's own heart. That is, divine law, true moral and spiritual behavior are often not being referenced or taken into account by people in their day-to-day life. This is because we intellectualize it, on one hand, and on the other, we distort it by allowing our views and behaviors to be driven by our emotional wants and needs. When Adam and Eve ate of the fruit of the Tree of the Knowledge of Good and Evil, the determination of good and evil became relative. It became subservient to our limited understanding of reality. The expulsion from the Garden of Eden was God's decision to force us to live out the consequences of that decision. A restoration to Eden would end that cycle and initiate a new era of human experience based on the unfulfilled, original design that God had in mind for humanity.

Within a restored Eden, the knowledge of good and evil has a definite place and purpose. Within Jewish belief, good and evil are not a strict duality. Rather, they are both seen as coming from the same basic source, God's Will. Adam and Eve ate from the Tree of the Knowledge of Good and Evil, and brought good and evil into the world as concrete realities as a direct result of their actions. The act of assimilating the knowledge of good and evil produced its emergence in the world.

In other words, before Adam and Eve's assimilation of the knowledge, good and evil were merely potentials. They only became actualities as a result of Mankind's conscious decision to take them upon itself. This was an act of will and volition on the part of humanity. Good and evil did not have to become manifest in the world or a concrete part of human experience. God, in fact, specifically had commanded the couple not to take that course of action.

It is important to remember that the Tree of the Knowledge of Good and Evil, along with the Tree of Life, stood at the heart of the Garden of Eden. It has a legitimate place in the structure of Creation. However, God makes it quite clear that this knowledge was not something humanity was supposed to take upon itself. The true knowledge of good and evil, the full understanding of the polar principles that govern the functioning of the universe, was not intended for human assimilation. Once mankind internalized it, it became subjective. Once this occurred, the basic polarity and dualism of existence was fundamentally changed as far as human experience was concerned.

Henceforth, humanity would be forced to make subjective determinations of good and bad, which were detached from their objective source—that of simple duality. Everything would now be seen through the lens of right and wrong. Positive and negative, then, could easily be confused with good and evil, because so much of man's experience is subjective.

When we make value judgements, we often overlay connotations of good and bad on basic dualities in the world. Everything in Creation is polarized into dualities. Living beings are male or female. The dimensions of space are polarized into up and down, left and right, forward and backward. Energy is the dualism of electricity and magnetism. Life takes place by movement within the dualism of Time–

Space. The basic duality of existence is inescapable. So, what did Adam and Eve do when they ate of the Tree? They introduced subjective value judgement into the equation. Now, instead of seeing something simply as left and right or as this or that, the dimension of good and bad was added. This added perception can produce great distortion.

If one is looking at two apples on a tree branch, one ripening and one rotting, it is not necessarily true to assume that the former is good and the latter bad. The rotting apple may fall to the ground and serve as badly needed fertilizer for nutrient-starved soil, which is good from nature's standpoint. Whereas the ripening apple may be one of too many apples on the tree, which are draining off much-needed resources and preventing the tree's crop from coming to full fruition. Hence, the whole crop of apples, ultimately, will be ruined.

Goodness and Evil, good and bad, are not always appropriate considerations. Much in life is actually neutral or an admixture of positive and negative. Often, good and bad are merely a function of how one is viewing something. Good and bad are not necessarily intrinsic. Rather, the reality of good and bad, goodness and evil, become realities based on how something is perceived, how one reacts to that perception, and the subsequent actions taken. Enormous harm, for example, and tremendous evil have been done to countless people over millennia by people reacting to what they viewed as an ultimate good.

The Tree of the Knowledge of Good and Evil stood in the Garden of Eden to regulate the balance of naturally opposing forces, that duality which constitutes the very core makeup of our world. That regulatory force was planted by God to support life on this plane of existence. The Tree was meant to serve Creation on a level of its own, beyond the pale of human comprehension and thought.

When Adam and Eve ate of this Tree, they took it upon themselves to decide what in this world was good and what was evil. The making of such distinctions would inevitably derive strictly from their own narrow frame of reference. This was the sin of mankind. Humanity set itself up as the ultimate judge of what is and is not reality. Moreover, we continue to make such decisions and do so through the distorted lens of subjective value judgement. By setting ourselves up as arbiters, we are preempting God—the true, eternal judge. Our distorted perceptions lead to inappropriate action, causing harm, damage, and destruction on many levels. We bring evil into the world through actions precipitated by confusion and misconception.

How can humanity escape this unending cycle of good and evil, of progress and retrogression? The answer is implied in the Book of Job. At the end of the story, God forces the issue. God demands to know why Job, or anyone else for that matter, thinks they can know the mind or intent of God? Job is forced to admit that he cannot fathom evil and suffering. The true roots of good and evil lie deep in the very fabric of Creation, in the hidden Will of God. This is far beyond the scope of human comprehension. No human explanation will ever be, even remotely, adequate to approximate the true of reality of existence. Why does mankind persist in distorting the world and human experience by playing God, by making subjective value judgements, and by casting them in terms of good and evil?

A return to Eden involves the surrender of this dualistic view of the universe and the permanent modification of the capacity to judge, away from judgment toward discernment. Mankind must move beyond the cycle of good and evil that has dominated human experience from the beginning. The future of humanity, as both biblical literature and the Dead Sea literature see it, involves returning to the original pattern of experience symbolized by Eden. Mankind must again allow itself to be guided by God directly, rather than by the limited insight of purely human reason. The question, then, is how exactly can this be achieved?

Before Mankind was created, God judged all of Creation to be Good. The universe, according to the teachings of the Torah, is innately good. No mention of evil whatsoever is made when Creation is being depicted and described. This suggests that there is a universal Good that transcends good and evil as we understand it. There is a transcendent good that stands at the very core of all Creation.

Good and evil are interdependent realities that are relative to each other. Without one, the other ceases to exist. This relative good, which we usually experience, is then only a reflection of the transcendent Good that underlies Creation. It is not Good itself. This relative good is the counterpart to evil. Evil is simply the shadow that allows good, as we perceive it, to exist through contrast. Evil is the dark underside of the cycle of good. Good, in large part, is defined by its relationship to evil. Both good and evil define each other, depend on each other for their existence, and contend with each other in an unending struggle.

It is mankind who brought this dichotomy into the world. Because of that, the literature suggests that God has allowed man to suffer the ramifications and consequences of this action ever since. The dichotomy of good and evil is a process of experience that has ruled human life since Eden. It has put man's soul to the test.

Ultimately, all souls will be judged by God and their fate sealed, if we understand the scrolls' messages clearly. The righteous will retain connection with this level of reality and will prosper and grow. They will inherit this world and have a share in the world beyond. The souls of the evil, who have taken the road of darkness, will be judged by God and cut off. The righteous souls, with a preponderance of light in their souls, will inherit the light. The wicked, who have darkened their souls, will inherit the darkness.

Having chosen in Eden to take on good and evil, mankind has lived for millennia with the consequent realities of relative good. Mankind has internalized light and dark to the extent that the soul of each individual has become molded by the experience. In the End of Days, the future position of every soul, relative to its composition of light and dark, will be determined by God's Judgement as the new era of the Restored Eden emerges. For millennia, the dichotomy of good and evil, which man brought into this world, has interfered with humanity's ability to experience the true, transcendent Good. With the reestablishment of Eden, this will no longer be the case. The elimination of evil also means the demise of relative good. Both must give way to true and enduring Good.

According to the Book of Deuteronomy, the duality of good and evil functions as a set of choices that each person is forced to make continually. Humanity has been confronted with the dichotomy of good and evil since the beginning of time. The Law of Moses set down moral choice as the basic operating principle between man and God. Choose life and good, or choose evil and death. Opt to serve God, or decide on abandoning God. The choices are clear and so are the consequences. According to the Dead Sea literature, the ultimate consequences become clear as well.

Deuteronomy teaches that one should not assume that understanding what God wants from us is hidden away somewhere or far beyond our reach. Nothing could be further from the truth. God's Will is very near to us. It is in our hearts and in our souls. To reach the ultimate Good, humanity has to pass through the dichotomy of good and evil. Humans must strive for the Good by connecting to the Will of God. That is accomplished by listening to the heart and working to serve God. The destruction of evil spoken of in the literature means the obliteration of the cycle of good and evil. The existence of relative good terminates with the extinction of evil. Mankind will then live in direct connection to God's Will and in the reality of transcendent Good.

With the demise of good and evil comes the elimination of egocentrism and emotionalism as prime factors in the process of decision making. Our own will becomes subordinate to that of the divine. Instead of resisting the inclination to evil and attempting to assert and develop the good, people will be connected directly with the transcendent Good, the light of holiness and of joy. Human life will be lived on a level previously unknown.

Eden represents living in accordance with God's Will. It is a state of human existence that experiences God's Presence in the universe continually. Man will live in the transcendent Good that replaces relative good and evil when the Kingdom of God is established on earth.

The question remains, how is this to be accomplished? Without the conflicting realities of good and evil, how does man know the Will of God and act in accordance with it? The answer is found in the biblical idea of Wisdom.

The Message of the Thanksgiving Scroll (1Q Hod)

"And I, the Instructor, have known You, my God, through the spirit which You gave me. I have listened loyally to Your wonderful secret, through Your holy spirit. You have opened within me the knowledge of the mystery of Your Wisdom, the source of Your power. . ." (1Q H, col. 20, ll. 11–13).

In this hymn near the end of the Thanksgiving Scroll, the leap from being caught in the cycle of good and evil to the point of transcending it is connected to reaching the level of Wisdom. The point of true knowledge, we are told, is reached when one's spirit is touched by, and then harmonizes with, the holy spirit. Then through this experience is Wisdom internalized and a true knowledge of the Divine Will revealed within.

Why is it important for the individual soul to be connected to the Divine Will? What is the purpose of experiencing true knowledge and understanding? According to the teaching, in column 18, lines 1–9, nothing actually takes place outside the Will of God.

Plans of the heart, the deepest motivations of the human soul, do not exist outside the Will of God. This does not mean that everything in life is preordained. Rather, it means that there is no dichotomy. God's Will allows for all things to exist and all choices to be made. The scroll here asks, what can be devised without God's agreement? Can any human act take place without God's consent? True, man can oppose God's Will, just as he can follow it and honor it. But man can take no action that is outside of God's Will.

God's Will is the reality that produces, underscores, maintains, and energizes all of Creation. To be outside of God's Will would be to be outside of Creation itself. This is simply an impossibility. This section of the scroll states that though no mortal man truly understands the full depth of God's Wisdom, it is attainable in sufficient part because God teaches it to man. Understanding Wisdom is to understand God's Will. We attune ourselves to the Divine through learning Wisdom.

The text asks, how can one be assertive if God does not give one the power to stand? How can one become learned, if God does not mold one? How can one answer, if God does not provide one with insight? Without God's involvement, nothing is truly known. Outside of God, nothing exists.

The implication here is that good and evil, as long as they continue to exist, both emanate from the Will of God. Mankind makes choices and activates one or the other. As a result of his actions, man experiences the ramifications and consequences of his acts. The way to transcendent Good is through the experience of internalizing Wisdom. Wisdom is the higher experience of true understanding and knowledge. This God teaches to man, if man is willing to accept it.

God's standard is truth and justice. By adhering to the Covenant and following the moral dictates of the Law, righteousness is achieved. Through righteousness one becomes truly aware, on the level of spirit, within the soul itself. One confesses one's sins, looks to strengthen oneself spiritually, learns to love God's Will and to serve God in truth. To those who love God, serving God in truth and through just actions, God is merciful and compassionate, accepting the evil they have done and forgiving the sins of the past (1Q H, col. 8, ll. 12–16).

A person who has become connected to the holy spirit through Wisdom is not only forgiven of his sins and transformed, he becomes spiritually far more aware. The implications of this transformed awareness are important in understanding the role of the "enlightened man."

Once a person becomes spiritually aware through the assimilation of Wisdom via the holy spirit, the closer he is drawn to God's Will. The more he approaches God, the more he detests the behavior of the wicked and the stronger his inclination is to follow God's instruction and not to alter the Word of God. What is more, by undertaking not to sin against God or do evil, he forces those around him to tow the line and make spiritual progress. He comes to perceive clearly the spiritual states of those around him, and by his actions comes to show them the consequences of their own deeds (1Q H, col. 6, ll. 11–18).

The formula expressed seems to be, to move beyond good and evil as the predominant influences in one's life by transcending them through connection with Wisdom, the embodiment of God's Will. Wisdom, when assimilated, brings connection with the holy spirit. This leads to personal transformation as well as spiritual transcendence. One then becomes a true servant of God. As such, one clearly perceives good and evil from the higher perspective. The result is that one's behavior becomes more moral, one's spiritual perspective becomes much clearer, and one becomes responsible for influencing others through example and through teaching. By doing so, the spirit of holiness becomes more pervasive in human life and experience.

During the Time of Wickedness leading up to the establishment of the Kingdom of God, the function of the "enlightened man" is to strengthen the forces of light and to rescue as many souls as can possibly be reached. The wicked have deliberately deluded the people. They have altered God's Law, imposing their own will over God's. They looked for God with a "double heart" (ulterior motives) that were not based on the truth. They looked for God among the idols. And prophets arose who spoke deceitfully, denying God's revealed Will and denying the path of Wisdom. Hence, the keys to transcendence were denied to the people. For this, God will inevitably punish the wicked. The judgement on those who perverted God's Covenant will, in the End, ultimately be annihilation (1Q H, col. 12, ll. 10–19).

In the End Time, during the period of Judgement, the sword of God will strike the Sons of Darkness and they will no longer exist (col. 14, ll. 29–30). For those who have chosen this course and held to it to the end, their demise will serve as a clear sign of God's glory and of God's Will. The consequence of rebellion was established at the beginning. The time of God's wrath was created for the annihilation of evil and of those who tenaciously cling to it (col. 6, ll. 22–24).

The path of every living being is grounded in God's Will. God's Will established the twin roads of good and evil as a testing ground for humanity (col. 6, l. 26). It also set down the consequences that would result from them. During the Age of Wickedness, the consequences would be learning experiences—those of reward and punishment. During the End Time, the final consequences would be either spiritual transformation or extinction.

The view of the Divine Will taken here is of the broadest possible perspective. A divine imperative was established at the beginning of human history and it will fully manifest itself at the end of human history as we have understood it. The Divine Will has set the ground rules by which man has had to live for millennia and sets the new rules for the coming age of mankind, the Kingdom of God.

The author of the Thanksgiving Scroll states that at one time, he thought himself unworthy. He felt that he was barred from God's Covenant. Then he remembered God's strength and compassion and remained firm. Out of compassion, God supported him, allowed him to atone for his sins, and through justice, cleansed him of his faults (1Q H, col. 12, ll. 35–37). Therefore, from personal experience, the author knows that there is hope for whoever is converted from wickedness, whoever relinquishes sin and walks in God's path, the way of righteousness and morality. In the End Time, there will be those who survive, those who inherit a new consciousness and are cleansed from guilt (col. 14, ll. 6–8).

Hope is held out until the very end for the salvation of the wicked. God's Will encompasses great mercy, holding the door of repentance and salvation open to the last minute. Those who grasp the truth and, through righteous action, cling to the light will be forgiven by God. They will be purified of sin and transformed through God's mercy. They will become fit to permanently stand in God's Presence (col. 25, ll. 28–31).

In the new age—the Kingdom of God—human depravity will have vanished and sin will exist no longer. Mankind will have a new name, a new character, a new reality. Humanity will inherit the Garden of Eden and the glory of Adam. The regeneration of mankind and the restoration of Eden, like the Age of Wickedness, the End Time, and the Judgement, are all part of the Divine Will, the divine plan. Like the preceding age and its climax, the coming age is designed to illustrate the mercy and compassion of God and to reflect His Wisdom. In the mystery of His Wisdom, God has apportioned all these things and made them unfold, in order to make known His glory, the reality of His Presence (col. 4, ll. 14–19).

Not only is the "enlightened man" the guiding light during the latter years of the reign of darkness, but it is reasonable to assume that this spiritual model is to serve as the basic paradigm for human behavior in the coming age. Scroll 1Q H, column 6, lines 1–10 refer to the men of truth as being chosen by justice. Righteous action, moral behavior, and a sensitivity to his relationship to others characterize the person who is spiritually attuned. Such an individual is chosen for leadership.

The man of truth is humble in spirit and is refined by external simplicity. Such an individual loves compassion and exercises it. He makes do with what he has and is ever alert to God's Will. Probing the mind, he continually searches out Wisdom. He is an exemplar of one acting in accordance with God's Will. God's Law is strengthened in the world by the righteousness and justice of his way of life. By living a life of moral principle, the Law of God is exemplified. Those following this example come to inherit God's blessing and promise. Because they are acting righteously, God acts righteously toward them.

The righteous will connect with Wisdom and know God by intimately knowing His Will. As a result, they will continually grow spiritually and increase in their connection to God and in their ability to serve Him. "And they know You, and in the era of Your glory, they rejoice. In accord with their knowledge and to the extent of their understanding, You allow them to improve. And in accord with their domain, they serve You . . ." (1Q H, col. 20, ll. 22–23).

The righteous, the enlightened of the coming age, will grow spiritually and increase continually in their ability to connect with God's Will. Subsequently, they will be able to manifest it through service. Spiritual growth is fostered through connection to the holy spirit and thereby to God's Will. This connectedness to God's Will impels the individual to greater understanding and to greater external action on a moral level. This indicates that there is an organic link, which binds inner knowingness to righteousness and to action, in accordance with God's Will.

The Mystery of "What We Will Become"

The linkage between Wisdom and knowing is the focus one has on the mystery of being. The righteous reach the point of connection with the holy spirit, the Will of God, through meditation and contemplation on the "Mystery of What We Will Become."

The term *Raz Niyeh*, if understood in the context of the future age of Eden, can also be taken to mean the "Mystery of What We Are," or even more precisely, the "Mystery of What We Are Becoming." The implication of the term *niyeh*, "we will be," in the framework of the Age of Eden, is that of humanity's continuing evolution.

The verb *niyeh* is not a static one. It is in the future tense. That projection into the future, the focusing on what we are becoming, is not limited to the immediate future, to the dawn of the Kingdom of God. Rather, it seems also to apply to the reality of spiritual life in the age to come. It appears as a central touchstone of the new order.

The great mystery is that of spiritual evolution itself. That quest for understanding the nature of our being does not cease with the advent of the Kingdom of God. Rather, it assumes even greater importance. It becomes the focal point for spiritual awareness and the trigger for spiritual growth in the coming epoch of human existence. By meditating and contemplating on this great mystery, one connects with Wisdom and penetrates deep into its meaning.

Since the pursuit of Wisdom is a continual process of inspiration and growth, then logically, delving into the mystery of *Raz Niyeh* is also meant to be a perpetual process. The key to understanding the connection between meditation on this mystery and "enlightenment"—the deepening penetration into Wisdom and all that implies—can be gained, in part, from a careful reading of Scroll 4Q 417, fragment 2, column 1. Below, I present my own translation of this text based on the transcription found in Fascicle Two of Wacholder and Abegg's *A Preliminary Edition of the Unpublished Dead Sea Scrolls*, Biblical Archeology Society, 1992, pp. 65–66.

Scroll 4Q 417, Frag. 2, Col. 1. lines 1–27

1. . . . you understand. . . .
2. . . . in the mysteries of His wonder . . . you will enlighten those who revere. . . .
3. . . . look . . . prior to what we will become and what we will become.
4. In what . . . to what

5. it is and to what we will become, in what . . . in all . . . you will do.
6. . . . [day and] night, meditate on the mystery of what we will become and always require. Then, you will know the truth and the yoke of Wisdom.
7. . . . a deed . . . on all their ways with their *pekudah* [ordained course] to all the ends of the earth and the *pekudah* [ordained course] of eternity.
8. And then, you will know between good and evil, according to their deeds. Because, to the knowledge of the secret of truth, and in the mystery of what we will become
9. He extended woman, an act . . . and to all . . . will trouble, and the rule [impact] of her actions toward all . . .
10. will produce all . . . He extended to the structure of every action, to walk together in the pattern of His structure.
11. And He extended . . . and with the ability of understanding the hidden secrets of His thought,
12. with the innocent who walk in His ways. These are of perpetual meaning. And He meditates on all
13. their results [ramifications]. And then, you will know eternal glory [or the glory of the universe], along with the mysteries of His wonder and the strength of His deeds.
14. Then, you understand the origin [beginning] of your action in the memory of time, because in the end are the laws. He will engrave every *pekudah* [fore-ordained course of action].
15. For an inscription is engraved by God regarding every . . . of the sons of Seth, and a reminder is written before Him,
16. for those that keep His word. And it is a vision of the *Hegui* [meditative insight] the Book of Remembrance has. And man will inherit it via spirit, because
17. his nature is like the structure of the holy ones. Yet, He has still not given *Hegui* [deep meditative understanding] to the spirit of flesh, because it does not know [has never known]
18. between good and evil as judgement of its spirit . . . and you, son, who understand, examine . . . the mystery of what we will become,
19. and the heritage of all the living, and walk together in the remembrance of the event. . . .
20. . . . between much and little and within your mystery . . .

21. . . . in the mystery of what we will become.
22. . . . every vision and in all . . .
23. and you will strengthen yourself continually. Do not touch the burnt offering . . .
24. by it, he will not be cleansed according to his inheritance . . .
25. For an enlightened one has meditated on your mysteries and with a person . . .
26. its foundation is within you . . . their . . . with the work of . . .
27. You shall not follow after your hearts and after your eyes. . . .

In line two, the instruction being given is to enlighten those who revere God. The implication in line three is that what is to be examined involves "what we will become." This seems to be the focus point for a deeper understanding our past and our future. Those who revere God need to view their own experience and that of humanity as a whole from the vantage point of the mystery of becoming. At the End of Time, the righteous will become cleansed of sin, purified, and forgiven. They will become whole and freed from evil, past and future. They will become saved and inherit dominion over the earth, as Adam had originally.

The sense of the first few lines of the text is that the key to reaching deeper levels of understanding God's purpose and comprehending the destiny of mankind is to focus on the *Raz Niyeh*. The enlightened are asked to view what we were and what we are, in terms of what we will ultimately be. By meditating on this great mystery, one comes to know the truth of existence and is thereby prepared to accept Wisdom. The implication here would be that meditating on the mystery of becoming opens one up to the deeper truths of reality and of human experience. Once the door of truth is opened, one has access to Wisdom, universal knowledge.

The term *pekudah* can be seen as playing an important role in describing the paths of truth and Wisdom. The *pekudah* of truth and Wisdom encompasses time and space. Through their deeds, through the actions of truth and Wisdom within the context of time and space, a true knowledge of what is good and what is evil emerges (lines 7–8). Truth and Wisdom manifest over time through *pekudah*. As truth and Wisdom manifest, the true nature of good and evil and a clear view of what truly is good and what is truly evil become apparent.

Pekudah seems to refer to a set course. On one hand, truth and Wisdom are eternal and encompass time and space. On the other hand, they are revealed over time and grasped by humanity only in stages. The verb *pakad* is used in the Bible in the sense of remembering something and bringing it about. The verb is used, for example, in describing God's remembering the promise to Sarah. God remembers that He promised that she would have a son, and so she becomes pregnant and gives birth to Isaac. God remembers (*pakad*) the Covenant with Abraham, Isaac, and Jacob and, taking note of what the Egyptians had done to their descendants, prepared to take them out of Egypt (Exodus 3:6).

The term implies a commitment being made, being recorded, and, at the appropriate time, being fulfilled. Truth and Wisdom are said to have their own *pekudah*. God ordained, at the beginning of time, several realities: the end of Eden, the first age of mankind, the conflict between good and evil during the Age of Wickedness, the destruction of evil, the redemption of the righteous during the End Time, and the restoration of Eden, the third age of mankind.

These realities are to play themselves out. They are promises made to man, backed by His truth and based in God's Wisdom. At the appointed time, they will be fulfilled. The promise of Eden, the promise of life in full accord with truth, justice, and Wisdom, will emerge with the Kingdom of God as the governing principles of all human life.

When living one's life in truth and being intimately connected to God's Will through Wisdom, true good and true evil will become immediately apparent in any action. In the coming age, the knowledge of good and evil will no longer be dependent on human subjectivity or be a matter of human definition. The knowing of good and evil will be inherent within us.

The secret of truth and the mystery of human evolution were imparted to Eve. The feminine element of Creation embodies these principles. The woman receives man and gives birth. The child develops, and through interaction, parents and child evolve. Truth is received from God. Wisdom is God's vehicle for transmitting truth and expressing His Will. The key to assimilating God's Will is to receive Wisdom and to meditate on what one is to become.

One evolves and becomes something more, through action and deed. Within every action is a structure. A deed or action plays itself out in a certain way and along certain lines. That structure corresponds to a part of the structure of Creation itself (line 10). So, whatever a person does, it resonates with Creation and follows certain universal principles, which affect its lines of development. An action or course of action will affect other levels of reality because of the resonance. It follows, then, that given the course of development determined by these universal principles being tapped into, there will be certain predictable ramifications and consequences.

Meditating on the relationship between one's actions and the structure of Creation, as well as on the ramifications that follow from it, one walks in the Ways of God. One penetrates the hidden levels of divine thought and is struck by the mystery and strength of His deeds. Through this meditation, one also comes to understand the roots of one's own actions as they have been registered in time/space. One comes to know the reasons why one's deeds unfolded the way they did and produced certain consequences. They all follow the laws of Creation. Everything one does, good or evil, is recorded in time/space and will fulfill itself eventually. Every action taken creates a *pekudah*. It is engraved in time/space and hence, will follow a course of development in accordance with God's Law, the laws of Creation (ll. 10–16).

The Book of Remembrance appears to refer to time/space, in which every decision and action is written, engraved, and embedded. Accessing the Book of Remembrance opens up knowledge of the origins of one's actions, the course they follow, the ramifications they produce, and the consequences that will result from them. It is with this knowledge and insight, and from this level, that one truly can perceive good and evil in the more transcendent sense. From this experience of seeing the origins, the development, and the consequences of all one's actions, one can truly understand life from a vantage point far beyond the limited subjective, emotional, and intellectual determinations of good and evil that have dominated human experience for millennia.

Meditating on the *Raz Niyeh*, the "secret of becoming," gives one access to the Book of Remembrance. The Book itself, once accessed, opens up the vista of a true understanding of one's life and experience. Experiencing the truth of one's existence and the ramifications of one's actions reflects on an even higher reality. It produces a vision of *Hegui*. According to line 16, one gets a vision or reflected glimpse, as it were, of the *Hegui* from the Book of Remembrance. This means that from the experience of perceiving one's actions in the broad context of time/space, one is led to an even higher reality. The Book of Remembrance, then, is a dimension of *Hegui*, and a gateway to *Hegui*. The question remains: What is *Hegui*?

The word *HGVY* is not a word familiar to us from either biblical or rabbinic literature. Although presented to the modern reader for the first time in the Qumran literature, there are, nonetheless, several things that can be understood about it. Apparently this term was in use during the Second Temple period, since it appears several times in the scrolls. From its form and usage, it is clearly a noun, and it derives from the verb root *HGH*.

One of the most common meanings for this root, found in biblical and midrashic literature, is "to meditate." So it is quite appropriate to translate this term as "meditation." This is very clear. The question becomes, is meditation the extent of the terms's implication or are there more dimensions to it?

What is noteworthy is that in the Hebrew Bible, the noun meaning "meditation" is *Hegayon*. The term *Hegui* does not appear. One possible reason for this would be that the term developed later, as an alternate or abridged form of *Hegayon*. Another possibility is that the term was designed to be unequivocal and may have been a precise, technical term. The word *Hegayon* comes from the *paal* verb form of the Hebrew root *HGH*. *Hegui* would come from the same verb root, but would derive from the *piel* verb form, that form which expresses intensity.

In other words, because the verb form from which each of these two nouns developed is slightly different, their meanings are correspondingly different. Even though they come from the same verb root, because they are structured differently, there is a difference in meaning. *Hegayon* comes from the *paal* verb form and *Hegui* derives from the *piel*. The *paal* form is simple and basic. The *piel* form is intensive.

Let us take a classical example of the difference between these two verb forms. We will use, in both cases, the exact same verb root *ShBR*. In the *paal* form, the verb is *Shavar*, meaning "to break." In the *piel* form, the verb becomes *Shebair*, "to smash." The verb root is the same. However, there is a greater degree of intensity in the *piel*. If, therefore, the word *Hegayon* derives from the *paal* and means "meditation," then *Hegui*, deriving from the *piel*, would likely mean "intensive meditation," or "meditation and something beyond it."

In the Sectarian literature of Qumran, *Hegui* is a process of the utmost importance. In the Community, study of the Book of *Hegui* was mandatory on a daily basis. Leaders of the Community had to be proficient in it. The exposition of the Law, by the Interpreter, was based on an intimate knowledge of the Book of *Hegui*. The Book of

Remembrance reflects *Hegui*. In the *Hodayot* Scroll, it is referred to as The *Hegui*.

The term does not seem to represent meditation alone. It is a broader reality. In the sense it is being used in Scroll 4Q 417, *Hegui* is a high state of spiritual experience granted to worthy individuals by God. It is not something that connects or resonates with "the spirit of flesh." The person who is still caught in the cycle of emotional attachment to the earthly form remains referenced to the flesh and to the concerns of physical existence. Such an individual cannot see beyond it. He or she does not pierce the veil and therefore is not able to see transcendent Good but only the reflections: good and evil. The true workings of the universe are hidden from that person's gaze. Only through walking in truth, doing justice, and meditating on Wisdom does one come to understand the divine, universal laws that underlie Creation.

When one reaches an intimate understanding of the universal law of God, the bedrock of Creation, one achieves vision. This vision is *Hegui*. *Hegui* is spiritual clarity. It is the level of existence experienced by the holy beings, by the heavenly host. Man is capable of reaching the level of *Hegui*. He can experience this reality because his spiritual makeup, the underlying structure of the human soul, at its core, is the same as that of the holy beings.

A person reaches the level of *Hegui* through spirit. Having cleansed himself from sin, walking in the Law of God, in honesty, morality, and truth, he has prepared himself. Meditating on the *Raz Niyeh*, "the Secret of Becoming," he penetrates the mysteries of the universal, divine laws that rule Creation. Meditating intensively on their ramifications, the soul attains to a vision of *Hegui*, and in attaining it, the soul inherits *Hegui* itself, spiritual clarity. The soul becomes totally clear spiritually. The soul then is revealed in its pure form, that of pure holiness. It proceeds to experience existence at that point as a holy being.

The implication that can be drawn from lines 17–27 is that in the Kingdom of God, the *Hegui* will descend upon those of spirit. It will give light to those who have inherited this new world, the restored Eden. It will become the heritage of all mankind because it was toward this end that humanity has moved from the beginning. Mankind has been impelled, in accordance with divine law, to move toward reconnection with the holiness that is at man's spiritual core. The foundation of spirit is within each of us. When, in the Kingdom to come, we are finally able to experience life from the level of *Hegui*, spiritual clarity and transcendent Good, we will be holy beings. Innately, we will follow the Will of God and not chase after our own concepts and desires, which trap us in the unending cycle of good and evil.

The model for the coming age is the man of truth, the person connected directly with the holy spirit, the Will of God, who transformed himself and who continually learns and exemplifies Wisdom. To fully comprehend the implication of this profound concept, it is important to understand clearly the ancient Hebrew concept of Wisdom.

14

WISDOM:
THE CONNECTION TO GOD

The Biblical View of Wisdom

When encountering the concept of Wisdom—of *Hochmah*—in the biblical text, it is erroneous to interpret it as merely being wise or possessing great knowledge. Wisdom is a much vaster concept in Jewish thought and has its own set of meanings and connotations. In biblical literature, Wisdom is not merely knowledge or understanding. Wisdom is a specific state of being. It is a transcendent essence that is bestowed upon certain individuals. It is a state of holy consciousness. It is vehicle for the transmission of divine energy, direction, and instruction to the human level. Wisdom is both a level of holiness and a divine empowerment.

One of the subjects of the 28th chapter of the book of Exodus is the making of the vestments of the High Priest. God gives very explicit directions for the creation of the various garments that Aaron and later generations of High Priests were to wear when performing their sacred tasks. Poignantly, the text states, " Next you shall instruct all who are wise in their hearts, whom I have filled with Wisdom, to make Aaron's vestments . . ." (Exodus 28:3). Only those whose hearts God has deliberately filled with the gift of Wisdom are to be commissioned to work on producing the High Priestly vestments.

The vestments of the High Priest are of unique sanctity. They are of great holiness because they are the vessels for the work he is performing. The vestments facilitate the holy tasks of the High Priest. They elevate him beyond the status of the rest of the priesthood. What is the sacred work of the High Priest?

The High Priest intercedes with God on behalf of the entire people and it is he who communicates directly with God, seeking atonement and facilitating the flow of divine grace. It is through the High Priest's work that the flow of divine grace continues to be channeled, in order to reach the world. This communication and intercession by the High Priest cannot take place without the holy vestments. They serve as the vehicles for the ritual.

It is very significant that only those whom God has chosen and imbued with Wisdom are in a holy enough state to perform the most sacred task of bringing these holy vestments into physical existence. Moses is told to teach the skills necessary for performing the sacred task of making the vestments. He is then instructed to reveal the detailed plans only to those into whose hearts God has implanted Wisdom. Wisdom is the prerequisite for manifesting the tools by which communication with God is made possible. It is bestowed by God and is implanted into the heart.

This was also the case with Bezalel and Oholiav. Both men were designated, by name, to be the architects and builders of the Ark of the Covenant and of the Sanctuary. The *Mishkan*, the Sanctuary, was the Dwelling Place of God. The Ark facilitated communication directly with God. Here, once more, we are presented with the reality of communion and direct interchange with God. Again, only those who are imbued with Wisdom are in a position to deal with this level of reality. "And then Bezalel and Oholiav, and every man wise of heart, whom God had placed Wisdom and understanding within them, to intimately know to do all the skilled work of holy service, did all that Adonai commanded" (Exodus 36:1).

Besides facilitating the means of direct communication with God, Wisdom also encompassed divine empowerment. It bestowed upon the individual possessing it the ability to lead others through its influence. When Wisdom was bestowed upon the worthy individual, he or she spoke with a divine mandate and was responsible for leading the people, for acting as a vehicle for divine guidance. "Now Joshua ben Nun was filled with the spirit of Wisdom, because Moses laid his hands upon him. And the Israelites heeded him, doing as Adonai had commanded Moses" (Deuteronomy 34:9).

The implication here is that not only had God found Joshua worthy of taking up the mantle of leadership from Moses, but that Joshua was prepared to accept it and to handle the responsibility. At God's behest, when the appropriate time came, the authority Moses had as leader was transferred to Joshua. Joshua was able to receive the cloak of authority and utilize it, not only because had God granted it to him specifically, but also because He had prepared him for it by bestowing Wisdom upon him. The granting of Wisdom to Joshua rendered him capable of communicating with God and receiving His instructions. The possession of Wisdom is seen as a prerequisite for the receipt of divine empowerment. It is seen as the means to insure that God's instructions, and the authority that comes with them, are properly handled and utilized for the good.

This is verified in the teachings of the Prophet Isaiah. In describing the perfect King, Isaiah states that the worthy descendant of Jesse will be a soul possessed of Wisdom. The presence of Wisdom within will facilitate strength and leadership, because Wisdom embodies an intimacy with God and God's Will. "And upon him the spirit of Adonai will rest, the spirit of Wisdom and understanding, the spirit of counsel and courage, the spirit of intimate knowledge and awe of Adonai" (Isaiah 11:2).

Wisdom is reverence for God. It entails a deep intimacy with the divine Will. It is through this close, inner connection with the divine Will that one discerns the inner truth of things. The discernment, once achieved, allows the spirit of God to flow through the wise one. Via the Word of God, the wise person becomes a leader. He or she is transformed. Possessed of Wisdom, one becomes a conduit through which God's providence becomes manifest. Joshua and David were leaders. Bezalel and Oholiav were craftsmen. Others were prophets, teachers, and judges. The central quality, which they all shared, was the possession of Wisdom bestowed upon them by God.

Wisdom is the embodiment of the awe of God. The two are synonymous. Reverence for God is the most central element of Wisdom. It stands at its core. To attain Wisdom, one must be in awe of the Creator. By so being, one becomes open and able to receive. One becomes overwhelmed by God. The ego is silenced as one stands before the complete majesty of Creation and fully senses God's vast creative power. Reverence is the very core and basis for Wisdom. It opens up our being and allows us to operate at higher levels. As Scripture so eloquently states, "The beginning of Wisdom is awe of God" (Psalms 111:10).

This level of deep devotion is also the basis for righteous action. "And the movement [or: the excitation] of his spirit is through awe of Adonai. He will not judge based on what his eyes see nor reprove based on what his ears hear" (Isaiah 11:3). A truly wise person, one invested by God with Wisdom, reveres God. He stands in awe of God and thereby is his spirit motivated. As a result, the truly wise person leads and judges others based on the inner spiritual direction dictated by his connection to God's Will through reverence.

This is true not only of the Kings, of the priests, and of the Prophets. It is equally true of any righteous individual. "The mouth of the righteous will utter Wisdom and his tongue will pronounce judgement. The Law of his God is in his heart. His steps will never falter" (Psalms 37:30–31).

Wisdom is bestowed upon the righteous. They, in turn, live their lives in accordance with Wisdom. It is fully reflected through speech and through action. Because Wisdom is engraved in their hearts, the Law becomes an internal reality and affects everything they say and do. It is that deep connection between Wisdom and righteousness that enables them to teach and to lead others by their example.

Righteousness expresses Wisdom. Just action and the fulfilling of the commandments articulate it. Acting in accordance with God's Law makes Wisdom manifest in the world. This is so, because Wisdom is embedded in the heart first. Then the Law of God is internalized and becomes part of the wise person. Wisdom through consistent, righteous action affects the lives of all whom it touches. Blessing is brought to the daily life of the people by the words and deeds of the wise. The heart and the lips of the righteous, indeed, work together to express Wisdom and make it manifest. "By the lips of one who understands will Wisdom be found. The mouth of the righteous will sprout Wisdom. In the heart of one who understands will rest Wisdom" (Proverbs 10:13, 10:31, and 14:33).

Moreover, one must seek to embrace Wisdom. Through righteousness and the observance of the commandments, one strives to attain Wisdom. One must also be inwardly open and prepared to accept Wisdom within. One must receive it and consciously make it a part of oneself. The Sage Kohelet states it quite clearly. "I have given my heart over to an intimate knowledge of Wisdom" (Ecclesiastes 8:16).

There is a sense of great intimacy associated with the acquisition and assimilation of Wisdom. To be wise, one has to embrace Wisdom and become intimately associated with it. It is a process of spiritual preparation, of acceptance, and of deep internalization. The truly wise person must become one with Wisdom. Wisdom is not an attribute. It is not just being wise. It is not an intellectual trait alone. It is a state of being.

The verb *LaDaAT* "to know," and the noun *DaAt*, "knowledge," are often coupled with Wisdom in biblical literature. One of the primary meanings of *DaAt* is "intimate knowledge." When Adam knows Eve, she conceives. *DaAt* is "to know deeply, intimately, and fully." This concept of deep intimacy, which is connected to Wisdom, is particularly prominent in the book of Ecclesiastes (see Ecclesiastes 1:17, 8:16, 9:10). The connection between Wisdom and deep intimacy also appears in the Dead Sea literature.

Among the scroll fragments found at Qumran is the original Hebrew for the fifty-first chapter of the Book of Ben Sira. This chapter contains the poem named "The Wooing of Wisdom." The Hebrew text is rich in imagery that is itself full of double entendre. As the imagery unfolds, it simultaneously conveys a combination of progressive eroticism and an increasing ethical imperative. The sense of intimacy and of moral obligation are delicately and effectively interwoven as the stages of the lover's amorous pursuit is described.

What is symbolized here is the acquisition of Wisdom. As Wisdom is pursued, an intimate connection is developed. The relationship between the individual and Wisdom is strengthened and enhanced over time, as it passes through various stages of bonding. As Wisdom is internalized and deepens within the individual, his sense of moral obligation and ethical action is strengthened. The deeper the connection to Wisdom, the deeper the bond to the Covenant, the stronger the drive to live in accordance with the Law of God. "Fools despise Wisdom and Morality" (Proverbs 1:7). "The awe of God is the Morality of Wisdom" (Proverbs 15:33).

The biblical view of Wisdom sees it as a transcendent essence, a state of being encompassing the divine perspective. It imparts to one worthy to receive it a direct linkage to the Will of God. One who acquires Wisdom becomes intimate with the living Will of God. To possess Wisdom, one must become intimate with it in stages, letting it penetrate to the core of one's own being. Once one becomes possessed of Wisdom, one bonds with the Law, with morality, which is the ultimate human expression of God's Will.

Given this understanding of the nature of Wisdom, the question now becomes, what implications stem from this doctrine? What is the relationship of Wisdom to the Jewish people and to humanity as a whole? What is the future role of Wisdom in the Age to Come? To find those answers, we must look to the literature of the Second Temple era.

The View of Wisdom in the Greco-Roman Period

The earliest post-biblical account of the nature and importance of Wisdom is found in the apocryphal Book of Ben Sira, also known as Ecclesiaticus. It is in the twenty-fourth chapter of the Book of Ben Sira that Wisdom is discussed at some length. Here, with great clarity, Ben Sira sums up the true nature of Wisdom, the role it has played in Israel, and the role it will play in the coming age of the Kingdom of God. So it is here that we should begin, in seeking to gain a deeper insight into the importance of Wisdom and its central role in man's future.

Ben Sira's view of Wisdom can be summarized as follows: In the beginning, from eternity, God created Wisdom. It will endure throughout all eternity. It came forth from the mouth of the Most High and filled the earth. With the emergence of the people of Israel, God commanded Wisdom to make its home among Jacob's descendants, a heritage of Israel. Wisdom ministered in the holy Tabernacle for centuries and with the establishment of the Temple, Jerusalem became her dominion. She will glory in the midst of her people and express herself in the assembly of the Most High.

Wisdom is the Book of the Covenant of God, the Most High. It is reflected in the Law of Moses, an inheritance of the Congregation of Jacob. Whoever obeys the dictates of Wisdom will never be put to shame. Those who seek Wisdom and ally themselves with her will be aided and assisted by her and kept from sin. Wisdom's depth is greater than the seas. Her counsel is vaster than the abyss. The first human did not understand completely, nor will the last. In the future, Wisdom will once again shine forth like the dawn. Once more will she pour out teaching like prophecy and leave it to all future generations, making it shine everywhere. Wisdom does not labor for herself alone, but rather on behalf of all who truly seek instruction. Wisdom is like produce. It produces fruit for those who tend it, for those who work diligently at it. Wisdom, when it is taken in and internalized, nourishes those who are truly able to assimilate it.

Ben Sira is portraying Wisdom as the guiding light of Creation. It was formed from the very beginning and will endure for all time. It is eternally valid. It is a living force, expressing the Will of God. Wisdom issues forth from the mouth of God. It is the articulation of the divine Will. It filled the earth in the beginning, in the age of Eden, and will again guide the destiny of mankind in the future.

The basis of human existence in the coming age will be morality, justice, and peace. The Torah, the Law of Moses, reflects Wisdom. It exemplifies the moral base of action—acting justly—that is the highest human expression of the divine Will. Those who connect with Wisdom take on the mantle of consistent moral behavior. They are kept away from sin and are blessed with a close communion with God.

Israel has kept Wisdom alive over the centuries. Wisdom is synonymous with God's Presence. It rested on the Ark of the Covenant and dwelt within the *Mishkan*, the Sanctuary. God's Presence, and the Wisdom that emanates from it, found a home in the Temple in Jerusalem. In the future, Wisdom again will flourish among her people, providing light to the world. Wisdom will shine forth and pour out instruction in the deeper paths of truth, the true paths that accord with the Will of God. Like prophecy, it will be revealed directly to man from God. Wisdom will come to shape the relationship between the future generations of mankind and God, the Most High.

The picture of Wisdom being presented is one that accords with the return to Eden. Mirroring the relationship that Adam and Eve had originally with God, Wisdom is intimately connected to the communion with God. It flows to man and overcomes his consciousness like prophetic experience. It is that part of God's Presence which imbues man with the true knowledge and understanding of the divine Will. One becomes sensitized to the divine processes that underlie all of Creation. Wisdom, when bestowed upon the worthy individual, upon the seeker, is internalized. It becomes an intimate process that allows one to come to some understanding of the unfathomable, divine thought that stands at the very core of all reality.

The reign of Wisdom on earth corresponds to the coming age, to the Kingdom of God. At the dawn of this new age, mankind's experience of the divine Presence will be one akin to prophecy. It will be one of intimate connection, communion, and direct communication with God. In the Qumran Scroll 4Q 541, Wisdom—though itself a deep, vast mystery—is said to be very near. In the time to come, the books of Wisdom will be opened. The vision that humanity will experience as a result will be very profound. Wisdom will affect even the Messiah, whose connection to it will be very great. Through it, he will make atonement for the people of his generation.

The scroll entitled "The Admonitions to the Sons of the Dawn" instructs us to search the testimony, the writings of antiquity, in order to fathom the hidden things. By delving into the depths of the concealed, the heart of Wisdom, we will come to understand the era of eternity and we will be able to examine the past so as to know it truly. Righteousness and Wisdom are said to have their roots in the highest realms. It is they who set the boundaries of the earth. Through Wisdom, we are able to understand the deeper levels of meaning that regulate our earthly existence. Through it, we can connect with and perceive the broader meanings of our own past and live in closer harmony with the realities of the divine order of things in the future. That is the vision of Eden, the coming reign of God's Kingdom, the coming age of mankind.

Wisdom, which is often equated with the Torah, the Law of Moses, is seen as a guide to righteous living, both in the dark times before the coming of the End Time and also throughout the eternal age of the Kingdom of God. The author of Scroll 4Q 525 blesses those who walk in God's Law with a pure heart and do not slander, who hold fast to the ways of the Torah and not to the ways of evil. Blessed are they who seek Wisdom with clean hands and are free from deceit. Blessed are the righteous, because they accept the discipline of Wisdom and do not cast off the commandments in times of misery, affliction, and terror, out of a weakness of the soul.

We are admonished to protect the ways of the Torah. The Torah, as the Law of God, is the embodiment of Wisdom. If one holds fast to the Will of God, as it has been expressed through the Torah, one is operating within the guidelines of Wisdom. This will uphold one when others falter. It will free one from the reproach of one's enemies and allow one eventually to triumph over the dark forces. Those with true understanding will bring forth words of insight and the perfect will thrust evil aside. They will be guided by Wisdom, will understand the deeper meanings of the Law, and will be able to throw off evil influences, eventually leading to the defeat of the evil around them (4Q 525).

The implication here is both personal and universal. A righteous person is one who walks carefully within the perimeters of God's Law. On one level, that would mean within the structure of the biblical commandments. On another level, it means having one's life fashioned to conform to the moral laws underlying Creation as a whole. Scroll 4Q 525 states that one who is imbued with Wisdom, who truly understands, will bring forth great insights—that is, greater understanding of the deeper levels of meaning implicit in the Covenant and within the commandments.

There are many levels of meaning within the *mitzvot*, the commandments. These depths of meaning can only be penetrated through a personal connection with Wisdom. One must become wise by purifying oneself morally and by opening up spiritually to the holy spirit. Through a combination of practice, knowledge, and meditation, one connects with Wisdom and thereby gains deep insight into the true moral and spiritual nature of Creation.

This personal connection has a transformative effect on the individual. The Law and the commandments are now internal, embedded deep within the fabric of the soul of the righteous. Such an individual sees the deeper meaning of the laws and commandments and understands their wider moral and spiritual ramifications. They are seen through the focus of Wisdom. As such, he or she is drawn to a greater level of service and devotion.

The more one understands, the more one is obligated to do. The entire structure of Jewish Law is based on the concept that knowledge predicates action. Once a person knows what a commandment is, he or she is obligated to fulfill it. Therefore, as one understands the deeper levels of meaning within a commandment, one sees more of the ramifications of the law. One also perceives the interrelationship between it and other commandments. This brings both new understandings and new responsibilities for observance and for teaching. The more one understands of the true nature and implications of a commandment, the greater the obligation in making it a part of one's life.

Wisdom is the origin of the commandments. Through Wisdom, the commandments are most fully penetrated and understood. For the commandments are the external forms generated by Wisdom. The deeper levels of content and mystery that they embody lie hidden below the surface. It is only through adherence to the commandments and through openness to Wisdom that the Law can be delved into deeply, revealing its hidden levels of meaning and its universal applicability.

Since Wisdom gave birth to the Law, the Torah is an outward manifestation of Wisdom. Therefore, to truly understand the Law and the commandments, we have to move into the deeper levels that comprise and sustain them. We must become one with the realm of Wisdom. We must open ourselves up to divine inspiration, to the holy spirit, and must adjust our life and behavior in accordance with the knowledge bestowed. This is the true pursuit of Wisdom.

The pursuit of Wisdom involves both observance of the commandments and openness to divine guidance. The two processes are seen as inseparable. One adheres to the Law, studies it, and meditates on it. This leads to great insight into the true nature of the laws. The connection with Wisdom yields both insight and true knowledge. This knowledge, in turn, must be translated into an active good. Hence, the insight and understanding obligate the righteous to further action and deeper levels of practice. Through this dual process, one is able both to fathom the depths of meaning implicit in the Torah, in the Law, in order to walk more fully in the light of God's guidance, and is also able to cast away evil.

The further a righteous person is drawn into the light of God's Law and God's providence, the further away from evil and evil influence he is pulled. There is a direct correspondence that is evident here. The principles involved are, first, that light dispels darkness, and second, that there is only so much spiritual space within the human soul.

The view of the Sectarian literature is that the human soul is composed of both light and dark elements and that one's actions have a direct effect on the constituent balance between them. In other words, the soul of man has increasingly less room for evil and darkness as more room is taken up by the divine light. The increase of light within the soul is created by righteous action and by openness to divine guidance.

The result of this pursuit of Wisdom is the inner transformation of the righteous soul. Light and knowledge increase as Wisdom is pursued and adhered to. God's ability to guide the individual becomes more pronounced in the process, and evil becomes both easier to recognize and easier to dispense with personally as its position weakens. The course of pursuing Wisdom brings with it the banishment of the darkness through observance of the commandments, revelations of the deeper meanings of the Law, and a strengthening of the light within the soul of the righteous.

One of the most important functions of Wisdom, in the pre-Judgement era of the Age of Wickedness, is to assist the righteous person in overcoming the power of evil within himself and the community around him. By so doing, he prepares for the coming of the Kingdom of God on two levels. He prepares his soul for a fuller life in the coming Kingdom of God through the pursuit of Wisdom and lays the general groundwork for the coming of the Kingdom through being the model of integrity and justice.

Scroll 4Q 541 and the Testament of Kohath both are quite adamant in warning against exchanging Wisdom and the Law for foreign knowledge. The view here is very clear from the perspective of the Qumran literature. Foreign knowledge leads away from Wisdom and away from the commandments. Greek wisdom was not the Law of God, but rather the law of man. The exchange of the latter for the former leads away from the light and back into the sin of Adam and Eve, the sin of following only what was perceived as good and right in one's own eyes. That tendency was seen as leading to idolatry, corruption, and sin. It fostered rebellion against God, and ultimately brought devastation and destruction.

Rather than tread this road to destruction, one is advised to be holy, to walk the path of the Law, the path of truth, righteousness, integrity, and purity. The reader is admonished to walk the road of holiness and priesthood that the generations who inherited the Law of Sinai bequeathed to us. Do not forsake the Torah and the commandments, God's Law. For the truth is indeed eternal (Testament of Kohath).

Those striving to obtain Wisdom must keep several important factors in mind. First, one can learn nothing of moral benefit from people who are deceitful or who are unstable or inconsistent. What they teach, their way of living, does not hold up when put to the test. There is no moral foundation in the words or deeds of a deceptive person. There is no inner strength or integrity in the actions or beliefs of one who vacillates or is mercurial. Plaster on the outside of a house washes away with the rain. Lead melts when exposed to the heat of the fire.

Second, one cannot teach a person who is not committed. If a person does not have the conviction to pursue a righteous life, he or she cannot be taught to live righteously. Spiritual evolution, striving to acclimate one's life and attune one's deeds to the divine, to the Will of God, is a very primal and sacred course of action. It is of utmost importance in terms of service to God and spiritual growth. It requires deep conviction and determination to cling to the light and to make the light part of one's daily existence. A slackard cannot be trusted with such an important task. There is no reason to believe that a person who is only paying lip service or who is simply disinterested in spiritual growth is either going to pay attention to your instructions or bother to carry them out.

Third, one should not turn for counsel, advice, or adjudication to a person who makes judgements without investigating the facts. Such a person is presuming to operate on his or her own light. Truth has to be pursued. It cannot be assumed. No person is omniscient and no issue is generic. Decisions and judgements must be made based on knowledge of the unique circumstances of the issues involved and upon the principles of justice embedded in the Law of God. This involves openness and investigation.

No credence or authority should be given to an individual who makes decisions arbitrarily and on an uninformed basis. A person who decides something without proper investigation is like one who is gullible, believing anything. Such a person accepts a belief without pondering it, thinking it over fully, or understanding it at all. Such an individual should not be put in a position of authority over people who are actively searching and pursuing Wisdom. He or she has no basis for understanding their position and their views. As a result, he or she is not in a position to determine who is right and who is wrong or to justify the righteous or condemn the wicked (4Q 424).

It is incorrect, however, to assume that the pursuit of Wisdom is only a process designed to help individuals perfect themselves in anticipation of the End time. Although that is its function in the Age of Wickedness, obtaining Wisdom and becoming one with it also has a primary role in the life of the individual and society in the post-End Time, in the coming age. The pursuit of Wisdom is not merely a process necessary for banishing evil and preparing for the messianic age. It is also the fundamental prerequisite element for living a full life in the Kingdom of God.

According to the Aramaic fragments of the text, the Testament of Levi (found among the Dead Sea literature) one prays for Wisdom. If you seek Wisdom, it will find you. When one possesses Wisdom, one does justice and acts in accordance with true, clear judgement. One then lives fully and completely in the Divine Presence. These principles are not limited only to the pre-messianic era. Rather, they also represent the pattern for life in the Kingdom of God. The post-End Time represents the construction of a world based on justice, divine intervention, and guidance, a new higher form of the Law of God incumbent on all mankind.

Levi's admonition is always to teach God's Law, its interpretation, and the Wisdom upon which it is based. One's words and one's deeds must always be righteous and must always be based on the truth. Wisdom comes from this combination of adherence to the Law, consistency in truth and honesty, and from teaching what one has come to understand. Light produces light. It expands outward, beneficially effecting others. Wisdom is universal. It is respected universally. It provides its own rewards. The patriarch Joseph, Levi points out, taught Torah, interpretation of the Law, and Wisdom. As a result, he became a great and honored man. Not just among Jews was he revered, but by all men whom he came into contact with. The Torah, the deeper levels of God's Law, is seen here to consist of universal principles that will, in their purer forms, act as a guide to all of humanity in the era to come.

It is stated in Scroll 4Q 424, fragment 2, that a person whose heart is encased in fat—that is, it is buried, unexposed, and unavailable—should not be expected to penetrate the deep thought of Wisdom. Such a person is unable to fathom it or even attempt to. Because his or her actions do not accord with Wisdom, Wisdom remains hidden, buried deep within the heart, unable to emerge and rule over this person's life and consciousness. On the other hand, a person of intelligence will accept understanding. A person of knowledge [one who seeks to know God intimately] will derive Wisdom. One who is honest will seek judgement. Such an individual will be an opponent of and a source of contention to anyone trying to remove the behavioral boundaries set by divine law.

Scroll 4Q 525 explains that one whose life is ruled by Wisdom will meditate on God's Law always. The Torah and Wisdom will be before such a person all his life. Wisdom will lift up his head, raising his consciousness, his sense of self and sense of purpose. His eyes will be lifted continually to the light. Lovers of God will look upon Wisdom and walk carefully within her boundaries.

This enlightenment is predicted upon meditation. Meditating and seeking Wisdom is a lifelong process. When one reaches a new level of consciousness, new awareness of the divine laws surface and one is then responsible for making constructive use of the acquired knowledge. Fulfilling the laws from the higher perspective, in turn, leads one to spiritual transformation. Eventually, one completes this level of consciousness and must move on to the next. Meditation is a constant throughout this process. First, to reach new levels of awareness and then to understand them fully once reached, meditation and the use of meditative focus are involved. Wisdom is only accessed through meditation and practice. Wisdom is the key to both reaching higher consciousness and to learning to understand it and utilize it properly.

Seeking Wisdom involves meditation on the Law of God. Meditation on the Law is a gateway to Wisdom. One learns about something initially by studying the details. One learns even more deeply what one is dealing with by contemplating and pondering the details. Meditation leads beyond the details to the levels of reality that underlie it. Psalm 77, verse 13, reads, "I will meditate on all Your works and on Your designs will I focus meditation."

Meditation is the seeking of the heart, mind, and soul after Wisdom. "Allow me to remember my song during the night, with my heart I will meditate and my spirit will search out" (Psalms 77:7). Wisdom is the key to spiritual development. Meditation on the Law and the commandments is the key to Wisdom. "On Your statutes will I meditate" (Psalms 119:15). The true seeker, the wise man, understands this. He focuses his attention on the Law. He meditates on the commandments in a continuing quest for deeper knowledge and a closer bond to God through harmony with His Law. "For if his desire is in the Law of God, then on His Law will he meditate day and night" (Psalms 1:2).

The pursuit of Wisdom is central to the future life of humanity. It is the gateway by which mankind evolves and through which communication and bonding with God is furthered. This reality would seem to be a core element in the restoration of Eden and of human life in the coming Kingdom of God.

Wisdom reveals. It brings the wise, those who pursue Wisdom, to new states of consciousness. Wisdom enlightens. It opens up deeper truths and teaches the righteous new directions. Wisdom links mankind to the living Word of God, molding man's life and behavior in paths ever more acceptable to the Creator of all. Seeking Wisdom is the model of the righteous. It is the model both of the present and of the future age.

Wisdom: The Hallmark of the Coming Age

As has been noted already, Wisdom possesses several different components. Wisdom is transcendent. It resides at the highest levels of Creation and embodies the living Will of God. By clinging to Wisdom, mankind is influenced by it. Wisdom penetrating the human heart guides the spiritual evolution of the human race. The very foundation for serving God is the possession of Wisdom. Based on the awe of God and on reverence for the Divine, Wisdom links man's will to God's Will and transforms the individual into a vessel for holy service.

Within the Dead Sea Scrolls and in the literature of the Second Temple period, Wisdom is equated frequently with the Torah, with God's Law. The commandments, the statutes, and ordinances are all an articulation of the Divine Will and therefore an embodiment of Wisdom. Moreover, Wisdom is also seen as the blueprint for Creation itself. The inherent order of the universe is established through its dependency on God's plan, through an internal program that regulates all, allowing everything to exist and to function. Natural law and moral law are seen as implicit within Creation and another expression of Wisdom.

One more very salient feature of Wisdom needs to be clarified—that is the aspect of Revelation. Wisdom embodies the power of revealing that which is most concealed. Wisdom reveals the hidden Will of God to those who pursue it, cling to it, and internalize it. Wisdom is the vehicle for Revelation. Only through Wisdom can God's Law and God's plan be comprehended.

Deep are the layers of interconnection and of meaning that hold the fabric of Creation together. The Will of God is embedded in the structure of Creation. The plan of Creation forms the essence of God's creative purpose. Wisdom is itself the plan of Creation. Therefore, it alone is the only true vehicle available to humanity for understanding the Will of God. Connection to Wisdom is the key to Revelation.

In the Book of Daniel, the equation of Wisdom with Revelation is made very clear. In Daniel, chapter 2, the king demands that not only is it incumbent upon the wise men of Babylonia to interpret his troubling dream, but to do so without him revealing the dream to them. They are bid to inform him of both the nature and the content of the dream and then interpret it for him. This is seen as an impossible task. Only the gods are capable of such a feat.

The Prophet Daniel asks for time. He goes to his companions, Hananiah, Mishael, and Azariah. Together, they implore God to reveal to them this mystery. The term used here for mystery is the word *Raz*. It is the exact same term used by the Qumran literature, when discussing the "Secret of Becoming," the *Raz Niyeh*. The use of the term *Raz*, in this chapter, is the first time the term appears anywhere in Jewish literature.

The mystery is revealed in a night vision. It is a direct Revelation from God. The companions seek to know that which is most hidden and concealed, both the nature of the dream and its meaning. To access this hidden knowledge, they must connect with God's Will. The dream represents a manifestation of the Will of God. It projects what is going to happen in the future, as God has ordained it. Only through connecting with Wisdom can one access the Divine Will. Only through the vehicle of Wisdom is the hidden revealed.

> Daniel spoke and said: "May God's Name be blessed forever and ever, since Wisdom and power are certainly His. He changes the seasons and the times, removing kings and establishing kings, giving Wisdom to the wise and Knowledge to those who intimately know Understanding. He reveals the deep and the mysterious. He knows what is in the darkness, and light resides with Him. To You, God of my fathers, I bow down and give praise for the Wisdom and power that You have given to me. Now, You have made known to me what we asked of You. You have made known to us the King's matter." (Daniel 2:20–23)

Daniel is expressing the reality that Wisdom emanates from God and that it encompasses the power of Revelation. Wisdom is the Divine Will. It resides within God Himself. Access to it comes only through Revelation. God grants Revelation only to those whom He deems worthy. It is bestowed upon those who have developed an intimacy with Wisdom and can call upon God in truth and sincerity.

Revelation of the Divine Will often comes in the form of dreams and visions. Much of the Book of Daniel is preoccupied with the interpretation of dreams, seen as revelations of God's Will. The meanings are, in turn, revealed through visions. "To these four young men,

God gave knowledge and intelligence regarding all books and Wisdom. And Daniel understood every vision and all dreams" (Daniel 1:17). Moreover, dreams and visions were interpreted periodically with the added assistance of angels. In dealing with visions of the End Time, for example, the archangel Gabriel is instructed to elucidate the full meaning to Daniel (Daniel 8:16–19).

Revelation also comes through study of the sacred texts. In Daniel, chapter 9, Daniel is confessing his sins. He verbalizes several deep truths regarding the destruction of the state and its relationship to the sins of the fathers. This knowledge is revealed to Daniel through his study of the writings of Jeremiah. His revelation of the truth comes from a deep meditation over the words of the Prophet. The subsequent understanding causes him great pain and anguish. He prays fervently to God, and the devotion of his prayers brings him further revelations brought by the angel Gabriel.

Within the Sectarian Community and among the Essenes, study of the sacred texts of the Torah and the prophetic writings was a gateway to Revelation. The Pesher Commentaries on prophetic texts certainly point in this direction. All members of the Community were required to study the Book of Meditations, the *Sefer Hagui*, daily. The Interpreter of the Community spent most of his time studying the Laws and meditating on them. From such a course of action, he merited Revelation.

According to Scroll 4Q 298, the Sons of Light pursue justice, love, piety, and increase patience and tolerance. They study the secrets of God's testimony and interpret them for the purpose of understanding the way things are to be in the time of eternity. A Son of the Dawn must always examine, take to heart, and know the ancient words.

Revelation through study of the sacred Word of God, through meditation, through the interpretation of dreams, and through the experience of visions are all dimensions of Wisdom. They all reveal God's Will to those who possess Wisdom internally and who seek God continually. This paradigm is one of continuing interaction and communication with God, through Wisdom and its multiple paths.

This pattern is not necessarily restricted to the present age. It is even more characteristic of the future relationship between man and God in the post-messianic Kingdom of God. The Community believed that its way of life was setting the groundwork for teaching Israel the true way of life, which would be implemented in the Kingdom of God. It felt it was establishing the prototype of man's relationship to the Creator, for Israel and for the world, by illustrating several basic principles that would apply to all of humanity in the coming age. In the view of the literature of the Second Temple period, Wisdom in its fullest context is to dominate human experience in the coming Kingdom of God.

With the restoration of Eden, God will make mankind truly great. Our greatness will stem from a way of life based on Wisdom. Humanity will be taught Wisdom. It will become our guide. God's Will will be known to us through an intimate, interactive process connecting us with a higher knowledge. Our rejection of all evil will be complete and final. As a result, we will inherit the knowledge of God's truth, generation after generation (4Q 413).

Wisdom is the pursuit of justice. It is the adherence to God's Law. It is living one's life in absolute steadfastness in the truth. It is being pure of heart and studying God's ordinances with clean hands. It is pursuit of the path of Wisdom by walking in the Law of the Most High and keeping Wisdom before one's eyes throughout one's entire life (4Q 525).

In the coming age, we are to walk on the path that was set by the Patriarchs. Blessed is the person who follows the road God commanded to Isaac and established for Jacob, walking in accordance with the words of God. We are to bear in mind that man's life is transitory. It blossoms and thrives. Then it withers and dies, being blown away without leaving a trace. We are to trust in God's saving and sustaining power, remembering the miracles God did for our forefathers in Egypt. Trusting in miracles, the manifested power of God, we are to seek out a way of life guided by Wisdom, directed by the hand of God. Then will we be united with the angels. As did our fathers Abraham, Isaac, and Jacob, we, too, are to draw Wisdom from the great power of God. Our lives are to be a dialogue with God. If we grasp Wisdom, then it becomes a way of life and it is passed on to coming generations as an inheritance. Blessed is the person to whom Wisdom is given (4Q 185).

The guiding principle of the Kingdom of God will be the possession of Wisdom by humanity. Reverence and awe for God will be the core of man's renewed relationship with God as Eden is restored. Wisdom has always guided individuals of great spiritual stature and devotion to God throughout the ages. In the coming age, it will be the inheritance of the righteous. Evil having been eradicated from our midst, the world will be in a state pure enough to house the Presence of God. Wisdom, the guiding light of God's Will, will become ever-present. It will facilitate the deep and continuing dialogue with the Almighty that is to be the hallmark of the new age of Eden. That is the vision of the scrolls.

EPILOGUE:
A PERSONAL DEDICATION

By way of conclusion, I want to take a moment to dedicate this volume to the memory of the holy Community whose writings have come down to us amid the literature of the Qumran caves. Hidden from view for two millennia, the courage, faith, and devotion shown in the writings they held dear speak boldly to us. The message they were annunciating rings as clearly and as poignantly today as it no doubt did to the Jews of their own time.

This Community of devout souls had a clear vision of Israel's mission and place in the world. They had great faith in the ultimate triumph of God's Will and a deep belief in the potential of humanity to evolve beyond turmoil and struggle to intimacy with God—from what we have been to what we will become. The teachings and piety of these devout souls reach out to us with a message of hope and of faith that is truly moving and inspiring.

Their vision and their way of life was as a community of the spirit. It was not family or tribe or nation that bound them together. It was trust in God, allegiance to God's Law, and faith in His promise, faith in the ultimate redemption of humanity. The way of the Community was submission to a totally moral way of life based on mutual respect and responsibility for one another. They formed a community whose very structure was designed to implement the dictates of God's Word from Sinai.

The members of the Community were willing to sacrifice everything, to break away completely from materialism, from the focus on survival as the centerpiece of existence. Rather, they chose to concentrate their lives on faith and on spiritual growth. Their daily routine was one that continually strived for intimacy with God and was based solidly and consistently on service to mankind. The Community sought to lead the way. They sought to be a model for all of Israel to follow and for the nations of the world to emulate. Their struggle was to remain steadfast during the dark days, before the final triumph of God. Their vision was fixed on the Kingdom of God and the resurrection of mankind, the full return to Eden.

In understanding the piety of these holy souls and the eternal truths they were trying to convey, it is important to bear in mind that their teachings, their beliefs, and their way of life all reflect each other. They are all different dimensions of the same thing. Cumulatively, they are all aspects of the message. To study their doctrines, to come to understand their way of life, and to see the world as they did is to assimilate a spiritual perspective of great depth and perception.

In this modest work, I have tried to present a glimpse into the life and thought, the devotion and the piety of this holy Community. It is a look into the spirituality of a past age. It is an endeavor done in the hope that others will be inspired to search this rich literature carefully. Working so closely with this literature, the energy and intensity of the material has had a profound and indelible effect on my own spiritual development. It has helped provide me with a workable spiritual approach to life that speaks to my soul. Personally, I have been enriched greatly by the deep insights and the spiritual direction these writings provide. For that, I am eternally grateful.

The Dead Sea Scrolls, the Apocrypha, and pseudo-epigraphical writings all form a great corpus of Jewish religious and theological literature. This literature spans the entire Second Temple period and it bridges the theological gap between the Bible and rabbinic literature. It reflects the vast diversity of thinking and speculation in the Judaism of the Greco-Roman age. It is rich in spiritual content and religious insight. Its texts are worthy of deep study and elucidation. My hope is that these works will reclaim their position as a vital part of Jewish religious literature and will help provide direction, insight, and inspiration to future generations of spiritual seekers.

There is no one road to God. There is no one doctrine. The true spiritual seeker searches, grows, and evolves continually. The Community knew this. They have left for us their thoughts and their experiences, their understanding and their visions. They have left us, as well, copies of the works that spoke to them on a deep spiritual level. For those who seek to draw close to God and to know His ways, an intimate knowledge of the Dead Sea literature is an important step on the road of spiritual evolution.

May the memory of these holy souls be cherished by those whose lives they affect, in our own day and in the years to come. May the vision of mankind's future be as bright and hopeful as they have foreseen. May their teachings shed light on the road to communion with God, for all who will take them to heart. May God's Kingdom come to reign on earth, soon and in our own day. And may the hearts of all humanity be opened to intimacy with God. Amen.

BIBLIOGRAPHY

The Dead Sea Scriptures. Trans. Theodore Gaster. Garden City, NY: Anchor Press, 1976.

The Dead Sea Scrolls in English. Third Ed. Trans. G. Vermes. New York: Penguin, 1987.

The Dead Sea Scrolls Translated. Trans. Florentino Garcia Martinez. Leiden: Brill, 1994.

The Dead Sea Scrolls Uncovered. Ed. Robert Eisenman and Michael Wise. Rockport, MA: Element, 1992.

A Facsimile Edition of the Dead Sea Scrolls. Ed. Robert Eisenman and James Robinson, vol. 1. Washington, D.C.: Biblical Archeology Society, 1991.

A Facsimile Edition of the Dead Sea Scrolls. Ed. Robert Eisenman and James Robinson, vol. 2. Washington, D.C.: Biblical Archeology Society, 1991.

The Old Testament Pseudoepigrapha. Ed. James H. Charlesworth, vol. 1. Garden City, NY: Doubleday, 1983.

The Old Testament Pseudoepigrapha. Ed. James H. Charlesworth, vol. 2. Garden City, NY: Doubleday, 1985.

The Oxford Annotated Apocrypha. Ed. Bruce Metzger. New York: Oxford University Press, 1965.

A Preliminary Edition of the Unpublished Dead Sea Scrolls: The Hebrew and Aramaic Texts from Cave Four, Fascicle One. Ed. Ben Zion Wacholder and Martin Abegg. Washington, D.C.: Biblical Archeology Society, 1991.

A Preliminary Edition of the Unpublished Dead Sea Scrolls: The Hebrew and Aramaic Texts from Cave Four, Fascicle Two. Ed. Ben Zion Wacholder and Martin Abegg. Washington, D.C.: Biblical Archeology Society, 1992.

A Preliminary Edition of the Unpublished Dead Sea Scrolls: The Hebrew and Aramaic Texts from Cave Four, Fascicle Three. Ed. Ben Zion

Wacholder and Martin Abegg. Washington, D.C.: Biblical Archeology Society, 1995.

Songs of the Sabbath Sacrifice. Ed. Carol Newsom. Atlanta: Scholars
Press, 1985.

Die Texte aus Qumran: Hebraisch und Deutsch. Ed. Eduard Lohse.
Munchen: Kosel, 1971.

Baumgarten, Joseph. *Studies in Qumran Law.* Leiden: Brill, 1977.

Bickerman, Elias. *The Jews in the Greek Age.* Cambridge: Harvard
University Press, 1988.

Hengel, Martin. *Judaism and Hellenism.* Philadelphia: Fortress Press,
1974.

Russell, D.S. *The Method and Messsage of Jewish Apocalyptic.* Philadelphia: Westminster Press, 1964.

Saldarini, Anthony. *Pharisees, Scribes and Sadduccees.* Wilmington, DE:
Michael Glazier, 1988.

Sanders, E.P. *Jewish Law from Jesus to the Mishnah.* Philadelphia: Trinity Press International, 1990.

Sanders, E.P. *Judaism: Practice and Belief 63 BCE to 66 CE.* Philadelphia:
Trinity Press International, 1992.

Tcherikover, Victor. *Hellenistic Civilization and the Jews.* New York:
Atheneum, 1970.

Wacholder, Ben Zion. *The Dawn of Qumran.* Cincinnati: Hebrew Union
College Press, 1983.

Zeitlin, Solomon. *The Rise and Fall of the Judean State.* Philadelphia:
Jewish Publication Society, 1968.

מגילת המקדש: ליקם: יגדל ידין: ירושלים, היכל הספר, 1977.

מקורות לתולדות הכיתות בימי בית שני: ליקם: ד. רוקח: ירושלים, אקדמון, 1970.

הספרים החיצונים: מתורגם: אברהם כהנא: ירושלים. מקור, 1970.

Articles

Abegg, M. "Messianic Hope in 4Q 285: A Reassessment." *Journal of
Biblical Literature* 113:1 (1994): 81–91.

Brin, Gershon. "The Laws of the Prophets in the Sect of the Judean
Desert: Studies in 4Q 375." *Journal for the Study of the Pseudoepigrapha* 10 (1992): 19–51.

Laato, A. "The Chronology of the Damascus Covenant of Qumran."
Revue de Qumran 60 (1992): 605–607.

Qimron, Elisha, and Strugnell, John. "For This You Waited 35 Years: The MMT Reconstructed." *Biblical Archeology Review* (November–December, 1994): 56–63.

Schiffman, Lawrence. "The Deuteronomic Paraphrase of the Temple Scroll." *Revue de Qumran* 60 (1992): 543–567.

Schiffman, Lawrence. "The Law of Vows and Oaths in the Zadokite Fragments and the Temple Scroll." *Revue de Qumran* 57–58 (1991).

Schiffman, Lawrence. "Miqsat Ma'aseh HaTorah and the Temple Scroll." *Revue de Qumran* 55 (1990): 435–457.

Stallman, Robert. "Levi and the Levites in the Dead Sea Scrolls." *Journal for the Study of the Pseudoepigrapha* 10 (1992): 163–189.

Stone, M., and Greenfield, J. "The Prayer of Levi." *Journal of Biblical Literature* 112:2 (1993): 247–266.

Tov, E. "Deuteronomy and 11Q Temple LII–LIII." *Revue de Qumran* 57–58 (1991): 169–173.

Vanderkam, J., and Milik, J. "The First Jubilees Manuscript from Qumran Cave Four: A Preliminary Publication." *Journal of Biblical Literature* 110:2 (1991): 243–270.

Weinfeld, M. "God versus Moses in the Temple Scroll." *Revue de Qumran* 57–58 (1991): 175–180.

Wise, M. "4Q Florilegium and the Temple of Adam." *Revue de Qumran* 57–58 (1991): 103–132.

INDEX

breakers of boundaries, 118,
125
force for evil, 53, 271
opponents of Law, 97, 117–
118
source of impurity, 124–125,
205–207
sinful acts, 53–54, 83
war with Sons of Light, 230,
253
Sons of God as Elect of God,
258
Sons of Light, 230–254, 258,
281, 317
Sons of the Pit. *See* Sons of
Darkness
Sons of Zadok. *See also* Zadok
connection with Sectarians,
32–33, 36–37, 49
Covenant Community
authority, 64, 65, 68,
78
Damascus Covenant, 32, 49,
64
Sectarian history, 32, 49,
64
Zadokim as Sadducees,
32–33
Sukkot. *See* Holidays

Tabernacle. *See also* Sanctuary,
Temple
at Shilo, 2, 32, 169
consecration, 157
creation, 134, 169
Mikdash (Mishkan), 136
structure, sacred elements,
169–171
symbolism, 74–75, 88, 120,
136

Talmud. *See also Mishnah*
2 Esdras chs. 5, 6, 9, 242
Noah, Covenant laws, 21
Yoma 38b, 237
Teacher of Righteousness, 68,
256
as Interpreter of Law, 49–50,
60, 107, 118, 128
as Onias III. *See* High Priests
identity, historical
background, 35–39
Temple. *See also* Jerusalem
architectural symbolism,
169–175
as sanctuary, 135–137, 139–
140, 143
design, Temple Scroll
elements. *See* Temple of
the Scroll
focus of worship, 120–121,
131, 133, 135, 138–139,
225
Jerusalem, role of priesthood,
33, 85–86
Mishkan (Mikdash), 135–137,
169–170, 172–174
nature, function, 135–141, 225
plans, building, 32, 136
profanation, 60–61, 119, 205,
235–237
ritual, Temple Scroll
provisions, 127–128
sanctuary, 134–136,
143–144
Sectarian Community beliefs,
123, 125–126
service. *See* Priesthood,
Temple service
services, purity, impurity
laws, 202

About the Author

Rabbi Steven A. Fisdel has studied and lectured on the Dead Sea Scrolls and their spiritual significance for over twenty-five years. Rabbi Fisdel holds a master's degree in Judaica from Spertus College in Chicago and a bachelor's degree in Jewish History and World History from the Hebrew University in Jerusalem. He received rabbinic ordination from the Pnai Or Fellowship in Philadelphia. Rabbi Fisdel is on staff with the Chochmat HaLev Institute for Jewish Learning in Berkeley, California and has been affiliated for many years with Foothill College in Los Altos, and with the College of Early Christian Studies in San Jose. Rabbi Fisdel serves as the spiritual leader of Congregation Bnai Torah in Antioch, California.